MW00803085

INTERNATIONAL GOVERNANCE AND THE RULE OF LAW IN CHINA UNDER THE BELT AND ROAD INITIATIVE

This edited volume examines China's role in the field of international governance and the rule of law under the Belt and Road Initiative. The authors' approach is holistic and seeks alternative analytical frameworks that not only take into account legal ideologies and legal ideals but also local demand, and sociopolitical circumstances, to explain and understand China's legal interactions with countries along the Road; this allows more useful insights into predicting and analysing China's and other emerging Asian countries' legal future. Authors from Germany, Korea, Singapore, Mainland China, Taiwan and Hong Kong contributed to this edited volume in order to encourage academic dialogue and to conduct intellectual exchange in specific sub-themes.

YUN ZHAO is Professor and Head of Department of Law at The University of Hong Kong; he gained his PhD from Erasmus University Rotterdam; an LLM from Leiden University; and an LLM and LLB from China University of Political Science and Law. Zhao is also Chen An Chair Professor in International Law at Xiamen University (2015), and Siyuan Scholar Chair Professor at Shanghai University of Foreign Trade (2012–14). He is listed as arbitrator in several international arbitration commissions.

INTERNATIONAL GOVERNANCE AND THE RULE OF LAW IN CHINA UNDER THE BELT AND ROAD INITIATIVE

Edited by

YUN ZHAO

The University of Hong Kong

CAMBRIDGE
UNIVERSITY PRESS

CAMBRIDGE
UNIVERSITY PRESS

University Printing House, Cambridge CB2 8BS, United Kingdom

One Liberty Plaza, 20th Floor, New York, NY 10006, USA

477 Williamstown Road, Port Melbourne, VIC 3207, Australia

314–321, 3rd Floor, Plot 3, Splendor Forum, Jasola District Centre, New Delhi – 110025, India

79 Anson Road, #06–04/06, Singapore 079906

Cambridge University Press is part of the University of Cambridge.

It furthers the University's mission by disseminating knowledge in the pursuit of education, learning and research at the highest international levels of excellence.

www.cambridge.org
Information on this title: www.cambridge.org/9781108420143
DOI: 10.1017/9781108332651

© Cambridge University Press 2018

First published 2018

Printed and bound in Great Britain by Clays Ltd, Elcograf S.p.A.

A catalogue record for this publication is available from the British Library.

Library of Congress Cataloging-in-Publication Data
Names: Zhao, Yun, editor.
Title: International governance and the rule of law in China under the Belt and Road Initiative / edited by Yun Zhao.
Description: New York : Cambridge University Press, 2018. | Includes bibliographical references and index.
Identifiers: LCCN 2018024257 | ISBN 9781108420143 (hardback)
Subjects: LCSH: Rule of law–China. | Soft law–China. | Globalization–China. | International economic relations. | Regional economics–China. | Trade routes–Eurasia. | Infrastructure (Economics)–China. | China–Foreign economic relations. | China–Commerce–Eurasia. | Eurasia–Foreign economic relations–China. | BISAC: LAW / International.
Classification: LCC KNQ2025 .I58 2018 | DDC 340/.11–dc23
LC record available at https://lccn.loc.gov/2018024257

ISBN 978-1-108-42014-3 Hardback

CONTENTS

FIGURES

TABLES

CONTRIBUTORS[1]

YONGMIN BIAN is Professor and Head of the Department of International Law at the School of Law, University of International Business and Economics, Beijing. She obtained her PhD from the University of International Business and Economics; and LLM and LLB from the China University of Political Science and Law. She is a member of the Committee on the Role of International Law in Sustainable Natural Resource Management for Development under the International Law Association. Bian is the winner of the An Zijie Award for Research in International Trade, 2006 by the An Zijie Award Committee in China. Her research interests focus on international environmental law and environment-related trade and investment issues.

YUHONG CHAI studied at Kobe University in Japan (LLM and PhD) and was Research Fellow there from 2014 to 2015. He currently teaches at the Law School of Lanzhou University. He is a council member of the China Society of International Private Law and a member of the China Academy of Arbitration Law. Chai is also a member of the Academy for International Business Transactions in Japan. His main research topics are as follows: international private law and international commercial arbitration.

CHRISTOPHER CHEN is Associate Professor of Law at the Singapore Management University (SMU). He received a PhD from the University of London (UCL) and LLM from the University of Michigan, after completing law degrees at the National Taiwan University. His main research interests include financial regulation, derivatives and risk management,

---

[1] Chinese names in this list and in the rest of the volume are in Western order so that a person's forename comes first, and then the surname, unless the name forms part of a title, is quoted matter or an award name. Where names are given in traditional Chinese, surnames appear first.

financial consumer protection, corporate governance and transplantation of law in Asia in broad areas of corporate, banking, insurance and financial laws. Chen has published in both English and Mandarin Chinese in the United States, United Kingdom, Europe, Singapore and Taiwan.

WEIXIA GU is Associate Professor of Law at The University of Hong Kong. She obtained her SJD and MCL degrees from The University of Hong Kong, and LLB degree (International Economic Law) from East China University of Political Science and Law. Her research interests are in arbitration, commercial dispute resolution and private international law, focusing on Greater China. Before joining The University of Hong Kong, Gu was Fulbright Fellow at the New York University School of Law where she taught arbitration and dispute resolution courses with Jerome A. Cohen. She is a member of the Chartered Institute of Arbitrators (London and East Asia), and serves on the Executive Council Board of the China Society of Private International Law. She also sits on the editorial team of the *Hong Kong Law Journal* (SSCI).

SHENGLI JIANG is Doctor of Laws and Assistant Researcher, Institute of Social Sciences, East China University of Political Science and Law, from where he obtained his LLB and PhD, majoring in public international law. He is also a visiting scholar at the Faculty of Law, The University of Hong Kong; guest professor at Faculty of Law, Shanghai Maritime University; and a distinguished expert of the "Shanghai Outstanding Legal Talents (Foreign Affairs) Education Program". Jiang is a member of the council at the Chinese Institute of Space Law, and a member of the Asian Society of International Law, Chinese Society of International Law. He has published around forty papers in several SSCI and CSSCI journals and many other academic journals.

KELVIN HIU FAI KWOK is Deputy Director and Fellow of the Asian Institute of International Financial Law, and Assistant Professor of Law at The University of Hong Kong. He obtained his LLM from the University of Chicago, and his LLB and BBA (Law) from The University of Hong Kong. Kwok has served as Associate/Articles Editor of the Oxford University Commonwealth Law Journal, Hong Kong Law Journal, and China Antitrust Law Journal; as Non-Governmental Advisor to the International Competition Network; and on the Competition Policy Committee of the Hong Kong Consumer Council, the Special Committee on Competition Law of the Hong Kong Bar Association, and the Executive Committee of the Hong Kong Competition Association. He is a barrister of the High Court of Hong Kong.

JAEMIN LEE is Professor of Law of the School of Law, Seoul National University in Seoul, Korea. He also serves as Associate Dean for Academic Affairs for the law school. He obtained his LLB, LLM and PhD from Seoul National University; LLM from Georgetown University Law Center; and JD from Boston College Law School. His major areas of teaching and research are public international law, international trade law and international investment law. Lee has published articles and books (including book chapters) on various topics of public international law, international trade law and international investment law.

YUE PENG is Professor of Law at Nanjing University. He obtained his PhD, LLM and LLB from Nanjing University. Between 2008 and 2010, he was Postdoctoral Fellow in the Law School of Fudan University. Peng is a director member of the Chinese Society of International Economic Law and China Securities Law Research Association. His interests lie in the domestic regulation of global economic activities and the international economic regulatory coordination and cooperation between sovereign states. He has published more than sixty articles on various topics including international trade law, international investment law and international finance law.

SAMULI SEPPÄNEN is Assistant Professor at the Faculty of Law of the Chinese University of Hong Kong. He holds an SJD from Harvard University and an LLM from the University of Helsinki. His research focuses on legal and political thought in China and developmental aspects of international law.

WEI SHEN is Dean and Professor of Law at Shandong University Law School. He obtained his PhD from the London School of Economics; LLM from the University of Cambridge (UK); LLM from the University of Michigan; and LLM and LLB from the East China University of Political Science and Law. He qualified as a lawyer in New York and has been practising for the last ten years, mostly in Hong Kong, in foreign direct investment, private equity and mergers and acquisitions. He is an arbitrator with Hong Kong International Arbitration Centre, Singapore

International Arbitration Centre, Shanghai International Arbitration Centre, Shanghai Arbitration Commission and Shenzhen International Court of Arbitration. His main research interests include financial regulation, corporate governance, international investment law and commercial arbitration. He has published 6 books and more than 160 articles in Chinese and English journals, and one of his articles was cited by the Supreme Court of Singapore.

JINGXIA SHI is Professor of Law and Dean, School of Law, China University of International Business and Economics (UIBE) based in Beijing. She also serves as Director for the International Law Institute, and Director of the Research Center for Unification of Commercial Law, both at UIBE. She obtained her JSD and LLM from Yale Law School; her PhD, LLB and BA from Wuhan University. She was appointed as Chen An Chair Professor in International Law at Xiamen University (2012). Shi is a member of the Governing Council of UNIDROIT and of the Panel of Conciliators at the International Centre for Settlement of Investment Disputes (ICSID), and she is listed as arbitrator in several international arbitration commissions. She has published widely on various topics including trade in services, cross-border insolvency and international investment law.

SARAH WERSBORG is currently completing her doctoral degree program at the University of Würzburg, Germany. Her fields of research are the anti-monopoly law and the law of conflicts with a focus on comparing Chinese and German law. She will obtain her LLM degree from the University of California at Berkeley in August 2018. In August 2011, she successfully passed the German First State Exam in law after her studies at the Humboldt University in Berlin. Wersborg has extensive experience in Chinese Law due to her research interests and several stays in China, including as a visiting scholar at The University of Hong Kong where she gave several lectures. She has also published several articles in the German Journal of Chinese Law.

YUN ZHAO is Professor and Head of the Department of Law at The University of Hong Kong. He gained his PhD from Erasmus University Rotterdam; an LLM from Leiden University; and LLM and LLB from China University of Political Science and Law. Yun Zhao is also Chen An Chair Professor in International Law at Xiamen University (2015) and

Siyuan Scholar Chair Professor at Shanghai University of Foreign Trade (2012–14). He is listed as an arbitrator in several international arbitration commissions. He sits on the editorial teams of several SSCI journals, including *Hong Kong Law Journal* (as China law editor) and *Journal of East Asia and International Law* (as executive editor). Zhao is the winner of the Prof. Dr. I.H.Ph. Diederiks-Verschoor Award 2006 by the International Institute of Space Law in France, the first winner of Isa Diederiks-Verschoor Prize in the Netherlands and also the first winner of SATA Prize by the Foundation of Development of International Law in Asia (DILA). He has published widely on various topics, particularly dispute resolution and space law.

~

Introduction

YUN ZHAO

Building on the concept of the ancient Silk Road networks, President Xi Jinping formally announced the Belt and Road Initiative (BRI) in September 2013, with the aim of strengthening the cooperation between China and other countries along the old Silk Road on a wide range of issues, in particular the fields of trade and investment. The BRI, covering more than sixty countries in Asia, Africa and Europe, encourages economic integration in the region leading ultimately to the formation of a new regional trading and investment bloc.

This initiative currently attracts considerable academic and policy attention. It is believed that the BRI is instrumental in promoting economic cooperation and cultural exchange among countries along and beyond the road. One of the central themes under the initiative is rule of law, which has important implications for the public and individual good in both the domestic and international arenas. While sufficient discussions have taken place on the economic and domestic legal aspects of the initiative, it is no less important to consider other aspects of the initiative, in particular to look at what changes it might bring to the field of international law and international governance.

International law is playing an increasingly important role in furthering economic reform and development in China. Focusing on both comparative pragmatic and theoretical aspects of international governance and rule of law under the BRI, this edited volume brings together scholars from China and other jurisdictions along the road to share their perspectives and discuss its future impact from the perspective of international law.

Using a holistic point of view to examine China's role in the field of international governance and rule of law under the BRI, this edited volume seeks alternative analytical frameworks that not only take into account legal ideologies and legal ideals, but also local demand and sociopolitical circumstances, to explain and understand China's legal interactions with countries along the road so that more useful insights can be gained in predicting and analysing China's and other emerging Asian countries' legal future. Authors from Germany, Korea, Singapore, Mainland China, Taiwan and Hong Kong contributed to this volume, with the intention of fostering academic dialogue and conducting intellectual exchange in the identified sub-themes.

The theme of international governance and rule of law in China under the BRI was further divided into sub-themes, where Chinese legal development will often interact/conflict/integrate increasingly with the world's legal order/powers: (i) convergence of international rules; (ii) development of substantive international rules and China's contribution; and (iii) development of international dispute resolution. Correspondingly, this edited volume is divided into three parts. The first part (two chapters) provides macroscopic discussions on the impact of the BRI and convergence of relevant rules in the region. The second part (eight chapters) focuses on specific areas for cooperation under the initiative, including trade and investment, finance, environment and space. The last part (three chapters) examines different aspects of dispute resolution mechanisms under the BRI.

Some scholars in the areas of international law, international public relations or international politics have already contributed various academic works related to the BRI. Research topics related to the initiative strategy, and its impact on domestic and international aspects are prevalent in China among Chinese scholars. On the one hand, the initiative is positioned as a top-level and long-term development strategy by the Chinese government. On the other, Chinese scholars get easier access to first-hand information concerning recent development trends in the initiative; thus, they have the advantage of being in a position to produce more research in the field.

With the principle of rule of law taking a more prominent position, the initiative will no doubt bring change to China's role in international relationships in a wider and more comprehensive manner. This adjustment will affect China's attitude towards international governance. This edited volume includes contributions not yet published elsewhere, representing the latest research in legal reforms and development in China with special focus on international legal relationships. These contributions will lead to a better understanding of the ongoing legal adjustment and provide a fuller picture of the developing Chinese legal system under the BRI at the international level. It will be an excellent resource for the study of Chinese law and the Chinese legal system under this increasingly globalised society.

More importantly, the extensive coverage of the chapters organised in such a book format is more reader-friendly for scholars, and avoids the time-consuming search for various journal papers published on the theme of the BRI. Furthermore, this edited volume can fill the gap left by insufficient research and discussions concerning the rule of law in the BRI in respect of topics such as: legal frameworks; implementation of international law, rules and agreements; the integration of new rules with existing rules; related IPR customs enforcement; and others. The scholars involved in this book project can also take the opportunity to generate more creative ideas through mutual exchange, and present valuable academic discussions to the readers.

Jingxia Shi (Chapter 1) examines the kind of role international law can play in promoting the implementation of the BRI and argues that China should attach more importance to international law in order to create a more friendly environment to strengthen the implementation of the initiative. In analysing why and how international law can promote the initiative, Shi makes reference to the theory of international public goods (IPGs) and studies the role of international law in providing these IPGs. The analysis is premised on the examination of whether the initiative has the characteristic of non-rivalry and non-excludability, and thus can be regarded as IPGs. Shi concludes with some suggestions on how China can move forward in formulating new-generation international economic and trade rules and how the BRI can serve as an optimal opportunity for China to develop into an active player in international rule-making.

Samuli Seppänen (Chapter 2) re-examines received perceptions on Chinese conceptions of sovereignty and argues that the received narrative is flawed in two significant ways. First, it overemphasises the distinction between the 'absolutist' and 'relativist' conceptions of sovereignty. Second, it fails to account for the performative nature of Chinese uses of sovereignty. Seppänen argues that the absolutist statements on sovereignty by Chinese leaders are better seen as performative acts rather than as logical propositions about the actual nature of sovereignty. The 'Three Nos' doctrine, as part of the BRI, is used to illustrate the argument that absolutist statements about sovereignty are intended for international use and they are not constitutive of conceptions of state power within China.

Jaemin Lee (Chapter 3) points out the importance of a proper framework under the BRI. Depending on how the initiative is implemented and through which legal vehicles, Lee posits that we may need to answer such questions as whether such a new cooperative agreement and regime are indeed compatible with provisions of the World Trade Organization (WTO) agreements, free trade agreements (FTAs) and bilateral investment treaties (BITs).

Sarah Wersborg (Chapter 4) picks up the enforcement of the Anti-Monopoly Law in China as a starting point to examine the latest developments in administrative and private enforcement of the law under the BRI. Wersborg not only reflects on the developments of the Anti-Monopoly Law, but also analyses the practical implications of the enforcement of the law to date by the authorities and courts.

Kelvin Hiu Fai Kwok (Chapter 5) looks at China's BRI from the perspective of cooperation in trade liberalisation and anti-trust enforcement between China and other countries which form part of the initiative. It argues that the initiative can only succeed in achieving its goal of 'unimpeded trade' with three essential components: (i) reduction in transportation costs for foreign imports; (ii) removal of government-imposed trade barriers by cooperation in trade liberalisation; and (iii) elimination of anti-competitive behaviour of private firms which affects cross-border trade by cooperation in anti-trust enforcement.

Wei Shen (Chapter 6) investigates whether the Belt and Road Initiative can be used to solidify China's efforts to frame a global investment governance regime, alongside its aggressive stance in negotiating BITs with the United States and the EU as well as regional investment treaties in Asia Pacific. Sheng concludes that deepening China's BIT network in the regions covered by the BRI is crucial for widening China's outbound investment in these regions.

Christopher Chen (Chapter 7) explores legal challenges and business opportunities for Chinese banks in the face of continuing efforts of financial integration in Southeast Asia under the Association of Southeast Asian Nations (ASEAN) framework, amid China's grand BRI in 2015 and the establishment of the ASEAN Economic Community effective from 2016. Chen outlines the current development in banking regulations and financial integration in ASEAN, and discusses how current regimes and legal obstacles might affect Chinese banks in the future.

Yue Peng (Chapter 8) examines the relationship between the loans of multilateral development financial institutions (MDFIs) and the Asian Infrastructure Investment Bank (AIIB). To facilitate the AIIB's cooperation with the MDFIs, Peng argues that the AIIB should follow current models established by World Banks, and the International Finance Cooperation and Asian Development Bank, and apply laws in line with the different characteristic of loan agreements.

Yongmin Bian (Chapter 9) investigates the role of environmental impact assessment (EIA) in the governance of Nu-Salween river in order to identify the flaws in the current approaches and experience for sustainable use of shared water. EIA law has been implemented for more than a decade in China; but scholars cast doubt on its effectiveness. Bian's comparative study of the Chinese and Burmese approaches to EIA reveals one dilemma for the Chinese government: although its domestic governance for the environment has not been very successful, foreign investors may be required to follow higher or even best practice in the unfolding of the BRI. As such, with a big share of investments coming from the Belt and Road region, China will in the end come up with more policies to stimulate green development under the BRI.

Yun Zhao (Chapter 10) takes up the task of examining the role of regional cooperation in the Asia-Pacific region and discusses how such regional cooperation can contribute to the maintenance of space security. Zhao outlines the principles and guidelines that should be followed in future regional space cooperation. He concludes by stating that regional space cooperation is a vital element in furthering security in outer space and that the Asia-Pacific region should further strengthen space cooperation under the BRI.

Focusing on the East Asian region, Yuhong Chai (Chapter 11) analyses and discusses the role of the regional dispute resolution model for international disputes. Chai's comparative study shows that an appropriate model for resolving international civil and commercial disputes in the region can be established. Chai elaborates on how to deal with the relationship between regional dispute resolution and international dispute resolution from the perspective of competition and cooperation.

Weixia Gu (Chapter 12) argues that 'true' harmonisation of the public policy exceptions is necessary to promote a cogent and coherent system of arbitral enforcement across the globe and, hence, harmonisation of international commercial arbitration. It is perceived that the BRI actually provides the incentive and reason to contemplate the possibility of a regional or 'geo-legal' harmonisation of public policy in cross-border arbitral enforcement in Asia, against the backdrop of a prevalence of harmonisation of arbitration laws in Asia. Gu concludes that while the presence of different legal systems and cultures in Asia offers formidable challenges, harmonisation of public policy exception in cross-border arbitration in Asia will yield greater benefits in trade and investment interests both with respect to China and extending to Asia alongside the Belt and Road jurisdictions.

Shengli Jiang (Chapter 13) explores the ways to effectively and reasonably resolve international trade disputes brought by China and other countries along the Belt and Road. Jiang argues that it is not feasible to resolve the trade disputes by simply copying or directly resorting to the existing global or regional trade dispute settlement mechanisms and that a new international mechanism should be established to meet demand. Jiang proposes that an appropriate mechanism should be established in a flexible form, which would take arbitration and diplomatic measures as its main dispute settlement channels. Jiang further suggests that the new mechanism should set up a specialised dispute settlement institution, taking 'optional compulsory jurisdiction' over the disputes.

This edited volume is the final product of an international conference organised by the Centre for Chinese Law, Faculty of Law, University of Hong Kong in June 2016. It would not have been possible without the support from all the contributors and the financial sponsorship from the Faculty of Law. I would like to thank Shelby Chan and Erika Hebblethwaite for their capable assistance in the editorial process.

PART I

Convergence of International Rules

1

The Belt and Road Initiative and International Law

An International Public Goods Perspective

JINGXIA SHI*

Since it was first advocated by Chinese President Xi Jinping, the Belt and Road Initiative (BRI)[1] has drawn international attention and become something of a buzzword. The BRI undoubtedly presents unprecedented development opportunities, but it is also associated with a variety of risks and challenges both for China and other countries worldwide. This chapter examines the role that international law can play in promoting BRI implementation. Its central argument is that China needs to attach greater importance to international law to create a friendly international environment and smoother landing for the initiative. In analysing why and how international law can promote BRI implementation, the chapter

* The author greatly appreciates the opportunities to present earlier versions of this chapter at the Faculty of Law, The University of Hong Kong on 5 June 2016, at the invitation of Yun Zhao; at the Biennial Conference of the American Society of International Law's International Economic Law Interest Group on 1 October 2016, at the invitation of Sonia Rolland; and at the Silk Road Institute for International and Comparative Law's Tenth Anniversary Symposium at Xi'an Jiaotong University on 1 November 2016, at the invitation of Wenhua Shan. Sincere gratitude also goes to the commentators at these conferences for their opinions and comments on the earlier versions and to the peer reviewers of this chapter for their helpful suggestions. The research presented herein was partly funded by the UIBE Collaborative Innovation Center for Chinese Enterprises Going Global (Project No. 201501YY001A). All errors are the author's alone.

[1] In August 2015, China's National Development and Reform Commission (NDRC), together with the Ministry of Foreign Affairs and Ministry of Commerce, clarified that the Belt and Road Initiative (BRI), also known as 'One Belt, One Road', is the official English translation, and that such words as 'strategy', 'programme', 'agenda' and 'project' are inaccurate. The word 'initiative' has been incorporated into the official abbreviation to stress the BRI's openness and to avoid any misunderstanding over 'China-centred institution building' as the initiative progresses. See National Development and Reform Commission (NDRC), 'NDRC and other related ministries set "BRI" as the official translation in English', 21 September 2015, accessed 12 March 2018 at www.ndrc.gov .cn/gzdt/201509/t20150921_751695.html.

makes references to the theory of international public goods (IPGs) and explores international law's role in IPG provision. The analysis herein is premised on an examination of whether the BRI features the characteristics of non-rivalry and non-excludability, and can therefore be deemed an IPG. Then, in discussing the role that international law can play in fulfilling the BRI's ambitions, the chapter looks at the existing bilateral, regional and international legal arrangements between China and the other BRI countries. Its primary conclusion is that China needs to extend its newly established 'law-based governance'[2] to the international arena by employing international legal mechanisms in BRI implementation. The chapter concludes with some observations on how China can move forward in realising its goals in the face of competition in formulating new-generation international economic and trade rules. The BRI provides an ideal opportunity for China to become an active player in international rule-making.

Recent years have witnessed the slow recovery of the global economy following the 2008 financial crisis, as well as emerging markets taking a larger share of that economy.[3] The international trade and investment landscape and multilateral rules are undergoing the most substantive adjustments seen since the establishment of the World Trade Organization (WTO) in 1995.[4] There is a pressing need to redress the limited role

---

[2] It was put forward on 23 October 2014 in the *Communiqué of the Fourth Plenary Session of the 18th Central Committee of the Communist Party of China* that China was to comprehensively advance 'the law-based governance of the country' ('*yi fa zhi guo*'); translated by Communist Party of China (CCP) Compilation and Translation Bureau, accessed 8 June 2018 at www.china.org.cn/china/fourth_plenary_session/2014-12/02/content_34208801.htm. Then, on 5 January 2016, China issued a guideline promoting 'law-based governance', vowing to build a rule-of-law government by 2020. See, e.g. Xinhua News Agency, 'China issues guideline to promote law-based governance', 5 January 2016, accessed 8 June 2018 at http://news.xinhuanet.com/english/2016–01/05/c_134979341.htm.

[3] These observations are based on recent economic statistics. See, e.g. Organisation for Economic Co-operation and Development (OECD), 'Gross domestic product (GDP)', accessed 8 June 2018 at http://doi:10.1787/dc2f7aec-en; 'FDI flows', accessed 8 June 2018 at http://doi:10.1787/99f6e393-en; 'FDI stocks', accessed 8 June 2018 at http://doi:10.1787/80eca1f9-en.

[4] See, e.g. Friends of the Earth International, *Dangerous Liaisons: The New Trade Trio – How the US and the EU are Using TTIP, TPP and TiSA to Outmanoeuvre Other WTO Members*, accessed 8 June 2018 at www.foei.org/wp-content/uploads/2016/11/foe-trade-bookletWEB.pdf.

traditionally played by developing economies in existing international institutions.[5] This is particularly true of China, a rising power whose economy has grown from strength to strength in recent decades.

The BRI[6] has been described as a key element of China's 'new round of reform and opening-up to the world', the phrase used by President Xi to advocate for his economic blueprint in foreign relations.[7] The countries along the BRI contain almost two-thirds of the world's population, and account for one-third of global GDP and three-quarters of known energy reserves.[8] The BRI's primary aims are to promote closer connections amongst nations and boost development by creating additional opportunities for cross-border trade, investment, technological innovation and other economic activities and the cross-border movement of people.[9] As a major component of China's overall reform-based economic strategy, the BRI also constitutes a response to the new global economy in which markets, energy resources and trade and investment are increasingly integrated. In developing the initiative, China has also been adjusting

---

[5] See Hongtao Zhang, 'China's road to participate in international rule-making' (2016) 12 (4) *Canadian Social Science* 51–5; see also Jeffrey J. Schott, Cathleen Cimino-Isaacs and Euijin Jung, *Implications of the Trans-Pacific Partnership for the World Trading System*, Policy Brief 16–8 (Washington, DC: Peterson Institute of International Economics (PIIE), July 2016).

[6] The BRI comprises the Silk Road Economic Belt (SREB) and New Maritime Silk Road (NMSR). Chinese President Xi Jinping unveiled the SREB on 7 September 2013 during a state visit to Kazakhstan, and the NMSR was announced before the Indonesian Parliament on 3 October 2013 as part of his state visit to Indonesia.

[7] President Xi used the phrase during a Politburo study session. See Jinping Xi, 'Accelerating the implementation of a free-trade zone strategy, accelerating the construction of a new economic model based on openness', *Xinhua News Agency*, 6 December 2014, accessed 12 March 2018 at http://news.xinhuanet.com/politics/2014–12/06/c_1113546075.htm.

[8] Given these statistics and the vast geographic expanse involved, the BRI has been described as 'the most significant and far-reaching initiative that China has ever put forward'. For the quote, see Jianmin Wu, '"One Belt and One Road," far-reaching initiative', *China-US Focus*, 26 March 2015, accessed 12 March 2018 at www.chinaus focus.com/finance-economy/one-belt-and-one-road-far-reaching-initiative/. See also Jianmin Wu, 'China to play a bigger role as a world contributor', *China Daily*, 20 April 2015, accessed 8 June 2018 at http://usa.chinadaily.com.cn/opinion/2015-04/20/content_20481447.htm.

[9] NDRC, Ministry of Foreign Affairs and Ministry of Commerce of China, Vision and Action Plan on the China-proposed Belt and Road Initiative (BRI Vision and Action Plan hereafter). The BRI Vision and Action Plan was jointly issued by these bodies with State Council authorisation in March 2015. See http://en.ndrc.gov.cn/newsrelease/201503/t20150330_669367.html (accessed 12 April 2018).

its domestic economic structure to further promote economic transformation and upgrading.[10] Thus, from the policy perspective, the BRI
has been prioritised within China's national development strategy, and
become an integral part of the country's new round of reform and
opening up to the world.[11]

In recognition of the BRI's significance and potential impact on the
international economic and trade order, this chapter examines the role
that international law can play in helping to develop the initiative. It
argues that China should attach more importance to international law in
order to create a friendly international environment to smooth the BRI's
implementation. Instead of merely contemplating the potential contribution of international law in this regard, the chapter forges its thesis from
the perspective of IPGs. The analysis proceeds as follows. Subsequent to
this introduction, Section 1 addresses the question of whether the BRI
can be viewed as an IPG by examining whether it features the characteristics of non-rivalry and non-excludability and/or other related features.
Section 2 then discusses the various risks and challenges associated with
the BRI's ambitions, a discussion that serves to demonstrate the great
value of legal mechanisms at both the public and private levels. Section 3
turns to the role of international law in providing IPGs in general, and
then focuses on existing bilateral, regional and multilateral institutions
to highlight the significance of both upgrading current instruments and
putting new mechanisms in place to boost BRI development effectively.
Section 4 closes the chapter with concluding remarks concerning the
necessity for China to capitalise on the opportunities the BRI affords to
enhance its ability to make international trade and economic rules in
addition to the economic opportunities the initiative offers.

1   The BRI as an International Public Good

This section considers whether the BRI can be regarded as an international (if not yet truly global) public good by examining whether the

---

[10] The BRI is expected to have a major domestic impact in China. One of its key domestic
objectives is to accelerate the development of the country's western and central provinces.
See Hill-Choi Lee, 'China's One Belt One Road initiative set to transform economy by
connecting with trading partners along ancient Silk Road', *South China Morning Post*,
21 June 2016.

[11] See, e.g. Yiwen Hua, 'The time is just right for comprehensively advancing "One
Belt, One Road"', *People's Daily* (overseas edition), 11 March 2015; see also Nathan
Beauchamp-Mustafaga, 'NPC meeting touts new Silk Road as new driver for economic
growth', *China Brief*, No. 6, 19 March 2015.

initiative has the two basic properties of IPGs and the extent to which it may be deemed to constitute a man-made global commons. The section thus lays the foundation for the discussions in subsequent sections concerning the link between international law and IPG provision and the role of international law in BRI implementation.

1.1   Background: The Concept and Properties of IPGs

The theory of global public goods (GPGs) is, in essence, grounded in the neoclassical economic theory of (national) public goods.[12] Thus, its roots lie outside international law, which renders it necessary to present some background information on the emergence, evolution and essentials of the IPG concept (the author uses the terms GPGs and IPGs interchangeably). In the economic literature, contrary to such private goods as a cake or a car, public goods are traditionally defined as both non-rivalrous (*in the sense that anyone can benefit from them without diminishing the quantity available to others*) and non-excludable goods (*in the sense that no one can realistically be excluded from their consumption*).[13] Because of these two characteristics, public goods often produce externalities, and are structurally affected by the free-rider dilemma and the problems of over-consumption and under-provision.[14] Hence, GPGs (or IPGs) are

[12] See Meghnad Desai, 'Public goods: a historical perspective', in Inge Kaul, Pedro Conceição, Katell Le Goulven and Ronald U. Mendoza (eds.), *Providing Global Public Goods: Managing Globalization* (Oxford: Oxford University Press, 2003), p. 63.

[13] For a discussion of non-rivalrous consumption, see Paul A. Samuelson, 'The pure theory of public expenditure' (1954) 36 *Review of Economics and Statistics* 387. For a description of how Samuelson reshaped the way in which economists and political philosophers think about the distinction between public and private goods, see William D. Nordhaus, 'Paul Samuelson and global public goods: a commemorative essay for Paul Samuelson', in Michael Szenberg, Lall Ramrattan and Aron A. Gottesman (eds.), *Samuelsonian Economics and the Twenty-First Century* (Oxford: Oxford University Press, 2006), pp. 88–98. See also Richard Cornes and Todd Sandler, *The Theory of Externalities, Public Goods, and Club Goods*, 2nd edn (Cambridge: Cambridge University Press, 1996), pp. 144–5; Samuel Cogolati, Linda Hamid and Nils Vanstappen, 'Global public goods and democracy: what role for international law?' Leuven Centre for Global Governance Studies, Working Paper No. 159, May 2015.

[14] The free-rider problem occurs when a person or entity is able to consume a good without paying for it. Classic examples include national defence, public roads and police protection. The free-rider problem means that private companies face considerable challenges in producing public goods. Externalities occur whenever the benefit or cost of consuming a good affects people who are not actually consuming it, and come in two forms: positive and negative. Negative externalities are always oversupplied in the market, whilst positive externalities are always undersupplied. See Tyler Cowen, 'Public goods and externalities', in David Henderson (ed.), *The Concise Encyclopedia of Economics*, 2nd edn (Carmel, IN:

goods that are non-rivalrous and non-excludable worldwide.[15] GPGs are not a new phenomena. Indeed, more than a decade ago Kaul et al. linked GPGs and globalisation[16] and defined GPGs as 'outcomes (or intermediate products) that tend towards universality in the sense that they benefit all countries, population groups, and generations'.[17] It has also been maintained that GPGs should be redefined to be seen not as goods that are purely non-rivalrous and non-excludable at the global level, but as 'goods that are in the global public domain'.[18]

Over the past two decades or so, IPGs have stood at the centre of the policy discourse of prominent international organisations, state and non-governmental alike, particularly concerning the topic of development.[19] For instance, the World Bank defines GPGs as commodities, resources, services, regulations and policy institutions that have strong cross-border externalities, are critical to development and rooting-out poverty, and

---

Liberty Fund, 2007); James M. Buchanan, 'Public goods in theory and practice: a note on the Minasian-Samuelson discussion' (1967) 10 *Journal of Law and Economics* 193–7; Paul A. Samuelson, 'Pitfalls in the analysis of public goods' (1967) 10 *Journal of Law and Economics* 199–204; Jora R. Minasian, 'Public goods in theory and practice revisited' (1967) 10 *Journal of Law and Economics* 205–7. Also compare with 'club goods', which are non-rivalrous but excludable (e.g. a toll road), and 'common pool resources', which are rivalrous but non-excludable (e.g. high-seas fisheries). See Nordhaus, 'Paul Samuelson and global public goods'; Daniel Bodansky, 'What's in a concept? Global public goods, international law and legitimacy' (2012) 23 *European Journal of International Law* 652–3; Katharina Holzinger, 'Common goods, matrix games and institutional responses' (2003) 9 *European Journal of International Relations* 173, 176. There are several possible reasons for the GPG supply shortage, including issues of sovereignty and differing preferences and priorities. See International Task Force on Global Public Goods (ed.), *Meeting Global Challenges: International Cooperation in the National Interests*, final report (Stockholm, Sweden: International Task Force on Global Public Goods, 2006).

[15] See Devesh Kapur, 'The common pool dilemma of global public goods: lesson from the World Bank's net income and reserves' (2002) 30(3) *World Development* 337–54.

[16] See Inge Kaul, Pedro Conceição, Katell Le Goulven and Ronald U. Mendoza (eds.), *Providing Global Public Goods: Managing Globalization* (Oxford: Oxford University Press, 2003). The book emphasises that the pursuit of GPGs, along with the prevention of global public 'bads', facilitates the attainment of a more equitable, and hence more stable, world order.

[17] Inge Kaul, Isabelle Grunberg and Marc A. Stern, 'Defining global public goods', in Inge Kaul, Isabelle Grunberg and Marc A. Stern (eds.), *Global Public Goods: International Cooperation in the 21st Century* (New York, NY: Oxford University Press, 1999), p. 16.

[18] See Maurizio Carbone, 'Supporting or resisting global public goods? The policy dimension of a contested concept' (2007) 13 *Global Governance* 183.

[19] Ibid.; see also Kapur, 'The common pool dilemma'.

can be supplied only through international cooperation and collective action.[20] The World Bank further divides GPGs/IPGs into two categories: (i) final public goods, which are outcomes such as the UN's Millennium Development Goals (MDGs),[21] and (ii) intermediate public goods, which are all goods contributing to some final public good, such as international health regulations that prevent the cross-border spread of infections.[22]

The problem at the international level, however, is that there is no centralised state-like entity available to provide public goods that know no national boundaries, such as, inter alia, the mitigation of climate change.[23] This reality, coupled with the process of globalisation, prompted the United Nations Development Programme (UNDP) to take the lead in the process of understanding the conceptual and methodological developments involved, as well as the public policy dimensions surrounding the IPG phenomenon. In particular, the institution organised a series of research efforts and published three books on the topic in 1999,[24] 2003[25] and 2006.[26]

Beyond the efforts of the World Bank and UNDP, the IPG discourse is becoming ever more important in the face of globalisation, rapid technological innovation and the astounding decline in transport and communication costs. Economic globalisation demands more IPGs. In the same way that the concept of public goods has served to justify the welfare function of the state at the national level in Samuelson's theory,[27] the concept of IPGs has been developed 'to enhance the scope for global

---

[20] Vinay Bhargava (ed.), *Global Issues for Global Citizens: An Introduction to Key Development Challenges* (Washington, DC: World Bank, 2006).

[21] The eight MDGs, which range from halving extreme poverty rates to halting the spread of HIV/AIDS and providing universal primary education, form a blueprint agreed to by all countries and leading development institutions. The UN is also working with governments, civil society institutions and other partners to build on the momentum generated by the MDGs. For further details, see www.un.org/millenniumgoals/ (accessed 12 April 2018).

[22] See Bhargava, *Global Issues for Global Citizens*.

[23] See Scott Barrett, *Why Cooperate? The Incentive to Supply Global Public Goods* (Oxford: Oxford University Press, 2007); Todd Sandler, *Global Collective Action* (Cambridge: Cambridge University Press, 2004).

[24] Kaul et al., 'Defining global public goods'.

[25] Kaul et al., *Providing Global Public Goods*.

[26] Inge Kaul and Pedro Conceição (eds.), *The New Public Finance: Responding to Global Challenges* (New York: Oxford University Press, 2006).

[27] See Cogolati et al., 'Global public goods and democracy'.

governance and thus legitimise their [IPGs] pursuit'.[28] On the one hand, in response to the ever-growing size of international trade and investment, it is necessary to increase the supply of IPGs. On the other, the economic imbalances seen in recent decades are one of the root causes of conflicts amongst a growing number of countries,[29] and an increase in the IPG supply could well serve to mitigate those conflicts.

1.2   BRI Characteristics of Non-Rivalry and Non-Excludability

In general, IPGs are goods whose benefits could in principle be consumed by all governments and their peoples. Thus, in order to be deemed an IPG, the BRI should conform to the two basic characteristics of an IPG outlined above, namely, non-rivalry and non-excludability. The BRI does indeed have these characteristics thanks to its openness to the participation of all countries and the potential benefits for all countries and population groups interested in participating.

In recent years, in conjunction with its status as a rising power and in response to demands that it shoulder more responsibility in terms of IPG provision, China has been playing a more active role on the world stage.[30] The BRI constitutes a significant step towards the country's goal of tackling the under-delivery of IPGs. According to the BRI Vision and Action Plan, the initiative is open and inclusive, rather than exclusive.[31] Its open nature affords it greater flexibility with respect to future operations. In stressing the open and cooperative nature of the BRI, Chinese diplomat and politician Wang Yi has employed the metaphor of a

---

[28] See Gregory Schaffer, 'International law and global public goods in a legal pluralist world' (2012) 23 European Journal of International Law 670.

[29] François Godement and Agatha Kratz (eds.), One Belt, One Road, China's Great Leap Outward (Brussels: European Council on Foreign Relations), p. 7; see also 'Foreign Minister Wang Yi meets the press', Ministry of Foreign Affairs of the People's Republic of China, 8 March 2015, accessed 12 April 2018 at www.fmprc.gov.cn/mfa_eng/wjb_663304/wjbz_663308/2461_663310/t1243662.shtml.

[30] See Angang Hu, China in 2020: A New Type of Superpower (Washington, DC: Brookings Institution Press, 2011), p. 17. Former US President Barack Obama also urged China to provide more public goods for the international community. See, e.g. 'Remarks by President Obama and President Xi of the People's Republic of China in joint press conference', The White House Office of the Press Secretary, 25 September 2015, accessed 12 April 2018 at https://obamawhitehouse.archives.gov/the-press-office/2015/09/25/remarks-president-obama-and-president-xi-peoples-republic-china.joint.

[31] BRI Vision and Action Plan, Part II (Principles).

'symphony' to highlight that the initiative will involve the participation of many countries rather than being a 'solo' effort by China alone.[32] As currently envisaged, the BRI covers, but is not limited to, the area of the ancient Silk Road, and is open to all countries that want to enjoy peace and development, with no additional conditions attached. All countries, regardless of their proximity to the geographic BRI area, are invited to participate in the initiative to contribute to the economic prosperity of their respective nation or region.[33] The initiative is also open to the engagement of international and regional organisations to ensure broader benefits. In this sense, the BRI is compatible with the non-excludability requirement of an IPG.

Furthermore, IPGs must produce benefits that are available across countries. The BRI promises such benefits in the form of increased connectivity, which can result in improved quality of life in developing countries and the opening up of economic opportunities for their developed counterparts. The potential secondary benefits include greater international security and bolstered state capacity arising from development.[34] At the same time, China is following the principle of shared benefits in the BRI's implementation, which means that the initiative is to be jointly undertaken by all countries involved, and accordingly benefit all countries involved, through mutual cooperation and consultation.[35] In this sense, it is compatible with the non-rivalry requirement of an IPG to some extent.

It should be noted that after sixty years of development, the concept of public goods has evolved from a traditional and static one to a modern and dynamic one. Public goods are now generally divided into three categories: *pure public goods*, that is, non-exclusive, non-rivalrous public goods; *club goods*, whose consumption is non-rivalrous, but can be easily

---

[32] Wang used the metaphor during a press conference on 8 March 2015, during which he stated that the BRI was 'not China's solo, but a symphony performed by all relevant countries'. See 'Foreign Minister Wang Yi meets the press', *China Daily*, 8 March 2015; Mingjie Li, 'How to play the 'One Belt, One Road' symphony well', *Liaowang (Outlook)*, 24 March 2015.

[33] Yi Hu, 'China's One Belt and One Road Policy Is Open to All Nations', 20 March 2015, accessed 15 June 2018 at www.larouchepub.com/eiw/public/2015/eirv42n12-20150320/27-29_4212.pdf.

[34] Alek Chance, 'The belt and road initiative and the US-China relationship', Institute for China-America Studies (ICAS) Bulletin, 15 November 2016, accessed 8 June 2018 at http://chinaus-icas.org/materials/belt-road-initiative-us-china-relationship.

[35] BRI Vision and Action Plan, Part VIII (Embracing A Brighter Future Together).

excludable; and *common resources*, which are non-rivalrous in consumption, but are not effectively excludable. The latter two are also known as 'quasi-public goods'. Hence, if the BRI does not constitute a pure public good, it at least matches the characteristics of a club good or common resource.

1.3   BRI as Man-Made Global Commons

The IPG concept, as reconstructed by the UNDP, covers a very large spectrum of global issues,[36] ranging from (1) 'natural global commons' such as climate stability; (2) 'human-made global commons' such as cultural heritage and knowledge;[37] to (3) 'global policy outcomes' such as distributive justice.[38] The BRI may fall within the ambit of the second category, i.e. it is a China-advocated initiative with the capacity to be transformed into a global commons. At another level, IPGs have developed, and indeed come to include, economic governance and trade integration.[39] The BRI's declared aim is to provide more balanced economic governance and trade, investment and financial integration. Reflecting the common ideals and pursuits of humane societies, the BRI can be seen as a positive endeavour to seek new models of international cooperation and global governance and to inject new energy into the pursuit of world peace and development.

In this way, China is attempting to contribute to a more reasonable, balanced and sustainable system of global governance than that which exists now. As Kaul et al. point out, there are three central weaknesses to the current system of global governance in terms of providing IPGs: (1) the 'jurisdictional gap', i.e. the absence of a state-like entity at the global level to supply IPGs; (2) the 'participation gap', i.e. the exclusion of certain countries, population groups (including future generations), civil

---

[36] The three classes of GPGs are detailed in Kaul et al., 'Global public goods: concepts, policies and strategies', in Kaul et al., *Global Public Goods*, pp. 454–5.

[37] See Ismail Serageldin, 'Cultural heritage as public good: economic analysis applied to historic cities', in Kaul et al., Global Public Goods, p. 240.

[38] See Joseph E. Stiglitz, 'Knowledge as a global public good', in Kaul et al., Global Public Goods, p. 308.

[39] See World Bank Development Committee, *Poverty Reduction and Global Public Goods: Issues for the World Bank in Supporting Global Collective Action*, DC/2000–16, 5–8 (Washington, DC: World Bank, 2000).

society and businesses from the decision-making process surrounding IPG provision; and (3) the 'incentive gap', i.e. the lack of perceived benefits for all parties involved in international cooperation to produce and finance IPGs.[40]

Owing to its open nature and China's commitment to openness, the BRI duly fills these three global governance gaps. First, it constitutes an ambitious economic vision for transparent cooperation between China and all countries interested in participating. In addition, the BRI plan contemplates long-term projects aimed at promoting a better-integrated, more communicative international community that prospers both economically and culturally, thereby filling the jurisdictional gap with respect to the under-supply of IPGs. Second, under the auspices of the BRI, all participating countries are encouraged to work in concert and move towards the objectives of mutual benefit and common security. More specifically, the aims of the BRI are to improve regional infrastructure and put in place a secure and efficient land, sea and air network, thereby boosting connectivity, and further to enhance trade and investment facilitation by establishing a network of free-trade areas that meet high standards and maintain close economic ties.[41] Such openness and cooperation are conducive to filling the aforementioned participation gap. Third, given its economic power and strength, China is committed to shouldering more responsibilities and financing obligations within its capabilities. As previously noted, the BRI is not only a comprehensive plan for international cooperation, but also a blueprint for China's own development, which is said to be entering a 'new normal' stage.[42] In essence, the initiative thus offers a ride on China's economic express train, which, to a large extent, is helpful in filling the incentive gap. Significant progress has been made towards BRI implementation in the past three years,[43] and thus it is hoped that the initiative will become a new type of global commons for the twenty-first century.

---

[40] Kaul et al., 'Defining global public goods', p. xxvi.

[41] BRI Vision and Action Plan, Part IV (Cooperation Priorities).

[42] See, e.g. Xiaoming Liu, 'New Silk Road is an opportunity not a threat', *Financial Times*, 24 May 2015, accessed 13 April 2018, www.ft.com/content/c8f58a7c-ffd6-11e4-bc30-00144feabdc0.

[43] For detailed information on the main achievements of the BRI, see the Belt and Road Progress Research Team of Renmin University of China, *Adhering to the Planning, Orderly and Pragmatically Build the 'Belt and Road'* (Beijing: Renmin University of China, 2016).

2   Risks and Challenges Associated with BRI Implementation

Although it may be a good international economic strategy, navigating the BRI's implementation will be no easy task for China. The initiative presents both unprecedented development opportunities and a variety of risks and challenges for both China and the other countries involved. This section draws on the perspectives of legal security and risk prevention to assess those risks and challenges, providing a basis for the subsequent discussion of the role that international law may play in realising the BRI's ambitions.

The BRI brings the Chinese government's 'going out' initiative into strategic focus. That initiative encourages Chinese enterprises to go abroad in search of new markets and/or investment opportunities to absorb the overproduction capacity in the country's current stage of economic transition. Although the BRI promises opportunities for Chinese companies, the path is unlikely to be smooth. The initiative encompasses countries as diverse as Singapore and Syria,[44] with the geographical, geopolitical, economic and legal conditions varying widely, particularly along continental routes.[45] Consequently, the companies that decide to take part may be heading into territories that are strategically important in terms of foreign relations, but present some potentially overwhelming difficulties from the business perspective. It is clear that there are myriad risks, including political, commercial, environmental, cultural and religious risks, associated with BRI implementation. Political instability constitutes the major risk, and it is highly likely it will slow down implementation efforts. For example, a China-funded water pipe construction project in Libya was burnt down in 2014, and more than 200 container trucks had to be abandoned on the roadside in Kyrgyzstan because of protests by angry locals in the same year.[46] Similarly, elections in Sri Lanka

---

[44] See 'The Belt and Road Initiative: country profiles', Hong Kong Trade Development Council (HKTDC) Research, 21 January 2016, http://china-trade-research.hktdc.com/business-news/article/The-Belt-and-Road-Initiative/The-Belt-and-Road-Initiative-Country-Profiles/obor/en/1/1X000000/1X0A36I0.htm. The countries listed have been selected based on a list compiled by the Chinese Academy of Social Sciences (CASS). Note, however, that according to the BRI Vision and Action Plan, the BRI is open to participation by all countries.

[45] The Economist Intelligence Unit (EIU), 'Prospects and challenges on China's "one belt, one road": a risk assessment report', *EIU*, accessed 8 June 2018 at www.eiu.com/public/topical_report.aspx?campaignid=OneBeltOneRoad.

[46] See Raffaello Pantucci and Qingzhen Chen, 'The geopolitical roadblocks', *China Analysis*, 10 June 2015.

disrupted the construction of a key port in 2015,[47] and in the same year the Cambodian government suspended a US$400 million dam project to be built by the Sinohydro Corporation until at least 2018 on environmental grounds.[48] An earlier example is the difficulties that China Power Investment encountered in its efforts to develop the Myitsone hydroelectric dam in Myanmar following the appointment of the new reformist government in 2011.[49]

All of these examples concern infrastructure projects, which typically require both the political stability of the host government and large sums of investment. Those involved need to be able to anticipate political shifts, which can alter the outcome of a large-scale project. At the same time, as facility connectivity is listed as one of the priorities for BRI implementation,[50] China has committed itself to investing heavily in a variety of infrastructure projects to strengthen the economic capacity of and connectivity amongst the nations involved. Several policy-orientated mechanisms have been designed and put into place entirely or in part to support the BRI's development, including the Silk Road Fund (SRF)[51] and Asian Infrastructure Investment Bank (AIIB).[52] Up to US$300 billion is slated for infrastructure financing in the coming years, not counting the leveraging effect on private investors and lenders. Financing for BRI projects is also provided by China's commercial banks.[53]

---

[47] The election in January 2015 of new Sri Lankan Prime Minister Maithripala Sirisena delayed the start of a US$1.4 billion port project in the country's capital, Colombo. The project had been awarded by the China-friendly former prime minister, Mahinda Rajapaksa. The delay imposed significant financial costs on the developer. See Jianxiong Ge, 'The history of one belt one road is misunderstood', *Financial Times* (Chinese version), 10 March 2015.

[48] EIU, 'Prospects and challenges on China's "one belt, one road"'.

[49] Ibid.

[50] BRI Vision and Action Plan, Part IV.

[51] The SRF was established in Beijing on 29 December 2014 as a long-term development and investment fund to provide investment and financial support for trade and economic cooperation and connectivity under the BRI. For more information, visit the SRF website: www.silkroadfund.com.cn/enweb/23773/index.html (accessed 8 June 2018).

[52] China proposed the AIIB in 2013, and the initiative was launched at a ceremony in Beijing in October 2014. It began operating on 25 December 2015. The AIIB serves as the financing arm of the BRI, and it began with authorised capital of US$50 billion, which is eventually to be raised to US$100 billion. The projected investment for the BRI is about US$1.4 trillion. For more information, visit the AIIB website: www.aiib.org/en/index.html (accessed 8 June 2018).

[53] For example, the Bank of China (BOC) has increased its financial support for enterprises implementing the BRI. In March 2015, the BOC promised US$5 billion in credit to Anhui Conch Cement to support its BRI endeavours abroad. The company is a state-owned

The financial firepower needed to promote BRI development has attracted mixed responses. Although the idea of enhancing connectivity has drawn considerable interest, given the huge infrastructure gaps across Asia and the world, scepticism regarding China's potential ambitions under cover of the BRI is prevalent amongst both regional rivals and the United States.[54] For instance, some see the BRI as a strategy for asserting China's leadership role in Asia in response to the US pivot towards Asia; as economic outreach to Asian countries as a means of resolving territorial and maritime disputes and exporting China's domestic development policies; as a means of tapping into new sources of growth to check the marked downturn in the Chinese economy; as a tool for tackling the socioeconomic divide between China's inland and coastal provinces; and as a vehicle to address the security challenges on the country's western periphery, as well as energy security issues.[55] These mixed responses to the initiative and the complicated international environment in which it must be implemented add another layer of risk.

In short, the BRI holds rich promise for Chinese enterprises looking to expand overseas, as well as for China's economic transition towards the 'new normal'. However, its implementation requires a new approach encompassing careful modelling of the associated risks and challenges. In this respect, it cannot be overemphasised that the BRI's forward development needs to operate by market principles and abide by market rules and international norms, give play to the decisive role of the market in resource allocation, as well as the primary role of private enterprise, and allow the governments involved to perform their due functions.[56] These factors hold the key to the BRI's success. To observe market rules and norms, a proper assessment of the risks and challenges in destination countries is advisable, given the wide range of countries involved and the magnitude of Chinese investment at stake. Failure to assess the risks involved appropriately will likely lead to huge financial losses and the

---

enterprise and the largest cement manufacturer in China. Over the next few years, the bank expects that its BRI construction-related credit will reach as high as US$100 billion. See the BOC website (in Chinese), accessed 8 June 2018 at www.bankofchina.com.

[54] See Godement and Kratz, *One Belt, One Road*.

[55] See, e.g. Gisela Grieger, *One Belt, One Road (OBOR): China's Regional Integration Initiative* (Brussels: European Parliamentary Research Service, July 2016); Colonel Chris Mills, 'The United-States' Asia-Pacific policy and the rise of the dragon' (2015) Spring *Indo-Pacific Strategic Digest* 185–99.

[56] BRI Vision and Action Plan, Part II.

waste of domestic preparations.[57] If companies encounter non-commercial problems in implementing BRI projects, there will be ramifications for both the companies themselves and the lenders backing their projects.[58] Accordingly, at the private law level, financial institutions need to be cognisant of the range of legal and credit-related risks present in BRI countries. In summary, although the BRI may be a grand initiative by China, considered planning and risk assessment and prevention mechanisms at the levels of both private and public law are needed if the initiative is to succeed.

3   Role of International Law in BRI Implementation

Given the various risks and challenges involved with BRI implementation, a question that naturally arises is how China can smooth the initiative's landing and protect the legitimate interests of the stakeholders involved. It is clear that the country needs to find an appropriate way to address what is a highly complex undertaking. The author of this chapter maintains that the BRI's successful implementation requires powerful and effective legal mechanisms suited to the complex issues that are likely to arise. This section first examines the role of international law in BRI implementation from the perspective of IPG provision in general, and then moves on to the international legal mechanisms that should be put in place to support the BRI in particular.

3.1   International Law and IPG Provision

The IPG concept has evolved from a technical economic concept into a powerful advocacy tool for greater international cooperation and regulation in today's globalised world,[59] particularly in the form of international law,[60] which can be used as a tool to aid the provision of IPGs.[61] Similar to the way in which national governments function to provide

---

[57] EIU 'Prospects and challenges on China's "one belt, one road"'.

[58] Ibid.

[59] See Jean Coussy, 'The adventures of a concept: is neo-classical theory suitable for defining global public goods?' (2005) 12 Review of International Political Economy 177.

[60] On the role of international law in providing IPGs, see Joel P. Trachtman, The Future of International Law: Global Government, ASIL Studies in International Legal Theory (New York: Cambridge University Press, 2014), p. 28.

[61] Schaffer, 'International law and global public goods', 670.

public goods, international law 'comprises a kind of rudimentary government' to provide IPGs.[62] Schaffer notes that international law 'is required
to produce global goods',[63] and Bodansky straightforwardly states that,
because IPGs 'cannot be adequately produced by the market, international institutions and international law are needed to help provide
them'.[64] Whilst the burgeoning scholarship in the IPG area is enlight-
ening, international legal scholarship remains fairly silent on the link
between IPGs and international law, with Bodansky describing international law as a relative 'late-comer' to the IPG debate.[65] Some authors
use IPG rhetoric to rehash specific issues of international law, whereas
others see the provision of IPGs as a new challenge for international
law.[66] The latter argue that this is the case primarily because, on the one
hand, public goods exacerbate ubiquitous collective-action problems
in the decentralised setting of global politics, whilst, on the other, both
the structure of international law itself and political power impose huge
obstacles to obtaining the unanimous or near-unanimous consent of
sovereign nations needed to take collective international action.[67] In part,
the situation reflects the reality that international law, in its classical
form, appears ill-suited to tackling these challenge because its consent-
based structure imposes high hurdles to, and thus creates a structural bias
against, effective action concerning IPGs, particularly in light of the large
number of sovereign states in existence today.[68] In the age of globalisation, according to a UNDP study, there are increasing numbers of GPGs
that transcend national boundaries and require cross-border collective
action for their provision,[69] which renders it necessary to take the limits
of international law into consideration in designing appropriate mechanisms for such provision.

However, from the economic perspective, certain types of IPGs do not
involve collective-action problems, and therefore suffer less from the
hurdles of the so-called Westphalian decision-making process.[70] Such

---

[62] Trachtman, *The Future of International Law*, pp. 7–9, 68.
[63] Schaffer, 'International law and global public goods', 670–1.
[64] Bodansky, 'What's in a concept?', 652.
[65] Ibid., 657.
[66] Ibid.
[67] Nordhaus, 'Paul Samuelson and global public goods'.
[68] Nico Krisch, 'The decay of consent: international law in an age of global public goods' (2014) 108 *American Journal of International Law* 1–40.
[69] Cogolati et al., 'Global public goods and democracy'.
[70] See Barrett, *Why Cooperate?*, chapters 1–3; Bodansky, 'What's in a concept?', 658–65; Schaffer, 'International law and global public goods', 675–81.

'single best-effort' goods, which can be provided by a single actor or group of actors, do not necessarily require joint rule-making and legal efforts, illustrating why China is now in a position to provide the BRI as a single actor thanks to its economic strengths and stated objective of benefiting all participating countries. Nevertheless, when it comes to effective IPG provision, even in the case of single best-effort goods, the contributions of partners are generally necessary.[71] Successful cooperation in IPG provision also helps to avoid the free-rider problem. Consequently, the joint construction of the BRI would conform to the participating countries' common interest in pursuing national development. At the same time, the sheer size of the investment required means that Chinese investors are increasingly looking for foreign partners to collaborate on projects. Notable projects already in the pipeline include construction of the US$11 billion Bagamoyo Port in Tanzania, which is being jointly funded by China Merchants Holdings International, a state-owned Chinese investment firm, and the State Government Reserve Fund of Oman.[72] This type of cooperation requires the safeguards of international law.

3.2   International Legal Mechanisms to Promote the BRI

As it currently stands, the BRI is a development strategy inspired by the land and maritime routes of the ancient Silk Road rather than a formal entity or treaty arrangement such as the Trans-Pacific Partnership (TPP).[73] Accordingly, it contrasts sharply with existing treaty-based integration concepts wherein the geographic scope, partner countries and principles and rules are clearly defined at the outset. Despite its seemingly loose form, however, a smooth landing for the BRI will require formal legal mechanisms that protect the rights and interests of the parties involved. The author maintains that China should further enhance the role of international law in implementing the BRI through bilateral, regional and multilateral mechanisms to attract the participation of more countries and regions. As noted above, international law faces difficulties in

---

[71] Barrett, *Why Cooperate?*, chapter 4.

[72] See Fumbuka Ng'wanakilala, 'Tanzania starts work on $10bln port project backed by China and Oman', *Reuters*, 16 October 2015, accessed 8 June 2018 at http://af.reuters.com/article/kenyaNews/idAFL8N12G3FZ20151016.

[73] The TPP and BRI have distinct cooperative frameworks. Whilst the aim of both is to expand and intensify the degree of connectivity amongst their participating states, they differ in their organising principles and modes of connectivity. See, e.g. Alice D. Ba, 'TPP, BRI and ASEAN: where will they lead to?' *RSIS Commentary*, No. 108, 11 May 2016, accessed 8 June 2018 at www.rsis.edu.sg/wp-content/uploads/2016/05/CO16108.pdf.

responding effectively to collective-action problems, and its consensual structure has often been seen as the main obstacle to the provision of IPGs. Those difficulties partly explain the potential barriers to formulating a multilateral instrument between China and other BRI participants, but also suggest instruments better suited to the current reality. Given the often-clogged channels of multilateralism,[74] China may opt instead to move towards bilateralism or regionalism, or even to turn to informal settings, although doing so would mean forgoing some of the benefits of formal, binding laws and institutions.[75] Examples of the bilateral or regional arrangements that might be practical options for China in promoting BRI implementation include bilateral investment treaties (BITs), bilateral or regional free trade agreements (FTAs) and double-taxation treaties (DTTs).[76] With regard to the substantive subjects on which these instruments should focus, the areas involving the most urgent legal issues include unimpeded trade and investment, dispute settlement, international finance integration, maritime transport, competition, e-commerce, consumer rights and protection and conflicts of law. In particular, the BRI is closely tied to China's ongoing pursuit of overseas investment and trade, and its implementation will open up new economic opportunities for Chinese enterprises. Thus, investment and trade cooperation is a major building block of the initiative's success, with particular emphasis on investment and trade facilitation, removing investment and trade barriers and creating a sound business environment in all countries involved. The need for such cooperation underscores the importance of BITs, FTAs and DTTs to realising the BRI's ambitions.

---

[74] The impasse surrounding the Doha Development Agenda (DDA) under the WTO framework is an example of the hurdles multilateralism has encountered. For the reasons for and analysis of multilateralism's predicament, see, e.g. Euan MacMillan, 'Explaining rising regionalism and failing multilateralism: consensus decision-making and expanding WTO membership' (2014) 11 *International Economics and Economic Policy* 599; Arvind Panagariya, 'Challenges to the multilateral trading system and possible responses', *Economics*, Discussion Papers No 2013-3, Kiel Institute for the World Economy, 10 January 2013, accessed 8 June 2018 at www.economics-ejournal.org/economics/discussionpapers/2013-3.

[75] See Krisch, 'The decay of consent', 1, 16.

[76] As of 30 June 2016, China had signed 102 tax treaties, 53 of them with BRI countries, thereby creating a tax treaty network that covers major investment sources and foreign investment destinations and helping to eliminate tax barriers to investment between China and the other signatory countries. For more information, see 'Tax treaty', State Administration of Taxation of the People's Republic of China, accessed 8 June 2018 at www.chinatax.gov.cn/eng/n2367756/index.html.

3.3   A Case in Point: BITs

Let's take BITs as an example. One of the BRI's pillars is the promotion of policy coordination amongst the countries along its route with respect to economic cooperation. BITs are essential to realising the increased flow of goods, services and capital envisioned by the BRI. From the outset of large-scale projects and throughout their lifespans, Chinese investors should ensure that their investments are protected by appropriate international laws to prevent any unjustifiable conduct that would harm the viability or profitability of the projects they fund and to mitigate any other potentially catastrophic effects. A BIT concluded between China and a partner BRI country would be of considerable relevance to a Chinese investor in the event of a discriminatory administrative system or poor corporate governance. Hence, the protection afforded investors by BITs would no doubt help China to attract investment for BRI projects.

If a Chinese investor is thinking about investing in a particular country, a key consideration will be whether a BIT is in force between that country and China and, if it is, which specific terms will protect his or her investment. Whilst the BRI without question presents attractive investment opportunities for Chinese investors, the very nature of investing in the countries involved, which carries significant risk, highlights the need for BITs that protect investors' rights and interests. As widely noted, much of the Chinese investment in the BRI countries flows to large-scale infrastructure projects such as energy, mining, construction and transport. Such projects not only require huge amounts of funding, but also rely on political stability and positive government attitudes towards foreign investment. Foreign investors often shy away from nations that suffer from political instability and corruption. Effective BITs can ensure that investors are treated fairly in host states, thereby mitigating the risks of direct or indirect expropriation without compensation.

China regards BITs as an important means of achieving unimpeded investment and trade amongst the BRI nations. The BRI Vision and Action Plan clearly states that countries along the BRI route should push forward negotiations on bilateral investment protection agreements 'to protect the lawful rights and interests of investors'.[77] Statistics show that

---

[77] BRI Vision and Action Plan, Part IV.

more than fifty BITs have been concluded between China and the BRI countries,[78] most of them signed in the 1980s and 1990s. However, the quality of these BITs is relatively low, particularly with regard to investment protection and market access. As a result, in addition to negotiating new BITs, alongside the negotiation and conclusion of the China–US[79] and China–EU BITs,[80] there is a pressing need for China and the BRI countries to update their existing BITs to cover both investment protection and market access on the basis of pre-entry national treatment and a negative list. It remains to be seen, however, the extent to which such BIT enhancement will take place, given the varying stages of negotiation taking place amongst such divergent countries.

At the same time, whilst the BITs agreed between China and the BRI countries may provide some comfort to Chinese investors at the public law level, that should not detract from the need for them to conduct proper due diligence for any BRI-related investments and to carefully consider the legal, regulatory and political risks associated with those investments. At the private law level, investors also need to give serious thought to how the foreign investment regime of the host country affects the types of investment that can be made and the way in which they are made.

---

[78] For information on the specific BITs concluded between China and the BRI countries, refer to the comprehensive database on international investment agreements compiled by the United Nations Conference on Trade and Development, accessed 13 April 2018 at http://investmentpolicyhub.unctad.org/IIA.

[79] China and the United States began negotiating a BIT in 2008, with thirty-one rounds of negotiation conducted by the end of 2016. The negotiations are based on a negative list approach, coupled with pre-entry national treatment, and the two sides were close to sealing a deal at the end of 2016. For further details, see Peterson Institute of International Economics (PIIE), *Toward A US-China Investment Treaty*, February 2015, PIIE Briefing 15-1; Congyan Cai, 'China-US BIT negotiations and the future of investment treaty regime: a grand bilateral bargain with multilateral implications' (2009) 12(2) *Journal of International Economic Law* 457–506.

[80] A China–EU BIT is also in the pipeline, with both sides agreeing to accelerate negotiations to achieve progress. Negotiations were launched in November 2013, with twelve rounds conducted by the end of 2016. Like the China–US BIT negotiations, the negotiations with the EU are based on a negative list approach and pre-entry national treatment. For further information and analysis, see Wenhua Shan and Lu Wang, 'The China-EU BIT and the emerging "Global BIT 2.0"'(2015) 30(1) *ICSID Review* 260–7; Francois Godement and Angela Stanzel, *The European Interest in an Investment Treaty with China*, European Council on Foreign Relations Policy Brief, ECFR/127, February 2015.

Recent years have witnessed a trend towards the convergence of trade and investment rules.[81] Accordingly, in addition to BITs, China may also employ FTAs to accelerate trade and investment liberalisation between itself and the BRI countries. Compared with BITs, FTAs are a more comprehensive means of promoting economic integration beyond investment liberalisation. To date, China has concluded fourteen FTAs involving twenty-two countries and regions.[82] A newly formulated Chinese FTA strategy is 'to start from neighboring countries, then expand to BRI nations, and further to the globe'.[83] The BRI nations will thus play a key role in shaping China's envisioned FTA network. The Regional Comprehensive Economic Partnership (RCEP)[84] under current negotiation holds the key to China's economic cooperation and development in the Asia-Pacific region. RCEP will serve to counterbalance the potential effects exerted on China's economy and trade by other mega-FTAs, although its substantive content, and whether it is up to new-generation standards, remains to be seen. Interestingly, the recent US withdrawal from the TPP may provide impetus for China's successful conclusion of the RCEP negotiations or even for it to join the TPP.[85]

---

[81] See Sergio Puig, 'The merging of international investment and trade law' (2015) 33(1) *Berkeley Journal of International Law* 1; Roger P. Alford, 'The convergence of international trade and investment arbitration' (2014) 12 *Santa Clara Journal of International Law* 35.

[82] The Chinese government views FTAs as a new platform for further opening up to the outside world and speeding up domestic reforms, an effective approach for integration with the global economy and strengthening economic cooperation with other economies, and as a particularly important supplement to the multilateral trading system. China currently has nineteen FTAs under construction, fourteen of which have already been signed and implemented. For more information on China's FTAs, refer to Ministry of Commerce, 'China FTA network', accessed 8 June 2018 at http://fta.mofcom.gov.cn/english/index.shtml.

[83] See, e.g. Narziga Salidganova and Iacob Koch-Weser, *China's Trade Ambitions: Strategy and Objectives behind China's Pursuit of Free Trade Agreements*, US-China Economic and Security Review Commission, Staff Research Report, 28 May 2015.

[84] RCEP is a proposed FTA between the ten member states of the Association of Southeast Asian Nations (ASEAN), namely, Brunei, Cambodia, Indonesia, Laos, Malaysia, Myanmar, the Philippines, Singapore, Thailand and Vietnam and the six countries with which ASEAN has existing FTAs, namely, Australia, China, India, Japan, South Korea and New Zealand.

[85] The US withdrawal from the TTP in January 2017 by the new administration led by President Donald Trump has generated considerable discussion, including on the withdrawal's potential impact on China. See, e.g. Justin Sink, Toluse Olorunnipa and Enda Curran, 'China eager to fill the political vacuum created by Trump's TPP withdrawal', *Bloomberg Politics*, 24 January 2017, accessed 8 June at www.bloomberg.com/news/articles/2017-01-23/trump-s-withdrawal-from-asia-trade-deal-viewed-as-boon-for-china

Whatever the international legal mechanisms chosen to safeguard BRI implementation, it should be emphasised that China does not intend the BRI to replace the existing mechanisms and institutions of regional and international cooperation.[86] To the contrary, China is trying to supplement the international economic order and build upon it to help countries to align their development strategies and achieve complementarity. With respect to informal mechanisms, China has thus far signed memoranda of understanding (MOUs) on the joint development of the BRI with approximately seventy countries and more than thirty international organisations. These MOUs concern regional and cross-border cooperation and mid- and long-term development plans for economic and trade promotion with neighbouring countries. China has also proposed outlines for regional cooperation plans with several adjacent countries.[87] These informal mechanisms provide a useful supplement to BITs, DTTs and FTAs with respect to further development of the BRI.

4   Concluding Remarks

As part of China's grand strategy to deepen its reform and opening up, the BRI is a long-term project whose aim is to build a community of shared interests, destiny and responsibility. Although proposed by China, the BRI should be seen as the common aspiration of all countries pursuing peace and development in today's globalised world. China welcomes the active participation of all countries and international and regional organisations. The initiative is unprecedented in terms of China's financial engagement and the development of innovative network-based projects designed to contribute to more inclusive global governance. In that sense, the BRI can be viewed as an IPG initiated and provided by China.

Instead of merely advocating for international law to play a significant role in BRI implementation, this chapter draws on the theory of IPGs to furnish a solid theoretical foundation for China's need to attach more importance to international legal mechanisms. On the domestic front, subsequent to the establishment of 'law-based governance of the country'

(accessed 16 April 2018); Knowledge@Wharton, 'TPP: why the U.S. withdrawal could be a boon for China', Knowledge@Wharton podcast, 27 January 2017, accessed 13 April 2018 at http://knowledge.wharton.upenn.edu/article/trans-pacific-partnership/.

[86] Jinping Xi, 'Towards a community of common destiny and a new future for Asia', keynote speech, Boao Forum Asia Annual Conference, 28 March 2015; see also BRI Vision and Action Plan, Part V.

[87] See, e.g. Renmin University, *Adhering to the Planning*.

in October 2014,[88] China issued guidelines for boosting such governance and vowed to build a 'rule of law' government by 2020.[89] The BRI thus provides an opportune moment for China to extend its domestic law-based governance beyond its borders to foster a more sustainable system of global governance.

International legal mechanisms such as BITs, FTAs and DDTs should be put in place and/or strengthened, given their important role in IPG provision. Such mechanisms will also facilitate the BRI's success in the face of fiercely competitive international rule-making. The world's major powers stress the importance of sound institutions within the international economic structure. To date, China has lagged far behind with respect to international rule-making, a situation that is incompatible with its current economic strength. The negotiations over the TPP, TTIP[90] and TiSA[91] (the 'triple T') in recent years have created a new global economic and legal bloc that is imposing unprecedented pressure on China, not only economically but also with respect to its rule-making capabilities. It would be wise for China to build the BRI as an IPG while enhancing its capacity-building in the area of international rule-making. In doing so, the country may gradually transform itself from a rule-taker or rule-follower into a rule-shaker or even rule-maker in the international economic and trade arena.

---

[88] The Fourth Plenary Session of the Eighteenth Central Committee of the Communist Party of China (CPC) was held in Beijing from 20 to 23 October 2014. At this session, it was announced that China would establish the 'law-based governance of the country' and elevate the 'rule of law' to unprecedented heights. See *Communiqué*. This milestone session witnessed 'three firsts' in CPC history: making rule of law a central topic; passing a significant resolution on comprehensively advancing law-based governance in China; and establishing an overall objective for such comprehensive advancement.

[89] Xinhua, 'China issues guideline'.

[90] TTIP stands for the Transatlantic Trade and Investment Partnership, a proposed trade agreement between the EU and the United States whose aim is to promote trade and multilateral economic growth. TTIP negotiations began in July 2013, with fifteen rounds of negotiation conducted by the end of 2016. For more information, consult the EU's TTIP website at http://ec.europa.eu/trade/policy/in-focus/ttip/ and the United States Trade Representative's (USTR) TTIP website at https://ustr.gov/ttip (both accessed 13 April 2018).

[91] TiSA, the Trade in Services Agreement, is a proposed international trade treaty between twenty-three parties considered 'really good friends of services', or RGFs, including the United States, EU and Australia, amongst others. A major aim of the agreement is to liberalise the global trade of such services as banking, healthcare and transport. All negotiation meetings have taken place in Geneva, but outside the auspices of the WTO. For more information, see the EU's TiSa website at http://ec.europa.eu/trade/policy/in-focus/tisa/ and the USTR's TiSA website at https://ustr.gov/TiSA (both accessed 8 June 2018).

2

Performative Uses of Sovereignty in the Belt and Road Initiative

SAMULI SEPPÄNEN

The Chinese conception of sovereignty is customarily pictured as slanted towards an 'absolutist' model, whereas Western governments are said to approach it in more 'relativist' terms. In this view, the absolutist perception – typically presented as an outdated but still influential concept – regards sovereignty as the foundation of international law and the absolute right of the sovereign, whereas the more recent relativist perception views it as a disaggregated bundle of rights. The absolutist model of sovereignty is thought to legitimise domestic policies and practices that diverge from various international standards, whilst the relativist model is thought to promote the establishment and enforcement of those standards. This dichotomous view (or, more accurately, diluted forms of it) is held by many scholars in both China and internationally. In the West, it is usually presented as a criticism of Chinese isolationism, while in China it is generally presented as a defensive stance against Western interventionism.[1]

---

[1] For seminal texts producing and reproducing this view, see, e.g. Oscar Schachter, 'Sovereignty: then and now', in Ronald St. John Macdonald (ed.), *Essays in Honour of Wang Tieya* (Boston, MA: M. Nijhoff Publishers, 1994), pp. 671–88 at pp. 676, 688 (noting that China gives primacy to sovereignty, although it does not accept the absolutist conception, and alluding to the 'excesses so often associated with claims of sovereignty'); Anne-Marie Slaughter, 'International law in a world of liberal states' (1995) 6 *European Journal of International Law* 503–38 at 514 (noting that the world of contemporary international politics, and 'of ... China', is not the world of liberal states, which is characterised by 'disaggregated sovereignty'). Scholars of China usually take a more nuanced view. See the references in Allen Carlson, 'More than just saying no: China's evolving approach to sovereignty and intervention since Tiananmen', in Alistair Iain Johnston & Robert S. Ross (eds.), *New Directions in the Study of China's Foreign Policy* (Stanford, CA: Stanford University Press, 2006), pp. 217–41; Bates Gill and James Reilly, 'Sovereignty, intervention and peacekeeping: the view from Beijing' (2000) 42(3) *Survival* 41–59. For a defence of the Chinese emphasis on sovereignty, see Muzheng Duan (端木正) (ed.), *International Law*, 2nd edn. (国际法:第2版) (Beijing: Peking University Press, 1997), pp. 53–4; Tieya Wang

It is true that Chinese government ideologues and international jurists have responded to the relativist project by adopting self-consciously non-interventionist (and according to some, absolutist) positions on sovereignty. However, this chapter argues that the received narrative on the Chinese conception of sovereignty on the whole overemphasises the distinction between the absolutist and relativist models in a way that is both untenable and unfair to Chinese uses of the concept. Rather than viewing sovereignty exclusively through the absolutist–relativist dichotomy, Chinese uses of sovereignty should also be examined through what can be called a 'post-relativist' (or simply 'postist') conception. This conception of sovereignty – as articulated by prominent Chinese international jurists – rejects the absolutist–relativist dichotomy of mainstream international law, and instead views arguments about sovereignty (whether seemingly absolutist or relativist) as attempts to achieve specific political aims.[2] The postist approach, in short, sees sovereignty as a contested term, while finding considerable use for the concept.

Uses of the three conceptions of sovereignty, that is, absolutist, relativist and postist, become understandable when they are analysed in terms of their performative qualities. From this perspective, proclamations on sovereignty by Chinese political ideologues and international lawyers are better seen as speech acts that change things in the world rather than as propositions about the actual nature of sovereignty.[3] For the purposes of this analysis (and one would assume for much academic research on international law), it is pointless to speculate about the 'true' nature of sovereignty: what matters are the intended and actual effects of statements concerning it. A necessary caveat, however, is that the political

---

(王铁崖) (ed.), *International Law* (国际法) (Beijing: Law Press China, 2005), pp. 81–2. For general overviews of the role of sovereignty in international law, see Anthony Anghie, *Imperialism, Sovereignty and the Making of International Law* (Cambridge: Cambridge University Press, 2007); Jean L. Cohen, *Globalization and Sovereignty: Rethinking Legality, Legitimacy, and Constitutionalism* (Cambridge: Cambridge University Press, 2012); Hent Kalmo and Quentin Skinner (eds.), *Sovereignty in Fragments: The Past, Present and Future of a Contested Concept* (Cambridge: Cambridge University Press 2010); Neil Walker, *Sovereignty in Transition* (Oxford: Hart, 2003).

[2] Hanqin Xue, *Chinese Contemporary Perspectives on International Law: History, Culture and International Law* (The Hague, Netherlands: Hague Academy of International Law, 2012), p. 69; Wang, *International Law*, p. 95.

[3] For the origins of this methodological approach, see John L. Austin, *How to Do Things with Words: The William James Lectures Delivered at Harvard University in 1955* (Oxford: Clarendon Press, 1962).

objectives underpinning arguments about sovereignty may well be influenced by absolutist, relativist and postist conceptions of sovereignty, conceptions that are an important element of the ideological conflicts amongst Chinese foreign policy elites. Nevertheless, behind these political objectives we can find no coherent theory of sovereignty.[4]

In line with the main subject matter of this volume, this chapter discusses the uses of sovereignty in the context of China's Belt and Road Initiative (BRI). My aim is to demonstrate that the BRI cannot in the main be seen as driven by an absolutist, relativist or even postist conception of sovereignty. Instead, Chinese legal scholars and political ideologues deploy various arguments about sovereignty for specific political ends in the promotion of particular goals relating to the initiative, or, less purposefully, simply to express their ideological views concerning and attitudes towards China's standing in the world. For instance, self-consciously absolutist statements about sovereignty are useful for legitimising the BRI as an attempt to promote local development models in contrast to what is perceived as the United States–led development model. Relativist arguments about sovereignty, in contrast, are helpful for establishing ideological and legal grounds for the protection of Chinese investments abroad. The postist perspective, finally, enables Chinese legal scholars and political ideologues to imagine the initiative as an effort to recast international legal norms in China's own image. This assumption is ideologically important for a number of Chinese legal scholars and political ideologues, although its actual policy implications are unclear.

The remainder of the chapter is structured as follows. It first points out that the distinction between the absolutist and relativist conceptions of sovereignty can be seen as ahistorical and theoretically untenable. The distinction – which remains a staple of international legal scholarship – emerged in the twentieth century in conjunction with a self-consciously internationalist agenda. After the end of the Cold War, that agenda took a 'liberal interventionist' form that sought to establish legal and moral

---

[4] This part of my argument is not novel. The *Max Planck Encyclopedia of Public International Law*, a benchmark for commonly accepted views on international law, points out that the concept of sovereignty is made 'intractable by its essentially contestable nature'. See Samantha Besson, 'Sovereignty', in Wolfram Rüdiger (ed.), *Max Planck Encyclopedia of Public International Law*, online edition (Oxford: Oxford University Press, 2011), para. 150.

grounds for interventions in foreign countries to further specific liberal causes.[5] The chapter then describes the post-relativist approach to sovereignty, as well as its attempt to reclaim the concept from the liberal interventionist project. Turning to China, the chapter then moves on to an examination of how the three conceptions of sovereignty play out in the context of the BRI. The concluding section then brings the discussion briefly back to general international law, casting doubt on the assumption that sovereignty exists beyond its performative uses.

1 Three Conceptions of Sovereignty

1.1 Before: Absolutism and Relativism

A popular notion concerning the Chinese conception of sovereignty – apparent, for instance, in the international commentary on the Responsibility to Protect initiative and the Diaoyu-Senkaku Islands dispute – holds that Chinese leaders and legal scholars have fallen behind the curve in the development of international legal conceptions of sovereignty. In this narrative, the classical, absolutist conception of sovereignty posited in the late nineteenth and early twentieth centuries viewed the state as the ultimate source of legal rights and obligations under international law.[6] Under this conception, supposedly embodied by such decisions as *Wimbledon* and *Lotus*, sovereignty is 'self-limited at the most'.[7] The increasingly sophisticated relativist notions of sovereignty put forward in the course of the twentieth century then supposedly limited sovereignty by appointing international law as the ultimate source of international legal rights and obligations.[8] Rather than seeing sovereignty as the foundation of international law, the relativist conception views it as a disaggregated

---

[5] Anghie, *Imperialism, Sovereignty and the Making of International Law*, pp. 113–14, 297; Cohen, *Globalization and Sovereignty*, pp. 172–3.

[6] In a book published in the mid-1990s, Abram and Antonia Chayes explain that '[t]raditionally, sovereignty ... signified the complete autonomy to act as it chooses, without legal limitation by any superior entity... If sovereignty in such terms ever existed outside books on international law and international relations, however, it no longer has any real world meaning.' See Abram Chayes and Antonia Handler Chayes, *The New Sovereignty: Compliance with International Regulatory Agreements* (Cambridge, MA: Harvard University Press, 1995), p. 27.

[7] See Besson, 'Sovereignty', paras. 75, 97; *The SS 'Wimbledon', United Kingdom and ors* v. *Germany* (1923) Permanent Court of International Justice (PCIJ), Series A, no. 1; *The SS 'Lotus', France* v. *Turkey, Judgment* (1927) PCIJ, Series A, no. 10.

[8] See Cohen, *Globalization and Sovereignty*, p. 48.

bundle of rights. Sovereignty thus stands for the 'body of rights and attributes which a state possesses in its territory, to the exclusion of all other states, and also in its relations with other states'.[9]

The concept of sovereignty has been questioned in Western legal academia to such an extent that it may no longer be possible to insist that classical conceptions of sovereignty were absolutist in any meaningful way.[10] As David Kennedy has pointed out, the rejection of classical conceptions 'may have been largely the retrospective fantasy of those who would define their politics by its rejection'.[11] Not even Hobbes, who is viewed as the foremost promoter of the absolutist conception of sovereignty,[12] promoted the absolutist credo on the international plane. True, Hobbes' description of international society in terms of the war of all against all is at odds with today's relativist sensibilities.[13] However, as Friedrich Kratochwil has observed, it follows from Hobbes' premises that 'the laws of nature' also govern normative expectations on the international plane.[14] There is, for instance, 'a general rule of reason ... that every man ought to endeavor to peace, as far as he has hope of obtaining it'.[15] This rule exists, in Hobbes' view, because it can 'never be that war shall preserve life and peace destroy it'.[16]

As is the case with Hobbes' perceptions of sovereignty on the international plane, early decisions in the absolutist canon can also be reinterpreted in both absolutist and relativist terms. For instance, the *Lotus* decision, the high-water mark of the supposedly absolutist conception of sovereignty, can be seen to make use of both absolutist and relativist

---

[9] *Corfu Channel, United Kingdom v. Albania, Assessment of the Amount of Compensation* (1949) International Court of Justice (ICJ), Report 244, p. 44.

[10] This is indeed the suggestion made by Chayes and Chayes in *The New Sovereignty*, p. 27.

[11] See David Kennedy, 'International law and the nineteenth century: history of an illusion' (1996) 65 *Nordic Journal of International Law* 385–420 at 388.

[12] See Besson, 'Sovereignty', para. 75.

[13] Hobbes famously wrote that 'though there had never been any time wherein particular men were in a condition of war one against another, yet in all times kings and persons of sovereign authority ... are in continual jealousies, and in the state and posture of gladiators'. Thomas Hobbes, *Leviathan or the Matter, Forme, & Power of a Commonwealth Ecclesiasticall and Civill* (Hamilton, ON: McMaster University Press, 1999), p. 79.

[14] Friedrich Kratochwil, *Rules, Norms, and Decisions: On the Conditions of Practical and Legal Reasoning in International Relations and Domestic Affairs* (Cambridge: Cambridge University Press, 1989), p. 4.

[15] Hobbes, *Leviathan*, p. 80.

[16] Ibid., p. 97. Hobbes' views are of course intricate. For instance, he assumes that the laws of nature govern 'desires' rather than actions.

statements about sovereignty. While the Permanent Court of International Justice (PCIJ) insisted, in the absolutist parlance, that '[t]he rules of law binding upon States ... emanate from their own free will',[17] it also deemed it appropriate to limit the sovereignty of states whenever the 'prohibitive rules' of international law exist.[18] To ascertain whether such rules exist, the PCIJ examined 'precedents offering a close analogy to the case under consideration'.[19] Despite its absolutist language about respecting 'the independence of States',[20] the court thus designated international law as the ultimate source of international legal rights and obligations.[21]

Similarly, the PCIJ's decision in *Wimbledon*, another landmark decision in the development of sovereignty within international law, can be read in both absolutist and relativist terms. The court held that international treaty obligations ultimately derive from state consent. According to the court, 'the right of entering into international engagements [is] an attribute of State sovereignty',[22] rather than a limitation upon state sovereignty. Whilst the PCIJ offered an ostensibly absolutist justification for the binding nature of treaties, it ended up through that justification establishing a relativist perception of sovereignty, a perception that allows states to contract away specific components of their sovereign powers. As Jan Klabbers has pointed out, the *Wimbledon* decision established sovereignty as 'a relative, disaggregated phenomenon, as such devoid of contents but encompassing a bundle of rights'.[23] Finally, the *Island of Palmas* case, yet another landmark decision in the supposedly absolutist canon, can also be seen as having mixed absolutist and relativist conceptions of sovereignty.[24] In his decision in the case, Max Huber, the sole arbitrator, asserted in absolutist terms that '[s]overeignty in

---

[17] *The SS 'Lotus'*, para 44.

[18] Ibid., para. 46.

[19] Ibid., para. 53.

[20] Ibid., para. 44.

[21] Moreover, when it came to exercising power in the territory of another state, the court did not justify the limitations on the basis of sovereign will: 'the first and foremost restriction imposed by international law upon a State is that – failing the existence of a permissive rule to the contrary – it may not exercise its power in any form in the territory of another State.' Ibid., para. 45.

[22] *The SS 'Wimbledon'*, p. 25.

[23] Jan Klabbers, 'Clinching the concept of sovereignty: Wimbledon redux' (1998) 3 *Austrian Review of International and European Law* 345–67 at 357–8, 362–3.

[24] *Island of Palmas Case (or Miangas), United States v. Netherlands, Award* (1928) II Results of International Arbitral Awards (RIAA), 829.

the relations between States [signifies] independence. Independence in regard to a portion of the globe is the right to exercise therein, to the exclusion of any other State, the functions of a State'.[25] At the same time, Huber recognised that sovereignty and its component, 'the exclusive right to display the activities of a State', have a 'corollary duty', namely, 'the obligation to protect within the territory the rights of other States'.[26] That duty effectively renders sovereignty relativist in nature.

Hence, conceptions of sovereignty may never have been as absolute as the proponents of the self-consciously relativist approach argued during the latter part of the twentieth century.[27] As David Kennedy has observed, the dichotomy between the two conceptions of sovereignty emerged only in the course of the twentieth century as part of a 'progressive and humanist discipline' marked by its 'hostility to what [was] remembered as the classical system' and its project to 'demystify' a conception of sovereignty that had actually been, according to Kennedy, a secular and practical matter.[28] The relativist credo was presented in terms of analytical and descriptive arguments about the nature of sovereignty, but in reality served as an intellectual justification for the moderately progressive agenda of decolonisation and internationalism.[29] For instance, one of the most prominent promoters of the self-consciously relativist approach, Judge Alejandro Alvarez, argued in 1949 that 'the new conditions of social life' had superseded the old conception of 'sovereignty as an absolute and individual right of every State'.[30] He insisted that, 'owing to social interdependence and to the predominance of the general interest', states were now 'bound by many rules which have not been ordered by their will'.[31] Martti Koskenniemi has argued that Alvarez developed the absolutist view as a 'straw man' to advance his moderate (and unthreatening) political agenda.[32]

---

[25] Ibid., 838.

[26] Ibid., 839.

[27] See, e.g. the Corfu Channel decision, p. 43 (stating that '[w]e can no longer regard sovereignty as an absolute and individual right of every State').

[28] Kennedy, 'International Law and the Nineteenth Century', pp. 388, 405.

[29] Martti Koskenniemi, The Gentle Civilizer of Nations: The Rise and Fall of International Law 1870–1960 (Cambridge: Cambridge University Press, 2001), p. 304.

[30] Corfu Channel, p. 43.

[31] Ibid.

[32] Koskenniemi, The Gentle Civilizer of Nations, p. 304. Koskenniemi notes that this agenda did not, for instance, allow a legal personality for the indigenous peoples in Alvarez's home country, Chile. Such restrictions were not of course the result of Alvarez's

In the latter part of the twentieth century, the self-consciously relativist conception of sovereignty became the mainstream view amongst Western international lawyers.[33] Whilst newly independent developing countries sought to assert absolute sovereignty within their territories, the Western scholarly mainstream learnt to look back to the supposedly absolutist conception of sovereignty, and to perceive it as a conception that was not only theoretically crude but also morally reprehensible.[34] As Louis Henkin, the doyen of American international lawyers during the Cold War, noted, '[t]he meaning of "sovereignty" is confused and its uses are various, some of them unworthy, some even destructive of human values'.[35] For Henkin and others, claims about sovereignty hampered efforts to protect universal human values.

Towards the end of the twentieth century, the academic debate about sovereignty – the 'S word' for Henkin – was influenced by developments in the international arena. The end of the Cold War and collapse of the Socialist Bloc in Europe, combined with the expansion of international trade regimes, growing awareness of global environmental risks and perhaps even the emergence of global information networks, contributed to the perception that sovereignty was on its way out from the international law domain. In the jubilant words of Anne-Marie Slaughter, '[e]ven legislators, the most naturally parochial government officials due to their direct ties to territorially rooted constituents', were now 'meeting to adopt and publicize common positions on the death penalty, human rights and environmental issues'.[36] Again, the old-fashioned conception of sovereignty stood in the way of the liberal interventionist agenda to tackle human rights violations (as defined by the opponents of absolutism), supposedly ineffective economic policies and harmful environmental practices. In the new era of relativised sovereignty, the legitimacy of

---

theoretical argument about sovereignty, which could easily have accommodated expansion of the concept of legal personality.

[33] The ICJ, for instance, disaggregated the various competences that various subjects of international law possess in an advisory opinion in 1949. See 'Reparation for injuries suffered in the service of the United Nations (advisory opinion)' (1949) 174 *ICJ Reports* 178.

[34] Anghie, *Imperialism, Sovereignty and the Making of International Law*, p. 254.

[35] Louis Henkin, 'That "S" word: sovereignty, and globalization, and human rights, et cetera' (1999) 68 *Fordham Law Review* 1–14.

[36] Anne-Marie Slaughter, 'Disaggregated sovereignty: towards the public accountability of global government networks' (2004) 39 *Government and Opposition* 159–90 at 161.

governments was to be based on their ability to deliver local and global welfare improvements. What was needed was a 'transition from a culture of sovereign impunity to a culture of national and international accountability'.[37]

1.2 After: Self-Awareness about the Uses of Sovereignty

Today, the relativist conception of sovereignty is part of the textbook wisdom of international law. Although the proponents of this now mainstream conception have not quite reached the eschatological heights of the most ardent liberal interventionists of the 1990s and 2000s – sovereignty is not a dirty word for mainstream international lawyers – international law textbooks nonetheless regard claims about sovereignty with considerable scepticism. According to Brownlie's *Principles of Public International Law*, a standard treatise on international law, the concept of sovereignty 'carries limited substantive consequences'.[38] Another textbook on international law asserts that 'the concept of state "sovereignty" has been increasingly challenged and exaggerated'.[39] Although such views have won widespread acceptance amongst Western international lawyers, there is something of a backlash against the relativist progress story in the field of international law. Today it is the self-consciously relativist conception of sovereignty, rather than the absolutist straw man, that is increasingly described as a politically outdated, theoretically crude and morally reprehensible construct.[40] Although sovereignty's next

---

[37] International Commission on Intervention and State Sovereignty, *Summary of the Responsibility to Protect: The Report of the International Commission on Intervention and State Sovereignty* (Ottawa, ON: International Development Research Centre, 2001), accessed 30 May 2018 at http://responsibilitytoprotect.org/ICISS%20Report.pdf, p. 3. According to the report, 'where a population is suffering serious harm, as a result of internal war, insurgency, repression or state failure, and the state in question is unwilling or unable to halt or avert it . . . the principle of non-intervention yields to the international responsibility to protect'. See ibid., p. 4. See also José E. Alvarez, 'The schizophrenias of R2P', in Philip Alston and Euan Macdonald (eds.), *Human Rights, Intervention, and the Use of Force* (Oxford: Oxford University Press, 2008), pp. 275–94.

[38] James Crawford, *Brownlie's Principles of Public International Law*, 7th edn. (Oxford: Oxford University Press, 2008), p. 13.

[39] Lori F. Damrosch and Sean D. Murphy, *International Law: Cases and Materials*, 6th edn. (St. Paul, MN: West Academic Publishing, 2014), p. 36.

[40] See Anghie, *Imperialism, Sovereignty and the Making of International Law*, pp. 88–90 (describing the uses of the disaggregated approach to sovereignty for Western imperialism); Kennedy, 'International law and the nineteenth century', 103 (describing the uses of the absolutist–relativist dichotomy and the disaggregated approach to sovereignty

chapter is still being written, a number of common themes are apparent. Most obviously, the reappraisal of the self-consciously relativist conception of sovereignty is taking place with reference to actual developments in the international arena, such developments as the centrifugal forces tearing apart international organisations (such as the European Union), the apparent irrelevance of the United Nations in international conflict resolution, the rise of nationalism, illiberalism and protectionism in both developed and developing countries, and, perhaps most importantly, the widespread disillusionment with universal development models and trade liberalisation. All of these factors are eroding confidence in the relativist progress narrative, which views sovereignty as a problematic relic.[41]

Scholars have also attacked the theoretical assertions of the self-consciously relativist notion of sovereignty. The seminal argument, presented by Martti Koskenniemi at the end of the 1980s, holds that the prevailing international legal doctrine of sovereignty is a consequence of the incoherent structure of liberal international law.[42] On the one hand, Koskenniemi argues, international law needs as its basis a conception of inherent state sovereignty that gives rise to, amongst other things, claims to independence and self-determination.[43] On the other, it must limit state sovereignty to protect the sovereignty of other members of international society.[44] Because of this dualistic structure, the international legal doctrine of state sovereignty simultaneously assumes that sovereignty precedes law and that law precedes sovereignty. The relativist perception of sovereignty cannot escape this dichotomy because it continues to base the validity of restrictions on sovereignty on the notion of state consent. It is not credible to claim that international law is independent of state consent – how else does international law come

---

for American foreign policy); Koskenniemi, *The Gentle Civilizer of Nations*, p. 304 (describing the relativist approach to sovereignty as a 'deeply conservative technique that deflects criticism away from "reality" and those responsible for it').

[41] See, generally, José E. Alvarez, 'The return of the state' (2011) 20 *Minnesota Journal of International Law* 223–64 at 251–3.

[42] Martti Koskenniemi, *From Apology to Utopia: The Structure of International Legal Argument*, reissued with a new epilogue (Cambridge: Cambridge University Press, 2005), pp. 226–8.

[43] Ibid., pp. 225–6, 236.

[44] Ibid., p. 225.

to be? – just as it is not credible to claim that international law is whatever a state says it is.[45]

The political force of the postist attack lies in its suggestion that all arguments about sovereignty are politically motivated, regardless of whether they are made on the basis of the supremacy of international law or with reference to supposedly inherent state sovereignty. A principal target of such critique is the liberal interventionist assumption that there are universal human values, such as economic development, the rule of law and human rights, that ought to be promoted through global, expert-run organisations in defiance of 'outdated' and sociologically unfounded claims about sovereignty.[46] From the postist perspective, the liberal interventionist project cannot claim to possess knowledge about universally shared conceptions of human values. Importantly, the post-relativist critique does not constitute a wholesale rejection of either sovereignty or efforts to restrict it on the basis of international law. Its aim instead is to cultivate awareness of the political uses of various conceptions of sovereignty. From this perspective, the concept appears to be a useful tool for protecting diverse local political projects. Such projects are necessary for human flourishing, being the forums in which we 'constitute ourselves, not only as social beings, but also as beings equally entitled to bring our Utopias to bear in the organization of social life'.[47] At stake in the sovereignty debate is thus the protection of local political projects and the agency to define those projects. The proponents of the relativist progress story, as the post-relativist argument goes, end up supporting exploitative and undemocratic transnational arrangements, particularly in the arena of international trade. From the postist perspective, the liberal interventionist critique of sovereignty is not only

---

[45] An exposé of this structure may appear overtly 'theoretical' for many mainstream international lawyers, but elements of it have appeared in the International Court of Justice (ICJ) jurisprudence, as Koskenniemi points out in his seminal text. In the *Nuclear Tests* case, the dissenting Judge Ignacio-Pinto noted that 'Australia can invoke its sovereignty over its territory and its right to prevent pollution caused by another State. But when the French Government also claims to exercise its right of territorial sovereignty, by proceeding to carry out tests in its territory, is it possible legally to deprive it of that right, on account of the mere expression of the will of Australia?' See *Nuclear tests, Australia* v. *France, interim protection order* (1973) 99 *ICJ Reports* 131, order of 22 June 1973; Koskenniemi, *From Apology to Utopia*, pp. 246–7.

[46] Martti Koskenniemi, 'What use of sovereignty today?' (2011) 1 *Asian Journal of International Law* 61–70 at 64–5.

[47] Martti Koskenniemi, 'The wonderful artificiality of states' (1994) 88 *Proceedings of the American Society of International Law* 22–9 at 29.

self-contradictory (because it cannot achieve its aims), but it also constitutes a 'tragical thesis' that surrenders political communities 'to an exterior purpose, to some self-evident certainty in no need of public reflection'.[48]

At the end of the day, the postist view is also a balancing act between domestic sovereignty and its international limitations. Koskenniemi, for instance, acknowledges that giving up moral arguments against foreign intervention in the case of 'a massive violation of human rights' is neither convincing nor authentic.[49] Other scholars have identified a 'trend in favour of greater sovereign "policy space"' instead of the wholesale rejection of sovereignty as a bundle of rights.[50] Hence, the post-relativist perspective does not dispute the legal or moral force of all interventionist arguments, and nor does it seek to consolidate the bundle of sovereign rights into a single, remystified concept of sovereignty. Its aim instead is to revive 'sovereignty' for its project to facilitate human flourishing in more diverse forms than mainstream international law, the liberal interventionist fringe in particular, would allow. This is indeed how prominent Chinese international jurists such as International Court of Justice (ICJ) Judge Hanqin Xue describe the Chinese approach to sovereignty. According to Judge Xue, 'China reserves its positions on the principles of sovereignty and non-interference, because it believes that sovereignty, in the final analysis, is not so much about the concept itself, relevant or obsolete', but a concept that 'serves to maintain that each State has the autonomy to freely choose the development model for its own country'.[51]

2 Uses of Sovereignty in the BRI

2.1 Absolutism and Relativism

As noted above, Chinese conceptions of sovereignty have been seen as threatening both the well-being of the Chinese people[52] and international peace, much like the supposedly absolutist notion of sovereignty has been blamed for its failure to prevent World War I.[53] Indeed, Judge Xue has

---

[48] Ibid., 27, 29.
[49] Ibid., 28.
[50] Alvarez, 'The return of the state', 254.
[51] See Xue, *Chinese Contemporary Perspectives*, p. 95.
[52] See W. Michael Reisman, 'Sovereignty and human rights in contemporary international law' (1990) 84 *American Journal of International Law* 866–76 at 872.
[53] Kennedy, 'International law and the nineteenth century', 102.

suggested that the repudiation of sovereignty in the 1990s was formulated partly in response to Chinese uses of the concept.[54] A central exhibit in the relativist case against the Chinese conception of sovereignty is the so-called Five Principles of Peaceful Coexistence, which were first enunciated in 1954. The Five Principles, once a cornerstone of Chinese foreign policy and still a prominent talking point in advocacy of the BRI, comprise: (i) mutual respect for one another's sovereignty and territorial integrity, (ii) mutual non-aggression, (iii) mutual non-interference in one another's internal affairs, (iv) equality and mutual benefit and (v) peaceful coexistence.[55] According to one telling description, intended for educational use in the United States, the Five Principles

> offer an alternative to the American conception of a new kind of world order – one in which international regimes and institutions, often reflecting U.S. interests and values, limit the rights of sovereign states to develop and sell weapons of mass destruction, repress opposition and violate human rights, pursue mercantilist economic policies that interfere with free trade, and damage the environment.[56]

More nuanced descriptions of Chinese foreign policy have pointed out that the Chinese government's conceptions of sovereignty are rather diverse. The People's Republic of China has understood itself as part of a relativist bundle of rights and obligations at least since the end of the Maoist era.[57] Chinese textbooks on international law, which can be seen as broadly representative of the government's views, portray sovereignty as being limited in many ways by international legal norms. Thus, while a prominent Chinese textbook on international law, edited by Tieya Wang, contains nothing of the millennial, end-of-sovereignty excitement of Western textbooks, it consistently describes sovereignty as being restricted by both the customary rules of international law and treaty law.[58] The assumption is *not* that states have the final say about all such

---

[54] Xue, *Chinese Contemporary Perspectives*, p. 69; Louis Henkin, 'The mythology of sovereignty', in Ronald St. John Macdonald (ed.), *Essays in Honour of Wang Tieya* (Boston, MA: M. Nijhoff Publishers, 1994), pp. 351–8.

[55] Samuel S. Kim, 'Sovereignty in the Chinese image of world order', in Ronald St. John Macdonald (ed.), *Essays in Honour of Wang Tieya* (Boston, MA: M. Nijhoff Publishers, 1994), pp. 425–45 at 428.

[56] See Columbia University, 'Principles of China's foreign policy', Asia for Educators, accessed 30 May 2018 at http://afe.easia.columbia.edu/special/china_1950_forpol_principles.htm.

[57] For the development of Chinese conceptions of sovereignty, see Carlson, 'More than just saying no', 217–41; Gill and Reilly, 'Sovereignty, intervention and peacekeeping', 41–59.

[58] See Wang, *International Law*, pp. 76–7.

norms. Rather, Chinese textbooks adhere to mainstream global views on non-derogable *jus cogens* norms and aspirational respect for (generally ill-defined) human rights norms.[59]

Nevertheless, it is true that Chinese international jurists and political ideologues occasionally describe sovereignty in a manner that appears to accept the absolutist–relativist dichotomy and positions itself in the backseat of the relativist progress story. Judge Hanqin Xue, for instance, justifies 'China's persistent stand on the primacy of sovereignty' on the basis of the country's 'miserable experience in its modern history'.[60] It is also clear that the self-conscious rejection of the relativist progress story – and the particular legal doctrines promoted by liberal interventionists – belongs to mainstream accounts of international law in China. The aforementioned international law textbook edited by Tieya Wang, for instance, explains that modern international law (in contrast to 'traditional' international law and 'some contemporary international lawyers') prohibits all forms of intervention in the domestic affairs of sovereign states, including those supposedly made for humanitarian reasons and to protect human rights.[61] It is telling that this blanket statement appears in connection with a discussion of foreign interventions to protect human rights; elsewhere, the textbook acknowledges that drawing boundaries between legal and illegal interventions is difficult.[62] (China has now moved on from this unqualified position on foreign interventions as far as the protection of its nationals abroad is concerned.[63])

The self-consciously non-interventionist (and according to its critics 'absolutist') stance on sovereignty is also apparent in policy documents promoting the BRI. A report by the State Council's National Development and Reform Commission (NDRC) notes that the initiative 'upholds China's non-interventionist foreign policy dogma, the so-called Five Principles of Peaceful Coexistence'.[64] It further stresses that China respects 'the paths and modes of development chosen by different countries', and

---

[59] See Duan, *International Law*, pp. 44–5, 578; Wang, *International Law*, pp. 34–7, 41.

[60] Xue, *Chinese Contemporary Perspectives*, p. 71.

[61] Wang, *International Law*, pp. 81–2.

[62] Ibid., 84.

[63] Ming Li (李鸣), 'International law and "one belt, one road"' ('国际法与"一带一路"研究') (2016) 1 *Legal Science Magazine* (法学杂志) 11–17 at 16.

[64] National Development and Reform Commission (NDRC), *Vision and Actions on Jointly Building Silk Road Economic Belt and 21st-Century Maritime Silk Road*, 28 March 2015, accessed 30 May 2018 at http://en.ndrc.gov.cn/newsrelease/201503/t20150330_669367 .html.

seeks the 'biggest common denominator' between the interests of the states participating in the BRI.[65]

While such non-interventionist principles are endorsed as a matter of course in Chinese commentary on the BRI,[66] they and other ostensibly absolutist statements form only a small part of the uses of sovereignty within the initiative. Rather than reinforcing the absolutist credo, the bulk of statements relating to sovereignty with respect to the BRI are made to qualify and restrict the use of governmental powers in the target countries of Chinese foreign investments. This approach is understandable: rather than constituting an ideological justification for Chinese isolationism, the BRI seeks to promote and protect Chinese investments abroad.

Accordingly, one major aim of the initiative is to facilitate the opening up of foreign countries to Chinese investments.[67] The aforementioned NDRC report emphasises that China 'should speed up investment facilitation, eliminate investment barriers, and push forward negotiations on bilateral investment protection agreements and double taxation avoidance agreements to protect the lawful rights and interests of investors'.[68] It goes on to welcome 'companies from all countries to invest in China', and encourages 'Chinese enterprises to participate in infrastructure construction in other countries along the Belt and Road, and make industrial investments there'.[69] The NDRC report also notes that the initiative's implementation 'will abide by market rules and international norms, give play to the decisive role of the market in resource allocation and the primary role of enterprises, and let ... governments perform their due functions'.[70]

Once Chinese investments have flowed into foreign countries, BRI advocates will attempt to protect those investments from government intervention. At the current stage, at least, promoters of the initiative are

---

[65] Ibid.

[66] Li, 'International law and "one belt, one road"', 12.

[67] In its 2013 decision on the reform programme, the Chinese Communist Party promised to 'work hard to build a Silk Road Economic Belt and a Maritime Silk Road, so as to form a new pattern of all-round opening'. See 'Decision of the Central Committee of the Communist Party of China on some major issues concerning comprehensively deepening the reform', USC US-China Institute, 12 November, 2013, accessed 30 May 2018 at http://china.usc.edu/decision-central-committee-communist-party-china-some-major-issues-concerning-comprehensively.

[68] NDRC, Vision and Actions.

[69] Ibid.

[70] Ibid.

not proposing the establishment of new trade rules to protect overseas Chinese investments, but instead intend to use 'existing bilateral and multilateral cooperation mechanisms' to that end.[71] In this context, implementers of the initiative are concerned about similar 'abuses' of governmental power as promoters of the self-consciously relativist version of sovereignty. For instance, a Hong Kong government report on the BRI (as well as a mainland Chinese commentator cited by the report) discusses the 'political risks' (政治风险) associated with the initiative.[72] These risks are due to the 'political systems' of the countries participating in the initiative being 'very different from China's'.[73] The Hong Kong report and a number of commentators have also noted the 'legal risks' (法律风险) associated with the BRI. Those risks range from Chinese companies' inadequate understanding of foreign laws and international regulations to indeterminate foreign laws, unexpected changes in foreign legislation and the threat of litigation abroad.[74]

The more closely the commentary on the BRI relates to the protection of Chinese investments abroad, the more explicitly it seeks to constrain the use of governmental power and limit the role of 'politics' in international relations. For instance, Chinese commentators urge the Chinese government to address political risks by requiring, in international treaties, that investment protections in foreign countries be enacted as domestic laws.[75] According to some commentators, the BRI will have to extend

---

[71] Ibid.

[72] HKSAR Commission on Strategic Development, *One Belt One Road*, SD/2/2015, 3 July 2015, p. 17, accessed 8 June 2018 at www.pico.gov.hk/en/CSD_2015_2017/csd_2_2015e.pdf, p. 17. For mainland Chinese comments, see Bo Liu (刘波), 'Six risks that need to be resolved as Chinese railways go global' ('中国铁路走出去需化解六种风险'), *Huanqiu*, 3 February 2015, accessed 8 June 2018 at http://opinion.huanqiu.com/opinion_world/2015-02/5582296.html. For another comment on the political risks, see, e.g. Yuanming Li (李元明), 'The international risks facing the "one belt, one road" and their countermeasures' ('浅谈"一带一路"面临国际风险与对策思考'), in Guiguo Wang (王贵国) (ed.), International Law Perspective of the Belt and Road Initiative: Collected Papers from the 2015 Hong Kong International Forum on the 'One Belt, One Road' ('一带一路'的国际法律视野:香港2015'一带一路'国际论坛文集) (Hangzhou: Zhejiang University Press, 2016), pp. 22–6.

[73] HKSAR Commission on Strategic Development, *One Belt One Road*, p. 17.

[74] Ibid. See also Liu, 'Six risks'; Li, 'The international risks', 25.

[75] Yuejiao Zhang (张月姣), 'Legal considerations in the implementation of the "one belt, one road" strategy' ('"一带一路"战略实施的法律思考'), in Guiguo Wang (王贵国) (ed.), International Law Perspective of the Belt and Road Initiative: Collected Papers from the 2015 Hong Kong International Forum on the 'One Belt, One Road' ('一带一路'的国际法律视野:香港2015'一带一路'国际论坛文集) (Hangzhou: Zhejiang University Press, 2016), pp. 12–21 at 19.

to many areas of domestic legislation in BRI countries, including 'trade law, foreign investment law, tax law, company law, contract law, labor law, environmental protection law, intellectual property law, civil law, property law, law of obligations, land expropriation rules, and so forth'.[76] Hence, even though the commentary on the BRI makes use of the absolutist language of the Five Principles, it also encourages scepticism about non-interventionism and establishes new intellectual grounds for closer engagement with the domestic policies of other countries. Some Chinese commentators are explicit about this. For instance, Professor Ming Li, a prominent international lawyer who teaches at Peking University, argues that 'sufficient flexibility should be reserved in the application of the principle of non-intervention' in the BRI context.[77]

Certainly, the relativist uses of sovereignty in the BRI do not amount to the vilification of sovereignty that defines the liberal interventionist agenda. Most commentators on the initiative do not call for the transfer of elements of sovereignty to new China-led international organisations,[78] even if some aspects of sovereign powers are to be internationalised and 'depoliticised' through international treaties. It is also noteworthy that most promoters of the BRI do not argue that the legitimacy of the governments along the new Silk Road is conditional on their capacity to promote public welfare within their jurisdictions, and neither is the initiative unambiguously promoted as a welfare-creating policy in the countries targeted for Chinese investment. For instance, the aforementioned Hong Kong report (and mainland Chinese commentator) identifies the 'cultural risks' (文化风险) in BRI implementation, for example, in powerful overseas labour unions that 'attach great importance to the

---

[76] Ibid., p. 14. See also Xinli Zhu (朱新力) and Jun Zhao (赵骏), 'International legal aspects of the "one belt, one road" strategy' ('"一带一路"战略中的国际法律问题'), Guiguo Wang (王贵国) (ed.), International Law Perspective of the Belt and Road Initiative: Collected Papers from the 2015 Hong Kong International Forum on the 'One Belt, One Road' ('一带一路'的国际法律视野:香港2015'一带一路'国际论坛文集) (Hangzhou: Zhejiang University Press, 2016), pp. 318–23.

[77] Li, 'International law and "one belt, one road"', 13. Professor Li also notes that China has traditionally respected the principle of non-intervention, and should not imitate the United States in this respect.

[78] For this point, see Jörg Fedtke, 'The European end of the Silk Road: current perceptions and future prospects', in Guiguo Wang (王贵国) (ed.), International Law Perspective of the Belt and Road Initiative: Collected Papers from the 2015 Hong Kong International Forum on the 'One Belt, One Road' ('一带一路'的国际法律视野:香港2015'一带一路'国际论坛文集) (Hangzhou: Zhejiang University Press, 2016), pp. 98–109 at 103.

welfare of local labour'.[79] The solution to cultural risks offered by the Hong Kong report is to keep the '[amount] of foreign labour ... minimal'.[80] Such statements explicitly acknowledge that the initiative's focus is, at least in part, the promotion of Chinese national interests rather than the promotion of values to which other BRI countries 'attach great importance'.[81]

Nevertheless, BRI promoters do make use of some of the same argumentative strategies as the liberal interventionists. They suggest, however subtly, that limiting sovereign rights and reducing the role of 'politics' in international relations will be helpful for promoting public welfare in the BRI region. The aforementioned NDRC report, for instance, argues that Chinese foreign investments – and the limitations of sovereignty needed to protect those investments – are beneficial for the economic development of target countries.[82] The initiative has also been described as an instance of the simultaneous progress of the 'rule of law' (法治) and development.[83] Moreover, a number of commentators have justified the far-reaching plans to establish investor-friendly legislation in BRI countries on the basis of meeting the UN's Millennium Development Goals.[84] The initiative's promoters thus imagine a world in which the benefits of the domestic and international rule of law, trade liberalisation, foreign investment protection and economic development are juxtaposed with the sins of unpredictably applied local politics, obscure local laws, protectionist policies and underdevelopment. Human rights notwithstanding, such an attitude is in line with much of the liberal interventionist agenda. Moreover, this attitude it has its roots in domestic Chinese development policies: economic growth is also a key argument for legitimising legal reforms and development interventions in China. Indeed, it is telling that the very name of the BRI – which conveys the construction of a conveyor belt (带) for the delivery of development goods – refers to the industrial and managerial quality of development.[85]

[79] HKSAR Commission on Strategic Development, *One Belt One Road*, p. 19.
[80] Ibid.
[81] Ibid.
[82] NDRC, *Vision and Actions*.
[83] Zhu and Zhao, 'International legal aspects', 323.
[84] Zhang, 'Legal considerations', 15.
[85] Ministry of Foreign Affairs, the People's Republic of China, 'President Xi Jinping delivers important speech and proposes to build a Silk Road economic belt with Central Asian countries', 7 September 2013, accessed 30 May 2018 at www.fmprc.gov.cn/mfa_eng/topics_665678/xjpfwzysiesgjtfhshzzfh_665686/t1076334.shtml.

2.2   The Performative Perspective

To better understand the various arguments about sovereignty in the BRI context, the foregoing arguments need to be examined in terms of their performative qualities without presuming there to be any coherent (whether absolutist, relativist or postist) doctrine behind them. The absolutist parlance on sovereignty typically appears in statements concerning territorial sovereignty in which such sovereignty is to be 'vigorously safeguarded' (大力维护).[86] In the BRI, absolutist claims about sovereignty are particularly helpful for warding off Western influence and liberal interventionist claims about legitimate development policies. In other words, the aim of absolutist language – say, references to mutual non-interference in member states' internal affairs – is to clear space for China's political influence in the region. At the same time, the absolutist recognition of sovereign equality is useful for reassuring countries on the new Silk Road of China's benevolent intentions. In a widely disseminated column, Professor Maochun He of Tsinghua University argues that the BRI is not tantamount to building a new Chinese 'vassal system' (宗藩体系).[87] According to Professor He, such a system would be impossible because 'the world entered a new era of sovereign equality a long time ago'.[88] He further assures readers that China will not implement the BRI by imposing its own rules on other countries because it is 'the presently recognized rules of international law [that] govern the implementation of the "One Belt One Road" initiative'.[89]

Relativist arguments about sovereignty in the BRI context also serve Chinese foreign policy objectives. Assurances that China will abide by international norms in the initiative's implementation situate the BRI within the existing structures of global governance,[90] thereby potentially

---

[86] In an article on American foreign policy, Dr Ruan Zongze, Vice President of the China Institute of International Studies, first discusses the US strategy vis-à-vis the BRI without mentioning the concept of sovereignty. He then moves on to a discussion of US activities in the South China Sea as a challenge to China's sovereignty. See Ruan Zongze (阮宗泽), 'The US rebalance towards Asia: quo vadis?'('美国"亚太再平衡"战略前景论析') (2014) 4 *World Economics and Politics* (世界经济与政治) 17–18. See also Li, 'International law and "one belt, one road"', 13, in which Professor Li also mentions 'sovereignty' in the context of the Diaoyu-Senkaku Islands dispute.

[87] Maochun He (何茂春), 'Ten misconceptions about the "one belt one road"' ('"一带一路"的十大误解'), *Xinhuanet*, 12 May 2015, accessed 30 May 2018 at http://news.xin huanet.com/comments/2015–05/12/c_1115338341.htm.

[88] Ibid.

[89] Ibid. Note that the BRI is sometimes called the 'One Belt, One Road' initiative.

[90] NDRC, *Vision and Actions*.

reducing concerns about the direction of China's foreign policy. At the same time, relativist arguments about sovereignty play a role within domestic policy-setting in China. As demonstrated above, a number of prominent Chinese international jurists argue that China ought to reconfigure its conception of sovereignty to allow for a more aggressively interventionist approach in the initiative's implementation.[91] As also pointed out above, some lawyers would like China to adopt a more legalistic approach to implementation of the initiative and to internationalise certain elements of domestic politics in the BRI countries.[92]

While policy documents and academic commentary on the BRI contain a number of relativist arguments about sovereignty, it would be a mistake to view the initiative as an unequivocal step in the direction of the liberal-interventionist camp. A number of prominent commentators have described the BRI as a self-conscious effort to make use of the established international legal discourse to create a new, China-led regional polity. One commentator notes, for example, that the initiative 'transcends different Free Trade Agreements (FTAs)', claiming further that it 'envisions regional integration beyond pure economic union, forming a political community founded on common interest in an attempt to forge, as much as possible, a common cultural identity'.[93] The aforementioned China-led regional polity is to be established through the present rules of international law, although its ultimate aim, according to several prominent commentators, is to contest and modify the rules of the Western international order. This ambitious agenda is a common talking point, particularly amongst the more conservative-minded Chinese commentators on the BRI (in contrast to more liberal-minded scholars who would be satisfied to play along with international rules).[94] Professor Lei Zhao of

---

[91] Li, 'International law and "one belt, one road"', 13.

[92] Zhang, 'Legal considerations'; Zhu and Zhao, 'International legal aspects'.

[93] Yafei He, 'Connecting the world through "Belt & Road"', China-US Focus, 13 October 2015, accessed 30 May 2018 at www.chinausfocus.com/foreign-policy/the-belt-road-initiative-offers-new-model-of-cooperation-in-global-governance.

[94] In the Chinese context, I use the word 'conservative' (or 'conservative socialist') to describe a group of Chinese legal scholars who seek to preserve China's political status quo and the word 'liberal' to describe scholars who seek to subject the party to democratic and judicial controls. See Samuli Seppänen, *Ideological Conflict and the Rule of Law in Contemporary China: Useful Paradoxes* (Cambridge: Cambridge University Press, 2016), pp. 2–3.

the Central Party School, for instance, describes the BRI as the start of a new Chinese-style discourse on international relations that emphasises inclusiveness and tolerance and embodies an 'anti-polarising' (非极化) tendency in international relations.[95] China will not seek to defeat the United States, he says, but instead will 'expand its cultural influence in Central Asia, Southeast Asia and other core regions'.[96] Similarly, Professor Ming Li of Peking University argues that the BRI transforms the established logic of international relations, in which the rising power challenges and overthrows the waning dominant power. Professor Li views the initiative as a result of China's transformation into a great power. Referring to the Chinese language translation of Martti Koskenniemi's essay 'What is international law for?',[97] he argues that China should learn from the realist perception of international law and depart from its single-minded focus on formal such law. 'Every great power', Li avers, 'wishes to impose its own will on international law, have an adequate say in the international order and realize its ambitions through international law'.[98]

Finally, arguments about sovereignty may be used to establish the speaker's position in the scholarly avant-garde and portray his or her opponents as theoretically outdated apologists for ethically compromised causes. This is the theoretical move deployed by both the promoters of the self-consciously relativist conception of sovereignty and their postist critics. In a similar vein, Chinese commentators on the BRI note that China's 'civilizational values' are built on respect for 'the diversity of the world's civilizations and their unique national development models'.[99] The counterpoint to this supposedly more enlightened approach is formed by the Western promoters of relativist conceptions of sovereignty, who of course also claim to represent the avant-garde of international law.

---

[95] Lei Zhao (赵磊), 'One belt, one road promotes the emergence of the Chinese civilisational model' ('"一带一路"助推中国的文明型崛起'), Think Tank Salon, 15 January 2016, accessed 30 May 2018 at www.china.com.cn/opinion/think/2016–01/15/content_3758 2134.htm.

[96] Ibid.

[97] See Martti Koskenniemi (trans. by Yifeng Chen (陈一峰), 'What is international law for?' ('国际法的目的是什么?') (2013) 1 *Peking University International and Comparative Law Review* (北大国际法与比较法评论) 71–101. It is perhaps worth noting that Li makes reference to instrumentalism and realism, which are tendencies opposed by Koskenniemi.

[98] Li, 'International law and "one belt, one road"', 14.

[99] Zhao, "One belt, one road".

Appreciating the performative quality of statements about sovereignty does not imply support for a conspiracy on behalf of Chinese international lawyers (although some Chinese commentary on the BRI does take on a conspiratorial tone). The aim of such analysis is to bypass the debate about the true nature of conceptions of sovereignty and focus instead on the effects of statements making use of those conceptions. Such statements may or may not be made in good faith. Further, even if one assumes that a number of Chinese international jurists view international law in bad faith without having truly internalised any of its values, it is still possible to conclude that it would not be helpful for those jurists to discard the mainstream discourse on international law. As Professor Li points out, China benefits from the present Western-built international order as a 'free rider' (搭便车).[100] The current international legal order not only offers legal protections for (Chinese) investments abroad, but also the possibility of using force in aid of humanitarian causes, for instance, when a powerful country such as China chooses to evacuate its nationals from combat zones.[101]

On the whole, however, the BRI literature suggests that Chinese international jurists do not view international law in exclusively strategic and self-interested terms. Chinese commentators on the initiative assert that international law not only constitutes a tool for states to pursue their own interests, but also an idealist enterprise in which Chinese international lawyers are eager to take part. Professor Li, for instance, sees the initiative as both a vehicle for advancing China's interests and a policy that takes into account the common interests of the international community through the established principles of international law.[102] Given the cosmopolitan aspirations of the Chinese legal profession, such statements need not be viewed as implausible or disingenuous.[103] In fact, the legal safeguards supporting the BRI are bolstered by (almost Fullerian) arguments about the 'internal morality of law'.[104] In Chinese

---

[100] Li, 'International law and "one belt, one road"', 14.
[101] Ibid., 16.
[102] Ibid., 15.
[103] I discuss the professional identities of Chinese mainstream and liberal legal scholars in Seppänen, *Ideological Conflict and the Rule of Law*, pp. 36–45.
[104] The connection to Fuller is made explicit in at least one text on the BRI. See Yuncheng Bao (包运成), 'Legal considerations in the construction of the "one belt, one road"' (2015) 375 *Forward Position* ('"一带一路"建设的法律思考前沿') 65–9 at 66. For Fuller's ethics, see Lon L. Fuller, *The Morality of Law*, revised edition (New Haven, CT: Yale University Press, 1964), p. 106. For the Chinese language translation of this text

writings on the initiative, such arguments are apparent in the view that
the Chinese have often been treated unfairly in the application of the law
in foreign countries. From this perspective, law is not just an instrument
for promoting economic development, but also an ethical enterprise. The
Hong Kong government report on the BRI, for instance, describes a
bidding competition in Mexico in which a Chinese company was dis-
qualified owing to the insufficient 'transparency of the tender process'.[105]
The incident was reported in the Chinese press as a cautionary lesson for
BRI implementation.[106] In the moralist commentary on the initiative,
China is on the side of the angels. As Professor Li notes, 'it is impossible
to deny that some countries simply lack the contractual spirit', a spirit
that is presumably present in China.[107]

Instead of being outsiders to the Western-built global legal discourse,
Chinese international jurists and government ideologues have arguably
absorbed some of the central attitudes of that discourse, including its
conflicting views on sovereignty as both the foundation of international
law and as a bundle of powers conferred by international law. It is these
attitudes, amongst many others, that are expressed through various arguments about sovereignty in the context of the BRI. Perhaps particularly
interesting for the global audience is the belief of some Chinese legal
scholars and government ideologues that Chinese 'civilisational values'
are able to transcend what they perceive as the Western-constructed international legal order. The present commentary on the BRI provides few
glimpses of how Chinese civilisational values might differ from their
Western counterparts in the context of sovereignty. Emphasis on non-
intervention and peaceful coexistence is hardly novel in the West, particularly if the former Eastern Bloc is considered part of the West. However,
as is the case with other statements about sovereignty, those about a new
China-led international order should not be seen as earnest arguments
about the nature of that order. Instead, such visionary statements express
their speakers' resentment of the present international system, their hope
that the coming international order will afford China a more prominent

---

cited by Professor Bao, see Lon L. Fuller (富勒) (trans. by Ge Zheng (郑戈), *The
Morality of Law* (法律的道德性) (Beijing: Commercial Press, 2005).

[105] HKSAR Commission on Strategic Development, *One Belt One Road*, p. 17.

[106] Xinrong He (何欣荣) and Ruifang Yue (岳瑞芳), 'High-speed train becomes a boost for
the "one belt, one road" strategy' ('高铁走出去成"一带一路"战略助推器'), *Xinhuanet*,
5 January 2015, accessed 30 May 2018 at http://news.xinhuanet.com/fortune/2015–01/
05/c_1113885333.htm.

[107] Li, 'International law and "one belt, one road"', 15.

role on the international stage and their pride in China's ancient civilisation and its newly recovered status as a dominant world power. The details will be worked out later – or not.

3   Conclusion

A focus on the performative uses of sovereignty makes it apparent that many arguments about 'sovereignty' are about something other than the nature of sovereignty. In the BRI context, the absolutist parlance on sovereignty allows China to keep the United States and other Western countries out of what it considers to be its sphere of influence and to assure its partners of the non-interventionist nature of its foreign policy. The relativist version of sovereignty then operates between China and other countries in the Chinese sphere of influence, assuring those countries of China's reliance on established rules of international law, while also affording China the ideological and legal means to safeguard its interests within its sphere of influence. China respects sovereign equality and is not at all interested in creating a system of vassal states; it is just that Chinese investments must be protected according to international norms and the common values of BRI countries. There are interesting twists in this project. It is ironic that China protects its interests abroad not only through recourse to the relativist conception of sovereignty, but also through self-consciously absolutist language. It is also interesting to note that Chinese foreign policy elites share a number of attitudes with Western liberal interventionists, particularly with respect to the disdain for nationalist politics in developing countries.

With regards to general international law, one conclusion to draw from the discussion herein would be that sovereignty is 'in the final analysis' a relative concept, that is, a bundle of rights that is unbundled and reassembled afresh for specific purposes. Such a conclusion would fall squarely within the mainstream view of international law in both the West and China. However, whatever one thinks about the true nature of sovereignty, it is also true that absolutist and postist statements about that nature have had effects on promotion of the BRI. A more challenging observation about the various uses of sovereignty in the initiative suggests that there is no 'there' there. One aspect of that observation is the conclusion that Chinese (and Western) international lawyers do not possess a coherent theory about the highest political authority in the international arena. Statements about sovereignty concern context and nuance – an exaggeration here and an oversight there – and are made with ad hoc policy objectives in mind or as a result of personal predilections. 'Sovereignty', it may even be argued, can be understood only as a term that achieves or is intended to achieve certain social effects. Of course, one may seek to make absolutist, relativist or post-relativist arguments about the nature of sovereignty to change things in the world. However, 'sovereignty' itself has no logic, structure or existence beyond those effects.

PART II

Development of Substantive International
Rules and China's Contribution

3

The Belt and Road Initiative under Existing Trade Agreements

Some Food for Thought on a New Regional Integration Scheme

JAEMIN LEE

China's Belt and Road Initiative (BRI) is a crucial long-term national project which aims to establish and operate infrastructure facilities in and through Central Asia, the Middle East and parts of Europe.[1] The overarching aim is to establish a new Silk Road connecting these regions, namely, a land-based Silk Road Economic Belt and ocean-based Maritime Silk Road.[2] These two 'Silk Roads' are together envisaged to enable China to increase its influence both in the BRI region and globally while also expanding its export markets.[3] National infrastructure development projects are currently in great demand in many of the countries on the BRI route, meaning that China is expected to mobilise its vast capital and manpower reserves for regional infrastructure construction under the initiative's auspices. In this regard, the China-led Asian Infrastructure Investment Bank (AIIB), which was successfully launched in 2014, offers a financial platform for infrastructure project implementation.[4] The BRI constitutes a new scheme for international economic cooperation that

---

[1] 'Our bulldozers, our rules', *The Economist*, 2 July 2016, accessed 30 May 2018 at www.economist.com/news/china/21701505-chinas-foreign-policy-could-reshape-good-part-world-economy-our-bulldozers-our-rules.

[2] Ministry of Foreign Affairs & Ministry of Commerce of the People's Republic of China, *Vision and Actions on Jointly Building Silk Road Economic Belt and 21st Century Maritime Silk Road*, accessed 30 May 2018 at http://en.ndrc.gov.cn/newsrelease/201503/t20150330_669367.html.

[3] Price Waterhouse Coopers Growth Markets Centre, *China's New Silk Route, The Long and Winding Road*, accessed 30 May 2018 at www.pwc.com/gx/en/growth-markets-center/assets/pdf/china-new-silk-route.pdf.

[4] Thomas Renard, *The Asian Infrastructure Investment Bank (AIIB): China's New Multilateralism and the Erosion of the West*, Security Policy Brief No. 63, April 2015, accessed 30 May 2018 at http://aei.pitt.edu/64789/1/SPB63-Renard.pdf.

differs from and/or is independent of such conventional trade liberalisation agreements as free trade agreements (FTAs).

Despite the many positive aspects of the BRI projects contemplated, there are also a number of concerns and challenges. Unless efficiently managed, those concerns and challenges run the risk of eroding any benefits that may accrue from the BRI scheme's expansion. A particular concern requiring our attention is that of the scheme's legal implications. Whilst it is too early to find answers to all outstanding legal questions at this point, further discussion and analysis are necessary to ensure a proper structure and framework from the outset. Otherwise, non-participating states and entities that stand to be negatively affected by the advent of the new regime will have sufficient reasons to file trade and investment disputes.

Depending on how the BRI scheme is implemented, and through which legal vehicles, questions may arise concerning whether the new cooperation agreement and regime are indeed compatible with the existing provisions of the World Trade Organization (WTO) Agreements, FTAs and bilateral investment treaties (BITs) regulating international economic cooperation amongst contracting parties in a specified manner. Hence, when a new scheme or regime is contemplated in the arena of international trade and investment, which is already heavily regulated by relevant trade agreements and BITs, it is crucial to examine the associated legal issues to ensure the sustainability of that scheme/regime under the umbrella of existing norms. If consistency is not guaranteed to a satisfactory extent, then ongoing controversies are almost inevitable, leading to conflict over the dispute settlement mechanisms of trade agreements and BITs. Accordingly, a consistency check or compliance assessment merits careful attention when a new scheme or regime such as the BRI is contemplated for the first time.

The aim of this chapter is to discuss a number of these legal issues and suggest ways to implement BRI projects in a manner consistent with the participating states' existing obligations under relevant trade and investment agreements. As the number of trade and investment disputes has risen steadily over the years, ensuring consistency with those agreements will avoid unnecessary and unintended disputes arising from BRI projects, thereby helping to safeguard their long-term sustainability.

1   Distinct Characteristics of BRI

The BRI has a number of distinct characteristics deserving appropriate scholarly attention. It is a scheme whose aim is to establish a new type of economic cooperation network.

1.1   From Market Penetration to Connection

Regional trade agreements continue to proliferate globally. Most FTAs exhibit similar structures and contain similar provisions. It appears, however, that China's BRI seeks to achieve different goals than conventional FTAs.[5] The BRI is, by nature, designed to introduce and implement new types of economic cooperation in the central Asian region to enhance the connections and connectivity amongst participating states in a way similar to the original Silk Roads of yesteryear.[6] Such connections/connectivity have not been the main objectives of the conventional FTAs negotiated to date. Under the initiative, a new land-based Silk Road Economic Belt and an ocean-based Maritime Silk Road are envisioned.[7] Together, these two 'roads' are anticipated to expand China's influence in global affairs and help to expand its export market to absorb the country's current overproduction.[8] In a nutshell,

---

[5] See Kim Taehwan, 'Beyond geopolitics: South Korea's Eurasia initiative as a new Nordpolitik', *The ASAN Forum*, 6 February 2015, accessed 30 May 2018 at www.theasanforum .org/beyond-geopolitics-south-koreas-eurasia-initiative-as-a-new-nordpolitik/; see, generally, European Parliament, 'One belt, one road (OBOR): China's regional integration initiative', European Parliament Think Tank, 7 July 2016, accessed 30 May 2018 at www.europarl.europa.eu/thinktank/en/document.html?reference=EPRS_BRI(2016)586608. This report explains that the basic objective of the BRI is to implement China's new integration strategy or integration initiative in Central Asia. It summarises the BRI objectives as follows: 'China's new development vision has been seen as an alternative to regional trade agreements which do not include it; as a strategy for asserting its leadership role in Asia in response to the US pivot to Asia; as an economic outreach towards Asian countries for resolving territorial and maritime disputes by exporting China's domestic development policies; as a means of tapping into new sources of growth to check the marked downturn in its economy; as a tool for tackling the socioeconomic divide between its inland and coastal provinces; and finally, as a venue for addressing security challenges on its western periphery as well as energy security issues.' See also 'Our bulldozers, our rules'.

[6] Ping Ai, 'One belt one road, new diplomacy and public diplomacy, China and world' (2014) 4 *International Understanding* 2; Ministry of Foreign Affairs of the People's Republic of China (MOF), 'Speech on the belt and road initiative by Chinese Ambassador Qu Zhe (From Chinese Embassy in Estonia)', MOF website, 13 April 2015, accessed 30 May 2018 at www.fmprc.gov.cn/mfa_eng/wjb_663304/zwjg_665342/zwbd_665378/ t1254259.shtml; MOF, 'Foreign ministry spokesperson Hong Lei's regular press conference', MOF website, 17 April 2015, accessed 30 May 2018 at www.fmprc.gov.cn/mfa_eng/ xwfw_665399/s2510_665401/t1255670.shtml.

[7] Jingping Xi, 'Develop further the Silk Road spirit and deepen China-Arab cooperation – Speech at the opening ceremony of the sixth Ministerial Conference of China-Arab Cooperation Forum', *People's Daily*, 6 July 2014, p. 2.

[8] See Scott Kennedy and David A. Parker, 'Building China's "one belt, one road"', CSIS, 3 April 2015, accessed 30 May 2018 at http://csis.org/publication/building-chinas-one-belt-one-road.

China's aim is to construct a 'new bridge' to Europe through Central Asia by implementing its BRI policy.[9]

Accordingly, China does not appear to be pursuing the creation of an integrated market or common market in the region, which is the goal of conventional FTAs. Rather, the emphasis of the ambitious BRI scheme is on specific construction and infrastructure projects and infrastructure establishment that will benefit all participating states and, in turn, facilitate the speedy transport of goods and services.[10] Most prospective participating states in the region are in great need of national infrastructure development plans. In that respect, the AIIB's successful launch in 2014 will provide a welcome financial platform for the implementation of those plans.[11]

1.2   New Type of Economic Cooperation Regime

More than anything else, the BRI project stands for the proposition that a new breed of economic cooperation regime is needed in the region.[12] It differs from present FTAs in that its priority is not to further market liberalisation or market penetration amongst the contracting parties but rather to connect constituent states in a way conducive to close economic cooperation.[13] That connection can take the form of transport route creation, infrastructure construction and/or the exchange of peoples and cultures. It is thus argued here that the BRI's focus is distinct from that of the FTA's.[14] At the same time, to the extent that it does not aim to create a common market such as the European Union (EU), the scheme is also distinguishable from economic integration plans.

[9] 'China's policy paper on the EU: Deepen the China-EU comprehensive strategic partnership for mutual benefit and win-win cooperation', *China Daily*, 2 April 2014, accessed 6 June 2018 at www.chinadaily.com.cn/world/cn_eu/2014-04/02/content_17401044.htm.

[10] Ai, 'One belt, one road, new diplomacy', 3.

[11] 'Why China is creating a new "world bank" for Asia', *The Economist*, 11 November 2014, accessed 30 May 2018 at www.economist.com/blogs/economist-explains/2014/11/economist-explains-6.

[12] The State Council of the People's Republic of China, *Action Plan on the Belt and Road Initiative*, 28 March 2016, accessed 30 May 2018 at http://english.gov.cn/archive/publications/2015/03/30/content_281475080249035.htm; see also Price Waterhouse Coopers, *China's New Silk Route*, p. 2.

[13] Lucio Blanco Pitlo III, 'ASEAN connectivity and China's "one belt, one road": could there be a convergence of interests between these two grand projects?', *The Diplomat*, 26 March 2015, accessed 30 May 2018 at http://thediplomat.com/2015/03/asean-connectivity-and-chinas-one-belt-one-road/.

[14] Ibid.

1.3 Regional Financial Stability Scheme

The effects of the 2008 global financial crisis persist today.[15] Although the initial atmosphere of emergency that prevailed in the autumn of 2008 when the crisis first unfolded has gradually dissipated over the years, the legacy of the crisis is still being felt in many corners of the world.[16] More importantly, the possibility of another financial crisis is as real as ever, as China discovered in July 2015.[17] By all indications, the 2008 global financial crisis and post-2008 repercussions offer an important turning point for the global economic and financial regulatory system. Efforts to reform the financial governance system have been mobilised by numerous governments and relevant international organisations.[18] More critically, in an effort to overcome the ill-effects of the financial crisis, many states are exploring a wide range of measures (or countermeasures) to aid their domestic industries and companies.[19]

---

[15] United Nations Conference on Trade and Development (UNCTAD), *Trade and Development Report, 2016: Structural Transformation for Inclusive and Sustained Growth Countries in World Trade* (Geneva and New York: United Nations, 2016), pp. 1–2.

[16] It should be noted that in this chapter, the terms 'financial crisis' and 'economic crisis' are used interchangeably. Whilst the latter is by definition broader in scope than the former, when used without any qualification 'economic crisis' is deemed to mean the same thing as 'financial crisis'. An example of the ongoing nature of the financial crisis is Greece's continued economic suffering in the summer of 2015 that began with the 2009 Eurozone crisis. See 'Greece's debt crisis explained', *The New York Times*, 17 June 2016, accessed 30 May 2018 at www.nytimes.com/interactive/2015/business/international/greece-debt-crisis-euro.html?_r=0.

[17] By way of example of ongoing financial crises, on 12 June 2015, the Chinese stock market began to crash. In the three weeks that followed, the Shanghai Composite Index fell by as much as 30 per cent. The Chinese government intervened in the market, announcing the suspension of trading in more than half the companies listed as well as the prohibition of short selling. See also Isabel Hilton, 'China's stock market crash is a problem for the whole world', *The Guardian*, 9 July 2015, accessed 30 May 2018 at www.theguardian .com/commentisfree/2015/jul/10/china-stock-market-crash-world-problem-struggling-economy-small-invesots; Charles Riley and Sophia Yan, 'China's stock market crash . . . in 2 minutes', *CNN Money*, 29 June 2015, accessed 30 May 2018 at http://money.cnn .com/2015/07/09/investing/china-crash-in-two-minutes/index.html.

[18] The aim of the Basel Accords – Basel I, Basel II and Basel III – issued by the Basel Committee on Banking Supervision (BCBS) is to provide a series of recommendations on regulating the banking industry. The most recent accord, Basel III, was agreed upon by BCBS members in 2010–2011 and established a voluntary framework on bank capital adequacy, stress testing and market liquidity risk in response to the lack of regulation revealed by the 2008 global financial crisis. See Bank for International Settlements (BIS), *International Regulatory Framework of Banks (Basel III)*, BIS website, accessed 30 May 2018 at www.bis.org/bcbs/basel3.htm.

[19] UNCTAD, *Trade and Development Report 2016*, pp. 1–2.

Developed countries such as the United States and the member states of the EU are no exception, with all of them having adopted a variety of measures over the years to counter the effects of economic crisis.[20] Notable amongst those measures are the ongoing and, to a great extent, intensifying bailouts of key financial institutions and banks by many of these countries.[21] Those bailouts are somewhat ironic because it was, after all, the financial industry that sparked the chain reaction that began in the autumn of 2008.

Given the scope and nature of the recent crisis, the bailouts of key domestic entities, banks in particular, seem both inevitable and necessary, as entire national economies could easily have collapsed. Through the bailouts of domestic banks, governments ensured that a funding mechanism was in place to channel financing through national economic arteries. The funds used for those bailouts came in the main from national treasuries. They thus constituted 'public money', as it is colloquially termed.

The AIIB's purported objective is to operate as an institution offering regional financial stability and providing facilities and loans to other financial institutions in the region.[22] It thus aims to be the Asian version of the International Monetary Fund (IMF).[23] Accordingly, as an international financial organisation, the AIIB will presumably help states and domestic banks to overcome the ongoing effects of the 2008 financial crisis and avert future crises. The AIIB's advent thus suggests that states in Asia have realised the importance of having an international financial organisation that can address problems on a local level.

2   Legal Implications of the BRI Scheme

In addition to the aforementioned benefits of the BRI scheme, there are also a number of legal concerns and problems that we need to be aware of, as it represents a new breed of international economic cooperation regime. Whilst we cannot, and do not have to, find answers to all of these

---

[20] Ibid.

[21] Ibid., p. 3.

[22] European Political Strategy Centre, 'The Asian Infrastructure Investment Bank: a new multilateral financial institution or a vehicle for China's geostrategic goals', EPSC Strategic Notes, Issue 1/2015, 24 April 2015, accessed 30 May 2018 at http://ec.europa.eu/epsc/pdf/publications/strategic_note_issue_1.pdf.

[23] Rebecca Liao, 'Out of the Bretton Woods: how the AIIB is different', Foreign Affairs, 27 July 2015, accessed 30 May 2018 at www.foreignaffairs.com/articles/asia/2015-07-27/out-bretton-woods.

Table 3.1 *Number of BITs/FTAs of Countries Situated on the Ancient Silk Road*

Country	Number of signed BITs (in force)[a]	Number of signed FTAs[b]
China	129 (110)	15
Pakistan	46 (32)	10
India	76 (66)	13
Kazakhstan	47 (42)	11
Uzbekistan	50 (47)	4
Iran	66 (52)	2

[a] UNCTAD, International Investment Agreements Navigator, accessed 30 May 2018 at http://investment policyhub.unctad.org/IIA/IiasByCountry#footnote.
[b] WTO, Participation in Regional Trade Agreements, accessed 30 May 2018 at www.wto.org/english/tratop_e/ region_e/rta_participation_map_e.htm.

legal questions at this juncture, relevant analyses are required to structure a proper framework and avoid structural incoherence amongst different regimes. It should be noted that economic cooperation issues often lead to trade and investment disputes being brought by states and/or entities that are negatively affected by the advent of a new regime. Given that the BRI scheme is a novel concept, it raises several legal issues that need to be explored. For the scheme to be implemented successfully, it needs to be analysed and examined within the framework of the WTO Agreements to ensure consistency with those agreements. With that in mind, this section discusses the legal issues pertaining to the scheme's implementation. Given that an amendment to the WTO Agreements is not feasible at present,[24] it needs to be proven that the gist of the BRI as currently conceptualised can be implemented within the parameters of the existing WTO regime. Depending on how it is implemented, and through which legal vehicles, questions remain concerning whether such a new cooperation agreement and regime can be compatible with the WTO Agreements and the existing FTAs and BITs that affect the countries concerned (see Table 3.1).

---

[24] See World Trade Organization (WTO), *WTO Eighth Ministerial Conference: Chairman's Concluding Statement*, Official Documents of the Geneva Ministerial, WT/MIN(11)/11, p. 3, accessed 30 May 2018 at www.wto.org/english/thewto_e/minist_e/min11_e/official_ doc_e.htm.

2.1   GATT 1994

For instance, it is possible that questions will be raised concerning the prospective regime's compatibility with the 1994 General Agreement on Tariffs and Trade (GATT 1994) if it results in participating countries agreeing preferential treatment towards one another. Depending on the circumstances, most favoured nation (MFN) and national treatment (NT) issues may arise. Ordinary FTAs, of course, can rely upon the exception contained in Article XXIV of GATT 1994. However, it is not entirely clear whether the new types of cooperation networks and agreements that will be required under the BRI scheme can indeed satisfy that exception. Careful reading of Article XXIV makes it clear that what is permitted under the exception therein is a preferential measure that is 'necessary for the formation of the FTA' concerned,[25] but does not place any non-party in a more disadvantageous position than it previously held.[26] Therefore, it arguably does not cover *all* consequences flowing from the creation of a new economic cooperation agreement.

2.1.1   Most Favoured Nation (MFN) Issue

Preferential treatment under the BRI scheme would raise the possibility of an MFN violation by an importing country under Article I of GATT 1994. If the products of certain WTO members were accorded preferential treatment by an importing member, the question of whether that member had violated its MFN obligation would naturally arise. Article I, which covers MFN treatment, reads as follows:

> With respect to customs duties and charges of any kind imposed on or in connection with importation or exportation or imposed on the international transfer of payments for imports or exports, and with respect to the method of levying such duties and charges, and with respect to all rules and formalities in connection with importation and exportation, and *with respect to all matters referred to in paragraphs 2 and 4 of Article III,** any advantage, favour, privilege or immunity granted by any contracting party to any product originating in or destined for any other country shall be accorded immediately and unconditionally to the like product originating in or destined for the territories of all other contracting parties. [emphasis added]

---

[25] See GATT 1994, Article XXIV(5), introductory chapter.
[26] See GATT 1994, Article XXIV(4) and (5)(b).

Preferential treatment afforded to a select number of countries, regardless of whether they are developing countries, apparently constitutes a violation of the MFN obligation enshrined in Article 1 of GATT 1994. MFN analysis of BRI measures, however, requires in-depth examination. As the BRI is designed to introduce a specific sales and distribution mechanism for the products of a particular group of countries, the most relevant phrase in Article I is 'with respect to all matters referred to in paragraphs 2 and 4 of Article III'. Other phrases in the article are concerned with the imposition of duties and charges and the ways in which duties and charges are imposed. Assuming that the BRI does not involve differentiation in the amount of duties and charges and their payment mechanisms, those phrases would probably not be implicated. However, Article III(2) and (4) directly discuss the sales and distribution mechanism.[27] Thus, according to Article I, with respect to that mechanism, an importing member is obligated to provide MFN treatment to all WTO members.[28] Hence, the preferential provision of goods to certain developing members in the form of a different sales and distribution mechanism would certainly raise an issue under Article I of GATT 1994. There is one important thing to note, however. Article III provides for an exception to paragraphs 2 and 4 in paragraph 8.[29] Put differently, the

---

[27] GATT 1994, Article III(2) and (4) respectively provide that: 'The products of the territory of any contracting party imported into the territory of any other contracting party shall not be subject, directly or indirectly, to internal taxes or other internal charges of any kind in excess of those applied, directly or indirectly, to like domestic products. Moreover, no contracting party shall otherwise apply internal taxes or other internal charges to imported or domestic products in a manner contrary to the principles set forth in paragraph 1'; '[t]he products of the territory of any contracting party imported into the territory of any other contracting party shall be accorded treatment no less favourable than that accorded to like products of national origin in respect of all laws, regulations and requirements affecting their internal sale, offering for sale, purchase, transportation, distribution or use. The provisions of this paragraph shall not prevent the application of differential internal transportation charges which are based exclusively on the economic operation of the means of transport and not on the nationality of the product.'

[28] See WTO, 'Principles of the trading system', Understanding the WTO: Basics, accessed 30 May 2018 at www.wto.org/english/thewto_e/whatis_e/tif_e/fact2_e.htm.

[29] GATT 1994, Article III(8) provides as follows: '(a) The provisions of this Article shall not apply to laws, regulations or requirements governing the procurement by governmental agencies of products purchased for governmental purposes and not with a view to commercial resale or with a view to use in the production of goods for commercial sale; (b) The provisions of this Article shall not prevent the payment of subsidies exclusively to domestic producers, including payments to domestic producers derived from the proceeds of internal taxes or charges applied consistently with the provisions of this Article and subsidies effected through governmental purchases of domestic products.'

application of Article III(2) and (4) for the purpose of meeting the MFN obligation outlined in Article I(1) is also subject to the exception stipulated in Article III(8).[30]

As mentioned in the NT discussion in Section 2.1.2, the exception under Article III(8) is carved out for government procurement. The measures adopted by importing developed members to implement the BRI scheme could be considered to constitute a government procurement project, which would mean that the paragraph 8 exception might apply. Hence, government procurement would provide an exception to both potential MFN and NT issues, as further discussed in the following section. Another question is whether an enabling clause can justify preferential treatment for developing members in the BRI context. The exception authorised by the enabling clause in GATT 1994 as an exception to the MFN obligation under Article I is applicable only to preferential tariff measures for developing members.[31] It does not apply to non-tariff measures such as sales and distribution, which are the measures contemplated under the BRI scheme.

2.1.2   National Treatment (NT) Issue

The next item requiring examination on the part of an importing developed member is the NT issue under Article III of GATT 1994. The BRI does not discriminate against products from participating developing members; rather, it accords them preferential treatment. Thus, exporters from participating developing countries would be unlikely to claim that their products were being discriminated against vis-à-vis the domestically produced products of participating developed countries. It is other, non-participating countries that could make such an NT claim. BRI implementation will require domestic entities, both governmental and private, in participating developed countries to collectively provide preferential treatment to the participating developing countries. The participation of private entities may possibly negate the existence of a given measure, but if they participate in a governmental scheme under the control of the government, the recent WTO Appellate Body precedent in *US AD/CVD*

---

[30] See WTO, *European Communities – Measures Affecting Trade in Commercial Vessels*, Panel Report WT/DS301/R (adopted 22 April 2005), para. 7.81 (*EC-Commercial Vessels (Panel)*).

[31] See GATT, 1994, Article 2(c) of the Enabling Clause.

signals that they may be captured as a governmental measure.[32] The participation of government agencies, which seems inevitable for BRI implementation, would automatically constitute a measure subject to examination under Article III of GATT 1994.

In fact, a similar issue was examined in *EC-Bananas III*. The appellate body in the dispute examined so-called hurricane licences issued to the European Community's (EC) domestic representatives. Such licences allowed those representatives to import additional quotas of bananas from the African, Caribbean and Pacific Group of States (ACP) and developing countries in other regions in the case of tropical storms. The WTO Appellate Body found the additional quotas assigned to EC representatives to constitute a violation of Article III of GATT 1994.[33] The dispute was not brought by the ACP countries receiving preferential treatment from the EC, but by other banana-exporting countries that did not receive such preferential treatment.[34] Thus, if a developed country participating in the BRI establishes a system in which its domestic entities are engaged, it is possible that a similar claim could be raised by a non-participating country whose market share in that developed country could potentially be damaged. Article III(4), which covers NT of international taxation and regulation and stipulates the following, is directly relevant in this respect:

> The products of the territory of any contracting party imported into the territory of any other contracting party shall be accorded treatment no less favourable than that accorded to like products of national origin in respect of all laws, *regulations and requirements affecting their internal sale, offering for sale, purchase, transportation, distribution or use*. The provisions of this paragraph shall not prevent the application of differential internal transportation charges which are based exclusively on the economic operation of the means of transport and not on the nationality of the product. [emphasis added]

---

[32] See WTO, *United States – Definitive Anti-Dumping and Countervailing Duties on Certain Products from China*, Appellate Body Report WT/DS379/AB/R (adopted 25 March 2011), para. 322 (*US AD/CVD(AB)*).

[33] See WTO, *European Communities-Regime for the Importation, Sale and Distribution of Bananas*, Appellate Body Report WT/DS27/AB/R (adopted 25 September 1997), paras. 212–14 (*EC-Bananas III (AB)*).

[34] See WTO, *European Communities-Regime for the Importation, Sale and Distribution of Bananas*, Panel Reports WT/DS27/R/ECU, WT/DS26/R/GTM, HND, WT/DS27/R/ MEX, and WT/DS27/R/USA (circulated 25 September 1997), paras. 3.1–3.36 (*EC-Bananas III (Panel)*).

The most relevant phrase in the foregoing paragraph is 'regulations and requirements affecting their internal sale, offering for sale, purchase, transportation, distribution or use'. Arguably, BRI implementation by importing developed members could directly implicate that phrase.

2.1.3   Uniform Administration of Laws and Regulations

At the same time, BRI implementation could also raise the issue of whether an importing developed member is applying its domestic laws and regulations in a non-uniform manner. Article X:3(a) of GATT 1994 imposes an obligation on members to administer their laws and regulations in a uniform, reasonable and impartial manner: 'Each contracting party shall administer in a uniform, impartial and reasonable manner all its laws, regulations, decisions and rulings of the kind described in paragraph 1 of this Article.' It is likely that importing developed members would be required to adopt new laws and regulations, or amend existing ones, to administer or implement the BRI concept domestically. For instance, a provision designed to effectuate the purchase, sale and distribution of products from developing members may substantiate a claim that laws and regulations are being applied in a non-uniform manner contrary to the requirements of Article X. After all, the importing member is adopting a different set of laws and regulations for a particular group of countries. It is not clear how such a claim would be resolved. The WTO Appellate Body decision in *EC-Customs Matters* sheds light on this issue:

> In order to find that an administrative process has led to non-uniform administration of a measure under Article X:3(a), a panel cannot merely rely on identifying the features of an administrative process that it may view as non-uniform; a panel must go further and undertake an analysis to determine whether those features of the administrative process *necessarily lead to non-uniform administration* of a legal instrument of the kind described in Article X:1. [emphasis added][35]

The reasoning of the Appellate Body in that case further demonstrates that merely showing the existence of non-uniform features is not sufficient to prove an Article X:3(a) violation. Rather, the key to Article X analysis is to determine whether those features '"necessarily" lead to non-uniform administration'. In other words, the requirement of 'uniformity,

---

[35] See WTO, *European Communities – Selected Customs Matters*, Appellate Body Report WT/DS315/AB/R (adopted 13 November 2006), para. 239 (*EC-Selected Customs Matters (AB)*).

impartiality and reasonableness' does not apply to the laws, regulations, decisions and rulings *themselves*, but rather to the *administration* of those laws, regulations, decisions and rulings.[36] Under the rationale of the Appellate Body in the aforementioned case, if importing developed members can implement the BRI scheme without administering different laws or regulations relating to importation or exportation for the purpose of achieving the BRI's goals, then the possible implications of Article X:3 (a) can be avoided. This discussion provides further evidence showing that a sophisticated implementation mechanism can help to avert possible violations of GATT 1994.

2.2   General Agreement on Trade in Services (GATS)

One aim of the BRI is to provide support to domestic entities in participating states. China will take the lead by providing financial, material and human resources, but the other participating countries will also add their own resources to the pool.[37] Those pooled resources will then be used to support various projects launched by the participating states.[38] In short, BRI constitutes an internal cooperation and mutual support scheme.

To the extent that support for domestic entities amongst the participating states is not covered by the conditions inscribed in the schedules of specific commitments agreed under the General Agreement on Trade in Services (GATS) and respective FTAs, such support can be declared a violation of those commitments.[39] The schedules of specific commitments rarely contain internal support measures. By way of example, the schedules in the financial services sector submitted by China set forth China's broad obligations in terms of regulating its services market.

---

[36] See also WTO, *European Communities – Regime for the Importation, Sale and Distribution of Bananas*, Appellate Body Report WT/DS27/AB/R, DSR 1997:II (adopted 25 September 1997), para. 589 (*EC-Bananas III (AB)*).

[37] Gregory T. Chin, 'Asian Infrastructure Investment Bank: governance innovation and prospects' (2016) 22 *Global Governance* 11.

[38] Makmun Syadullah, 'Prospects of Asian Infrastructure Investment Bank' (2014) 5(3) *Journal of Social and Development Sciences* 155–67, accessed 30 May 2018 at https://ifrnd.org/journal/index.php/jsds/article/view/816/816.

[39] See Gary N. Horlick and Peggy A. Clarke, 'WTO subsidies discipline during and after the crisis' (2011) 13(3) *Journal of International Economic Law* 859, 872–3; Bart De Meester, 'The global financial crisis and government support for banks: what role for the GATS?' (2010) 13(1) *Journal of International Economic Law* 30–2; Fabio Leonardi, 'A bailout for the international trade system: rescuing the WTO from TARP' (2011) 14 *International Trade and Business Law Review* 291, 304.

More specifically, with respect to 'Banking and Other Financial Services (excluding insurance and securities)', the schedules stipulate that these services include:

(a) Acceptance of deposits and other repayable funds from the public;
(b) Lending of all types, including consumer credit, mortgage credit, factoring and financing of commercial transaction;
(c) Financial leasing;
(d) All payment and money transmission services, including credit, charge and debit cards, traveller's cheques and banker's drafts (including import and export settlement);
(e) Guarantees and commitments; and
(f) Trading for own account or for account of customers: foreign exchange.[40]

Thus, banking services are defined sufficiently broadly to cover the various types of lending, financing and transaction services conducted in China. With respect to the 'market access' obligation for the banking and other financial services sector, China imposes specific conditions. For mode 3 services (commercial presence), which are generally regarded as the most critical by foreign service providers, China's Schedules of Specific Commitments impose specific requirements concerning geographic coverage, clients and licensing, as discussed in turn in the following subsections.

2.2.1 Geographic Coverage

There was no geographic restriction for foreign currency business upon China's accession to the WTO. For local currency business, the geographic restriction was to be phased out as follows: upon accession, Shanghai, Shenzhen, Tianjin and Dalian; within one year of accession, Guangzhou, Zhuhai, Qingdao, Nanjing and Wuhan; within two years of accession, Jinan, Fuzhou, Chengdu and Chongqing; within three years of accession, Kunming, Beijing and Xiamen; and within four years of accession, Shantou, Ningbo, Shenyang and Xi'an. Within five years of accession, all geographic restrictions were to be removed.

---

[40] See WTO, Schedules of Specific Commitments Submitted by People's Republic of China in accordance with its obligation under GATS. See in particular '7. Financial Services, B. Banking and Other Financial Services'.

2.2.2   Clients

For foreign currency business, foreign financial institutions were permitted to provide services in China without any restrictions concerning clients upon accession. For local currency business, they were to be permitted to provide services to Chinese enterprises within two years of accession. Finally, within five years of accession, foreign financial institutions were to be permitted to provide services to all Chinese clients. Further, those licensed for local currency business in one region of China are to be allowed to service clients in any other region that has been opened up to such business.

2.2.3   Licensing

The criteria for gaining authorisation to deal in China's financial service sector are solely prudential (i.e. they contain no economic needs test or quantitative limits on licences). Within five years of accession, any existing non-prudential measures restricting the ownership, operation and juridical form of foreign financial institutions, including those concerning internal branching and licences, were to be eliminated. Foreign financial institutions that meet the following condition are permitted to establish a subsidiary of a foreign bank or foreign finance company in China: total assets of more than US$10 billion at the end of the year prior to filing the application. Those that meet the following condition are permitted to establish a foreign bank branch in China: total assets of more than US$20 billion at the end of the year prior to filing the application. Those that meet the following condition are permitted to establish a Chinese-foreign joint bank or Chinese-foreign joint finance company in China: total assets of more than US$10 billion at the end of the year prior to filing the application. The criteria for a foreign financial institution to engage in local currency business include three years of business operation in China and being profitable for two consecutive years prior to the application.[41]

In other words, the geographic coverage and client requirements in the aforementioned schedules merely offer a phase-out schedule following China's WTO accession. As China is now entering its seventeenth year of accession, all of those requirements have now been phased out. The licensing requirement is not tied to a time schedule, but merely addresses

[41] Ibid.

the issue of prudential regulation, and it is the responsibility of the financial regulatory agencies to monitor the financial soundness of banking institutions and protect consumers. Accordingly, the licensing requirement is not directly related to the restriction of market access to potential foreign service providers that wish to provide financial services in China, including participation in BRI projects.

However, the column headed 'Limitation of National Treatment' in China's Schedules of Specific Commitments stipulates that 'except for geographic restrictions and client limitations on local currency business (listed in the market access column), [a] foreign financial institution may do business, without restrictions or need for case-by-case approval, with foreign invested enterprises, non-Chinese natural persons, Chinese natural persons and Chinese enterprises'.[42] In short, with respect to national treatment, there is no substantive limitation on foreign service providers in the banking services sector. Non-discriminatory treatment between Chinese and foreign banking institutions is therefore essentially guaranteed by the Schedules of Specific Commitments that China submitted to the WTO. Thus, assuming that foreign banking institutions will desire to participate in BRI projects, preferential approval of the participation of Chinese domestic banking institutions and *de jure* or *de facto* restriction of participation by foreign banking institutions have the potential to violate commitments made under GATS. Similar violations may also arise in the respective schedules of specific commitments made under the FTAs concluded by China.

2.3   Subsidies and Countervailing Measures (SCM) Agreement

In addition, it seems that the BRI is based on a commitment of full support by the governments of participating states. As with any other signature national project, it is quite likely that various types of government support measures will be introduced to encourage domestic companies and entities to take part in BRI projects. Such measures are inevitable because it is, after all, individual businesspeople and corporations that actually participate in infrastructure projects in neighbouring states, and they are likely to do so only when they are certain of receiving an economic return or other benefits. Because commercial returns/ benefits are not always guaranteed, particularly in the initial stage of the

---

[42]   Ibid.

BRI scheme, participating governments may try to provide incentives in the form of, for example, affordable loans, tax exemptions, loan guarantees, and the provision of government goods and services. Such support, albeit necessary and appropriate within the confines of the BRI, runs the risk of violating the WTO's Agreement on Subsidies and Countervailing Measures (SCM Agreement hereafter), which rather strictly regulates the provision of government support to domestic industries and companies.[43]

However, the governmental support captured by the SCM Agreement is in fact quite broad, covering not only the provision of cash grants, tax exemptions or goods, but also the provision of government support in a variety of other forms. As evidenced in recent currency disputes between the United States and China, a government's policy to operate an economic or financial system can sometimes lead to the filing of claims under the SCM Agreement.[44] One segment of the process for implementing the BRI scheme may involve the provision of assistance by the government of an exporting developing member to domestic industries to facilitate the export of the goods they produce. Even if no money changes hands, the provision of such support could lead to a finding that the government in question was violating Article 1.1(a)(1) of the SCM Agreement.

2.3.1   General Infrastructure

Another issue that requires careful consideration is the general infrastructure exception in the SCM Agreement. As shown above, Article 1.1 (a)(1)(iii) of that agreement explicitly excludes the provision of general infrastructure from the definition of 'financial contribution by the government'.[45] Although every infrastructure project is different, an argument could be made that the construction of a nationwide distribution channel by a developing member should be regarded as a general infrastructure project, and thus should fall under the Article 1.1 exception. The ordinary meaning of the term 'general infrastructure', as interpreted

---

[43] See Articles 1, 2 and 14 of the SCM Agreement.

[44] See WTO, *United States – Definitive Anti-Dumping and Countervailing Duties on Certain Products from China*, Appellate Body Report WT/DS379/AB/R (adopted 25 March 2011), paras. 217–72 (*US AD/CVD(AB)*).

[45] See WTO, *United States – Preliminary Determination with Respect to Certain Softwood Lumber from Canada*, Panel Report WT/DS236/R (adopted 14 April 1999) (*US-Softwood Lumber* III (Panel)). Para. 7.26 reads '[W]e find further confirmation of this broad meaning in the fact that the drafters of the Agreement considered it necessary to explicitly exclude "general infrastructure" [in drafting] Article 1.1(a)(1)(iii) of the SCM Agreement'.

by Article 31 of the 1969 Vienna Convention on the Law of Treaties, is 'basic physical and organizational structures needed for the operation of a society or enterprise where such structures are (i) affecting or concerning all or most people or things; or (ii) not specialized or limited'.[46] Depending on how the domestic collection and processing system is established and operated, it may be considered to constitute general infrastructure.[47]

Whilst the SCM Agreement does subject WTO members' provision of illegitimate subsidies to specific private economic entities within their territories to rigorous discipline, the agreement is also mindful not to interfere with governments' inherent authority to pursue otherwise legitimate public objectives within the agreement's parameters, as is well-summarised by the panel in *Canada–Aircraft*.[48] Viewed from this perspective, the explicit exclusion of 'general infrastructure' in Article 1.1(a) (1)(iii) of the SCM Agreement, in enumerating specific forms of financial contribution by a government, is a reflection of that consideration to ensure that the governments of WTO members have room to manoeuvre

---

[46] The *Concise Oxford English Dictionary* defines 'general' as 'affecting or concerning all or most people or things; not specialised or limited'. See Catherine Soanes and Angus Stevenson (eds.), *Concise Oxford English Dictionary*, 11th edition (Oxford: Oxford University Press, 2004), p. 592. 'Infrastructure' is defined as 'the basic physical and organizational structures (e.g. buildings, roads, power supplies) needed for the operation of a society or enterprise'. Ibid., p. 730.

[47] In *EC-LCA*, in exploring the meaning of 'general infrastructure', the panel highlights the importance of managing the programme in question over time for it to be eligible for general infrastructure status. For instance, it points out that a programme considered general infrastructure at one point in time might not be so considered at other times. The panel thus held that: 'Such situations would have to be carefully evaluated, based on all the relevant facts in each case, in order to determine whether the provision of the infrastructure in question is general or not, and whether that determination changes over time. Thus, we consider that the proper point of reference in determining whether a provision of goods or services is "other than general infrastructure" is the time when the act of provision that is alleged to constitute a subsidy takes place. That might be at the time the infrastructure in question is created, in the sense of being brought into existence, or a subsequent point in time, when the conditions surrounding the provision of that infrastructure are changed by the government providing it. Moreover, the determination of whether a provision of goods or services is "other than general infrastructure" may involve a time period of limited or indefinite duration.' See WTO, *European Communities – Measures Affecting Trade in Large Civil Aircraft*, Panel Report WT/DS316/AB/R (adopted 18 May 2011), para. 7.1044 (*EC and Certain Member States – Large Civil Aircraft (Panel)*).

[48] See WTO, *Canada – Measures Affecting the Export of Civilian Aircraft*, Panel Report WT/DS70/R (adopted 14 April 1999), para. 9.119 (*Canada-Aircraft (Panel)*).

in pursuing legitimate public objectives. The BRI arguably fits the profile of legitimate economic policies by its members.

In fact, it is noteworthy that the government procurement market is explained in relation to, or in the context of, general infrastructure in the revised WTO Agreement on Government Procurement (GPA) issued in December 2011.[49] Although the recognition of such a market largely reflects foreign business entities' increased access to the global infrastructure construction market, thanks to the amended GPA,[50] it also indirectly supports the proposition that the overall administration of a member's government procurement market, such as distribution channel management, constitutes general infrastructure in itself. The administration or operation of projects relating to general infrastructure arguably falls under one segment of the establishment of general infrastructure, as long as such administration/operation is closely related to the establishment of infrastructure. Article 1 of the SCM Agreement, which covers the definition of a subsidy, states:

> For the purpose of this Agreement, a subsidy shall be deemed to exist if (a)(1) there is a financial contribution by a government or any public body within the territory of a Member (referred to in this Agreement as "government"), i.e. where: (iii) a government provides goods or services other than general infrastructure, or purchases goods.

As can be seen, sub-paragraph (iii) of the article stipulates three items as instances of a financial contribution by a government in the form of 'in-kind' assistance: the provision of goods, the provision of services and the purchase of goods. Interestingly, the term 'purchase of services' does not appear. Its explicit omission, as opposed to the inclusion of 'purchase of goods', indicates that the drafters of the SCM Agreement made a deliberate decision to exclude the purchase of services from the agreement's ambit.[51]

---

[49] See WTO, 'Historic deal reached on government procurement', 2011 News Items, accessed 30 May 2018 at www.wto.org/english/news_e/news11_e/gpro_15dec11_e.htm. In the article, Pascal Lamy, the WTO Director-General in 2011, opines: 'This extremely important deal means better disciplines for awarding government contracts. And this also means better use of public resources in a moment when, more than ever, the economic crisis calls for fiscal discipline. It will also provide a needed stimulus for the world economy because it will apply to many sectors of it, namely to the suppliers of infrastructure, public transport, hospital equipment and many other government services.'
[50] Ibid.
[51] The interpretation of the principle of 'ordinary meaning' codified in Article 31 of the Vienna Convention leaves us with few choices when a provision lists certain items and

The intention of the BRI scheme is to introduce a system whereby the government of a developing member state can facilitate access to the international trading system by products manufactured by its domestic exporters. If such a government enters into contracts with domestic entities involved in BRI administration (e.g. collection, processing and distribution), then the argument could be made that those contracts constitute the purchase of a service on the part of that government. If so, the entire mechanism of the country could remain outside the scope of financial contribution within the meaning of Article 1.1(a)(1) of the SCM Agreement. The absence of the financial contribution element would resolve all subsidy-related issues. Thus, it may prove crucial to how a developing country government formulates transactions inside its territory before products are exported.

2.4   Free Trade Agreements (FTAs)

Similar circumstances may arise with respect to the FTAs that BRI participating states already have in place. For instance, China's preferential treatment of goods and services from another country may constitute a possible MFN or NT violation under the terms of its FTAs with non-participating countries.

2.5   International Investment Agreements (IIAs)

Investment issues have recently taken centre stage in international economic law. International Investment Agreements (IIAs) have become one of the most frequently negotiated and concluded treaties between and amongst states, whether they carry the title of BITs or FTAs.[52] The

---

omits others in no uncertain terms. If a particular item is missing, that means the negotiators wanted to exclude the item from the scope of the application. As noted, in this sub-paragraph, only three items are listed. In these circumstances, unless a compelling reason is identified, adding a fourth one through interpretation might exceed the scope of the provision's ordinary meaning. Such interpretation is also apparently disfavoured by international law scholars. See Anthony Aust, *Modern Treaty Law and Practice* (Cambridge: Cambridge University Press, 2002), p. 188. He writes: 'Thus, although paragraph 1 [of Article 31 of the Vienna Convention] contains both the textual (or literal) and the effectiveness (or teleological) approaches, it gives precedence to the textual.'

[52] The number of BITs and FTAs with investment chapters has increased steadily. According to official statistics, by the end of 2015, the IIA regime consisted of 3,304 agreements, including 2,946 BITs and 358 'other IIAs' such as integration or cooperation

surge in IIAs has also brought about a dramatic increase in the number of investment disputes.[53] Not surprisingly, the contents of such disputes have also become increasingly complex and controversial. A variety of novel issues have been raised, and different views juxtaposed.[54] Also, given that infrastructure projects are a frequent subject of investment disputes, efforts to treat Eurasian states preferentially in the context of those projects may bring BITs into the equation as well. BITs also contain MFN and NT arrangements, together with fair and equitable treatment (FET) principles whose support and arrangement under the auspices of the BRI may potentially raise investment dispute issues. By way of example, Article 5(1) of the Korea-China-Japan trilateral investment treaty of 2012 provides for FET as follows:

> Each Contracting Party shall accord to investments of investors of another Contracting Party fair and equitable treatment and full protection and security. The concepts of 'fair and equitable treatment' and 'full protection and security' do not require treatment in addition to or beyond any reasonable and appropriate standard of treatment accorded in accordance with generally accepted rules of international law. A determination that there has been a breach of another provision of this Agreement, or of a separate international agreement, does not ipso facto establish that there has been a breach of this paragraph.

Korea and the United States concluded an FTA on 15 March 2012,[55] attracting robust domestic attention in both countries. Amongst the many

---

agreements with an investment dimension. That year also saw the conclusion of 31 IIAs (20 BITs and 11 'other IIAs'). See UNCTAD, *World Investment Report 2016, Investor Nationality: Policy Challenges* (New York and Geneva: UNCTAD, 2016), p. 101.

[53] As of 1 January 2016, the total number of known cases (concluded, pending or discontinued) reached 696, and the total number of countries that had responded to one or more ISDS claims increased to 107. The majority of cases continued to accrue under the ICSID Convention and ICSID Additional Facility Rules and the UNCITRAL Rules. Other arbitral venues have been used only rarely. Ibid., p. 104. See also Susan D. Franck, 'The legitimacy crisis in investment treaty arbitration: privatizing public international law through inconsistent decisions' (2005) 73 *Fordham Law Review* 1521; Stanimir A. Alexandrov, 'Breaches of contract and breaches of treaty – the jurisdiction of treaty-based arbitration tribunals to decide breach of contract claims in SGS v. Pakistan and SGS v. Philippines' (2004) 5 *Transnational Dispute Management* 555.

[54] Jarrod Wong, 'Umbrella clauses in bilateral investment treaties: of breaches of contract, treaty violations and divide between developed and developing countries in foreign investment disputes' (2006) 14 *George Mason Law Review* 135–6.

[55] For the chronological history of the Korea–US FTA negotiations and conclusion, see Yong-Shik Lee, Jaemin Lee & Kyung Han Sohn, *The United States – Korea Free Trade Agreement: Path to Common Economic Prosperity or False Promise?*, U. Pa. E. Asia. L. Rev. Vol. 6 Issue 1 (2011) pp.117–120.

issues raised in the course of negotiating and concluding the agreement, the issue of the investor-state dispute settlement (ISDS) mechanism drew the most acute controversy in Korea,[56] a controversy that persists today. Many people are watching how the ISDS mechanism of the Korea-US FTA[57] is applied and implemented in practice.

3 Conclusion

China's BRI is a new breed of international economic cooperation scheme covering Asia and the eastern part of Europe. As the scheme is not necessarily concerned with the market liberalisation of the constituent countries, but rather with infrastructure construction, joint energy resource development and transport/communication networks, it is distinct from traditional FTAs. The BRI scheme is in fact focused on ensuring enhanced connection and connectivity – both figuratively and culturally – to achieve the varying objectives of participating states. However, the scheme is also likely to have a number of unintended side effects. Its legal implications, in particular, should not be underestimated. As with any other new attempt to establish an international economic cooperation scheme, a myriad of trade and investment agreements apply to the new BRI scheme.

---

[56] The ISDS mechanism has become one of the most important issues in BITs. See John H. Jackson, Marco C. E. J. Bronckers and Reinhard Quick, *New Directions in International Economic Law: Essays in Honour of John H. Jackson* (The Hague: Kluwer Law International, 2000), pp. 392–3. As of 31 December 2017, the total number of BITs stood at 3,322. See UNCTAD, *World Investment Report 2018*, p. 89, accessed 6 June 2018 at http://unctad.org/en/PublicationsLibrary/wir2018_en.pdf. The total number of known treaty-based arbitration (ISDS) cases had reached 568 by the end of 2013. See UNCTAD, 'Recent developments in investor-state dispute settlement (ISDS)', IIA Issues Note, No. 1, April 2014, accessed 30 May 2018 at http://unctad.org/en/PublicationsLibrary/webdiaepcb2014d3_en.pdf. Of those ISDS cases, at least 57 were initiated in 2013. See ibid., pp. 2, 7.

[57] The Free Trade Agreement between the Republic of Korea and the United States of America (Korea-US FTA) entered into force on 15 March 2012. See FTA Korea website, accessed 10 March 2017, www.fta.go.kr/korus/main/index.asp.

4

Anti-Monopoly Law in China

Administrative and Private Enforcement and the Belt and Road Initiative from an Anti-Monopoly Law Perspective

SARAH WERSBORG

It has now been nearly ten years since the Anti-Monopoly Law (AML) of the People's Republic of China (PRC)[1] came into effect on 1 August 2008. In the years since, several general provisions and juridical interpretations have been issued. The first judgments of the Chinese courts and decisions made by the PRC authorities are also now available. It is thus an opportune moment to reflect not only on the developments of monopoly law in China, but also on the practical implications of the enforcement of the AML to date by the country's authorities and courts. In particular, private enforcement of the AML is gaining increased importance and attention in China, although administrative enforcement of the law by the AML enforcement authorities has also recently come under public scrutiny.

This chapter provides an overview of the developments in merger and abuse control, the prohibition of monopolies and private enforcement. It discusses both the new provisions in the arena of merger control and private enforcement in China, as well as the latest decisions of both the PRC authorities and courts in all areas of the AML. In addition, the chapter offers a new perspective on the connections between China's Belt and Road Initiative (BRI) and the AML.

1 Developments in Merger Control

1.1 General Overview

Merger control is governed in detail by Articles 20–31 of Chapter 4 of the AML. According to Article 20, a concentration of business operators is present if there is:

---

[1] See www.lawinfochina.com (accessed 30 May 2018).

1. a merger of business operators;
2. acquisition of control by a business operator over other business operators through acquisition of the latter's equity assets; or
3. acquisition of control or the exertion of a decisive influence over another business operator by a business operator via a contract or other means.

The PRC Ministry of Commerce (MOFCOM) is in charge of merger control, which constitutes a major, and important, component of the country's AML. [2] In 2014 alone, MOFCOM completed the inspection of 245 out of the 262 mergers registered. Four of the 245 were eventually authorised subject to certain provisions, and one was rejected, the other 240 mergers were unconditionally approved.[3] In 2014, Chinese companies were involved in mergers and acquisitions valued at a total of US$396.2 billion.[4] Unfortunately, however, there is a lack of transparency in the mergers and acquistions (M&A) arena, as not all MOFCOM decisions are required to be published, pursuant to Article 30 of the AML.[5]

1.2 General Provisions and Juridical Interpretations

As is the case with nearly every law in China, juridical interpretations and general provisions have been passed in connection with the AML. General provisions and juridical interpretations constitute a special feature of Chinese law, and stem from the partial compilation of Chinese laws in a basic and general manner.[6] Juridical interpretations are passed by the Supreme People's Court (SPC), and are intended to supplement generally formulated provisions, close any existing gaps in those provisions and

---

[2] See Markus Masseli, *Handbook of Chinese Merger Control (Handbuch chinesische Fusionskontrolle)* (Berlin: Springer, 2011), p. 31.

[3] Michael Gu, 'Annual review of PRC anti-monopoly law enforcement (2015)', Anjie Law Firm, accessed 30 May 2018 at http://en.anjielaw.com/downloadRepository/46dbc187-d36c-43b0-a839-d3d4e70bc784.pdf.

[4] MOFCOM, 'Chinese companies are increasingly taking over business abroad. This is shown by the latest figures from Thomson Reuters', MOFCOM, 5 February 2015.

[5] Lukas Ritzenhoff, 'Chinese merger control: between law and reality' (Fusionskontrolle in China: zwischen Recht und Wirklichkeit) (2014) (1) *Industrial Property and Copyright International (Gewerblicher Rechtsschutz und Urheberrecht International)* 33–7 at 35.

[6] Yuanshi Bu, *Introduction to Chinese Law (Einführung in das Recht Chinas)* (Munich: Beck, 2009), p. 3.

serve as guidelines for the courts.[7] They therefore complement the law itself. Even before the AML entered into effect, it was expected that more than forty general provisions would be needed as supplements to render the AML complete.[8]

The first general provisions came into effect on 3 August 2008, just two days after the AML itself took effect. Called *Provisions of the State Council on the Standard for Declaration of Concentration of Business Operators* (Registration Provisions hereafter), they were essential for AML enforcement and contributed to strengthening legal security and clarity for investors and companies.[9] Some of the newer AML-related provisions pertain to the control of mergers. For example, MOFCOM's *Interim Provisions on Standards Applicable to Simple Cases of Concentration of Undertakings* (Interim Provisions hereafter)[10] were passed on 11 February 2014 and took effect the next day. Aided by the Interim Provisions, concentrations of business operators should be completed more quickly, as long as they do not exceed a certain market share. To enforce these provisions, MOFCOM published *Guidelines on the Filing of Simple Cases Regarding [the] Concentration of Business Operators (for trial implementation)* (Guidelines hereafter)[11] on 18 April 2014. It subsequently published the *Guiding Opinions of the Anti-Monopoly Bureau of the Ministry of Commerce on the Declaration of the Concentration of Business Operators* (Amended Guidelines hereafter)[12] on 6 June 2014.

1.2.1 Registration Provisions

The first general provisions for the AML concerned the control of mergers. As the provisions concerning the registration criteria for the concentration of business operators are rather short and generally formulated in the AML, these additional general provisions were regarded

[7] Ibid., p. 20.
[8] Markus Masseli, 'Chinese merger control in light of the first general provisions of the anti-monopoly law' ('Die chinesische Fusionskontrolle im Lichte der ersten Nebenbestimmungen zum Antimonopolgesetz' (2009) 16 (1) *German Journal of Chinese Law (Zeitschrift für Chinesisches Recht (ZChinR)*) 18–36 at 18.
[9] Masseli, 'Chinese merger control', 18–19.
[10] MOFCOM, accessed 5 June 2018 at www.mofcom.gov.cn/article/b/c/201402/20140200 487038.shtml.
[11] MOFCOM, accessed 5 June 2018 at http://fldj.mofcom.gov.cn/article/i/201404/20140400 555353.shtml.
[12] MOFCOM, accessed 5 June 2018 at http://fldj.mofcom.gov.cn/article/i/201406/20140600 614679.shtml.

as essential.[13] Article 2 of the Registration Provisions defines what constitutes a merger, namely, the merger of business operators or the taking of control by one business operator over others through the acquisition of their shares, the signing of contracts or other means.[14] The criteria that must be present to meet the registration obligation are also stipulated. In particular, the turnover thresholds pursuant to Article 3 of the Registration Provisions must be observed. According to the article, a merger must be registered if:

1. The total worldwide turnover of all business operators involved in the concentration exceeded RMB10 billion, and at least two of those operators each had turnover of more than RMB400 million in China, in the previous accounting year; or
2. the joint turnover in China of all companies involved in the concentration exceeded RMB2 billion in the previous accounting year and at least two of those companies made more than RMB400 million in that year.

According to Article 4 of the Registration Provisions, MOFCOM reserves the right to investigate in the event of any suspicion of a restriction on competition through concentration even if the criteria for the registration obligation required by those provisions are not present. As noted above, additional enforcement provisions and guidelines were passed in the initial phase of the AML, but they will not be examined in detail in this chapter.[15]

1.2.2   Provisions for Simple Cases

One of the newer sets of MOFCOM provisions relating to the AML concerns simple cases of business operator concentrations. These provisions were passed by MOFCOM on 11 February 2014 and entered into effect the following day. With only six articles, these Interim Provisions are relatively tightly scripted. They are intended to ensure that concentrations of smaller companies can be completed more quickly. Accordingly, they establish solely whether such a simple case is present, taking no stance on the concentration procedure itself.[16]

---

[13] Masseli, 'Chinese merger control', 19–20.
[14] Ibid., 20–1.
[15] See ibid. for further details.
[16] Hannah C. L. Ha et al., 'China: MOFCOM adopts interim provisions on the standards that apply to simplified cases of concentrations of undertakings: first steps toward a fast

1.2.2.1 Simple Case of a Concentration of Business Operators Article 2 of the Interim Provisions stipulates the circumstances under which a simple case of business operator concentration exists:

1. The business operators participating in a (horizontal) concentration are active in the relevant market, and the total combined market share is less than 15 per cent.
2. There is an upstream-downstream relationship amongst the business operators participating in the concentration, and the combined market share of those in the upstream and downstream markets is less than 25 per cent.
3. The business operators participating in the concentration do not operate in the same relevant market or have any upstream-downstream relationship, and the market share of the business operators in each market is less than 25 per cent.
4. The business operators participating in the concentration establish a joint venture outside China that does not engage in any business activities within China.
5. The business operators participating in the concentration acquire equity interests in other business operators that do not engage in any business activities within China.
6. An overseas entity that engages in no business activities in China is acquired by a concentration of business operators through an asset deal.
7. A joint venture under the joint control of several business operators is taken over by one of the parties.

The definition of 'relevant market' sometimes causes difficulties for the parties concerned, as MOFCOM has provided neither a definitive definition nor sufficient decisions or information.[17] It is therefore up for interpretation.

1.2.2.2 Exceptions If, according to the aforementioned criteria, a simple case of business operator concentration generally exists, then once

---

track procedure', *Mondaq*, 27 February 2014, accessed 5 June 2018 at www.mondaq.com/x/295934/Antitrust+Competition/MOFCOM+Adopts+Interim+Provisions+On+The+Standards+That+Apply+To+Simplified+Cases+Of+Concentrations+Of+Undertakings+First+Steps+Toward+A+Fast+Track+Procedure.

[17] Ilka Mauelshagen, 'Simplified merger control in China' ('Vereinfachte Fusionskontrolle in der Volkrepublik China - Mehr Schein als Sein?') (2014) (8-9) *Industrial Property and Copyright International (Gewerblicher Rechtsschutz und Urheberrecht International)* 780-5 at 782.

again exceptions are possible. Such exceptions are regulated by Article 3 of the Interim Provisions and are possible in the following cases.

1. If the business operator that takes control of a joint venture is a competitor of the joint venture.
2. If it is difficult to define the relevant market.
3. If the concentration of business operators may exert an adverse impact on market access or technological advancement.
4. If the concentration of business operators may exert an adverse impact on consumers or other business operators.
5. If the concentration of business operators may exert an adverse impact on national economic development.
6. If any others circumstances exist that may have an adverse impact on market competition in MOFCOM's opinion.

A clause such as number 6 above is often found in regulations concerning the AML, and this type of catch-all clause can also be found in the AML itself.[18] Although there is much to welcome in such an approach because the courts and authorities are left with a certain freedom of interpretation, and are thus able to subsume unplanned cases under the catch-all clause, it also leads to legal uncertainty, the consequences of which should not be underestimated.[19]

MOFCOM has reserved further exceptions in Article 4 of the Interim Provisions with respect to simple cases. Even if the criteria for a simple case are met, MOFCOM can still revoke its decision if

1. the applicants conceal important information or provide false or misleading information;
2. a third party claims – and provides sufficient evidence to show – that the concentration of business operators has had or may have the effect of eliminating or restricting competition in the relevant market; or
3. MOFCOM finds further material indicating that the circumstances in the relevant market in question have changed.

Article 5 of the Interim Provisions empowers MOFCOM to interpret those provisions, which once again can lead to legal uncertainty for the companies concerned, and thus does not actually make it any easier for small companies to concentrate, as the parties involved are often unsure how individual provisions should or will be interpreted.

---

[18] See AML sections 13, 14, 15, 17, 18 and 32.
[19] Mauelshagen, 'Simplified merger control', 783.

1.2.2.3 Open Questions Unfortunately, the Interim Provisions do not clarify the exact procedure for simple cases of business operator concentration or whether simplified provisions should be applied to accelerate drawn out processes. It would be desirable for such simple cases to be processed via a simplified, accelerated procedure. However, the Interim Provisions provide no indication of the maximum allowable schedule or other procedural benefits. Whether simple concentrations can be completed under the conditions of Article 25 of the AML within thirty days is thus unclear and requires further clarification by MOF-COM. Given that in 2015 alone, approximately 80 per cent, or 243 of 312, registered concentrations of business operators constituted simple cases, such a solution would be practical and efficient.[20] Particularly with regard to German–Chinese economic relations, simplified regulations on the control of mergers would be advantageous. Germany has become one of China's largest trading partners in Europe,[21] meaning that mergers and joint ventures between German and Chinese partners are no longer a rarity. Such a shortened and simplified procedure would be particularly beneficial to small and medium-sized German companies, which are highly active in China today.

1.2.3 Guidelines for Simple Cases of Concentration

The aforementioned Guidelines, published by MOFCOM on 18 April 2014, added some clarity to the procedure for simple cases of business operator concentration.

1.2.3.1 Preliminary Consultation and Filing To assure themselves that the case in question is a simple one, the parties involved can obtain advance appraisal from MOFCOM, as provided for in Article 1 of the Guidelines. Such a provision is already in place for the standard procedure. To be able to obtain advance appraisal for simple cases as a special procedure, the filing must be made expressly as a simple case; otherwise, the standard procedure must be followed (see Article 2 of the

---

[20] Michael Gu, 'Annual review of the public enforcement of China's anti-monopoly law (2016)', *China Law Vision*, 29 March 2016, accessed 5 June 2018 at www.chinalawvision .com/2016/03/articles/competitionantitrust-law-of-th/annual-review-of-public-enforce ment-of-chinas-antimonopoly-law-2016/.

[21] German Federal Foreign Office, 'China', accessed 5 June 2018 at www.auswaertiges-amt.de/ en/aussenpolitik/laenderinformationen/china-node/china/228916.

Guidelines). This also applies if all of the criteria for a simple case are fulfilled.[22] It is clear from Article 3 of the Guidelines which documents have to be submitted to file a simple case with MOFCOM, and Article 4 provides a registration form for simple cases that can be downloaded from the MOFCOM website.

If a concentration of business operators falls within the simple case definition, it can be filed with MOFCOM using the corresponding registration form, which requires far less information than the standard form.[23] It is particularly advantageous for a company to avail itself of the special filing procedure, which relieves it of the risk and burden of revealing a large amount of internal information.

1.2.3.2 Publication of Cases and Legal Consequences Articles 8 and 9 of the Guidelines stipulate that the information required for registration must be made publicly accessible to allow third parties – usually competitors – to make a statement regarding the proposed concentration within the ten-day deadline, which can render a case more difficult.[24] MOFCOM can also revoke a decision to treat a given concentration as a simple case at any time according to Article 10 of the Guidelines. It will certainly do so if the parties concerned make false statements about a concentration project (see also Article 11 of the Guidelines). Further, the parties are held legally responsible according to Article 52 of the AML, and may be fined in the case of any wrongdoing.

1.2.4   Amended Guidelines on Concentration Registration

On 6 June 2014, MOFCOM published the aforementioned Amended Guidelines to replace the *Guidelines on the Registration of the Concentration of Business Operators* promulgated on 5 January 2009 (2009 Guidelines hereafter).[25] The Amended Guidelines comprise thirty articles, and are thus considerably more extensive than the 2009 Guidelines, which contain just twelve.

---

[22] Mauelshagen, 'Simplified merger control in China', 784.

[23] Ibid. See also Guat Kim Toh and Minning Wei, 'China's merger clearance requirements – an update', *Deacons*, 17 July 2014, accessed 5 June 2018 at www.deacons.com.hk/news-and-insights/publications/chinas-merger-clearance-requirements---an-update.html.

[24] Xiang Wang, 'MOFCOM anti-monopoly bureau issued procedural rules for review on simple merger cases', Global Law Office (GLO), accessed 5 June 2018 at www.glo.com.cn/en/content/details_13_289.html.

[25] Masseli, 'Chinese merger control', 48–50.

1.2.4.1 Definition of 'Control' A special feature of the Amended Guidelines is that they, for the first time since the AML came into effect, allow the AML enforcement authorities specified in Article 3 to offer a more stringent definition of 'control'.[26] To determine whether control over a company is obtained in the event of concentration, several factors are taken into consideration. In accordance with Article 3, they include the following:

1. Purpose of the transaction and future plans.
2. Concentration-induced changes to the shareholding structure.
3. Voting rights' distribution during the post-concentration general share-holders' meeting, as well as documentation on the participation and voting distribution of previous general shareholders' meetings.
4. Composition of the board of directors after the concentration.
5. Appointment and removal of senior management after the concentration.
6. Post-concentration relationship amongst shareholders and directors.
7. Post-concentration relationship and cooperation agreements amongst the business operators concerned.

1.2.4.2 Turnover Figures and Joint Ventures Article 2 of the Amended Guidelines also stipulates the required turnover, although it was already evident from Article 3 of the Registration Provisions.[27] Additional clarity is achieved with regard to newly formed joint ventures, turnover thresholds and additional registration requirements. According to Article 4 of the Amended Guidelines, newly formed joint ventures controlled by only one party are not deemed to be a concentration of business operators. Only those controlled by two parties are considered to constitute such a concentration. As the latter account for approximately 40 per cent of all registrations for business operator concentrations in China, this clarification is particularly important.[28] Pursuant to Article 5, 'turnover' in the sense of the Amended Guidelines is defined as including only revenues derived from the sale of products or provision of services within China. Exports are therefore not considered part of the relevant turnover.

---

[26] Zhaofeng Zhou, 'Merger control finally gets makeover', *China Law and Practice*, 8 July 2014, accessed 15 June 2018 at www.chinalawandpractice.com/sites/clp/2014/07/08/merger-control-finally-gets-makeover/.

[27] See Article 3 of Registration Provisions.

[28] Zhou, 'Merger control finally gets makeover'.

1.2.4.3 Preliminary Consultation According to Article 9 of the Amended Guidelines, preliminary consultations can still be held with MOFCOM regarding a future concentration of business operators. The preconditions for such consultations are even more detailed than those in the 2009 Guidelines. However, they are not a prerequisite for registration. Companies remain free to choose whether they wish to apply for a consultation. According to Article 10 of the Amended Guidelines, those registering for a preliminary consultation must provide background information on the transaction and parties concerned, in addition to the questions and topics to be discussed with MOFCOM, and the names and contact details of all consultation participants. Article 11 specifies which questions can be discussed. Further, the consultation in question must concern a concentration of business operators that is actually being planned.[29] Article 11 stipulates that MOFCOM will accept no anonymous registrations. MOFCOM then decides whether a consultation will take place based on the documents submitted. If the documents and information submitted are insufficient or incomplete, MOFCOM may request additional documents, which must be submitted by a specified deadline (see Article 12 of the Amended Guidelines).

1.2.4.4 Filing Procedure According to Article 13 of the Amended Guidelines, one of the parties involved can be nominated as the party responsible for the filing. If that party does not meet its obligations, however, the other party is not freed from legal responsibility. The article also stipulates that the filing can take place after the contract for a merger has been signed, although it must take place before the merger has been executed (also see Article 14). Unfortunately, however, no clarification is provided concerning the circumstances that constitute the execution of a merger.[30]

Articles 20–24 of the Amended Guidelines provide a detailed description of the documents and materials that have to be submitted as part of the filing procedure. Article 26 states that companies involved in a simple business operator concentration case should refer to the aforementioned Guidelines.

1.2.4.5 Additional Information A merger that has already been filed or authorised can be revoked by MOFCOM at any time according to

---

[29] Ibid.
[30] Ibid.

Article 27 of the AML. Such revocation is particularly likely in the case of the submission of false documents or the withholding of documents. Article 50 of the AML stipulates that the parties concerned can also be forced to bear legal responsibility.

Companies can carry out the consultation and filing procedures themselves or hire legal representation, according to Article 28 of the Amended Guidelines. In the latter case, written power of attorney is required. Although MOFCOM's Amended Guidelines have resulted in clarifying some points that were previously unclear, such as the definition of the term 'control' and the detailed regulations for preliminary consultations, a number of questions remain unanswered. For example, we still lack detailed instructions on how to calculate the turnover of a joint venture, and no criteria have been set according to which a merger can be deemed complete. Additional guidelines or provisions are expected to come into effect in the near future to clarify these outstanding issues.[31]

1.3 Administrative Enforcement

China's AML enforcement authorities have become increasingly active in the past few years. To date, the control of mergers has accounted for the majority of AML enforcement measures. Since the AML took effect, MOFCOM has reviewed approximately 1,300 cases of business operator concentration.[32] Thus, it is not surprising that MOFCOM has already made a number of notable decisions. The AML enforcement authorities in China are completely independent in their decisions and reviews, and are not bound by the decisions of their counterparts in other countries or regions, including the European Union (EU) and United States. There are indications, however, that the Chinese authorities have begun to launch investigations after moves by other authorities, although there are notable differences between the final decisions reached. The following subsection provides examples of recent AML enforcement measures taken by MOFCOM to provide greater insight into the administrative enforcement regime.

---

[31] Ibid.
[32] From 2008 to July 2014, there were approximately 800 cases. See also Alec J. Burnside, Rocky T. Lee, Christian J. Lorenz and Brandon C. Kressin, 'China: making life simpler – China's anti-monopoly bureau has reformed the merger review regime', *Mondaq*, 30 July 2014, www.mondaq.com/x/331490/Antitrust+Competition/Making+Life+Simpler+Chinas +AntiMonopoly+Bureau+Has+Reformed+The+Merger+Review+Regime.

1.4   Decisions in Control of Mergers Framework

1.4.1   Prohibition of P3 Alliance Merger

Until 2015, only two mergers had been prohibited in China. The first prohibition was issued shortly after the AML came into effect on 18 March 2009 and concerned the proposed takeover by Coca-Cola of Hui-yuan, a Chinese juice manufacturer.[33] The second was issued on 17 June 2014, and concerned the so-called P3 Alliance, an alliance between the world's three largest shipping lines (AP Moller-Maersk from Denmark, CMA CGM from France and MSC from Switzerland). MOFCOM rejected the P3 Alliance because it believed that it would have an exclusionary or anti-competitive effect. The aim of the proposed alliance was to divide the capacities of the Europe–Asia, transpacific and transatlantic routes amongst the three companies. In MOFCOM's opinion, the P3 Alliance's market share of the Europe–Asia route would total approximately 47 per cent, thereby considerably restricting market access.[34] In addition, the parties concerned had not sufficiently demonstrated that the alliance's positive influence would outweigh its negative influence or that it served the public interest.[35] What is particularly notable about MOFCOM's decision in the P3 Alliance case is that both the US Federal Maritime Commission and European Commission had already approved the merger. However, both the US and European authorities examined the proposed alliance for its potential to restrict competition, whereas MOFCOM looked at it as a concentration of business operators. This example yet again demonstrates that concentrations of business operators, which require MOFCOM approval, have to be treated with particular care in China.[36] Chinese shipping lines openly opposed the P3 Alliance. As MOFCOM's decision differed from that of the US and EU authorities,

---

[33] For MOFCOM's decision, see Masseli, *Handbook of Chinese Merger Control*, pp. 341–4.

[34] Peter Wang and Sébastien J. Evrard, 'China: China blocks global shipping alliance', *Mondaq*, 25 June 2014, accessed 5 June 2018 at www.mondaq.com/x/322944/Cartels +Monopolies/China+Blocks+Global+Shipping+Alliance.

[35] Michael Gu and Yu Shuitian, 'No way: top three shipping liners proposed alliance was blocked by Chinese watchdog', *China Law Vision*, 24 June 2014, accessed 5 June 2018 at www.chinalawvision.com/2014/06/articles/competitionantitrust-law-of-th/no-way-top-three-shipping-liners-proposed-alliance-was-blocked-by-chinese-watchdog/.

[36] Gaby Smeenk, Yi Duan and Sjoerd Van Elferen, 'China: Chinese competition authority blocks P3 network', *Mondaq*, 17 July 2014, accessed 5 June 2018 at www.mondaq.com/x/ 328206/Antitrust+Competition/Chinese+Competition+Authority+Blocks+P3+Network.

questions have been raised over whether political considerations exerted an influence. In the context of this chapter, it is also not unlikely that the BRI was a hidden factor in the decision. China's anti-monopoly enforcement authorities may well be tougher in their actions and decisions concerning international companies than in purely national cases.[37] MOFCOM decisions are therefore certain to attract considerable international interest in the future.

1.4.2   First Fine Imposed by MOFCOM

For the first time since passage of the AML, MOFCOM levied a fine related to the control of a merger in 2014, publishing its decision on 2 December of that year.[38] The case concerned the merger of Tsinghua Unigroup and RDA Microelectronics. Although the merger did not in MOFCOM's opinion exert a negative impact on competition, the two companies had failed to meet the filing requirements and were thus forced to pay an RMB300,000 fine.[39]

According to Article 20 of the AML, a concentration of companies that attains the threshold set by the State Council must, according to Article 21 of that law, be registered, and the concentration can be completed only after MOFCOM approval is obtained.[40] In the event of an illegal merger, the fine could reach as high as RMB500,000 according to Article 48 of the AML. MOFCOM's decision in the Tsinghua-RDA case clearly shows that companies must take their filing obligations seriously. Particularly important is observing the thresholds set by the AML enforcement authorities. This example demonstrates that thresholds alone can be decisive, with the question of whether a merger restricts competition being exclusionary.

---

[37] See Wang and Evrard, 'China: China blocks global shipping alliance'.

[38] Michael Gu and Yu Shuitian, 'MOFCOM steps up: penalty decisions regarding merger control published for the first time', *China Law Vision*, 31 December 2014, accessed 5 June 2018 at www.chinalawvision.com/2014/12/articles/competitionantitrust-law-of-th/mofcom-steps-up-penalty-decisions-regarding-merger-control-published-for-the-first-time/.

[39] See Peter Wang, Sébastien J. Evrard and Yizhe Zhang, 'China's MOFCOM fines merging parties for failure to notify transaction under anti-monopoly law', *Mondaq*, 30 December 2014, accessed 5 June 2018 at www.mondaq.com/x/363078/Cartels+Monopolies/Chinas+MOFCOM+Fines+Merging+Parties+For+Failure+To+Notify+Transaction+Under+Anti Monopoly+Law.

[40] Ibid.

2   Prohibition of Cartels and the Control of Abusive Practices

2.1   General Information

The statutory provisions concerning the prohibition of monopolistic agreements can be found in Articles 13–16 of the AML, and those covering prohibitions against the abuse of dominant market positions in Articles 17–19.

Responsibility for the prohibition of cartels and control of abuse lies with the State Administration of Industry and Commerce (SAIC) or National Development and Reform Commission (NDRC), depending on whether the case in question is a matter of price fixing or an abuse of a dominant market position or other trade agreement. SAIC is responsible for judging monopolistic agreements, the control of abusive practices and administrative monopolies that do not contain any price fixing element or relation to price. The NDRC, in contrast, is responsible for all behaviour of a monopolistic nature that is price-related.[41] In the first years after the AML came into effect, the AML enforcement authorities were very reluctant to prohibit cartels and impose fines, a reluctance that has diminished significantly over the past few years. The authorities are now more active than ever when it comes to punitive actions against monopolistic behaviour. It is not only Chinese companies that are affected by such actions. International companies are also increasingly affected.

2.2   Decisions

2.2.1   LCD Cartel

The first sensational decision by the NDRC was taken on 4 January 2013[42] against six international flat screen display manufacturers, including Samsung, LG and HannStar. It appears that the Chinese authorities' attention was drawn to the cartel after decisions announced by the European anti-monopoly enforcement authorities and the US Ministry of

---

[41] Lars Mesenbrink, *The Anti-Monopoly Law of the PRC between Politics and Competition Law'* (*Das Antimonopolgesetz der VR China im Spannungsfeld zwischen Politik und Wettbewerbsrecht*), (Baden Baden: Nomos 2010), pp. 47–8.

[42] For the original decision, see NDRC, 'Six foreign enterprises to implement the LCD panel price monopoly investigated and dealt with according to the law', NDRC website, accessed 5 June 2018 at http://jjs.ndrc.gov.cn/gzdt/201301/t20130117_523203.html.

Justice, decisions that probably served as a reference for the NDRC.[43] The European authorities imposed fines amounting to EUR648.9 million in total against five of the six companies, with Samsung let off the hook as a key witness.[44] The RMB353 million fine levied against the cartel in China was thus relatively mild in comparison.[45] The price fixing in which the six companies engaged took place between 2001 and 2006. Hence, the AML was not applicable. Instead, the action was brought under the Price Law of 29 December 1997, which explains the relatively low fine. According to Article 46 of the AML, the relevant fine would have ranged between 1 and 10 per cent of the annual turnover of the company being penalised.[46]

2.2.2   Automotive Cartels (Volkswagen AG, Chrysler and Audi)

At the end of 2014, several further decisions reached by the Chinese AML enforcement authorities created a stir. For the first time in the history of the AML, a German automotive company was affected by a review and decision made by the Chinese authorities. The decision is also notable because it was the first time that both a horizontal and vertical monopolistic agreement had been made. FAW-Volkswagen made vertical agreements with Audi dealers in China to limit resale prices. Chrysler also made similar price-fixing deals with its dealers. The dealers in question subsequently made horizontal agreements with one another to set the relevant prices. This case constituted a breach of Article 14 of the AML (which prohibits vertical monopolistic agreements) by FAW-Volkswagen and Chrysler, as well as a breach of Article 13 (which prohibits horizontal monopolistic agreements) by the dealers. FAW-Volkswagen was fined RMB248.58 million, which corresponds to 6 per cent of its annual turnover. Chrysler's fine was somewhat milder at just RMB31.68 million,

---

[43] Catherine Shen, 'China: China fines Samsung, LG and four others in LCD price-fixing', *Mondaq*, 3 November 2014, accessed 5 June 2018 at www.mondaq.com/x/351512/Cartels +Monopolies/China+Fines+Samsung+LG+And+Four+Others+In+LCD+PriceFixing.

[44] European Commission, 'Antitrust: Commission fines six LCD panel producers €648 million for price fixing cartel', accessed 5 June 2018 at http://europa.eu/rapid/press-release_IP-10-1685_en.htm.

[45] Zhan Hao and Ying Song, 'NDRC imposed the penalty against LCD panel companies for their monopolistic behavior', *China Law Vision*, 11 January 2013, accessed 5 June 2018 at www.chinalawvision.com/2013/01/articles/competitionantitrust-law-of-th/ndrc-imposed-the-penalty-against-lcd-panel-companies-for-their-monopolistic-behavior/.

[46] Hao and Song, 'NDRC imposed the penalty against LCD panel companies'.

or approximately 3 per cent of its annual turnover. The eight Audi dealers involved had to pay fines amounting to RMB29.96 million, whereas the three Chrysler dealers were fined 'just' RMB2.14 million, which equates to between 1 and 2 per cent of their annual turnover.[47]

3   Private Enforcement Developments

3.1   General Information

Pursuant to Article 50 of the AML, a company that causes damage through monopolistic behaviour is required to compensate the injured party.[48] The number of cases accepted by the courts in connection with such behaviour has increased rapidly in recent years. As of May 2014, 188 such cases had been accepted for proceedings, 172 of which have been completed.[49]

3.2   SPC Anti-Monopoly Provisions

A huge step towards simplifying the private enforcement of the AML was the juridical interpretations on such enforcement issued on 31 January 2012 by the SPC. Called the *Provisions of the Supreme People's Court on Several Issues Concerning the Application of Law in the Trial of Civil Dispute Cases Arising from Monopolistic Conduct* (SPC Anti-Monopoly Provisions hereafter),[50] they took effect on 1 June 2012. These provisions

---

[47] Michael Gu, 'FAW-Volkswagen, Chrysler and related dealers fined nearly RMB280 million for monopolistic conduct', *China Law Vision*, 11 November 2014, accessed 5 June 2018 at www.chinalawvision.com/2014/11/articles/competitionantitrust-law-of-th/faw volkswagen-chrysler-and-related-dealers-fined-nearly-rmb280-million-for-monopolistic-conduct/.

[48] See Sarah Wersborg, 'The private enforcement of the anti-monopoly law in China – provisions of the supreme court regarding questions of the application of law in proceedings due to civil law suits on account of monopolistic behaviour' ('Die private Kartellrechts-durchsetzung in China – Die Bestimmungen des Obersten Volksgerichts zur Anwendung des Rechts bei monopolbezogenen Zivilstreitigkeiten') (2012) 19(4) *German Journal of Chinese Law* (*ZChinR*) 301–6.

[49] Zhan Hao and Song Ying, 'Private AML enforcement is catching up its public counter-part', *China Law Vision*, 3 December 2014, accessed 5 June 2018 at www.chinalaw vision.com/2014/12/articles/competitionantitrust-law-of-th/private-aml-enforcement-is-catching-up-its-public-counterpart/.

[50] Concerning the Application of Law in the Trial of Civil Dispute Cases Arising from Monopolistic Conduct, see www.lawinfochina.com (accessed 5 June 2018). See also Wersborg, 'The private enforcement of the anti-monopoly law', 379.

constitute the first judicial interpretations of the SPC concerning private AML enforcement, and they should make it easier for plaintiffs to assert damages before the courts. In addition, the SPC Anti-Monopoly Provisions also create clarity concerning the preconditions for a monopoly-related civil dispute.[51] They thus alleviate the general provisions on limitations in the General Principles of Civil Law in the PRC to a considerable degree.[52] Furthermore, the SPC Anti-Monopoly Provisions also contain regulations on the jurisdiction and local responsibility of the court in monopoly related civil disputes, as well as regulations on referrals to other responsible courts.[53] The core of the SPC Anti-Monopoly Provisions, however, is new rules on both the burden and type of proof. In particular, the reverse burden of proof specified therein should make it easier for a plaintiff to prove monopolistic behaviour on the part of the defendant.[54] Previously, most civil dispute cases concerning monopolistic behaviour were decided in favour of the defendant, as it was virtually impossible for a plaintiff to prove monopolistic behaviour or a market-dominating position on the defendant's part.[55]

3.3   Recent Examples

3.3.1   Qihoo 360 v. Tencent

The case of *Qihoo 360 v. Tencent* is not only the first monopolistic civil dispute affecting the Chinese internet industry, but also the first such dispute presided over by the SPC.[56] Qihoo 360 is one of the largest anti-virus software companies in China, and Tencent is the operator of the country's most popular instant-messaging software. In November 2011, Qihoo 360 filed suit against Tencent in the Guangdong High People's Court asking for damages of RMB150 million. Its complaint was that Tencent did not allow its users to utilise Qihoo 360 anti-virus software.

---

[51] Wersborg, 'The private enforcement of the anti-monopoly law', 301–6.

[52] Ibid., 306.

[53] Ibid., 303.

[54] Ibid., 304–5.

[55] See Vanessa van Weelden, 'Private enforcement of the Chinese anti-monopoly law' ('Private Rechtsdurchsetzung im chinesischen Kartellrecht') (2010) 17(3) *German Journal of Chinese Law (ZChinR)* 209–21 at 218.

[56] David M. Goldstein et al., 'China: China's supreme court upholds high court's AML ruling in Tencent case', *Mondaq*, 2 January 2015, accessed 5 June 2018 at www.mondaq .com/x/363584/Cartels+Monopolies/Chinas+Supreme+Court+Upholds+High+Courts +AML+Ruling+in+Tencent+Case.

In fact, the Tencent internet platform could be used only if Tencent anti-virus software was installed.

In this case, definition of the relevant market and proof of Tencent's abuse of its market-dominant position were particularly difficult. Both parties had experts testify in court to prove their respective positions. Despite the opinion of its expert witness, however, Qihoo 360 failed to prove that Tencent was guilty of monopolistic behaviour, both in terms of having a market-dominant position and of abusing that position. After losing its case in Guangdong on 28 March 2013,[57] Qihoo 360 appealed to the SPC in Beijing. In its first judgment on a monopolistic civil dispute, the SPC also ruled on 8 October 2014 in favour of the defendant in confirming the judgment reached by the Guangdong High People's Court.[58]

3.3.2   Rainbow v. Johnson & Johnson

Johnson & Johnson (Shanghai) (J&J) is one of the leading corporations in the healthcare arena. Rainbow is a Chinese distributor of J&J products. The two companies signed a distribution contract in which the product resale price was stipulated. Then, when Rainbow subsequently resold products under the agreed resale price, J&J terminated its business relationship with the company. Rainbow filed suit against J&J in April 2010 in the Shanghai No. 1 Intermediate People's Court, claiming RMB14 million in damages owing to a monopolistic agreement. The suit was rejected in the first instance on 18 May 2012 owing to a lack of proof that the agreement restricted competition. The fact that it is very difficult, albeit not impossible, to meet the standard of proof for a damage claim was confirmed by the decision in the second instance: on 1 August 2013, the Shanghai Higher Court ruled that J&J had to pay damages of RMB530,000 to Rainbow.[59]

---

[57] Zhan Ha and Annie Ying Xue, 'Tencent defeats Qihoo 360 in first antitrust litigation involving instant messaging services', *China Law Vision*, 1 April 2013, accessed 5 June 2018 at www.chinalawvision.com/2013/04/articles/competitionantitrust-law-of-th/tencent-defeats-qihoo-360-in-first-antitrust-litigation-involving-instant-messaging-services/.

[58] Goldstein et al., 'China: China's supreme court'.

[59] Zhan Hao, 'Chinese court's roadmap on vertical monopoly analysis: some comments on the final judgment on Rainbow vs. Johnson & Johnson case', *China Law Vision*, 29 October 2013, accessed 5 June 2018 at www.chinalawvision.com/2013/10/articles/competitionantitrust-law-of-th/chinese-courts-roadmap-on-vertical-monopoly-analysis-some-comments-on-the-final-judgment-on-rainbow-vs-johnson-johnson-case/.

4 The BRI: A State Monopoly?

As the foregoing discussion shows, developments in the AML arena are widespread in China, extending not only to administrative and private anti-monopoly enforcement but also to legislation. Another example of a notable type of monopoly in China is the so-called state monopoly. In a state monopoly, the state is the only supplier by means of a state-owned enterprise (SOE). In China, the state has market control in a number of special sectors in which SOEs alone operate. What does this situation mean for the BRI? Is there any link between the initiative and state monopolies or the AML? This section of the chapter addresses these questions.

To date, no dedicated legal rules have been established to govern the BRI, which means that the general laws of the PRC apply to it. The main purpose of the BRI is to contribute to and strengthen China's economic growth and global position, not only in Central and Southeast Asia, but also in Europe and North America. The BRI is definitely one way to achieve that purpose, and it is without doubt a visionary idea. Because the general laws of the PRC apply to the BRI, the initiative will almost certainly be affected by the AML. As the AML applies to all enterprises, it applies to SOEs as well. Unfortunately, such application is in theory alone. In practice, SOEs are privileged and enjoy government protection. However, some scholars argue that the AML regulations should in general be applicable to all SOEs.[60]

The most controversial article of the AML is article 7, which states:

> With respect to industries controlled by the state-owned economy and concerning the lifeline of national economy and national security or the industries lawfully enjoying exclusive production and sales, the state shall protect these lawful business operations conducted by the business operators therein, and shall supervise and control these business operations and the prices of these commodities and services provided by these business operators, so as to protect the consumer interests and facilitate technological advancements.
>
> The business operators mentioned in the previous paragraph shall operate according to law, be honest faithful and strictly self-disciplined, and accept public supervision, and shall not harm the consumer interests by taking advantage of their controlling or exclusive dealing.

---

[60] Masseli, 'Chinese merger control', 68.

State monopolies encompass the military, electricity, telecommunication, aviation and shipping sectors, as well as railway operations,[61] sectors that the state regulates and protects. Article 7(2) alone leaves space for enforcement action if consumer interests are harmed or business operators take advantage of their market dominance. There are only a very few examples of SOEs and state monopolies being suspected of monopolistic behaviour, and the AML enforcement authorities dropped all of the ensuing cases after a brief investigation[62] or allowed the merger in question without filing a declaration of concentration.[63] Nevertheless, according to Article 7 of the AML, it is possible for an SOE to violate the AML if consumer interests are harmed. The same applies to any other monopolistic conduct such as abuse of a dominant market position.[64]

Another issue to consider with respect to SOEs, state monopolies and the AML is the potential abuse of administrative power, which is governed by Articles 32–37 of the AML. According to those articles, no administrative organ or organisation may abuse its administrative power to restrict competition, block non-local business operators from entering the market or formulate provisions to restrict or eliminate competition. Unfortunately, however, the penalties for such abuse are relatively minor, which may create the impression that abuses of administrative power are neither harmful nor relevant.[65]

SOEs and state monopolies, particularly those involved in infrastructure, are likely to benefit from the BRI. It seems a given that the market position and market dominance of SOEs will be strengthened by the initiative, which means that the government will be supporting and protecting their market position/dominance. It is thus possible that foreign and/or private companies will be blocked from the BRI market or at least experience difficulties in accessing that market. With respect to the AML, Article 7 allows the state to protect business operators as long as they

---

[61] Masseli, 'Chinese merger control', 66.
[62] See Shuli Hu, 'China must rein its state owned monopolies', *South China Morning Post*, 29 August 2013, accessed 5 June 2018 at www.scmp.com/comment/insight-opinion/article/1300109/china-must-rein-its-state-owned-monopolies.
[63] Masseli, 'Chinese merger control', 70–1.
[64] Markus Masseli, 'The anti-monopoly law of the People's Republic of China' ('Das Antimonopolgesetz der Volksrepublik China') (2007) 14(3) *German Journal of Chinese Law (ZChinR)* 259–77 at 271.
[65] Ibid., 274–5.

do not harm consumer interests. The protection of and/or support for a favoured SOE by the state or its organs may well make it difficult for private companies to enter the market. In theory, however, no administrative organ or organisation is permitted to abuse its administrative power to support SOEs or restrict or eliminate competition in the market. In practice, though, it is not only state monopolies, SOEs and abuses of administrative power that may provide support for the BRI, or vice versa. There are other ways in which a connection may be created with the AML.

In infrastructure, for example, transport companies and harbour operators may benefit from implicit state support. As we saw with the case of MOFCOM's prohibition of the P3 Alliance, which strengthened the position of national shipping companies, the Chinese authorities are able and willing to use the AML to enforce their own goals, for instance those associated with the BRI. There is also a possibility of other monopolistic behaviour on the part of the companies and business operators involved in the initiative. However, those companies and business operators must abuse their market dominance to be accused of an AML violation, which is a formidable challenge. Hence, support from the government may well constitute tacit encouragement for monopolistic behaviour. Further, as we have already seen, it remains uncertain how the courts and anti-monopoly enforcement authorities are likely to react. The Chinese government's goal of strengthening the Chinese economy may lead to some kind of monopoly in the regions affected by the BRI, even if that monopoly cannot be regarded as a state monopoly in the classical sense. The enterprises leading the market on the road from China to Europe could either abuse their market dominance or restrict market access for other enterprises, for example by controlling infrastructure access. Even if that does not prove to be the case, foreign governments and their anti-monopoly enforcement authorities may well get the impression that such abuse/restriction is taking place.

Although the BRI is not a state monopoly in the classical sense, it may well provoke monopolistic behaviour, and therefore should be regarded with caution from the anti-monopoly perspective, particularly as it is far from unlikely that the Chinese authorities will make use of the AML to direct the BRI towards the pursuit of particular interests.

5 Conclusion

Chinese anti-monopoly law has seen significant advances in the past few years. Not only has its legal basis become more detailed through general provisions and interpretations, but considerable progress has been made in the areas of administrative and private enforcement. Alongside their counterparts in the EU and United States, China's AML enforcement authorities have developed into one of the world's most important institutions in fighting agreements that restrict competition and concentrations of business operators. Their importance in this arena is likely to continue as China grows in stature on the world stage.

In the merger control framework, the companies involved should always cooperate with the authorities because the relevant provisions are frequently insufficiently clear and the authorities usually grant themselves wide interpretation freedom. In the AML enforcement authorities' fight against monopolies, a number of record penalties have been levied on both national and international companies. The insight that we can glean from those penalties is that the Chinese authorities are not overly influenced by their counterparts in other countries and regions. To date, both the amount of the penalties levied and the decisions made differ considerably between China and other jurisdictions. Another notable development is that international companies are increasingly coming under the scrutiny of the Chinese authorities, which gives the impression that tougher controls are being exerted on foreign companies than on their domestic counterparts. The authorities have also been criticised for allowing considerations unrelated to competition to influence their decisions, particularly when it comes to controlling mergers.[66]

Further, as noted above, China's proposed BRI needs to be regarded with particular caution, as it has the potential to lead to monopolistic behaviour. It is even possible that the AML will be used to enforce and strengthen the initiative in a way that weakens the position of, and therefore discriminates against, foreign companies. State monopolies and SOEs may also be strengthened and supported by the BRI, and SOEs are certainly likely to support the initiative. In addition, the risk of abuses of administrative power should not be underestimated. It is to be welcomed that the Chinese authorities are becoming increasingly active against monopolies and other competition-limiting behaviour in view of growing demand for international competition and consumer protection. China is successfully implementing international standards, although it not infrequently follows its own path. At the current juncture, developments in

---

[66] Ritzenhoff, 'Chinese merger control', 35.

the private enforcement of the AML should be stressed. The assertion of damages is still associated with considerable difficulties, but doing so is not impossible, as demonstrated by the Rainbow case discussed herein. That case should motivate others who have suffered losses to take private action against monopolistic behaviour. It also offers a possible direction for foreign companies to fight against discrimination in the BRI context.

5

The Belt and Road Initiative

Cooperation in Trade Liberalisation and Antitrust Enforcement

KELVIN HIU FAI KWOK*

This chapter analyses China's Belt and Road Initiative (BRI) from the related perspectives of trade liberalisation and antitrust enforcement. The initiative, which was first announced by Chinese President Xi Jinping in late 2013, has the overarching purpose of 'promot[ing] the economic prosperity of the countries along the Belt and the Road and regional economic cooperation', 'strengthen[ing] exchanges and mutual learning between different civilizations' and 'promot[ing] world peace and development'.[1] Amongst the priorities of cooperation under the BRI – and the focus of this chapter – is the promotion of 'unimpeded trade' between China and the other countries participating in the BRI.[2]

It is argued in this chapter that, in order for the BRI to successfully achieve its objective of unimpeded trade, China and the other BRI countries need to work towards: (i) reducing transport time and costs for imports of products and inputs;[3] (ii) trade liberalisation

---

* The author wishes to thank the anonymous reviewer for his or her comments. All errors remain the author's own. This chapter was written for a conference organised by the Centre for Chinese Law, Faculty of Law, the University of Hong Kong in June 2016, although it has been subsequently updated to reflect some recent developments. The support of the Small Project Funding programme of the University of Hong Kong is gratefully acknowledged.
[1] National Development and Reform Commission (NDRC), Ministry of Foreign Affairs, and Ministry of Commerce of the People's Republic of China, *Vision and Actions on Jointly Building Silk Road Economic Belt and 21st-Century Maritime Silk Road* (Preface), 28 March 2015, accessed 5 June 2018 at http://en.ndrc.gov.cn/newsrelease/201503/t2015 0330_669367.html.
[2] Ibid., Section IV.
[3] Simeon Djankov, 'The rationale behind China's Belt and Road Initiative', in Simeon Djankov and Sean Miner (eds.), *China's Belt and Road Initiative: Motives, Scope, and Challenges* (Washington, DC: Peterson Institute for International Economics, March 2016), p. 7, accessed 5 June 2018 at https://piie.com/system/files/documents/piieb16–2_1.pdf.

cooperation with a view to removing government-imposed trade barriers; and (iii) antitrust enforcement cooperation with a view to eliminating cross-border anti-competitive behaviour that hampers free trade. Whilst the Chinese government has announced a range of infrastructure projects intended to facilitate transport between BRI countries,[4] there has been rather limited discussion of trade liberalisation and competition policies under the initiative or of the relevance of those policies to the aforementioned priority of promoting unimpeded trade. This chapter fills the gap by examining the BRI through the lens of trade liberalisation and antitrust enforcement cooperation.

The chapter begins with an introduction to the BRI, its relevance to free trade and the infrastructure projects planned under the initiative's auspices. It then considers the general relationship between trade and competition, and argues that comprehensive trade liberalisation and competition policies emphasising cooperation amongst BRI countries are essential components of the initiative insofar as its objective to promote unimpeded trade is concerned. The chapter then addresses the significance of trade liberalisation cooperation amongst BRI countries, as well as the design of a trade liberalisation policy suited to the initiative. It also considers the importance of antitrust enforcement cooperation amongst BRI countries and the design of a competition policy that encompasses such cooperation.

1   The BRI: The Story So Far

What is the BRI? As its alternative name – One Belt, One Road – suggests, the initiative consists of both a 'Belt' and a 'Road'. 'One Belt' refers to the Silk Road Economic Belt, which extends from China to various parts of Asia (including Southeast Asia, South Asia, Central Asia, the Middle East and Russia), and then further to Europe.[5] The Belt is land-based and comprises the highways and railroads connecting China

---

[4] Ibid., p. 8. See also Sean Miner, 'Economic and political implications', in Djankov and Miner, *China's Belt and Road Initiative*, p. 11.

[5] 'The Belt and Road Initiative', Hong Kong Trade Development Council (HKTDC), 21 January 2016, accessed 5 June 2018 at http://china-trade-research.hktdc.com/busi ness-news/article/One-Belt-One-Road/The-Belt-and-Road-Initiative/obor/en/1/1X000000/ 1X0A36B7.htm; China-Britain Business Council (CBBC) and the UK Foreign & Commonwealth Office (FCO), 'One Belt One Road: A role for UK companies in developing China's new initiative', p. 6, China-Britain Business Council/British Chamber of Commerce website, accessed 5 June 2018 at www.cbbc.org/events/one-belt-one-road/.

with numerous countries in Asia and Europe.[6] It is expected to grow into six economic corridors spanning China and many parts of Eurasia.[7] 'One Road' refers to the twenty-first century Maritime Silk Road, which comprises the sea routes connecting the significant ports of China with parts of Asia, Africa and Europe via the South China Sea, South Pacific Ocean, Indian Ocean and Mediterranean Sea.[8]

The BRI comes with five cooperation priorities, namely, 'policy coordination', 'facilities connectivity', 'unimpeded trade', 'financial integration' and 'people-to-people bonds'.[9] Unimpeded trade lies at the core of the initiative, which also has the following trade-related objectives.

> [P]romoting [the] orderly ... free flow of economic factors, highly efficient allocation of resources and deep integration of markets; encouraging the countries along the Belt and Road to achieve economic policy coordination and carry out broader and more in-depth regional cooperation of higher standards; and jointly creating an open, inclusive and balanced regional economic cooperation architecture that benefits all.[10]

The promotion of unimpeded trade between China and the other BRI countries will undoubtedly play a crucial role in the economic development of China for two primary reasons. First, such trade is widely believed to constitute an effective solution to the ongoing excess capacity problems experienced by many Chinese industries, including aluminium, cement, chemicals, glass, iron, oil refining, power generation equipment, solar panels and steel.[11] The many Asian countries participating in the

---

[6] Carolyn Dong et al., 'One Belt One Road – China's new outbound trade initiative', DLA Piper, 18 January 2016, accessed 5 June 2018 at www.dlapiper.com/zh-hans/china/insights/publications/2016/01/chinas-new-outbound-trade-initiative/; CBBC and FCO, 'One Belt One Road: a role for UK companies', p. 6.

[7] CBBC and FCO, 'One Belt One Road: a role for UK companies', pp. 6, 9–14. The six economic corridors are the New Eurasian Land Bridge Economic Corridor, China-Mongolia-Russia Economic Corridor, China-Central Asia-West Asia Economic Corridor, China-Indochina Peninsula Economic Corridor, China-Pakistan Economic Corridor and Bangladesh-China-India-Myanmar Economic Corridor.

[8] Ibid., p. 6; NDRC et al., *Vision and Actions*, Section III.

[9] NDRC et al., *Vision and Actions*, Section IV.

[10] Ibid., Section I.

[11] Wallace Cheng, 'Overcapacity a time bomb for China's economy', *South China Morning Post*, 28 September 2015, accessed 5 June 2018 at www.scmp.com/comment/insight-opinion/article/1862024/overcapacity-time-bomb-chinas-economy; 'Industrial overcapacity: Gluts for punishment: China's industrial excess goes beyond steel', *The Economist*, 9 April 2016, accessed 5 June 2018 at www.economist.com/business/2016/04/09/gluts-for-punishment; CBBC and FCO, 'One Belt One Road: a role for UK companies', p. 7; Dong et al., 'One Belt One Road – China's new outbound trade initiative'; 'A brilliant

BRI represent potential new sources of demand, and hence new export destinations, for the products of these industries.[12] The country's over-capacity problems are due in part to competition amongst Chinese local governments for GDP growth, which has prompted them to offer rental, tax and other incentives to Chinese manufacturers to stimulate capacity expansion.[13] A long-term solution to these problems would require the Chinese central government to exert tighter controls over the financial assistance rendered by local governments to local manufacturers,[14] which goes beyond the scope of the BRI.

The steel industry offers a good example of the overcapacity problems China faces, as extensively reported by the international media.[15] Statistics from the China Iron and Steel Association reveal that the capacity utilisation rate had dropped to 67 per cent by 2015.[16] Despite the decline, however, steel production in China has been gradually increasing since 1981,[17] reaching an unprecedented average daily production level of 2.314 million tonnes in May 2016.[18] Chinese steel manufacturers have aggressively sought to export their excess production to the United States and many European countries, resulting in frequent dumping complaints by the governments of those countries.[19] Excess capacity problems can

plan: One Belt, One Road', CLSA, accessed 5 June 2018 at www.clsa.com/special/onebeltoneroad/; 'Belt and Road Initiative', Mylo Trade, 30 November 2017, accessed 5 June 2018 at www.mylotrade.com/new-silk-road-one-belt-one-road.html.

[12] CBBC and FCO, 'One Belt One Road: a role for UK companies', p. 7; Dong et al., 'One Belt One Road – China's new outbound trade initiative'; 'A brilliant plan'; 'Belt and Road Initiative'; Miner, 'Economic and political implications', p. 11.

[13] Cheng, 'Overcapacity a time bomb for China's economy'.

[14] Ibid.

[15] David Stanway, 'China overcapacity problems worsen over 2008–2015: EU chamber', *Reuters*, 21 February 2016, accessed 5 June 2018 at www.reuters.com/article/us-china-overcapacity-idUSKCN0VV05R; Ruby Lian and David Stanway, 'China admits overcapacity not yet falling in bloated steel sector', *Reuters*, 16 May 2016, accessed 5 June 2018 at www.reuters.com/article/us-china-steel-overcapacity-idUSKCN0Y703A; Tom Mitchell and Christian Shepherd, 'China says its steel overcapacity will remain', *Financial Times*, 10 April 2016, accessed 5 June 2018 at www.ft.com/content/e62e3722-fee2-11e5-ac98-3c15a1aa2e62; 'Industrial overcapacity: gluts for punishment'.

[16] Stanway, 'China overcapacity problems worsen'.

[17] Ibid.

[18] Lian and Stanway, 'China admits overcapacity not yet falling'.

[19] Mitchell and Shepherd, 'China says its steel overcapacity will remain'; Stanway, 'China overcapacity problems worsen'; Lian and Stanway, 'China admits overcapacity not yet falling'.

also be found in many other industries.[20] For example, Chinese aluminium manufacturers, which recently accounted for more than half the worldwide aluminium supply, have continued to expand their capacity and production despite significantly depressed international aluminium prices.[21] Further, there are no signs that Chinese chemical manufacturers will cease capacity expansion in the near future despite below-capacity production.[22] Although China's oil refining industry suffers severe excess capacity, 2016 saw a 31 per cent increase in oil product net exports.[23]

The second reason for the importance of unimpeded trade is the potential for Chinese businesses to capitalise on sources of low-cost supplies and/or labour from other BRI countries.[24] On the one hand, many Central Asian and Middle Eastern countries have rich supplies of gas, hydropower, oil and other forms of energy that may be conveniently imported into China at low cost[25] via the BRI's land and sea routes.[26] On the other hand, China is gradually evolving into a 'high-wage producer' in Asia,[27] with salaries increasing at an annual rate of more than 10 per cent. Accordingly, Chinese businesses may consider establishing factories in Central Asia and other countries with an abundant supply of low-cost labour, and then transporting finished goods back to China or to other destinations via the cross-border transport facilities built under the initiative.[28]

Therefore, by facilitating trade between BRI countries, the BRI is expected to stimulate GDP growth both in China and in its trading partners amongst the other BRI participants.[29] Haggai has observed that

---

[20] 'Industrial overcapacity: gluts for punishment'.

[21] Ibid.

[22] Ibid.

[23] Ibid.

[24] Miner, 'Economic and political implications', p. 12; David Dollar, 'China's rise as a regional and global power: the AIIB and the "One Belt, One Road"', *Horizons*, 15 July 2015, p. 170, accessed 5 June 2018 at www.brookings.edu/wp-content/uploads/2016/06/China-rise-as-regional-and-global-power.pdf; 'Belt and Road Initiative'; Kanenga Haggai, 'One Belt One Road strategy in China and economic development in the concerning countries' (2016) 2 *World Journal of Social Sciences and Humanities* 10.

[25] 'Belt and Road Initiative'.

[26] Djankov, 'The rationale behind China's Belt and Road Initiative', p. 7; Miner, 'Economic and political implications', p. 12.

[27] Dollar, 'China's rise as a regional and global power', p. 170.

[28] Miner, 'Economic and political implications', p. 12.

[29] Haggai, 'One Belt One Road strategy', Section 3; Djankov, 'The rationale behind China's Belt and Road Initiative', p. 7.

[c]onceptually, the One Belt One Road project is expected to affect aggregate output in two main ways: (i) directly, considering the sector contribution to GDP formation and as an additional input in the production process of other sectors; and (ii) indirectly, raising total factor productivity by reducing transaction and other costs thus allowing a more efficient use of conventional productive inputs.[30]

Insofar as the promotion of unimpeded trade is concerned, the focus has thus far been on the building of infrastructure and facilities across BRI countries to facilitate the transport of products and inputs.[31] This has involved the construction of new transport facilities, including highways, railroads and bridges, linking China to a range of Eurasian countries.[32] In addition to transport facilities, the BRI also encompasses the building of pipelines and other facilities for the transmission of power and energy resources.[33] These capital-intensive construction projects may require funding from Chinese and multilateral financial institutions, including the Silk Road Fund, China Development Bank, Export-Import Bank of China, Asia Infrastructure Investment Bank (AIIB) and BRICS New Development Bank.[34] The Silk Road Fund, created in 2014, has made US$10 billion in funding available, part of which (i.e. US$1.65 billion) had already been committed to the Pakistan Card Lott Station.[35] As of March 2016, the AIIB had injected US$12 billion into the BRI, and it is expected to provide US$25 billion in loans annually going forward.[36]

The aforementioned infrastructure projects and their funding sources are no doubt essential to the implementation of BRI's objective of unimpeded trade. Infrastructure projects seeking to reduce transport costs across BRI countries[37] will play a particularly significant part in promoting free trade, and may also help to generate new sources of

---

[30] Haggai, 'One Belt One Road strategy', Section 3(3).

[31] Djankov, 'The rationale behind China's Belt and Road Initiative', p. 8; Miner, 'Economic and political implications', p. 11.

[32] Djankov, ibid.; Miner, ibid.

[33] 'Navigating the Belt and Road: financial sector paves the way for infrastructure', Ernst & Young, August 2015, p. 7, accessed 5 June 2018 at www.ey.com/Publication/vwLUAssets/EY-navigating-the-belt-and-road-en/$FILE/EY-navigating-the-belt-and-road-en.pdf.

[34] Ibid., p. 11; Djankov, 'The rationale behind China's Belt and Road Initiative', p. 8; Miner, 'Economic and political implications', p. 11.

[35] 'Navigating the Belt and Road: financial sector paves the way', p. 11.

[36] Djankov, 'The rationale behind China's Belt and Road Initiative', p. 8; Miner, 'Economic and political implications', p. 11.

[37] Djankov, 'The rationale behind China's Belt and Road Initiative', pp. 7–8; Miner, 'Economic and political implications', p. 11.

revenue for Chinese businesses (particularly manufacturers in industries experiencing overcapacity problems), as well as reduce their production costs by facilitating access to inexpensive supplies and labour.[38] Nevertheless, whilst initiatives aimed at reducing transport costs are of crucial importance,[39] the Chinese government should not overlook the significance of the other essential components of free trade, namely, comprehensive trade liberalisation and competition policies emphasising cross-country cooperation. The next section explains why such policies are important with reference to the general relationship between trade and competition.

2   The Importance of Trade Liberalisation and Competition Policies Emphasising Cooperation[40]

'Trade' and 'competition' are increasingly interconnected in today's globalised economy. Globalisation has rendered business competition increasingly less local and more international, with firms now facing competition from both domestic and international competitors. International trade, which facilitates international competition, means that locally produced goods have to compete with foreign imports. The foreign producers of certain products may enjoy a higher degree of efficiency than local producers, allowing them to produce those products at lower cost and/or with higher quality.[41] However, they also suffer the

---

[38] Miner, 'Economic and political implications', p. 11; Haggai, 'One Belt One Road strategy', Section 3(3).

[39] Djankov, 'The rationale behind China's Belt and Road Initiative', pp. 7–8; Miner, 'Economic and political implications', p. 11.

[40] This section draws in part from Kelvin Kwok, 'Antitrust enforcement and state restraints at the mainland China-Hong Kong interface: the importance of bilateral antitrust cooperation' (2017) 12 *Asian Journal of Comparative Law* 335, Part IIA.

[41] This is the argument underlying Adam Smith's 'theory of absolute advantage' in favour of trade. Another theory is David Ricardo's 'theory of comparative advantage', which posits that it can be mutually beneficial for two countries to trade following each country's decision to specialise in manufacturing a product over which it has comparative advantage vis-à-vis the other country, considering the relative opportunity cost of manufacturing that product. See Michael Trebilcock, *Understanding Trade Law* (Cheltenham: Edward Elgar Publishing, 2011), pp. 1–3; Paul Krugman, Maurice Obstfeld and Marc Melitz, *International Economics: Theory and Policy* (Boston: Pearson, 2015), p. 58; John Ravenhill, *Global Political Economy* (Oxford: Oxford University Press, 2017), p. 107; Dani Rodrik, *The Globalization Paradox: Democracy and the Future of the World Economy* (Oxford: Oxford University Press, 2011), p. 50.

inherent disadvantage of having to transport their output from the site of manufacture to the local site of consumption. Foreign imports may also be rendered uncompetitive vis-à-vis locally produced goods when local governments erect artificial trade barriers in the form of tariffs, quotas and/or discriminatory regulations, thereby raising the cost (and accordingly the price) of imports. Further, foreign trade and competition may be restricted by firms engaging in anti-competitive conduct. Therefore, free trade and competition can work effectively to the benefit of consumers only if there are policies in place to tackle both natural and artificial barriers to trade. As argued above, the BRI has thus far focused primarily on reducing transport costs and time (natural trade barriers) via various cross-country infrastructure projects.[42] However, in the longer term, the initiative also needs to tackle the artificial trade barriers imposed by governments or private entities to promote free trade and competition across BRI countries.

Despite the intertwined nature of trade and competition, policymakers and commentators alike tend to classify measures tackling *state-initiated* trade barriers as belonging to a state's 'trade liberalisation policy', and those tackling *business-initiated* trade barriers as belonging to its 'competition policy'. On the one hand, trade liberalisation policy

> aims at a more efficient use of scarce resources in the importing country (e.g. by replacing less efficient domestic production by imports) as well as in the exporting country (e.g. by promoting more productive export industries rather than less efficient import-substitution). Non-discriminatory trade liberalisation tends to enhance microeconomic 'technical efficiency' (use of fewer inputs for the production of the same level of output at the firm level), macroeconomic 'allocative efficiency' (use of national resources in the most productive and least costly manner at the country level) and consumer welfare (maximization of consumers' surplus).[43]

On the other hand, 'competition policy', which is commonly effectuated through the enactment and enforcement of domestic competition legislation against the anti-competitive behaviour of private firms,

---

[42] Djankov, 'The rationale behind China's Belt and Road Initiative', pp. 7–8; Miner, 'Economic and political implications', p. 11.

[43] Working Group on the Interaction between Trade and Competition Policy, 'Communication from Hong Kong, China', World Trade Organization (WTO), 10 September 1997, para. 2, accessed 5 June 2018 at https://docs.wto.org/dol2fe/Pages/FE_Search/FE_S_S009-DP.aspx?language=E&CatalogueIdList=28491,26452,28590,28568,5405,38233,38234,5290,10979,9763&CurrentCatalogueIdIndex=1&FullTextHash=.

aims at safeguarding and enhancing the process of price formation and other conditions of resource allocation thereby correcting restrictive practices and other anti-competitive measures which may otherwise develop in imperfect market conditions. An active competition policy enforced by public authorities remains a key guarantor for economic efficiency and consumer welfare and contributes to greater availability to the consumer of a broader range of products and services at lower prices. An open competitive environment also fosters innovation and efficiency, thereby contributing to the overall competitiveness of producers.[44]

Trade liberalisation and competition policy thus work together to improve economic efficiency and consumer welfare globally.[45] It has been correctly observed that

> open markets, liberal legal framework rules and a sound competition policy play a key role in fostering economic growth, innovation and continuous upgrading of productivity and product quality. In this regard, trade-liberalisation and competition policies foster development and economic growth by limiting protectionist abuses of both government and private market power. They reinforce one another and result in a more efficient use of resources.[46]

It might be thought that, for small market economies such as some of the BRI countries other than China, trade liberalisation alone is sufficient to guarantee efficient production and low prices for the benefit of consumers, given that local producers typically have limited capacity and face fierce competition from foreign imports.[47] This is the argument that

[44] Working Group on the Interaction between Trade and Competition Policy, 'Submission by the European Community and its member states', WTO, 24 November 1997, Section 1(1), accessed 5 June 2018 at https://docs.wto.org/dol2fe/Pages/FE_Search/FE_S_ S009-DP.aspx?language=E&CatalogueIdList=18644,33911,20028,37447,40140,54031,43051, 66442,41978,39801&CurrentCatalogueIdIndex=3&FullTextHash=.

[45] Working Group, 'Communication from Hong Kong', para. 6; Working Group on the Interaction between Trade and Competition Policy, 'Synthesis paper on the relationship of trade and competition policy to development and economic growth', WTO, 18 September 1998, para. 29, accessed 5 June 2018 at http://docsonline.wto.org/imrd/directdoc .asp?DDFDocuments/t/WT/WGTCP/W80.DOC; Working Group, 'Submission by the European Community', p. 4; Maher Dabbah, *International and Comparative Competition Law* (Cambridge: Cambridge University Press, 2010), pp. 594–5.

[46] Working Group, 'Communication from Hong Kong', para. 8.

[47] Working Group, 'Synthesis paper on the relationship of trade and competition policy', para. 30; Working Group on the Interaction between Trade and Competition Policy, 'Report on the meeting of 27 and 28 November 1997 – note by the secretariat', WTO, 26 February 1998, para. 48, accessed 5 June 2018 at https://docs.wto.org/dol2fe/Pages/ FE_Search/FE_S_S009-DP.aspx?language=E&CatalogueIdList=41089,27096,32965,4309, 18524,38479&CurrentCatalogueIdIndex=3&FullTextHash=.

underlies the so-called 'import-discipline hypothesis', which is premised on the 'large degree of substitutability between domestic and foreign goods, together with low freight costs brought about by efficient transport, and almost non-existent tariffs', such that 'domestic prices [are] kept in line with those of imports'.[48] The argument is, however, undermined by two significant considerations. First, local consumers remain dependent on local producers and suppliers for many kinds of perishable products and services, and the entry of foreign service suppliers may be obstructed by cultural and/or regulatory barriers.[49] Second, local firms in liberalised industries may engage in anti-competitive behaviour to prevent competition from foreign importers or entrants.[50] Thus, 'effective national competition policies are vital to ensure that the process of adjustment to external liberalisation and resulting benefits for efficient economic development are not circumvented by anti-competitive practices'.[51]

When it comes to trade liberalisation and trade-related competition law enforcement, the cooperative efforts of other countries are often necessary, as there may be incentive distortions to, or practical constraints on, the independent efforts of individual countries. Ironically, whilst trade liberalisation works to the advantage of local consumers, the incentives of local governments may nonetheless be distorted by the interests of local producers, leading to measures and policies against such liberalisation. Protectionist reasons may likewise undermine the enforcement incentives of local antitrust authorities, which may in any event face evidentiary and other obstacles in antitrust cases with a cross-border element. Such legal and political barriers constitute significant impediments to trade liberalisation and effective antitrust enforcement to ensure free trade between BRI countries. However, they can be substantially mitigated by comprehensive trade liberalisation and competition policies passed under the BRI that emphasise the need for cross-country cooperation. These arguments are further elaborated in the following section.

---

[48] Working Group, 'Report on the meeting', para. 48.
[49] Working Group, 'Synthesis paper on the relationship of trade and competition policy', para. 31.
[50] Ibid., paras. 31–2. See also Diane P. Wood, 'Antitrust: a remedy for trade barriers?', Antitrust Division, US Department of Justice, 24 March 1995, accessed 5 June 2018 at www.justice.gov/atr/speech/antitrust-remedy-trade-barriers; Dabbah, *International and Comparative Competition Law*, pp. 582, 584–5.
[51] Working Group, 'Synthesis paper on the relationship of trade and competition policy', para. 32.

3   Cooperation in Trade Liberalisation under the BRI

Trade liberalisation entails the removal of state-initiated trade barriers to encourage foreign imports and foreign competition generally.[52] Such barriers may take various forms. For instance, tariffs on imported products (which constitute a revenue source for local governments) must be factored into the eventual retail price of those products, thereby placing them at an unfair competitive disadvantage vis-à-vis their domestic counterparts.[53] Quotas and other quantitative restrictions exert a similar effect in creating artificially high prices for imported products to the detriment of consumers, although the ensuing economic rents end up in the hands of import licensors rather than local governments.[54] Subsidies to local producers represent wasteful government expenditure (in that the money could have been spent more productively in meeting social needs),[55] and may even entail consumer harm if they raise the costs of (and hence the prices charged by) foreign suppliers by depriving them of economies of scale (after losing sales to subsidised local suppliers). Unless local suppliers have the capacity to fully satisfy local demand, some consumers will have to purchase what they need from foreign suppliers at inflated prices. State-initiated trade barriers may also take the form of anti-competitive local regulations that discriminate against foreign producers.[56] Whilst a regulation that pursues some legitimate efficiency or public policy objective (for instance, reducing information asymmetries or ensuring consumer protection) may necessarily exclude some inefficient or incompetent firms from the market, such a regulation is anti-competitive only if it specifically excludes or create difficulties for foreign suppliers and cannot be justified by reference to any 'genuine, non-protectionist regulatory objective', taking into account the availability of any 'less restrictive alternative' that is equally effective in achieving the objective.[57] Sykes has argued that such 'regulatory protectionism' is

---

[52] For the economic arguments in favour of trade, please refer to Note 41 and the accompanying text on the theories of absolute advantage and comparative advantage.

[53] 'Tariffs', WTO, accessed 5 June 2018 at www.wto.org/english/tratop_e/tariffs_e/tariffs_e.htm.

[54] Robert Feenstra and Alan Taylor, *International Economics* (New York: Worth Publishers, 2014), p. 273; John McLaren, *International Trade: Economic Analysis of Globalization and Policy* (Hoboken, NJ: John Wiley & Sons, Inc., 2013), p. 119.

[55] Alan Sykes, 'Regulatory protectionism and the law of international trade' (1999) 66 *University of Chicago Law Review* 1, 10.

[56] Ibid., 3–5.

[57] Ibid.

often more economically harmful than such traditional state restraints as tariffs, quotas and subsidies because all of the unnecessary compliance costs incurred by foreign firms in meeting discriminatory regulatory requirements represent 'deadweight losses'.[58]

If state-initiated trade barriers restrict foreign trade and competition, and ultimately harm local consumers, why do local governments impose them or allow them to exist? In other words, why does trade liberalisation not occur automatically in the absence of cooperation from foreign countries? There are at least two possible explanations. First, the incentives of a local government may be distorted by the urge to boost government revenue by way of tariffs or by the lobbying efforts of domestic businesses keen to maintain trade barriers in order to restrict foreign competition.[59] Second, stimulating exports may be no less important than stimulating imports for a given country, which may use its own trade barriers as a bargaining chip in trade liberalisation negotiations with another country.[60] In a non-cooperative game, both countries have an incentive to maintain trade barriers against each other, becoming trapped in the 'prisoner's dilemma' in which

> trading partners who recognize that it is in the first country's interests to liberalize no matter what the trading partners do will withhold concessions in the hopes of gaining the benefits of the first country's liberalization for free. The dominant strategy becomes protectionism, and such individually rational action leads to an inefficient collective outcome of restrictive trade policies. Trade agreements incorporating reciprocal tariff reductions thus offer governments a means of escape from a Prisoner's Dilemma.[61]

Between-country cooperation in trade liberalisation is therefore essential to the promotion of free trade and competition. At the global level, credit must be afforded the multilateral efforts of the Word Trade Organisation (WTO) and its predecessor, the General Agreement on Tariffs and Trade (GATT), in this regard. On the basis of GATT,[62] participating states have over the years agreed on tariff reductions after numerous rounds of negotiations, with an average reduction of 15 per cent following the

---

[58] Ibid., 4–5, 10, 12.
[59] Feenstra and Taylor, *International Economics*, pp. 246–7; McLaren, *International Trade*, pp. 109, 122–4.
[60] Trebilcock, *Understanding Trade Law*, p. 5.
[61] Ibid.
[62] See Article I GATT and Article XXVIII *bis* GATT.

Kennedy Round and a less than 3.6 per cent reduction following the Uruguay Round.[63] Further, GATT Article XI provides for the 'general elimination of quantitative restrictions' such as import and export quotas, whilst Article XVI imposes notification and consultation requirements for local subsidies as between participating states. GATT also addresses the issue of 'regulatory protectionism', which is fundamentally inconsistent with the agreement's 'national treatment principle' (requiring imported products to be 'accorded treatment no less favourable than that accorded to like products of national origin in respect of all laws, regulations and requirements affecting their internal sale, offering for sale, purchase, transportation, distribution or use').[64] Article XX of GATT also makes it clear that any state measure imposed to 'protect human, animal or plant life or health' must not be a 'disguised restriction on international trade'.[65]

However, multilateral cooperative efforts to liberalise trade through the WTO have a number of limitations. First, despite the WTO's broad member base, membership is not universal. In fact, many of the developing countries participating in the BRI have yet to become WTO members. At the time of writing, Azerbaijan, Belarus, Bhutan, Bosnia and Herzegovina, Iran, Iraq, the Lebanese Republic, Serbia, the Syrian Arab Republic, Timor-Leste and Uzbekistan remain 'observer governments',[66] whereas Palestine and Turkmenistan are neither observers nor members.[67] Second, trade barriers such as tariffs still affect a wide range of goods despite the many rounds of WTO negotiations. The latest round, the Doha Round, kicked off in 2001 with the rather ambitious agenda of reducing tariffs and eliminating other trade barriers for a

---

[63] Carole Murray, David Holloway and Daren Timson-Hunt, *Schmitthoff: The Law and Practice of International Trade* (London: Sweet & Maxwell, 2012), p. 945; 'The GATT Years: From Havana to Marrakesh', World Trade Organization, accessed 5 June 2018, www.wto.org/english/thewto_e/whatis_e/tif_e/fact4_e.htm.

[64] GATT Article III(4); Sykes, 'Regulatory protectionism and the law of international trade', 16–17.

[65] As discussed in Sykes, 'Regulatory protectionism and the law of international trade', 17.

[66] According to the WTO, 'observers must start accession negotiations within five years of becoming observers'. See 'Understanding the WTO: the organization: members and observers', WTO, accessed 5 June 2018 at www.wto.org/english/thewto_e/whatis_e/tif_e/org6_e.htm.

[67] Gleaned from a comparison of the list of BRI countries on the HKTDC website and the countries listed as members and observers on the WTO website. See 'Belt and Road: country profiles', HKTDC, accessed 5 June 2018 at http://beltandroad.hktdc.com/en/country-profiles/country-profiles.aspx; WTO, 'Understanding the WTO: the organization: members and observers'.

variety of products.[68] However, there has been very little progress in the past decade or so owing to a lack of consensus amongst WTO members on many important agenda issues, particularly those concerning agricultural products.[69] The difficulty in reaching consensus is hardly surprising given the differing interests and circumstances of the numerous WTO member states.[70]

The obstacles to trade liberalisation agreements at the multilateral level may explain the gradual shift towards bilateral or regional free trade agreements (FTAs) in recent years,[71] with the past two decades seeing a sharp increase in the number of FTAs concluded.[72] In fact, China has already concluded FTAs with a number of BRI countries,[73] including member states of the Association of Southeast Asian Nations (ASEAN) (i.e. Brunei, Cambodia, Indonesia, Laos, Malaysia, Myanmar, the Philippines, Singapore, Thailand and Vietnam),[74] Georgia, Korea, the Maldives, New Zealand, and Pakistan, and a separate FTA with Singapore that was built on the basis of the FTAs concluded between China and ASEAN.[75] At the time of writing, China is also in the process of negotiating FTAs with the Gulf Cooperation Council (which comprises Bahrain, Kuwait, Oman, Qatar, Saudi Arabia and the United Arab Emirates),[76] and also with other countries.[77] The country is also engaged in discussions with a number of Asia-Pacific nations concerning forma-

---

[68] Katie Allen, 'World Trade Organisation: 20 years of talks and deadlock', *The Guardian*, 15 December 2015, accessed 5 June 2018 at www.theguardian.com/business/2015/dec/15/world-trade-organisation-20-years-of-talks-and-deadlock; Murray et al., *Schmitthoff*, pp. 954–5.

[69] Murray et al., *Schmitthoff*, p. 955; Allen, 'World Trade Organisation: 20 years of talks and deadlock'.

[70] See, generally, Anu Bradford, 'When the WTO works, and how it fails', University of Chicago Public Law & Legal Theory Working Paper No. 300 (2010).

[71] Allen, 'World Trade Organisation: 20 years of talks and deadlock'.

[72] Ibid.

[73] See the list of BRI countries at HKTDC, 'Belt and Road: country profiles'.

[74] 'ASEAN Member States', Association of Southeast Asian Nations, accessed 5 June 2018 at http://asean.org/asean/asean-member-states/.

[75] 'China's free trade agreements', China FTA Network, accessed 5 June 2018 at http://fta.mofcom.gov.cn/english/fta_qianshu.shtml.

[76] 'Member States', Secretariat General of the Gulf Cooperation Council, accessed 5 June 2018 at www.gcc-sg.org/en-us/Pages/default.aspx.

[77] 'A brilliant plan: One Belt, One Road'; 'Free trade agreements under negotiation', China FTA Network, accessed 5 June 2018 at http://fta.mofcom.gov.cn/english/fta_tanpan.shtml.

tion of the Regional Comprehensive Economic Partnership (RCEP).[78] In an important policy document discussing the 'Visions and Actions' for the BRI, the Chinese government specifically notes that 'China has signed MOUs of cooperation ... on regional cooperation and border cooperation and mid- and long-term development plans for economic and trade cooperation with some neighboring countries'.[79] The same document also urges BRI countries to 'strengthen bilateral cooperation' via 'the signing of cooperation MOUs or plans'.[80] The negotiation and conclusion of FTAs with other BRI countries should therefore be a top priority for China going forward.

China's existing FTAs with ASEAN countries, as major trading partners, provide a useful reference point for the trade liberalisation arrangements it could conclude with fellow BRI countries in future. China's economic cooperation with ASEAN began with the Framework Agreement on Comprehensive Economic Co-operation in late 2002.[81] That agreement forms the basis of the Agreement on Trade in Goods, which took effect on 1 January 2005.[82] Article 6 of the Framework Agreement established the 'Early Harvest Programme' for a range of products (namely, live animals, meat and edible meat offal, fish, dairy produce, other animal products, live trees, edible vegetables and edible fruits and nuts), under which China and the 'ASEAN 6' (i.e. Brunei, Indonesia, Malaysia, the Philippines, Singapore and Thailand) agreed to reduce tariffs progressively to 0 per cent by January 2006, with the remaining ASEAN members (Vietnam, Laos, Myanmar and Cambodia) following suit at later dates (i.e. by January 2008, January 2009, January 2009 and January 2010, respectively).[83] The timeline for tariff reductions on those

---

[78] 'Regional Comprehensive Economic Partnership', Association of Southeast Asian Nations, accessed 5 June 2018 at http://asean.org/?static_post=rcep-regional-comprehensive-economic-partnership.

[79] NDCR et al., *Vision and Actions*, Section VII.

[80] Ibid., Section V.

[81] 'Agreement on Trade in Goods of the Framework Agreement on Comprehensive Economic Co-operation between the Association of Southeast Asian Nations and the People's Republic of China', Association of Southeast Asian Nations (ASEAN), 29 November 2004, p. 1, accessed 5 June 2018 at www.asean.org/storage/2012/06/22201.pdf.

[82] ASEAN, 'Agreement on Trade in Goods of the Framework Agreement', p. 10.

[83] 'Framework Agreement on Comprehensive Economic Co-operation between the Association of Southeast Asian Nations and the People's Republic of China', ASEAN, 4 November 2002, Article 6, Annex 3, accessed 5 June 2018 at http://wits.worldbank.org/GPTAD/PDF/archive/ASEAN-China.pdf.

products depended on whether they belonged to the 'normal track', 'sensitive lists' or 'highly sensitive lists'.[84] Tariff reductions were effected most rapidly for normal track products, on which China and the ASEAN 6 committed to reducing tariffs to 0 per cent by 2010, with the other ASEAN countries doing so by 2015.[85] The year 2010 therefore marks the formation of the ASEAN-China Free Trade Area (ACFTA) amongst China and the ASEAN 6, with the remaining ASEAN countries joining ACFTA in 2015.[86] In addition to tariff provisions, the Agreement on Trade in Goods contains similar provisions to those in GATT on national treatment (Article 2), the prohibition of quantitative restrictions (Article 8) and general exceptions (Article 12).[87] The parties subsequently concluded the Agreement on Trade in Services in 2007 and Agreement on Investment in 2009.[88] In the latter year, they also signed Memorandums of Understanding (MOUs) on Intellectual Property, and on Standards, Technical Regulations and Conformity Assessment.[89] The successful experience of ACFTA provides a possible roadmap for future FTA discussions between China and the other participating BRI countries.

In devising a comprehensive trade liberalisation policy, China must also take into consideration the *strategy* used in negotiating and concluding FTAs with other BRI countries. There are two key strategy-related issues it must consider. The first is the mode and process of negotiation. Aside from the RCEP agreement, which is still under negotiation, China has thus far adopted a 'party-by-party' approach to negotiating FTAs with individual countries and economic associations (i.e. ASEAN and the Gulf Cooperation Council). Although ACFTA comprises 'a collection or combination of bilateral agreements between China and individual ASEAN members',[90] it is in fact a 'hub and spoke' deal, with ASEAN the

---

[84] ASEAN, 'Agreement on Trade in Goods of the Framework Agreement', Article 3, Annexes 1–2.

[85] Ibid., Article 3, Annex 1.

[86] Ibid., p. 1.

[87] JiangYu Wang, 'Association of Southeast Asian Nations – China Free Trade Agreement', in Simon Lester and Bryan Mercurio (eds.), *Bilateral and Regional Trade Agreements: Case Studies* (Cambridge: Cambridge University Press, 2009), p. 200.

[88] 'ASEAN – China Free Trade Agreements', ASEAN, 12 October 2012, accessed 5 June 2018 at http://asean.org/?static_post=asean-china-free-trade-area-2.

[89] Ibid.

[90] Wang, 'Association of Southeast Asian Nations – China Free Trade Agreement', p. 219.

'hub' and China the 'spoke'.[91] As it would be time-consuming for China to negotiate future FTAs with individual countries on an ad hoc basis, the country should seriously consider adopting the more efficient hub and spoke strategy, acting as the leader of an existing hub (e.g. ACFTA) and inviting an outside spoke country to join the free-trade area by agreeing to the trade liberalisation arrangements applicable to existing members.[92] On the one hand, such a strategy would provide an efficient and coherent way to gradually dismantle trade barriers across BRI countries; on the other hand, it would benefit China by strengthening its economic power vis-à-vis its trading partners as the trade hub leader.[93]

The second strategic point for China to consider is the extent of trade liberalisation that is desired. As many of the BRI countries are existing WTO members, most FTAs agreed with them will naturally involve liberalisation arrangements that go beyond existing WTO obligations, that is, 'WTO-plus' reductions in tariffs or other trade barriers.[94] China may also wish to engage in further economic cooperation with its BRI partners on such matters as the 'Singapore issues' (namely, investment, competition policy, government procurement and trade facilitation),[95] intellectual property, and even labour and environmental standards.[96] It is suggested here, however, that China should consider adopting a progressive approach to trade liberalisation, similar to the one it has taken towards the ASEAN countries. Such an approach would mean a cautious, step-by-step strategy beginning with less contentious issues on which the parties are likely to swiftly reach consensus before moving on to more difficult matters likely to cause disagreements and prolong negotiations. Similar to its approach with the ASEAN countries, China could in its discussions with the other BRI countries first propose tariff reductions on less sensitive goods before proceeding to the issues of tariff reductions on more sensitive goods, services and technical trade barriers, and more contentious matters.

---

[91] David Evans, 'Bilateral and plurilateral PTAs', in Simon Lester and Bryan Mercurio (eds.), *Bilateral and Regional Trade Agreements: Commentary and Analysis* (Cambridge: Cambridge University Press, 2009), pp. 54–5.

[92] See ibid., pp. 63–5.

[93] Ibid., p. 56.

[94] Wang, 'Association of Southeast Asian Nations – China Free Trade Agreement', p. 324.

[95] 'Singapore issues', WTO, accessed 5 June 2018 at www.wto.org/english/thewto_e/glossary_e/singapore_issues_e.htm.

[96] Evans, 'Bilateral and plurilateral PTAs', p. 60.

4   Cooperation in Antitrust Enforcement under the BRI[97]

Whilst trade liberalisation is important, China should not overlook the significance of implementing a competition policy emphasising antitrust enforcement cooperation under the BRI. Such a policy would ensure that the efficiency benefits derived from efforts to reduce natural and state-initiated trade barriers are not compromised by the anti-competitive conduct of private firms.[98] It is argued in this section that the effectiveness of a competition policy in the context of cross-border trade is crucially dependent on effective antitrust enforcement cooperation between the countries party to the free trade initiative. Owing to the legal and political complexities created by anti-competitive practices that impede free trade, joint enforcement efforts are often required to successfully tackle such practices. Here, two anti-competitive practices, export cartels and the abuse of power by local firms to exclude foreign entities, are examined in turn.

An export cartel is an agreement by which exporting firms fix the price of, restrict the volume of and/or divide the markets for products sold to overseas destinations. Such cartels generally have the effect of elevating the price of exports, thereby harming overseas purchasers. However, because their anti-competitive effects are felt overseas rather than domestically, export cartels may not be illegal under local competition law. It is common for national competition legislation to regulate conduct (whether it takes place locally or abroad) that restricts competition *in that nation* alone.[99] For example, the Competition Act of Singapore, which is modelled on the competition laws of the United Kingdom and European Union, renders illegal only undertakings that restrict 'competition within Singapore'.[100] In any event, some countries, the United States and India included, have specific laws that exempt export cartels from the scope of their competition legislation.[101] The

---

[97] This section draws in part from Kwok, 'Antitrust enforcement and state restraints', Part II.

[98] See Notes 50–1.

[99] Martin Taylor, *International Competition Law: A New Dimension for the WTO?* (Cambridge: Cambridge University Press, 2006), p. 121.

[100] Competition Act of 2004 of Singapore (Chapter 50B), Section 34(1); Brendan Sweeney, *The Internationalisation of Competition Rules* (London: Routledge, 2010), p. 67.

[101] Stephen Harris et al., *Anti-Monopoly Law and Practice in China* (New York: Oxford University Press, 2011), p. 85. See, e.g. Webb Pomerene Act of 1918 of the United States, 15 USC, Section 62; Competition Act of 2002 of India, Section 3(5)(ii).

stipulation in Article 2 of the Anti-Monopoly Law (AML) of China – China's competition legislation – providing that the AML is applicable generally to 'monopolistic conduct ... in economic activities within the territory of the People's Republic of China' (as well as 'monopolistic conduct ... outside the territory ... which serve to eliminate or restrict competition on the domestic market of China') is thus somewhat unusual, as it seems to encompass export cartels on Chinese-manufactured goods that affect only competition abroad.[102] However, some commentators have suggested that the general stipulation under Article 15(6) of the AML, which states that the relevant AML provisions are inapplicable where the agreements in question are meant for 'safeguarding legitimate interests in foreign trade and in economic cooperation with foreign counterparts', may amount to an exemption for export cartels.[103] This unresolved issue can be avoided in instances in which an export cartel has local anti-competitive effects that render it illegal under local competition law, such as when it facilitates local tacit collusion amongst the parties to it.[104]

Efforts by powerful local firms to exclude foreign competitors also warrant scrutiny under local competition law.[105] There are various ways in which established local entities may seek to exclude foreign rivals at the early stage of the latter's entry into local markets. First, a powerful local firm may engage in predation, that is, predatory pricing (selling its products at a loss in an attempt to exclude foreign entry) or predatory bidding (overbuying and thereby driving up the price of an essential input to deter foreign entry regardless of the loss incurred).[106] A local entity in control of a critical input or facility may find it profitable, at least in the long run, to deny a foreign competitor access to that input/facility at any price.[107] A variation of such an absolute refusal to deal is 'margin squeeze', whereby a local entity grants a foreign competitor

---

[102] For further analysis of this issue, see Kwok, 'Antitrust enforcement and state restraints', Part IIA.

[103] Harris et al., *Anti-Monopoly Law and Practice in China*, pp. 84–5.

[104] Stephen Martin, *Industrial Organization in Context* (New York: Oxford University Press, 2010), pp. 552–4. See further discussion in Kwok, 'Antitrust enforcement and state restraints', Part IIA.

[105] Dabbah, *International and Comparative Competition Law*, pp. 584–5. The remainder of this paragraph is partly based on the same source.

[106] See, generally, *Weyerhaeuser Company* v. *Ross-Simmons Hardwood Lumber Company*, 549 US 312 (2007).

[107] See, generally, Case 7/97, *Oscar Bronner* v. *Mediaprint* [1998] ECR I-7791.

access to a critical input or facility but at such a high access price (or such a low retail price downstream) that it is impossible for the latter to break even.[108] An established local entity may also seek to exclude foreign competition by imposing vertical restraints, such as exclusive dealing obligations that prevent distributors from wholesaling or retailing the products of foreign suppliers. When the cumulative effect of such obligations is substantial, a foreign supplier may struggle to find available distribution channels through which to penetrate the local market.[109]

The importance of transnational antitrust enforcement cooperation is obvious in the case of export cartels. Consider the situation of a manufacturing firm in a BRI country being party to an export cartel that fixes the price of products sold to China. As noted above, the country's competition laws may not apply to that manufacturer because the cartel's anti-competitive effects are external. And, in the absence of local consumer harm, the country's antitrust agencies may have no incentive to enforce those laws (even if applicable) against the manufacturer in question.[110] Because the cartel would exert a negative effect on both competition and consumers in China, the Chinese antitrust agencies would have an incentive to enforce the AML.[111] However, enforcing the AML against foreign entities is easier said than done. In reality, as Einer Elhauge and Damien Geradin have observed,

> ... even if enforcement incentives are adequate, the ability of the consuming jurisdiction to prosecute antitrust cases can be compromised if the case requires evidence within the exporting jurisdiction or remedies that only that exporting jurisdiction can impose because of where firm assets or personnel are located. Thus, making this allocation of enforcement authority effective requires that the exporting jurisdictions assist foreign antitrust authorities in discovering evidence about firms within their borders and in enforcing foreign judgments. As we shall see, this has been the main focus on international antitrust cooperation so far.[112]

---

[108] See, generally, Case COMP/C-1/37.451, 37.578, 37.579, *Deutsche Telekom AG* OJ 2003 No. L263/9; Case T-271/03, *Deutsche Telekom v. Commission* [2008] ECR II-477; Case C-280/08 P, *Deutsche Telekom v. Commission* [2010] ECR I-9555.

[109] See, generally, Case C-234/89, *Stergios Delimitis v. Henninger Bräu AG* [1991] ECR I-935.

[110] Einer Elhauge and Damien Geradin, *Global Competition Law and Economics* (Oxford: Hart Publishing, 2011), p. 1138.

[111] Ibid.

[112] Ibid, p. 1139.

The need for transnational antitrust enforcement cooperation may seem less obvious in cases involving the exclusion of foreign companies by Chinese firms, as the AML provisions (the Chapter III provisions on abuse of dominance in particular) clearly apply to anti-competitive practices by Chinese firms in a 'dominant market position'. Enforcement incentives also appear not to be an issue, as the local consumer harm ultimately resulting from the exclusion of foreign rivals should motivate the Chinese authorities to take action against the Chinese firms in question. However, the presence of legal and political barriers may impose enforcement difficulties and disincentives that can be resolved only by transnational enforcement cooperation. In terms of legal barriers, investigations of exclusionary cases involving foreign entities as victims rely heavily on complaints made by (or private actions initiated by) the victims themselves, as they are in the best position to offer incriminating evidence against the Chinese firms attempting exclusion. However, as foreign entities are likely unfamiliar with China's regulatory and judicial system, they may be reluctant to file a legal complaint under the AML or supply sensitive business information that would assist the Chinese agencies in conducting their investigations. These legal barriers would perhaps be surmountable if the foreign victims were in a financial position to engage law firms with a strong presence in China to act as their legal representatives in filing complaints or taking action against Chinese companies. However, they would still have to overcome the impediments imposed by political barriers, which are believed to be accountable for the under-enforcement of the AML against Chinese companies (state-owned enterprises in particular) and its over-enforcement against foreign entities since the law's inception.[113] Indeed, this chapter's author has struggled to find a single publicised AML case involving a Chinese entity as an antitrust defendant abusing its power to exclude a foreign rival. On the contrary, there have been quite a few AML investigations involving foreign companies as antitrust defendants.[114] The US Chamber of Commerce has complained that

---

[113] 'Competing interests in China's competition law enforcement: China's anti-monopoly law application and the role of industrial policy', United States Chamber of Commerce, pp. 1–2, 53–6, accessed 5 June 2018 at www.uschamber.com/sites/default/files/aml_final_090814_final_locked.pdf; Angela H. Zhang, 'Bureaucratic politics and China's anti-monopoly law' (2014) 47 Cornell International Law Journal 671, 700–6.

[114] US Chamber of Commerce, 'Competing interests in China's competition law enforcement', 56–67.

in many cases involving foreign companies, China's anti-monopoly enforcement agencies ... have skewed the implementation of the AML and related statutes to support China's industrial policy goals, including through discrimination and protectionism. ... The beneficiaries of these policies are often Chinese national champions in industries that China considers strategic, such as commodities and high technology. ... By contrast, foreign companies suffer disproportionately from China's patterns of enforcing the AML.[115]

Transnational antitrust enforcement cooperation could help to minimise the aforementioned legal and political barriers and signal China's commitment to the rule of law.[116] For instance, instead of dealing with the Chinese antitrust authorities directly, an excluded foreign company in a BRI country could file a complaint with the antitrust agencies in that country. With appropriate cooperation arrangements in place, those agencies could then channel the complaint and the evidence gathered to the appropriate Chinese antitrust authorities, accompanied by a specific request that they investigate the allegedly exclusionary Chinese firms under the AML. Such arrangements could also require the Chinese authorities to provide periodic updates on the investigation and liaise with the home country authorities to obtain further evidence from the allegedly victimised companies. The political pressure on the Chinese authorities to conduct investigations in a non-discriminatory, non-protectionist fashion in accordance with the cooperation arrangements could help to overcome the obstacles to effective antitrust enforcement and to strengthen China's commitment to the rule of law.

In order to facilitate the conclusion of such arrangements between China and the other BRI countries, the relevant parties may first need to agree on basic principles of national competition policy harmonisation. A basic level of substantive and procedural convergence is important, as '[s]hared beliefs about markets, law, and regulation facilitate collective action'.[117] In this regard, the 'competition policy' chapter of the

---

[115] Ibid., 1–2.

[116] See the 'sub-rules' of the rule of law discussed in Lord Bingham, 'The rule of law' (2007) 66 *Cambridge Law Journal* 67, 73, which include, amongst other things, the sub-rule that 'the laws of the land should apply equally to all, save to the extent that objective differences justify differentiation'.

[117] Brian Portnoy, 'Constructing competition: antitrust and the political foundations of global capitalism', PhD dissertation, University of Chicago (2000), p. 170, as cited in Anu Piilola, 'Assessing theories of global governance: a case study of international antitrust regulation' (2003) 39 *Stanford Journal of International Law* 207, 239.

Trans-Pacific Partnership (TPP) agreement[118] provides a basic framework for convergence that may serve as a useful reference point for China and the other BRI countries in their harmonisation efforts. Article 1 of the aforementioned chapter sets out a number of fundamental substantive principles, for example, 'national competition laws [shall] proscribe anticompetitive business conduct, with the objective of promoting economic efficiency and consumer welfare', and such laws shall generally regulate 'all commercial activities in [the party's] territory'.[119] Article 2, which covers 'procedural fairness', guarantees, amongst other things, a defendant's right to legal representation, to a fair hearing, to judicial scrutiny of the decisions of national competition authorities and to have its confidentiality safeguarded.[120] Article 3 provides for the right to standalone or follow-on private actions.[121] The two subsequent articles provide for cross-border cooperation between national competition authorities in the form of information exchange, enforcement cooperation and technical cooperation.[122] With respect to information exchange and enforcement cooperation, Article 16.4(2) specifically states that the relevant competition authorities 'may consider entering into a cooperation arrangement or agreement'.

Before commencing negotiations on antitrust enforcement cooperation arrangements with other BRI countries, China should consider two important issues: first, whether to include those arrangements in FTAs or separate memoranda or agreements, and, second, the extent of enforcement cooperation. In fact, China has already concluded a number of MOUs on antitrust cooperation with major competition law jurisdictions outside Asia,[123] including the European Union and the United States.[124]

---

[118] 'Chapter 16: Competition Policy', Office of the United States Trade Representative, accessed 5 June 2018 at https://ustr.gov/sites/default/files/TPP-Final-Text-Competition.pdf.

[119] TPP agreement, Article 16(1).

[120] Ibid., Article 16(2).

[121] Ibid., Article 16(3).

[122] Ibid., Articles 16(4)–(5).

[123] 'List of agency-to-agency memoranda of understanding (MOUs)', OECD, accessed 5 June 2018 at www.oecd.org/daf/competition/mou-inventory-list.pdf.

[124] 'Memorandum of Understanding on Cooperation in the Area of Anti-monopoly Law between the European Commission and the National Development and Reform Commission and the State Administration for Industry and Commerce of the People's Republic of China', 20 September 2012, accessed 5 June 2018 at http://ec.europa.eu/competition/international/bilateral/mou_china_en.pdf (abbreviated to China-EU MOU hereafter); 'Memorandum of Understanding on Antitrust and Antimonopoly Cooperation between the United States Department of Justice and Federal Trade Commission

The China–EU MOU states, amongst other things, that '[s]hould the two Sides pursue enforcement activities concerning the same or related matters, they may exchange non-confidential information, experiences views on the matter and coordinate directly their enforcement activities, where appropriate and practicable'.[125] Similarly, the China–US MOU stipulates that 'when a U.S. antitrust and a PRC antimonopoly agency are investigating related matters, it may be in those agencies' common interest to cooperate in appropriate cases, consistent with those agencies' enforcement interests, legal constraints, and available resources'.[126] As this chapter's author has argued elsewhere,[127] it is in China's best interests to formalise such cooperation arrangements into more formal bilateral agreements. An example of a formal bilateral agreement is that concluded between the European Union and the United States in 1991.[128] In addition to provisions for case notification (Articles II and III) and coordination and cooperation between the two jurisdictions' antitrust authorities (Article IV), the 1991 agreement contains arrangements for both 'traditional comity' (for avoiding conflicts in competition law enforcement; under Article VI) and 'positive comity' (for one party to notify the other of anti-competitive practices 'adversely affecting its important interests'; under Article V).[129]

and the People's Republic of China National Development and Reform Commission, Ministry of Commerce, and State Administration for Industry and Commerce', 27 July 2011, accessed 5 June 2018 at www.ftc.gov/sites/default/files/attachments/international-antitrust-and-consumer-protection-cooperation-agreements/110726mou-english.pdf (abbreviated to China-US MOU hereafter).

[125] The China-EU MOU, cl. 2.3.
[126] The China-US MOU, pp. 2–3.
[127] Kwok, 'Antitrust enforcement and state restraints', Part II.
[128] 'Agreement between the Government of the United States of America and the Commission of the European Communities regarding the application of their competition laws' (27 April 1995) 38(L95/47) *Official Journal of the European Communities*, accessed 5 June 2018 at http://eur-lex.europa.eu/legal-content/EN/TXT/PDF/?uri=CELEX:21995 A0427(01)&from=EN.
[129] The parties later signed an agreement in 1998 that provided the particulars of their 'positive comity' arrangement. See 'European Commission: competition: international: bilateral relations: United States of America', European Commission, accessed 5 June 2018 at http://ec.europa.eu/competition/international/bilateral/usa.html; 'Agreement between the European Communities and the Government of the United States of America on the application of positive comity principles in the enforcement of their competition laws' (18 June 1998) 41(L173/28) *Official Journal of the European Communities*, accessed 5 June 2018 at http://eur-lex.europa.eu/legal-content/EN/TXT/PDF/?uri=CELEX:21998A0618(01)&from=EN.

Comity arrangements of this kind can be quite effective in addressing anti-competitive cases involving a dominant local firm that is abusing its power to prevent the entry of foreign companies, particularly if the foreign antitrust authorities concerned can file a positive comity request with the local authorities (on account of the abuse adversely affecting the foreign government's important interests) seeking an investigation of the local firm's behaviour under local competition law.[130] However, such comity arrangements are unlikely to be effective in tackling export cartels lacking local anti-competitive effects that fall outside the scope of local competition law because the local antitrust authorities receiving a positive comity request from an importing jurisdiction would not be in a position to launch an investigation of, let alone impose sanctions on, the cartelists pursuant to local law.[131] Although the antitrust authorities in the two jurisdictions could exchange information on the cartelists to aid potential legal proceedings initiated in the importing jurisdiction, significant shortcomings remain. First, the local jurisdiction may have laws in place requiring the cartelists' consent to pass on confidential information to the importing jurisdiction's authorities,[132] consent that they may well refuse to provide. Second, in the absence of local anti-competitive effects, the local antitrust authorities may lack the legal authority to obtain information from cartelists – which are not suspected of any violation of local competition law – in the first place.[133]

The foregoing shortcomings may be overcome by legal amendments enabling a local jurisdiction's antitrust authorities to render legal assistance to their overseas counterparts. For example, the International Antitrust Enforcement Assistance Act of the United States was enacted in 1994 to enable the US antitrust authorities to 'conduct investigations to obtain antitrust evidence relating to a possible violation of ... foreign antitrust laws' pursuant to an antitrust mutual assistance agreement.[134] Such evidence may include confidential information pertaining to business

---

[130] Dabbah, *International and Comparative Competition Law*, p. 515.
[131] Ibid., p. 521.
[132] Ibid., pp. 517–8; Taylor, *International Competition Law*, pp. 112–13; Christine Laciak (ed.), *International Antitrust Cooperation Handbook* (Chicago: ABA, Section of Antitrust Law, 2004), p. 76.
[133] Dabbah, *International and Comparative Competition Law*, p. 521.
[134] International Antitrust Enforcement Assistance Act of 1994 of the United States, Section 6202(b).

entities in the United States, whose prior consent is not required.[135] Despite the Act's apparent advantages, however, it has resulted in only one antitrust mutual assistance agreement thus far – that between the United States and Australia.[136] A potential explanation, as several commentators have observed, is the tendency of many countries to 'guard their corporate information jealously, partly for the fear of cross-border industrial espionage'.[137] Further, unlike the United States and Australia,[138] many countries lack laws enabling a similar level of foreign assistance to be offered.[139]

Based on the antitrust cooperation experiences of other countries and the strategy proposed above for China's trade liberalisation negotiations with other BRI countries, it is suggested here that China similarly adopts a progressive strategy for antitrust cooperation negotiations under the BRI. For instance, the parties concerned may first strive to agree on a basic framework for competition policy convergence and antitrust enforcement cooperation under their existing trade liberalisation agreements before deepening their relationship through progressively extensive arrangements under separate incremental bilateral agreements on antitrust cooperation.

---

[135] Ibid., Section 6205; Laciak, *International Antitrust Cooperation Handbook*, p. 77; Dabbah, *International and Comparative Competition Law*, pp. 517–18; Taylor, *International Competition Law*, p. 114.

[136] 'USA/Australia Mutual Antitrust Enforcement Assistance Agreement', US Federal Trade Commission (FTC), April 1999, accessed 5 June 2018 at www.ftc.gov/policy/coopera tion-agreements/usaaustralia-mutual-antitrust-enforcement-assistance-agreement; Dabbah, *International and Comparative Competition Law*, pp. 517–20; Taylor, *International Competition Law*, p. 115.

[137] Taylor, *International Competition Law*, p. 115. See also 'First international antitrust assistance agreement under new law announced by FTC and DOJ Federal Trade Commission', FTC press release, 17 April 1997, accessed 5 June 2018 at www.ftc.gov/ news-events/press-releases/1997/04/first-international-antitrust-assistance-agreement-under-new-law.

[138] For Australia, see the country's Mutual Assistance in Business Regulation Act 1992, Sections 6–10, as discussed in Laciak, *International Antitrust Cooperation Handbook*, pp. 76, 81.

[139] Laciak, *International Antitrust Cooperation Handbook*, pp. 71, 76 (referring to Christine Varney, 'Cooperation between enforcement agencies: building upon the past', FTC, 25 July 1995, accessed 5 June 2018 at www.ftc.gov/es/public-statements/1995/07/cooper ation-between-enforcement-agencies-building-upon-past); FTC, 'First international antitrust assistance agreement under new law announced'.

5   Conclusion

This chapter addresses the important issue of how the BRI can best achieve its stated objective of promoting 'unimpeded trade' between China and the other BRI countries. Whilst many of the initiative's announced proposals relate to infrastructure projects facilitating the transport of products and inputs across BRI countries,[140] it is argued herein that it is equally important for the Chinese government to develop comprehensive trade liberalisation and competition policies emphasising cooperation between China and its BRI partners. The chapter has explained why cooperation in both trade liberalisation and antitrust enforcement across BRI countries is essential to the successful implementation of the initiative's unimpeded trade objective, and has also explored strategies for the negotiation and conclusion of FTAs and antitrust enforcement cooperation arrangements.

The BRI raises the broader question of what it takes for economic cooperation between countries of unequal power to succeed.[141] It is difficult for China to seek one-sided trade liberalisation in favour of its own exports (while restricting imports and investments from overseas) within the WTO system owing to the economic and political strength of some WTO members. At the same time, the disparity in power between China and some BRI countries means that one-sided liberalisation may possibly result from individual FTA negotiations. The initiative's unimpeded trade objective thus constitutes a significant commitment on China's part to *comprehensive* trade liberalisation.

The successful achievement of that objective may provide a turning point for the Chinese economy, with the country's GDP growth rate having recently declined to approximately 7 per cent per year.[142] In addition, the BRI may also act as a powerful stimulant to the economic growth of the other BRI countries[143] owing to the expected surge they will see in trade with China.[144] As the initiative encourages Chinese businesses to establish factories and offices in participating BRI states

---

[140] Djankov, 'The rationale behind China's Belt and Road Initiative', p. 8; Miner, 'Economic and political implications', p. 11.

[141] The author thanks the anonymous reviewer for raising the issue discussed in this paragraph.

[142] Dollar, 'China's rise as a regional and global power', p. 162.

[143] CBBC and FCO, 'One Belt One Road: a role for UK companies', p. 21.

[144] Djankov, 'The rationale behind China's Belt and Road Initiative', p. 7.

with low-cost labour,[145] it may also help to reduce the unemployment rates in those countries.[146] Indeed, one economic study has predicted that the BRI, if successful, 'will reestablish Eurasia as the largest economic market in the world'.[147]

According to one Chinese official, the initiative symbolises 'an innovative mode of cooperation in global governance' in all dimensions – economically, politically and culturally.[148] Economic cooperation is just the starting point, however. China's long-term strategy, as a number of commentators have observed, is to strengthen its economic and political power through the BRI and eventually to 'set . . . the rules of the game for future global governance'.[149] The success of both the initiative and China's international governance strategy are crucially dependent on China's commitment to trade liberalisation, antitrust enforcement cooperation and the rule of law.

---

[145] Miner, 'Economic and political implications', p. 12.

[146] Haggai, 'One Belt One Road strategy', Sections 3(3)–(4).

[147] Djankov, 'The rationale behind China's Belt and Road Initiative', p. 10.

[148] Yafei He, 'B&R: innovation for global governance', China-US Focus, accessed 5 June 2018 at https://chinausfocus.com/videos/obor-innovation-for-global-governance.

[149] William Callahan, 'Policy brief [22/2016]: China's Belt and Road Initiative and the new Eurasian order', Norwegian Institute of International Affairs, p. 2, accessed 5 June 2018 at https://brage.bibsys.no/xmlui/bitstream/handle/11250/2401876/NUPI_Policy_Brief_22-16_William_Callahan.pdf?sequence=3&isAllowed=y; James Paradise, 'The role of "parallel institutions" in China's growing participation in global economic governance' (2016) 21 *Journal of Chinese Political Science* 149.

6

The Belt and Road Initiative, Expropriation and Investor Protection under BITs

WEI SHEN

China announced its Belt and Road initiative (BRI), officially known as 'the Silk Road Economic Belt and the 21st Century Maritime Silk Road initiatives', in September 2014, immediately before the Asia-Pacific Economic Cooperation summit was held in Beijing that year.[1] The 'road' element of the initiative refers to the ancient maritime routes between China and Europe, whilst the 'belt' describes the overland trails of the ancient Silk Road. Chinese officials have somewhat diminished the initiative's exotic appeal by using the unlovely acronym BRI.

The purpose of the sprawling BRI is to revivify, reinvigorate and resurrect the old Silk Road trading routes that once carried treasures between China and the Mediterranean through Central Asia. The new Silk Road will connect China's western region, including the predominantly Muslim province of Xinjiang, to the Chinese-funded Pakistani port city of Gwadar. In the seventh century, the Silk Road was a vast network of trade routes connecting Chinese merchants with their counterparts in Central Asia, the Middle East, Africa and Europe. Its heyday was the golden age in which Chinese luxuries were coveted across the globe, with the Silk Road serving as a conduit for diplomacy and economic expansion.

The current BRI effectively constitutes the Chinese government's global economic strategy and action plan to resurrect the old Silk Road concept. The initiative will have broad international coverage, affecting 55 per cent of world GDP, 70 per cent of the global population and 75 per cent of the world's energy reserves. It will encompass 3.8 billion people

---

[1] President Xi Jinping first floated the idea of forming a 'New Silk Road Economic Belt' in a speech at Nazarbayev University in Astana, Kazakhstan in September 2013. One month later, he made the pitch for a '21st Century Maritime Silk Road' when addressing the Indonesian parliament in Jakarta.

and economies totalling US$21 trillion.[2] The BRI is amorphous, with no official list of member states, although China's rough count of countries along the BRI route is approximately sixty-five.[3] Most of those countries are in desperate need of infrastructure but lack sufficient capital to finance infrastructure projects. It has been reported that 900 deals worth US$890 billion are currently underway and that China will eventually invest US$4 trillion in BRI countries.[4] The initiative will effectively connect the supply and demand sides of the infrastructure equation. On the domestic front, the relatively poorer inland regions of China will also be key beneficiaries.

The underlying rationale of the BRI is to apply a bonding approach rather than a more assertive and muscular diplomatic and military approach to strengthen China's economic and political connectivity with neighbouring nations. For instance, China wants to secure a route to the Indian Ocean that will reduce its dependence on the chokepoint of the Strait of Malacca between the Malay Peninsula and the Indonesian island of Sumatra.[5] The Chinese government is trying to take advantage of the mostly benign security environment to achieve its aim of strengthening its global power without causing conflict. The BRI appears to be a 'soft' and 'smart' way to package that strategy. The initiative also fits into the 'Chinese dream' of recreating its past greatness. The country has made the BRI a central part of its foreign policy ever since it was first promoted as a promising yet ambiguous strategic concept. Economically, China can use the initiative to shift some of its vast manufacturing capacity overseas to deal with rising costs, not least the growing costs of complying with more stringent environmental protection measures and the ongoing anti-corruption campaign.[6] The initiative will allow China to extend its commercial and even political influences to neighbouring countries,

---

[2] François Godement, Agatha Kratz (eds.), 'One Belt, One Road': China's Great Leap Outward (London: ECFR and Asia Centre, 2015), p. 1.

[3] 'Our bulldozers, our rules', The Economist, 2 July 2016, accessed 5 June 2018 at www.economist.com/news/china/21701505-chinas-foreign-policy-could-reshape-good-part-world-economy-our-bulldozers-our-rules.

[4] 'Our bulldozers, our rules', p. 29.

[5] Farhan Bokhari, 'China urges Pakistan to give army role in silk road project', Financial Times, 22 July 2016, p. 5.

[6] It has been estimated that China's coal industry will have 3.3 billion tonnes of excess capacity within with years. Overcapacity within the aluminium, oil refining and chemical industries poses a threat not only to China but also internationally. The output of the overcapacity within Chinese industries may send global prices plunging and harm China's rivals in the global market. See 'Gluts for punishment', The Economist, 9 April 2016,

thereby reducing its economic dependence on infrastructure investment at home. However, the EU has expressed concerns regarding China's plan to export its excess industrial capacity in key industries, and has put in place a number of arrangements to address those concerns.[7]

In implementing the BRI, China wants to make use of the platform it provides to deepen economic ties with neighbouring countries. For instance, China made Pakistan an early stop on the BRI route in 2015 by proposing the China-Pakistan Economic Corridor (CPEC), a US$46 billion bundle of road, railway, electricity, oil and gas projects that marked the largest foreign investment in Pakistan to date. However, many of China's neighbours are wary of its ambitions and economic clout, and fear that China will derive disproportionate benefits from the links foreseen under the BRI. CPEC, for example, has stalled as the two sides struggle to work out how to turn proposals into concrete projects. In Pakistan, the internal debate centres on whether the government should take ownership of CPEC projects.[8]

There is considerable fear amongst the countries affected that Chinese goods will flood their markets and drown their own nascent industries. With respect to foreign direct investment (FDI), it is widely known that China places more emphasis on laying tarmac and extracting resources than on sharing technical know-how. However, it appears that China may have outgrown its fixation with commodities and energy. Chinese investors are hungry for Western brands and technology, and their demand for assets far afield of China remains quite robust. The world has witnessed a wave of China-led mergers and acquisitions sweeping the global economy.[9] Chinese investors announced nearly US$100 billion in cross-border merger and acquisition (M&A) deals in 2016, almost double 2015's US$61 billion. China's share of such cross-border deals has averaged roughly 6 per cent over the past five years, accounting for nearly 15 per cent of global GDP.[10] The country's FDI is increasingly flowing along the Silk Road, with FDI rising in the BRI countries twice as much

---

accessed 5 June 2018 at www.economist.com/news/business/21696552-chinas-industrial-excess-goes-beyond-steel-gluts-punishment.

[7] Alun John, 'Europe back on Chinese investors' radar, says official', *South China Morning Post*, 15 July 2016, p. B1.

[8] Bokhari, 'China urges Pakistan'.

[9] Asia as a whole has nearly doubled its volume of mergers and acquisitions in other regions. See Don Weinland and Jennifer Hughes, 'Asia overtakes US in value of outbound deals', *Financial Times*, 20 July 2016, p. 16.

[10] 'Money bags', *The Economist*, 2 April 2016, p. 61.

as China's increase in total FDI in 2015. A total of 44 per cent of contracts for new engineering projects announced by China in 2015 were signed with BRI countries.[11]

Some view the BRI initiative as a response or even challenge to US efforts to promote new US-centric economic zones such as the Trans-Pacific Partnership (TTP) and Transatlantic Trade and Investment Partnership (TTIP).[12] The United States is the focal point of two of the world's main trading blocs, the trans-Atlantic and trans-Pacific blocs. The two regional trade deals, TPP and TTIP, embody an approach by which the United States seeks to bind itself together with its closest Asian allies in an economic bloc that encircles a rising China.[13] In this sense, TPP, its advocates insist, is as much a geostrategic agreement as a trade deal. The BRI, in contrast, treats Asia and Europe as a single bloc, albeit with China at the centre. This treatment clearly matches China's strategy to promote its own regional trade arrangements in the Asia-Pacific region. Against this backdrop, the BRI, combined with China's other efforts to establish regional pacts, constitutes an institution-building strategy that is shifting the focal points of global trade and investment.

1   BRI, China's BITs and the Risks of Expropriation

Along with the BRI, China has been aggressively promoting outbound investment, and, looking back nostalgically to the Silk Road, the country envisages a web of bilateral agreements with the beneficiaries of the initiative's largesse. At the heart of that web of agreements lies China's eagerness to build up a vast trade and investment network by signing a

---

[11] 'Our bulldozers, our rules'.

[12] PRC Ministry of Commerce, 'China FTA network, China's free trade agreements', accessed 5 June 2018 at http://fta.mofcom.gov.cn/english/fta_qianshu.shtml.

[13] However, immediately upon taking office, President Trump, who has put trade protectionism at the heart of his economic policy, withdrew the United States from the historic twelve-nation TTP, which had been part of former President Obama's signature initiative to 'pivot' towards Asia. Senator John McCain criticised Trump's move as a 'serious mistake' and an agenda at odds with long-term US trade policy. McCain pointed out that 'it will create an opening for China to rewrite the economic rules of the road at the expense of American workers' and 'send a troubling signal of American disengagement in the Asia-Pacific region at a time we can least afford it'. See Demetri Sevastopulo, Shawn Donnan and Courtney Weaver, 'Trump puts protectionism at heart of US economic policy', *Financial Times*, 24 January 2017, accessed 5 June 2018 at www.businessday online.com/trump-puts-protectionism-heart-us-economic-policy/#. Meanwhile, Japan and other US allies along the Pacific Rim plan to press ahead with the pact despite the United States' withdrawal.

large number of bilateral investment treaties (BITs), free trade agreements (FTAs) and mega-regional investment pacts. In addition to its 129 BITs, China has negotiated and concluded more than a dozen FTAs. As of January 2013, it had signed FTAs with eighteen countries and regions, and is still in negotiations with numerous other countries and regional groupings, including Australia, the Gulf Cooperation Council, Norway and the Southern African Customs Union. According to figures from the Chinese Ministry of Commerce, a quarter of mainland Chinese foreign trade is with the country's FTA partners.[14] Furthermore, China has been proactive in promoting multilateral efforts aimed at regional integration by entering into regional or multilateral FTAs and economic cooperation agreements with regional organisations. The latest fruits of those efforts include the Agreement on Investment of the Framework Agreement on Comprehensive Economic Cooperation,[15] concluded with the Association of Southeast Asian Nations (ASEAN) in Bangkok on 15 August 2009 (the China-ASEAN Treaty hereafter), and the Agreement among the Government of the Republic of Korea, the Government of the People's Republic of China (PRC) and the Government of Japan for the Promotion, Facilitation and Protection of Investment (also known as the China-Japan-Korea trilateral investment treaty, or TIT), which was signed by those three countries on 13 May 2012 in Beijing. China's FTAs and multilateral investment treaties, including the China-ASEAN Treaty and TIT, often include a chapter providing for investment protection, and the expropriation clauses in these FTAs are more detailed, if not more advanced, than those in China's BITs.

China needs a BRI-based investment treaty not only to counter the impact of the US-led TPP and TTIP, should they materialise, but also to encourage other nations to rewrite the investment rules. More substantially, such a treaty would offer better protection for China's outbound investment. China is not only a major capital importer, but is also a significant capital exporter, becoming the world's third largest investor in 2016, after the United States and Japan.[16] In terms of FDI stock,

---

[14] 'Deal sealed with a handshake and fish', *China Daily*, 3 May 2013, accessed 5 June 2018 at http://europe.chinadaily.com.cn/epaper/2013-05/03/content_16471009.htm.

[15] ASEAN, Agreement on Investment of the Framework Agreement on Comprehensive Economic Cooperation between the Association of Southeast Asian Nations and the People's Republic of China, accessed 5 June 2018 at www.asean.org/wp-content/uploads/images/archive/22974.pdf.

[16] United Nations Conference on Trade and Development (UNCTAD), *World Investment Report 2018: Investment and New Industrial Policies* (New York and Geneva:

China is one of the largest developing country investors in Africa,[17] and is the top investing nation in some of the continent's least developed countries, such as Sudan and Zambia, as well as better off countries such as Nigeria and Algeria.[18] China shifted its policy in 2001, and in the years since has been steadily promoting outbound FDI to reduce its external surplus and secure access to natural resources in other developing countries. The ruling Communist Party of China took the initiative to craft its well-known 'go global' strategy in 1998.[19] The State Council then not only included that strategy in the Tenth Five-Year Plan for National Economy and Social Development in 2001, but also set out the clear objective to promote up to fifty globally competitive 'national champions' by 2010.[20] Continuing to play a guiding role in the promotion of overseas expansion,[21] the State Council in 2004 formulated regulations that replaced the substantial approval regime with a registration regime.[22] This regulatory and policy change may well explain the sharp surge in China's outbound FDI after 2004,[23] as seen in Figure 6.1.

UNCTAD), p. xiii; UNCTAD, *World Investment Report 2014: Investing in the SDGs: An Action Plan* (New York and Geneva: UNCTAD), p. 6.

[17] UNCTAD, *World Investment Report 2013*, p. xvi.

[18] Ibid., p. 5.

[19] Full text of Jiang Zemin's Report at 16th Party Congress on Nov 8, 2002, available at http://www.fmprc.gov.cn/mfa_eng/topics_665678/3698_665962/t18872.shtml. See also 'Implementing the "going out" strategy (2007)', MOFCOM.gov.cn, accessed 5 June 2018 at http://njtb.mofcom.gov.cn/subject/zcq/index.shtml; 'Decision on several issues of perfecting the socialist market economic system', *Xinhuanet*, 20 October 2003, accessed 5 June 2018 at http://news.xinhuanet.com/newscenter/2003-10/21/content_1135402.htm.

[20] See Usha C. V. Haley, 'Hearing on China's world trade compliance: industrial subsidies and the impact on U.S. and world markets statement before the U.S.-China Economic and Security Review Commission', USCC.gov, 4 April 2006, accessed 5 June 2018 at www.uscc.gov/hearings/2006hearings/written_testimonies/06_04_04wrts/06_04_04_haley.php.

[21] Florencia Jubany and Daniel Pvoon, 'Recent Chinese engagement in Latin America and the Caribbean: a Canadian perspective', FOCAL, March 2006, accessed 5 June 2018 at www.focal.ca/pdf/China-latam.pdf.

[22] 'Decision of the State Council on the reform of the investment system', *Xinhuanet*, 26 July 2004, accessed 5 June 2018 at http://news.xinhuanet.com/zhengfu/2004-07/26/content_1648074.htm.

[23] Peter J. Buckley et al., 'Explaining China's Outward FDI: An Institutional Perspective' in Karl P. Sauvant, Kristin Mendoza and Ince Irmak (eds.), *The Rise of Transnational Corporations from Emerging Markets: Threat or Opportunity?* (2008), pp. 104–57; Lide Liu, 'Lasting Sino-African Friendship', 31/2 African Insight (2001), pp. 35–7; Sithara Fernando, 'Chronology of China-Africa Relations', 43/3 China Report (2007), pp. 363–73.

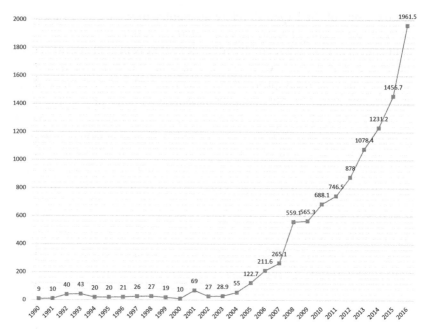

Figure 6.1   Growth in China's Outbound Investment (1990–2016)[24]
Note: Chart compiled by the author.

Given China's massive foreign currency reserves and ongoing efforts to liberalise its foreign exchange controls,[25] Chinese companies have an understandable desire to grow globally. Hence, the wave of outbound investment from China is likely to increase going forward.[26] Even in the midst of the recent global financial crisis, whose effects are still being felt, Chinese players failed to slow the pace of expansion. On the contrary, Chinese companies in a growing number of industries have actually

[24] Ministry of Commerce of PRC, National Bureau of Statistics of PRC and State Administration of Foreign Exchange, *Statistical Bulletin of China's Outward Foreign Direct Investment*, accessed 5 June 2018 at http://images.mofcom.gov.cn/hzs/accessory/201009/1284339524515.pdf. See also 'Statistics on China's foreign direct investment for 2013', Invest in China, 12 September 2014, accessed 5 June 2018 at www.fdi.gov.cn/1800000121_33_4266_0_7.html.

[25] *OECD Investment Policy Reviews: China 2008*, 5 December 2008. p. 69, accessed 15 June 2018 at www.oecd.org/investment/investmentfordevelopment/oecdinvestmentpolicyreviews-china2008encouragingresponsiblebusinessconduct.htm.

[26] Daniel H. Rosen and Thilo Hanemann, 'The rise in Chinese overseas investment and what it means for American businesses', China Business Review, accessed 5 June 2018 at www.chinabusinessreview.com/the-rise-in-chinese-overseas-investment-and-what-it-means-for-american-businesses/.

raised their international profiles.[27] It seems inevitable that Chinese companies will become a major FDI force in the global sphere.

However, Chinese investors face a number of challenges in the global market. Whilst China's growing economic dominance is clear in Central Asia, the investment security in that region is a pressing challenge. The BRI route covers a large part of Central Asia, which has historically provided a thoroughfare for Uighur militants who wish to join terrorist groups in Afghanistan and Pakistan. The Chinese government had already blamed a number of violent attacks within China on the radicalisation of the country's Muslim Uighur minority by international militant groups before the Chinese embassy in Kyrgyzstan was hit by a suicide attack on 30 August 2016. This was a worrying development at a time when China was stepping up investments in central Asia under the BRI. Kyrgyzstan's economy is increasingly reliant on Chinese trade and investment, including several Chinese-backed infrastructure projects such as a railway network linking China to Uzbekistan through the country. The attack's deliberate targeting of a Chinese embassy[28] caused consternation in China, particularly coming as it did in the wake of an earlier wave of protests that broke out across Kazakhstan in 2016 based on fears that a new land code would allow Chinese investors to buy up Kazakh land.

It is natural that China is placing greater emphasis on the use of BITs as legal instruments for the protection of Chinese investments overseas by signing new BITs with developing countries and upgrading old BITs with developed countries. Against this backdrop, China's stance concerning BIT practice has evolved from a restrictive to a balanced or even liberal stance. Starting with the Barbados-China BIT 1998, China began to provide foreign investors with stronger and more comprehensive substantive and procedural protections that are largely comparable to those of other capital-exporting states.[29] It is no coincidence that this change in China's BIT policy overlapped in time with the launch of its 'go global' strategy.

---

[27] Julie Jiang and Jonathan Sinton, 'Overseas investments by Chinese national oil companies: assessing the drivers and impacts', International Energy Agency Information Paper, February 2011, accessed 5 June 2018 at www.iea.org/publications/freepublica tions/publication/overseas_china.pdf.

[28] Christian Shepherd and Jack Farchy, 'Chinese embassy in Kyrgyzstan hit by suicide bomb attack', Financial Times, 30 August 2016, accessed 5 June 2018 at www.ft.com/content/23243e7e-6e82-11e6-9ac1-1055824ca907.

[29] Stephan W. Schill, 'Tearing down the great wall: the new generation investment treaties of the People's Republic of China' (2007) 15 Cardozo Journal of International and Comparative Law 73–118 at 73; Yuqing Zhang, 'The case of China', in Michael Moser (ed.), Investor-State Arbitration: Lessons for Asia (Hong Kong: HKIAC, 2008), p. 156.

Table 6.1 *China's BITs and FTAs with BRI Countries*

	Number of BITs and FTAs
FTAs	5 signed: China-ASEAN Asia-Pacific trade agreement (with India, Bangladesh and Afghanistan) China-Pakistan China-Singapore China-Georgia
	6 in negotiation: China-Gulf Cooperation Council FTA China-Sri Lanka China-Israel China-Pakistan FTA second phase China-Singapore Upgrade FTA China-Moldova
BITs	59 BITs With 56 countries = 65 BRI countries – 9 countries
Mega-regional	1 Regional Comprehensive Economic Partnership (RCEP)

The country's increased confidence in providing sufficient protection to foreign investors, as well as its growing outbound FDI and increasingly sophisticated legal system, may well explain its growing acceptance of modern BIT jurisprudence and related international investment law. Owing to a rise in the number of disputes raised on the ground of indirect expropriation, the recent BITs concluded by the United States and Canada have included more detailed provisions, a trend that China appears to have taken on board in its own BIT jurisprudence and practice.

Most of the sixty-five countries covered by the BRI had existing FTAs and BITs with China, as shown in Table 6.1. However, the focus of this chapter is on the expropriation clauses in China's BITs and FTAs, with the aim of formulating a picture of the evolution of those clauses. The main reason for the chapter's focus is the fact that most of the BRI countries are developing nations that lack a strong legal infrastructure for property rights protection, a situation that may damage China's economic interests when it seeks to protect outbound Chinese investment. Given the lack of an adequate domestic legal infrastructure in many BRI countries, reliance on the stronger protection standards in BITs (i.e. with regard to the avoidance of expropriation or provision of ample compensation) is a natural tool for outbound Chinese investors looking to invest in those countries.

In summary, this chapter focuses on the notion of expropriation and related compensation standards by examining the expropriation clauses in China's existing BITs. The underlying rationale of this focus is the correlation between expropriation, the most pressing risk facing outbound investment, and foreign investment protection.

2   Concept of Indirect Expropriation: Scope and Content

The doctrine of and case law on expropriation in international investment law is an unsettled area owing to a variety of factors, including the divergence of interests between capital-importing and -exporting states, divergence in legal, economic and cultural concepts concerning property rights and, more importantly, the regulatory role of states in cross-border investment activities. Although China has been an active treaty-maker in the realm of international investment arbitration, as evidenced by the nearly 130 BITs it has signed to date, the notion of expropriation within those BITs remains in a state of flux.

The origins of expropriation can be traced back to the international law standards on the protection of aliens. In modern international investment protection law, expropriation is permitted only if it is carried out on a non-discriminatory basis for some public purpose and in compliance with due process and the principle of compensation payment. BITs regulate the exercise of a state's power to expropriate investments. In fact, investors' chances of succeeding in an expropriation claim against a state are rather slim, particularly in cases in which the disputed expropriation is a regulatory matter. Tribunals have long found it difficult to conclude either that a state's actions amount to an actual taking or that the accumulative effect of the state's act reaches the threshold of expropriation.

Expropriation is a critically important issue in Chinese BITs,[30] considering China's enormous amount of foreign capital, history of nationalising foreign investment, which dates to the immediate aftermath of the founding of the PRC,[31] emerging 'new state order' and 'creeping renationalisation' in order to 'attack private enterprises' by grabbing state

---

[30] All of the BITs cited herein are available from http://investmentpolicyhub.unctad.org/IIA/CountryBits/42 (accessed 15 June 2018).

[31] Laurie A. Pinard, 'United States policy regarding nationalization of American investments: the People's Republic of China's nationalization decree of 1950' (1984) 14 *California Western International Law Journal* 148.

land from privately owned coal mines and residents.[32] However, the utility of the expropriation clauses in China's 129 BITs and a dozen FTAs remains something of a mystery given that very few BIT arbitration cases brought before the International Centre for Settlement of Investment Disputes (ICSID) have involved Chinese BITs.

Under investment treaty jurisprudence, it is almost a settled matter that, subject to the precise wording of the BIT in question, expropriation extends to both direct and indirect measures, as well as to 'creeping expropriation'.[33] However, investment treaties do not generally define expropriation, indirect expropriation in particular, leaving the specific contours of the concept to customary international law.[34] This approach is also recognised in BIT jurisprudence,[35] recent US BITs[36] and Chinese FTAs.[37] The lack of a uniform definition of indirect expropriation has become the greatest source of difficulty for both host governments and investment arbitration tribunals. Some Chinese BITs, such as the Germany-China BIT, touch upon indirect expropriation by stipulating that 'investments by investors of either Contracting Party shall not directly or indirectly be expropriated, nationalised or subjected to any other measure the effects of which would be tantamount to expropriation or nationalization in the territory of the other Contracting Party'.[38] In addition, the Mexico-China BIT expressly refers to expropriation enacted directly or 'indirectly through measures tantamount to expropriation or

---

[32] Jamil Anderlini and Geoff Dyer, 'Beijing accused of attacking private enterprise', Read and Think, 26 November 2011, accessed 5 June 2018 at http://beyondboundboy.blogspot .hk/2009/12/beijing-accused-of-attacking-private.html; Geoff Dyer, 'Crackdown on coal mines ignites fears of state land grab', *Financial Times*, 26 November 2009, p. 3.

[33] International investment jurisprudence often equates direct expropriation with the forcible taking by the government of tangible or intangible property owned by individuals or companies through administrative or legislative actions, while placing emphasis on the effect of the measures taken by host governments on the investment in adjudicating indirect expropriation even in the absence of the formal transfer of title or outright seizure. A situation in which an investment may be affected by measures gradually, but eventually results in expropriation, is known as 'creeping expropriation'. Campbell McLachlan, Laurence Shore and Matthew Weiniger, *International Investment Arbitration: Substantive Principles* (Oxford: Oxford University Press, 2007), Chapter 8.

[34] Jack Coe, Jr. and Noah Rubins, 'Regulatory expropriations and the TECMED case: context and contributions', in Todd Weiler (ed.), *International Investment Law and Arbitration: Leading Cases from the ICSID, NAFTA, Bilateral Investment Treaties and Customary International Law* (London: Cameron May, 2005), p. 601.

[35] *Saluka Investments BV* v. *Czech Republic*, UNCITRAL Ad Hoc Arbitration, Partial Award, 17 March 2006, para. 261.

[36] US Model BIT 2004, Annex B Expropriations, at 38.

[37] New Zealand-China FTA, Article 143; Peru-China FTA, Article 132(2)(c).

[38] Germany-China BIT, Article 4(2); Jordan-China BIT, Article 5(1); Uganda-China BIT, Article 4(1).

nationalization'.[39] The phrase 'tantamount to expropriation'[40] has allowed a number of tribunals to provide broad protection for the investments of foreign investors who suffer harm from being deprived of their fundamental investment rights.[41] For instance, the tribunal in *Eureko* v. *Republic of Poland* concluded that 'tantamount to deprivation' extends to frustration of the benefits of an investor's contractual rights.[42]

A large number of Chinese BITs have other variations with a similar effect. Examples include the Czech Republic-China BIT, Denmark-China BIT, Indonesia-China BIT and Iceland-China BIT, which incorporate the phrase 'having an effect equivalent to . . .',[43] the Greece-China BIT, which has the caveat 'tantamount to',[44] and the France-China BIT, which features the phrase 'same effect'. Based on extensive jurisprudence, any of these formulations may be held by tribunals to have the effect of bringing indirect expropriation into the ambit of a treaty,[45] as the state's actions effectively 'neutralise the benefit of the property of the foreign owner'.[46] In line with general BIT practice,[47] the Albania-China BIT, similar to most other Chinese BITs, contains the following generic expropriation clause.

> Neither Contracting Party shall expropriate, nationalize or take similar measure (hereinafter referred to as "expropriation") against investments of investors of the other Contracting Party in its territory, unless the following conditions are met:
>
> (a) for the need of social and public interests;
> (b) under domestic legal procedure;
> (c) without discrimination;
> (d) against compensation.[48]

---

[39]   Mexico-China BIT, Article 7(1).

[40]   Greece-China BIT, Article 4(1).

[41]   *Pope & Talbot Inc.* v. *Government of Canada* (Merits, Phase 1, 26 June 2000), para. 99; *Waste Management Inc.* v. *United Mexican States* (Merits), paras. 143–5; *GAMI Investments, Inc.* v. *Government of the United Mexican States* (Merits), para. 131; *Tecnicas Medioambientales Tecmed, SA* v. *United Mexican States* (Merits), paras. 113–15, 121; *Compania del Desarrollo de Santa Elena, SA* v. *Republic of Costa Rica* (Merits), paras. 71–2, 76.

[42]   *Eureko B.V.* v. *Republic of Poland*, Ad Hoc Arbitration, Partial Award, paras. 240–2 (involving the Netherlands-Poland BIT of 1992).

[43]   Indonesia-China BIT, Article 6(1).

[44]   Greece-China BIT, Article 4(2).

[45]   *ADC Affiliate Limited and ADC & ADMC Management Limited* v. *Hungary*, ICSID Case No. ARB/03/16, para. 426; *Waste Management, Inc.* v. *Mexico* (Number II), ICSID Case No. ARB(AF)/00/3, Final Award, 20 April 2004, para. 143.

[46]   *CME Czech Republic BV* v. *Czech Republic*, UNCITRAL Partial Award September 13, 2001, paras. 6–14.

[47]   Andrew Newcombe, 'The boundaries of regulatory expropriation in international law', (2005) 20(1) *ICSID Review–Foreign Investment Law Journal* 8–9.

[48]   Albania-China BIT, Article 4(1).

In many other Chinese BITs, including the Peru-China BIT and Malaysia-China BIT, 'for the need of social and public interests' is simplified as 'for the public interest'.

Unlike many other Chinese BITs or FTAs, the country's BITs with Albania and Malaysia do not refer to 'indirect expropriation'. That silence adds uncertainty over an investor's ability to bring a claim within investor-state arbitration. Further, apart from the phrase 'take similar measures', neither the Albania-China BIT nor Malaysia-China BIT contains a functional definition of indirect expropriation, which, as a consequence, may allow tribunals to adopt a more expansive approach to such expropriation.[49] Given the lack of guidance in these Chinese BITs concerning the application of the treaty standards to specific circumstances, the application of international law seems to be an option. Such application would be legitimate and reasonable for an investor bringing a claim to the ICSID for arbitration in accordance with the investment dispute clause in the Peru-China BIT, for example.[50] What is noteworthy is the completeness contributed by the Peru-China FTA to the definition of indirect expropriation, which not only covers an 'equivalent effect' scenario but also provides a two-pronged test to determine the existence of indirect expropriation, that is, the severity or indefinite nature of the expropriatory act and its proportionality to the public interest.

International investment treaty jurisprudence makes a structural distinction between full or substantial deprivation and regulatory takings, with the latter referring to measures taken in the context of a modern regulatory state, including strangulating taxation.[51] Although the distinction is not easily sustained,[52] it has been recognised as one of the most contentious issues in international investment law[53] by both

---

[49] The TIT Protocol, which also includes an identical definition of 'indirect expropriation,' details some of the key perspectives on such expropriation. See Article 2a(ii) of the Protocol, accessed 5 June 2018 at http://tfs.mofcom.gov.cn/article/h/at/201405/201405 00584828.shtml.

[50] Shen Wei, 'The good, the bad or the ugly?: a critique of the decision on jurisdiction and competence in *Tza Yap Shum v. The Republic of Peru*' (2011) 9(1) *Chinese Journal of International Law* 55–95.

[51] Stephan W. Schill, *The Multilateralization of International Investment Law* (Cambridge: Cambridge University Press, 2009), p. 82.

[52] Rosalyn Higgins, 'The taking of property by the state: recent developments in international law' (1982) 176 *Recueil des Cours* 331.

[53] Thomas Walde and Abba Kolo, 'Environmental regulation, investment protection and "regulatory taking" in international law' (2001) 50 *International & Comparative Law Quarterly* 811, 814.

international legislative documents[54] and case law. The general rule is that a diminution in value remains uncompensated as long as rights of use, exclusion and alienation remain untouched.[55] Most tribunals follow this legal approach,[56] although some integrate economic elements. In the latter case, those elements are taken into account in assessing issues of causation and damage. Some tribunals favour the economic approach. For example, the tribunal in *Telenor* required 'a major adverse impact on the economic value of the investment',[57] whilst that in *Parkerings* referred to 'a substantial decrease [in] the value of the investment'.[58] In *Tecmed*, the tribunal held that deprivation analysis should focus on the 'economic use and enjoyment of [the] investments as the rights related thereto – such as the income or benefits related to the expropriation – ha [d] ceased to exist'.[59] Even though some tribunals favour the economic approach, when the question comes to the economic conception, they have not provided any conclusive answer to the threshold for a diminution in value, with some exceptions, for example *GAMI v Mexico*.[60]

Most Chinese BITs, including the Albania-China, Malaysia-China and - Peru-China BITs, do not specify the evidentiary requirement for establishing a causal link between a measure of expropriation and subsequent damages. The tribunal in *Tza Yap Shum* v. *Peru* recognised that other tribunals had dealt with this issue based on general principles of international law.[61] In some cases, such as *LG&E Energy Corp et al.* v. *Argentinean Republic*, a decrease in an investment's capacity to maintain its activities or a deterioration in profit margins was deemed insufficient, particularly when the investment remains operational. As noted, international law traditionally evaluates whether various types of government interference leave essential

---

[54] The official commentary to the OECD Draft Convention of 1967 states that 'the taking of property, within the meaning of the Article [3], must result in a loss of title or substance – otherwise a claim will not lie'. See 'OECD draft convention on the protection of property, adopted by the council in its 150th meeting on 12 October 1967' (1968) 7 *International Legal Materials (ILM)* 117, 126.

[55] Higgins, 'The taking of property', 271.

[56] David J. Harris, *Cases and Materials on International Law*, 5th edition (London: Sweet & Maxwell, 1998), pp. 555–61.

[57] *Telenor Mobile Communications AS* v. *Republic of Hungary*, ICSID Case No. ARB/04/15, Award, para. 64.

[58] *Parkerings-Compagniet AS* v. *Republic of Lithuania*, ICSID Case No. ARB/05/8, Award, 11 September 2007, para. 455.

[59] *Tecmed*, para. 115.

[60] *Gami Investment, Incorporated* v. *The Government of the United Mexican States*, Final Award, 15 September 2004, Ad Hoc Tribunal (UNCITRAL).

[61] Ibid., para. 167.

rights intact,[62] with a diminution in value generally remaining uncompensated as long as rights of use, exclusion and alienation remain untouched.[63] The Peru-China FTA sides with the more legalistic approach, providing that '[t]he fact that an action or series of actions by a Party has an adverse effect on the economic value of an investment, standing alone, does not establish that an indirect expropriation has occurred'.[64]

Investment arbitration tribunals often follow a 'sole effect' doctrine or the 'orthodox' approach, one of the dominant conceptions in international law,[65] by centring their assessments on the effects of government measures.[66] Expropriation is found to exist if the government measure's effect is the complete or substantial deprivation of an investment,[67] a material decline in the value of its assets or an impairment in the ability of the business to function,[68] which would require compensation.[69] The focus in such assessment is the degree of interference with the investment, measured by the severity of the economic impact, which is the decisive criterion.[70] Judicial practice has confirmed the magnitude or severity of this test in determining whether indirect expropriation has taken place.[71] A tendency has emerged to equate indirect expropriation to 'a measure that effectively neutralizes the

---

[62] Grant T. Harris, 'The era of multilateral occupation', (2006) 24(1) *Berkeley Journal of International Law* 1–78.

[63] Mexico-China BIT, Article 7(1), at 271.

[64] Peru-China FTA, Annex 9, Article 4.

[65] Newcombe, 'The boundaries of regulatory expropriation', 10.

[66] Rudolf Dolzer, 'Indirect expropriations: new developments?' (2002) 11 *New York University Environmental Law Journal* 64, 78. See also Jan Paulsson and Zachary Douglas, 'Indirect expropriation in investment treaty arbitrations', in Norbert Horn and Stefan Kröll (eds.), *Arbitrating Foreign Investment Disputes* (The Hague: Kluwer Law International, 2004), p. 148.

[67] See *Pope & Talbot Inc.* v. *Government of Canada*, Interim Award, paras. 96, 102, 26 June 2000, Ad Hoc Tribunal (UNICITRAL); *Occidental Exploration & Production Company* v. *The Republic of Ecuador*, LCIA Case No. UN3467, 1 July 2004), reprinted in 43 (2004) ILM 1248.

[68] Peter Cameron, 'Stabilisation in investment contracts and changes of rules in host countries: tools for oil & gas investors', AIPN Research Paper Final Report, 5 July 2006, p. 60. See also Noah D. Rubins and Stephan Kinsella, *International Investment, Political Risks and Dispute Resolution: A Practitioner's Guide* (Oxford: Oxford University Press, 2005), p. 207.

[69] Ian Brownlie, *Principles of Public International Law*, 5th edition (Oxford: Oxford University Press, 1967), p. 546.

[70] Christoph Schreuer, 'The concept of expropriation under the ETC and other investment protection treaties', CSUN paper, 20 May 2005, accessed 5 June 2018 at www.univie.ac.at/intlaw/pdf/csunpublpaper_3.pdf, 28–9. See also Anne K. Hoffmann, 'Indirect expropriation', in August Reinisch (ed.), *Standards of Investment Protection* (Oxford: Oxford University Press August, 2008).

[71] *Metalclad Corp.* v. *United Mexican States*, ICSID Additional Facility Case No. ARB(AF)/97/1, 30 August 2000, para. 103; see also *LG&E Energy Corporation and Others* v. *the Republic of Argentina*, ICSID Case No. ARB./02/1 (2007).

enjoyment of the property' even if the measure itself does not involve an overt taking.[72] Interferences constitute expropriation if they 'approach total impairment',[73] that is, 'wip[e] out *all or almost all* [of] the investor's investments'.[74] This approach has been followed by a number of tribunals in determining whether interference constitutes expropriation.[75] In sum, a taking does not have to be complete, only to 'have the effect of depriving the owner, in whole or in significant part, of the use or reasonably-to-be-expected economic benefit of property even if not necessarily to the obvious benefit of the host State'.[76]

Doubts have been expressed over the question of whether the 'sole effect' doctrine should be the only factor in determining whether a regulatory measure in the arenas of tax, the environment, health, human rights and/or a state's welfare interests constitutes a taking.[77] It has been argued that the purpose and context of the measure should be taken into account. In the case of *Tza Yap Shum* v. *Peru*, for example, Peru's argument was reflective of a highly narrow, restrictive and obsolete approach that required Tza to prove an expropriatory 'purpose', a purpose-orientated approach that focuses on the host state's intention or motivation to expropriate.[78]

Greater clarity has been brought to China's newer BITs and FTAs. Both the Finland-China and Netherlands-China BITs, for instance, are closer to the US approach[79] to expropriation.[80] The most sophisticated definition of indirect expropriation, drawing on recent BIT case law, appears in the New Zealand-China FTA, under the terms of which it is

---

[72] Greece-China BIT, para. 200. See also *CME Czech Republic B.V.* v. *The Czech Republic*, UNCITRAL Arbitration Tribunal (2001), para. 591.

[73] Coe and Rubins, 'Regulatory expropriation and the TECMED case', p. 621.

[74] *LG&E Energy Corporation and Others LG&E Energy Corporation and* v. *the Republic of Argentina*, ICSID Case No. ARB/02/1 (2007), para. 191.

[75] *Metalpar SA & Buen Aire SA* v. *Argentina*, Award on the Merits, ICSID Case No. ARB/03/5, 6 June 2008, paras. 172–3.

[76] *Metalclad Corporation* v. *Mexico*, Award, ICSID Case No. ARB(AF)/97/1 (2000), para. 103.

[77] Dolzer, 'Indirect expropriations', 79–80.

[78] Hoffmann, 'Indirect expropriation', 156–8.

[79] The approach taken by the United States in negotiating its BITs is to ensure that the standards created by the takings clause of the Fifth Amendment to the US Constitution are also applied to investment protection. To this end, the term 'expropriation' explicitly covers both direct and indirect expropriation. Accordingly, any expropriation is required to be consistent with such general absolute treatment standards as 'fair and equitable treatment', 'full protection and security' and 'treatment in accordance with customary international law'. See Kenneth J. Vandevelde, *U.S. International Investment Agreements* (Oxford: Oxford University Press, 2009), Chapter 7.

[80] Finland-China BIT, Article 4; Netherlands-China BIT, Article 5.

confined to measures that are '(a) equivalent to direct expropriation in that [they] deprive . . . the investor in substance of the use of the investor's property' (b) either severe or indefinite and (c) disproportionate to the public purpose.[81] Clear interpretative guidelines are provided on what actions constitute expropriation.

In the protocol of the 2006 India-China BIT, the detailed criteria for indirect expropriation are stipulated as follows.

(2) The determination of whether a measure or a series of measures of a Party in a specific situation, constitute measures as outlined in paragraph 1 above requires a case by case, fact based inquiry that considers, among other factors:

    (i) the economic impact of the measure or a series of measures, although the fact that a measure or series of measures by a Party has an adverse effect on the economic value of an investment, standing alone, does not establish that expropriation or nationalization, has occurred;

    (ii) the extent to which the measures are discriminatory either in scope or in application with respect to a Party or an investor or an enterprise;

    (iii) the extent to which the measures or series of measures interfere with distinct, reasonable, investment-backed expectations;

    (iv) the character and intent of the measures or series of measures, whether they are bona fide public interest purposes or not and whether there is a reasonable nexus between them and the intention to expropriate.

(3) Except in rare circumstances, non-discriminatory regulatory measures adopted by a Contracting Party in pursuit of public interest, including measures pursuant to awards of general application rendered by judicial bodies, do not constitute indirect expropriation or nationalization.[82]

The foregoing criteria adhere closely to the provisions of the 2004 US Model BIT,[83] indicating China's intention to emulate the US approach to the issue of expropriation. Few BITs or FTAs specify an interpretative methodology. The Peru-China FTA, for example, calls for 'a case-by-case, fact based inquiry'.[84] This common-law type of case-by-case method is also codified in other BITs, including the 2004 Canadian Model BIT.[85]

---

[81] New Zealand-China FTA, Annex 13.

[82] Protocol to India-China BIT, Articles 3, 5.

[83] US Model BIT 2004, Annex B, Article 4.

[84] Peru-China FTA, Annex 9, Article 4. Identical terminology appears in Article 2b(1) of the TIT Protocol.

[85] Canadian Model BIT 2004, Annex B, Article 13(1)(b).

Such a pragmatic, realist approach was adopted by the tribunal in *Tza Yap Shum* v. *Peru*, which found that the constitution of expropriation 'cannot be answered in the abstract but only on the basis of particular circumstances and in the context of particular purposes'.[86]

3   Lawful Grounds for Expropriation

Expropriation is not unlawful under international law as long as certain formalistic conditions are met.[87] In general, a signatory state is able to expropriate, nationalise or take similar measures against the investments of investors of another party if the action is: '(a) for the public purpose; (b) under [a] domestic legal procedure; (c) without discrimination; and (d) against compensation'.[88] Most Chinese BITs, in their fairly traditional terms, have cloned Chinese investment treaty practice by imitating these four elements.

3.1   Public Purpose

'Public purpose' is germane to expropriation, as a government can authorise a regulatory measure for diverse reasons. The public purpose requirement for an act of expropriation is a widely accepted principle in both customary international law and investment treaties.[89] However, the phrase 'for a public purpose' has not been well-defined or -illustrated. Variations of the phrase include 'for public interests', which has been adopted by a large number of Chinese BITs, including the Cyprus-China and Benin-China BITs, and 'for public benefits', which appears in the Germany-China BIT. These differences in phrasing do not indicate substantial differences in meaning. The formula of 'public purpose, security or national interests' adopted by the Belgium-Luxembourg-China BIT makes the public purpose criterion more operative, even though doing so puts the host state in a more advantageous position because such an operative criterion is easier to satisfy. Other variations, such as 'the need[s]

---

[86] Robert Jennings and Arthur Watts (eds.), *Oppenheim's International Law*, 9th edition (London: Longman, 1992), pp. 916–17.

[87] Rudolf Dolzer and Christoph Schreuer, *Principles of International Investment Law* (Oxford: Oxford University Press, 2008), p. 91.

[88] See Article 8(1) of ASEAN Agreement on Investment of the Framework Agreement on Comprehensive Economic Cooperation concluded with China on 15 August 2009.

[89] See Article 13(1)(a) of Energy Charter Treaty, April 1998, p. 57; Article 1110(1) of NAFTA, reprinted in (1993) 32 ILM 289.

of social and public interest[s]' and 'national security and public interest', which appear in the Argentina-China BIT[90] and Philippines-China BIT,[91] respectively, are less operative owing to their wider or vaguer coverage. The Oman-China BIT uses the language 'for a public purpose related to the internal needs of that Contracting Party',[92] which can be interpreted in a more subjective manner. These varying terminologies indicate the scope and nature of the public purpose criterion, and all entail consideration of the detailed facts of the specific case at hand.

Some Chinese BITs[93] contain a carve-out for the reasonable exercise of a state's 'police powers', which is intended to offer a safe harbour for regulations that can be reasonably justified in the public interest. Given the lack of such a carve-out in many BITs, the public purpose criterion may function as a safe harbour for expropriation regulations. 'Public power', which refers to the authority of a state government to enact measures to protect public health, welfare and morals, serves the 'public purpose'. As it may also serve local protectionist purposes, it is difficult to discern from an international perspective. Accordingly, tribunals may weigh up such considerations as bad faith, arbitrariness and/or discrimination in determining whether an ostensibly public purpose is more targeted at domestic purposes.

3.2   Due Process

Due process is a necessary measure to satisfy the public interest exception. The tribunal in *Methanex*, for example, decided the taking question against the investor on more general terms:

> [A]s a matter of general international law, a non-discriminatory regulation for a public purpose, which is enacted in accordance with due process and, which affects, inter alia, a foreign investor or investment is not deemed expropriatory and compensable unless specific commitments had been given by the regulating government to the then putative foreign investor contemplating investment that the government would refrain from such regulation.[94]

---

[90] Argentina-China BIT, Article 4(1).
[91] Philippines-China BIT, Article 4(1).
[92] Oman-China BIT, Article 4(1); Israel-China BIT, Article 5(1).
[93] New Zealand-China FTA, Annex 13.
[94] *Methanex Corporation* v. *US*, UNCITRAL Arbitration Tribunal (2005), para. 7.

Any deficiency in due process may lead a tribunal to invalidate an expropriation. For instance, the tribunal in *Metalclad* equated the fact that the 'municipality [had] acted outside its authority' with the unlawful prevention of 'the Claimant's operation of the landfill'.[95] In *Middle East Cement*, the tribunal transformed a lawful seizure into an indirect expropriation because of a lack of due process (inter alia, a failure to properly notify the investor of the seizure and auction of its vessel, the *Poseidon*).[96] Most Chinese BITs include the phrase 'under domestic legal procedures'[97] or 'under the relevant domestic laws'.[98] Reference to domestic laws provides a state with greater flexibility and control, as the expropriation process will be subject to the domestic laws of the expropriating state. In any event, the due process criterion should be relatively easy for an expropriating state to satisfy when a domestic review procedure, fair hearing and impartial tribunal are available.[99]

Whilst some Chinese BITs, such as the Croatia-China BIT, list 'under domestic legal procedures' as one of the four conditions that must be fulfilled to justify the right to expropriate foreign property', others specify 'due process of law.[100] Legally speaking, a domestic legal procedure can be interpreted more narrowly than due process, thereby bringing more local legal elements into play. Because the Peru-China BIT offers no functional definition of 'under the domestic legal procedure', the tribunal in *Tza Yap Shum* v. *Peru* made reference to both international and domestic law, again confirming the hybrid nature of international investment arbitration jurisprudence comprising both international and municipal law.[101]

Under the terms of some Chinese BITs, the norm 'due process of national laws' or 'in accordance with its laws' is more operative, as the

[95] *Metalclad Corp.*, ICSID Case No. ARB(AF)/97/1 (2000), para. 79.
[96] *Middle East Cement Shipping and Handling Co. S.A. v. Arab Republic of Egypt*, ICSID Case No. ARB/99/6 (2002), paras. 139–44.
[97] Peru-China BIT, Article 4(1)(b); Peru-China FTA, Article 133(1)(b).
[98] United Arab Emirates-China BIT, Article 6(1).
[99] Dolzer and Schreuer, *Principles of International Investment Law*, p. 91.
[100] See France-China BIT, Article 4(3); Denmark-China BIT, Article 4(1); Spain-China BIT, Article 4(1). Most of the BITs that China has signed with Western European countries have adopted 'due process of law' instead of 'under domestic legal procedures'.
[101] Andrew Newcombe and Lluís Paradell, *Law and Practice of Investment Treaties* (The Hague: Kluwer Law International, 2009), pp. 86–7.

investor is granted the right to a judicial review of a completed expropriation and the amount of compensation due. The UK-China BIT, for example, provides that 'the national or company affected ha[s] a right, under the law of the Contracting Party making the expropriation, to prompt review, by a judicial or other independent authority of that Party, of his or its case and of the valuation of his or its investment in accordance with the principles set out in this paragraph'.[102] Similar rights are granted under other Chinese BITs, such as the Germany-China BIT, according to which an investor may request 'the legality of any such expropriation and the amount of compensation shall be subject to review by national courts'.[103] The ASEAN-China Treaty does not follow this route of providing investors with a review right. Accordingly, investors may have to rely upon investor-state arbitration in making a claim against expropriation.

3.3　Without Discrimination

Non-discrimination with regard to the status and treatment of aliens and property is a well-established principle in customary international law,[104] treaty law and case law.[105] A breach of the non-discrimination principle gives rise to international responsibility.[106] In practice, discrimination complaints are most likely to be raised with respect to due process and compensation issues. However, the discriminatory factor, owing to the lack of guidance and specificity, is 'extremely difficult to prove in concrete cases'.[107] Hence, a blanket exception for non-discriminatory measures may create complexity or a 'gaping loophole in international protections against expropriation'.[108] The non-discrimination requirement appears in many Chinese BITs, being

---

[102] UK-China BIT, Article 5(1).

[103] Germany-China BIT.

[104] *Alex Genin and Others* v. *Republic of Estonia*, ICSID Case No. ARB/99/2 (2001), para. 368.

[105] *BP* v. *Libya*, reprinted in (1979) 53 *International Law Reports* (ILR), 297, 329; *Libya* v. *Libyan Am. Oil Co.*, reprinted in (1981) 20 ILM 20, 58.

[106] Ian Brownlie, *System of the Law of Nations* (Oxford: Oxford University Press, 1983), p. 81.

[107] Malcolm Shaw, *International Law*, 5th edition (Cambridge: Cambridge University Press, 2003), p. 751.

[108] *Pope & Talbot Inc.* v. *Canada*, 26 June 2000, para. 99.

absent only from those China has agreed with Austria, Germany, Indonesia, Italy, Oman and the United Kingdom. The requirement adds more value to investor protection if the BIT does not offer national treatment protection.

4 Compensation

The payment of compensation is necessary in cases of expropriation,[109] but it has proved difficult to reach consensus on an acceptable standard of compensation for lawful expropriation. Whilst developed countries insist on full compensation in accordance with the so-called Hull formula, i.e. 'prompt, adequate, and effective compensation',[110] developing countries generally prefer either 'appropriate' compensation or no compensation at all.[111] The great majority of BITs adopt customary international law on lawful expropriation, including the Hull formula, with some variations.[112] In a few Chinese BITs, a close-to-Hull-formula principle is mentioned in the form of such phrases as 'reasonable, effective and non-discriminatory compensation',[113] 'reasonable compensation'[114] or 'appropriate and effective compensation'.[115]

---

[109] Brownlie, *Principles of Public International Law*, p. 546.

[110] See, e.g. Treaty between the United States of America and the Oriental Republic of Uruguay Concerning the Encouragement and Reciprocal Protection of Investment, U.S.-Uruguay, 4 November 2005, S. Treaty Doc. No. 109–9, Article 6(1)(c), reprinted in (2005) 44 ILM 268. See also Shain Corey, 'But is it just? The inability for current adjudicatory standards to provide "just compensation" for creeping expropriations' (2012) 81 *Fordham Law Review* 989; Tom Ginsburg, 'International substitutes for domestic institutions: bilateral investment treaties and governance', Illinois Law and Economics Working Paper No. LE06–027 (2006), p. 6.

[111] 1974 Charter of Economic Rights and Duties of States, GA Res. 3281, UN GAOR, 29th Session, Supp. No. 31, UN Doc. A/9631 (1974), p. 50. For further details, see Francesco Francioni, 'Compensation for nationalization of foreign property: the borderland between law and equity' (1975) 24 *International & Comparative Law Quarterly* 255–6.

[112] See *Bilateral Investment Treaties 1995–2006: Trends in Investment Rulemaking* (New York and Geneva: UNCTAD, 2007), accessed 5 June 2018 at http://unctad.org/en/docs/iteiia20065_en.pdf; para. 52 of UNCTAD/ITE/IIT/2006/5 (2007).

[113] United Arab Emirates-China BIT, Article 6(1).

[114] Israel-China BIT, Article 5(1).

[115] Laos-China BIT, Article 4(1).

4.1 Value

Investment treaty jurisprudence in the compensation arena is exhibiting increasing convergence on the view that compensation needs to be equivalent to 'fair market value'.[116] The Peru-China BIT, for example, stipulates that 'compensation ... shall be equivalent to the value of the expropriated investment at the time when the expropriation is proclaimed, be convertible and freely transferrable ... [and] paid without unreasonable delay'.[117] The Peru-China FTA adopts a nearly identical compensation clause: '[C]ompensation ... shall be equivalent to the fair market value of the expropriated investment immediately before the expropriation took place ("the date of expropriation"), convertible and freely transferrable. The compensation shall be paid without unreasonable delay.'[118]

These provisions pertain to adequacy and promptness, connecting the financial concept of fair market value to the abstract concept of adequate compensation, as the market value of the property that has been taken is supposed to be sufficient to compensate the investor. Fair market value is the price reached between a buyer and seller acting 'at arm's length in an open and unrestricted market when neither is under compulsion to buy or sell and when both have reasonable knowledge of the relevant facts'.[119] However, BITs do not usually define fair market value explicitly. Article 133(2) of the Peru-China FTA, for example, merely stipulates that 'the compensation ... shall be equivalent to the fair market value of the expropriated investments immediately before the expropriation took place, convertible and freely transferable', which suggests that the compensation is not reflective of any change in value that occurs because the intended expropriation became known earlier. In other words, this stipulation is meant to curb the negative impact on the value of the taken property that might result from advance public knowledge of the fact of expropriation. Few Chinese BITs offer clearer guidance to supplement the market value concept. For instance, the Oman-China BIT suggests 'generally recognized principles of valuation' and 'equitable principles taking into account, inter alia, the capital invested, depreciation, capital already repatriated, replacement value and other relevant factors' as a

---

[116] Schreuer, 'The concept of expropriation', p. 2.

[117] Peru-China BIT, Article 4(2).

[118] Peru-China FTA, Article 133(2).

[119] *National Grid plc* v. *The Argentine Republic*, UNCITRAL Arbitration Tribunal, 3 November 2008, para. 263.

backup when the market value cannot be readily ascertained.[120] The Germany-China BIT, however, specifies that 'compensation shall be paid without delay and shall carry interest at the prevailing commercial rate until the time of payment; it shall be effectively realizable and freely transferrable'.[121] Although both legal instruments are in line with general value formulae, their differences are obvious. The Peru-China FTA moves one step further by stipulating that compensation shall 'be equivalent to the fair market value of the expropriated investment'.[122] None of these value formulae are operative in a practical sense.

The adoption of more operative valuation methods and principles is recommended by the World Bank, incorporated by the North American Free Trade Agreement (NAFTA) and endorsed by a number of tribunals to increase the transparency of valuation methods.[123] One concern with the compensation formula in the Peru-China FTA is that it is unclear whether its wording refers to full market value. In this sense, the agreement has made little substantial progress in clarifying the issue of how to evaluate an expropriated investment. It could certainly be argued, however, that the Peru-China FTA's approach is closer to the Hull formula than other trade agreements, as its wording has absorbed some market-orientated factors.

4.2   Moral Damages

Few investors to date have sought moral damages under BITs, and in fact the case law granting moral damages in investment arbitration is scanty. However, there have been signs recently of an increasing role for this category of damages. The concept of moral damages encompasses all

---

[120] Oman-China BIT, Article 4(2).

[121] See Article 4(2) of Agreement between the Federal Republic of Germany and the People's Republic of China on the Encouragement and Reciprocal Protection of Investments, 1 December 2003, reprinted in (2003) 42 ILM 609.

[122] Peru-China FTA, Article 133(2).

[123] See Article IV(5) of World Bank Guidelines on the Treatment of Foreign Direct Investment, reprinted in (1992) 31 ILM 1366; NAFTA (list of criteria that must be taken into account by the tribunal, e.g. 'going concern value, asset value including declared tax value of tangible property, and other criteria, as appropriate to determine fair market value'). See also CME, UNCITRAL Arbitration Tribunal, March 2003, para. 103 (which recognises that a discounted cash flow valuation is the most widely employed approach to the valuation of a going concern).

compensatory but non-pecuniary and non-material damages.[124] The UN's Draft Articles on State Responsibility stipulate that 'the ... state is under an obligation to make full reparation for the injury caused by the internationally wrongful act. Injury includes any damage, whether material or moral, caused by the internationally wrongful act'.[125] This wording suggests the real importance of potential moral damages in providing a victim with full compensation under international law.

4.3   Valuation Date

Determining the appropriate date of expropriation is important in calculating interest.[126] The valuation date is an integral part of the total compensation awarded by a tribunal in an expropriation case, and can be the most keenly contested issue. Most Chinese BITs fix the valuation date by relying on one of two cut-off points, for example 'immediately prior to the time when the expropriation became public'[127] or 'immediately before the expropriation measures were taken'.[128] The Oman-China BIT opts for the time 'immediately prior to the point of time when the decision for expropriation was announced or became publicly known',[129] which can be earlier than the date on which the expropriation actually takes place. The Greece-China BIT adopts both: 'Such compensation shall amount to the value of the investments affected immediately before the measures ... occurred or became public knowledge'.[130] That level of clarity helps to guarantee that the 'value of the expropriated investment' will not depreciate once the expropriation is known to the public. It may also guarantee the investor full and adequate recovery in the case

---

[124] Sergey Ripinsky and Kevin Williams, *Damages in International Investment Law* (London: British Institute of International and Comparative Law, 2008), p. 307.

[125] See Article 31 of Draft Articles on Responsibility of States for Internationally Wrongful Acts, with commentaries (2001), accessed 5 June 2018 at http://legal.un.org/ilc/texts/instruments/english/commentaries/9_6_2001.pdf.

[126] However, it has also been suggested that the 'moment of expropriation' be distinguished from the 'moment of valuation', as the former is related to the question of liability, whilst the latter concerns the question of damages. For details, see W. Michael Reisman and Robert Sloane, 'Indirect expropriation and its valuation in the BIT generation' (2004) 74 *British Year Book of International Law* 115.

[127] Austria-China BIT 1985, Article 4(1).

[128] Netherlands-China BIT (2001), Article 5(1)(c); New Zealand-China FTA (2008), Article 145(2); Mexico-China BIT (2008), Article 7(2)(a).

[129] Oman-China BIT, Article 4(2).

[130] Greece-China BIT (1992), Article 4(2).

of 'creeping expropriation'. Finally, the Peru-China FTA uses 'the date immediately before the expropriation took place' as the date of expropriation. Whilst such a definition may be beneficial to the aggrieved investor, it offers little in the way of clarity or practicality. The general practice is that the accrual of interest should begin at the time the expropriation occurs and end on the date payment is made. In one case, the full compensation principle led the tribunal to determine the interest due from the date of expropriation to the actual payment of compensation.[131]

4.4   Interest Rates

Neither the Peru-China BIT nor Peru-China FTA makes reference to a specific interest rate. Both, however, require that compensation 'be paid without unreasonable delay'.[132] This ambiguity over interest rates provides prospective tribunals with some degree of flexibility. Several Chinese BITs have made an attempt to fill the vacuum. For instance, the Oman-China BIT stipulates that 'compensation shall include interest at the current LIBOR rate of interest applicable to the currency in which the investment was originally undertaken from the date of expropriation until the date of payment',[133] thereby helping to avoid any confusion over the calculation of the interest payment.

According to well-established practice, interest should be compounded semi-annually to recognise the realities of trade and fully compensate investors.[134] Compounding also counteracts to some degree the risk that investors assume against the accrual arising from an award, and ideally provides an incentive for its timely payment.[135] The final ruling on this issue in *Tza Yap Shum* v. *Peru* was that the interest rate on damages would be tied to the average monthly rate on ten-year US treasury bonds.[136]

---

[131] See *Tza Yap Shum* v. *The Republic of Peru*, ICSID Case No. ARB/07/6, accessed 5 June 2018 at www.italaw.com/sites/default/files/case-documents/ita0881.pdf; ICSID Tribunal, Final Award, July 7, 2011, paras. 286, 292.

[132] Peru-China BIT, Article 4(2); Peru-China FTA, Article 133(2).

[133] Oman-China BIT, Article 4(2).

[134] *Metalclad Corp.*, ICSID Case No. ARB(AF)/97/1,§128 (2000). See also Greece-China BIT, Article 4(2), Section 440.

[135] See *Tza Yap Shum* v. *Peru*, Final Award, para. 291.

[136] Ibid., para. 290.

4.5   Exchange Rate

Effective compensation is made in a form usable by the investor. Therefore, the currency of payment must be freely usable or convertible into a
freely usable currency.[137] Chinese BITs adopt several formulae, including
the 'average of the daily exchange rates',[138] the 'official exchange rate' on
the day of transfer[139] and the 'exchange rate applicable for the payment
of the compensation . . . on the date used to determine the value of the
investment',[140] all of which are helpful in avoiding potential disputes
over the exchange rate issue. Unlike these BITs, neither the Peru-China
BIT nor Peru-China FTA specifies the way in which the exchange rate
between the local currency and a freely usable currency should be determined. However, both require compensation to 'be convertible and freely
transferrable'.[141] In *Tza Yap Shum* v. *Peru*, Tza made his monetary claim
in the local currency, i.e., the Peruvian Nuevo Sol, but the tribunal
granted damages in US dollars.[142] The tribunal most likely took into
consideration the convertibility and free transferability requirement.[143]

5   Expropriation: A Summary

At present, there is no mechanically straightforward or uniform way of
applying the expropriation clause in BIT arbitration. The methodology
adopted by the tribunal in *Tza Yap Shum* v. *Peru* echoes the pragmatic
approach advocated in investment arbitration circles, that is, that the
constitution of expropriation 'cannot be answered in the abstract but
only on the basis of particular circumstances and in the context of
particular purposes'.[144] This pragmatic approach is also in line with the
Peru-China FTA, which, as we saw above, calls for 'a case-by-case, fact
based inquiry'.[145] This common-law type of case-by-case method is also
codified in some of the other BITs we have discussed, including the

---

[137] See Article IV(7) of World Bank Guidelines on the Treatment of Foreign Direct Investment, reprinted in (1992) 31 ILM 1366.
[138] Australia-China BIT (1988).
[139] Korea-China BIT (1992).
[140] Greece-China BIT (1992), Article 4(2).
[141] Peru-China BIT (1994), Article 4(2); Peru-China FTA (2008), Article 133(2).
[142] See *Tza Yap Shum* v. *Peru*, Final Award, para. 266.
[143] Peru-China FTA, Article 133(2).
[144] Jennings and Watts, *Oppenheim's International Law*, pp. 916–17.
[145] Peru-China FTA, Annex 9, Article 4. Identical terminology appears in Article 26(1) of
the TIT Protocol.

2004 Canadian Model BIT.[146] No BIT agreed to date is comprehensively useful in outlining an exhaustive list of elements upon which tribunals can technically rely in determining an expropriation occurrence.

At the two extremes of the spectrum are interpretive approaches dealing with the concept of indirect expropriation. One extreme is marked by the trend for tribunals to conceptualise or theorise the terminology of indirect expropriation with the aim of distinguishing between takings and police power.[147] The other is marked by a focus on the semantic components of the concept of indirect expropriation.[148] Interestingly, the treaty interpretation methodology deployed by the tribunal in *Tza Yap Shum v. Peru* reflects a hybrid character, combining efforts not only to conceptualise, but also to textualise, the notion of expropriation. This hybrid approach enriches the conceptual framework of indirect expropriation by striking a balance between the legalistic and economic elements of 'destructive harm'. It brings expropriatory acts into the investment arena, while relying on the textual dimensions of indirect expropriation illuminated in the Peru-China FTA rather than the Peru-China BIT. Such an approach may inevitably cause tension.[149] Compared with the Peru-China BIT, the Peru-China FTA draws upon a more comprehensive decisional matrix to activate key aspects of indirect expropriation, thereby transforming this ambiguous black-letter doctrinal concept into a more practical notion.

Relying on the textual framework of a legal instrument is a safe and useful undertaking. However, it is only convincingly helpful if the legal instrument is clear and comprehensive. By contrast, conceptualising the doctrine of indirect expropriation appears to be more important when all members of the international community are expected to normatively abide by publicly known and well-crafted limits. The real challenge facing international investment arbitration is to find a more consistent and

---

[146] Canadian 2004 FIPA (BIT) Model, Annex B, Article 13(1)(b), which provides that '[t]he determination of whether a measure or series of measures of a Party constitute an indirect expropriation requires a case-by-case, fact-based inquiry'.

[147] Wenhua Shan, *The Legal Framework of EU-China Investment Relations: A Critical Appraisal* (Oxford: Hart Publishing, 2005), Chapter 6.

[148] Ibid.

[149] Susan Franck, 'The nature and enforcement of investor rights under investment treaties: do investment treaties have a bright future?' (2005) 12 *UC Davis Journal of International Law and Policy* 47–99 (2005). See also Anna Joubin-Bret, 'BITs of the last decade: a ticking bomb for states?', in Catherine Rogers and Roger Alford (eds.), *The Future of Investment Arbitration* (Oxford: Oxford University Press, 2009), pp. 145–53.

institutionally coherent approach to evaluating indirect expropriation in investor-state arbitration proceedings.[150] Against this backdrop, the hybrid route adopted by the tribunal in *Tza Yap Shum* v. *Peru* can be seen as a realist approach: it combines the conceptual and textual methodologies to comprehensively address the current arbitral inconsistencies in the expropriation arena and foster clearer, more predictable jurisprudence concerning expropriation. In any event, the award rendered in that case is by no means the final word on interpreting and applying substantive terms in Chinese BITs, but it is a good start.

International investment law shares similarities with administrative law at the national level in terms of many factual instances of the protection of rights or entitlements. Expropriation law and due process are common grounds in both international investment law and municipal legal orders. In this sense, international investment law constitutes the main body of global administrative law.[151] Together, BITs and international investment law jurisprudence (which comprises a large number of investment arbitration awards) form the main body of a growing system of international administrative law comprising the key ingredients of foreign investment protection law and practice. Whilst neither customary international law nor international investment law reveals a recognisable consensus on many expropriation-related rules, capital-exporting countries have long been engaged in the process of shaping the international legal framework based on idealised versions of their own domestic legal doctrines[152] with the aim of providing sound legal standards to protect their outbound investments.

As a consequence, international investment law not only transfers bilateral legal doctrines to the multilateral level, but also lays a foundation for a de facto judicial review of national laws and regulations. Non-compliance with these oft-adjudicated ingredients may result in state responsibility under international law.[153] Naturally, internationally

---

[150] Susan Franck, 'The legitimacy crisis in investment treaty arbitration: privatizing public international law through inconsistent decisions' (2005) 73 *Fordham Law Review* 1521–625.

[151] Rudolf Dolzer, 'The impact of international investment treaties on domestic administrative law' (2005) 37 *New York University of International Law and Policy* 970.

[152] David Schneiderman, *Constitutionalizing Economic Globalization: Investment Rules and Democracy's Promise* (Cambridge: Cambridge University Press, 2008), p. 56.

[153] Ari Afilalo, 'Constitutionalization through the back door: a European perspective on NAFTA's investment chapter' (2001) 34 *New York University of International Law and Policy* 1.

recognised rules such as the minimum standard of treatment, compensable taking and standards of compensation are expected to influence domestic laws[154] and pro-investment alternatives. This will certainly be the case for China, which is in a transitional process leaning primarily in the direction of global constitutionalism. It is likely that the legal norms and doctrines of foreign investment law will be applied and embedded locally, thereby reshaping the property rights and foreign investment protection regime in China.[155]

6 Conclusion

This chapter argues that China should take advantage of the BRI to formulate a mega-regional investment agreement that covers all BRI member states. Doing so would be a sensible way for China to apply a lawfare approach to stronger collaboration at the mega-regional level. An investment treaty covering all BRI nations would help China to solidify its leading role in the BRI region and reshape its legalistic image on the global stage.

It is clear from the discussion herein that China's BITs have been undergoing a generational evolution, meaning that the overall evolutionary process can be divided into several generations. In terms of expropriation standards, the cut-off point was 2006, the year in which China signed a BIT with India that, for the first time, included the concept of indirect expropriation. Recognising indirect expropriation and applying stronger compensation standards on expropriation will offer better legal protection to both foreign and Chinese investors bringing expropriation cases to the ICISD for international investment arbitration. However, most BITs between China and the BRI counterparties were signed before 2006, as indicated in Table 6.2, which suggests that the expropriation and compensation standards in most do not meet the higher standards.

---

[154] For an account of Latin America, see Schneiderman, *Constitutionalizing Economic Globalization*, pp. 59–61.

[155] Although China is an increasingly important capital-exporting state, it remains a major capital-importing country. Different from the United States, whose goal in using BITs is to both entrench customary rights and improve the general investment environment of BIT partners, China's use of BITs has a de facto domestic dimension, a point that is often overlooked by international investment lawyers. For an account of the US goal with respect to BITs, see Akira Kotera, 'Regulatory transparency', in Peter Muchlinski, Federico Ortino and Christoph Schreuer, *The Oxford Handbook of International Investment Law* (Oxford: Oxford University Press, 2008), p. 623.

Table 6.2 *Existing BITs between China and Other BRI Countries*

Period	Countries	Number
1982–9	Singapore (1986), Thailand (1985), Kuwait (1986), Sri Lanka (1987), Poland (1989)	5
1990–9	Pakistan (1990), Malaysia (1990), Czechoslovakia (1992), Greece (1993), Hungary (1993), Mongolia (1993), Laos (1993), Ukraine (1993), Vietnam (1993), Turkey (1994), Turkmenistan (1994); Kazakhstan (1994), Tajikistan (1994), Uzbekistan (1994), Lithuania (1994), Estonia (1994), United Arab Emirates (1994), Bulgaria (1994), Croatia (1994), Indonesia (1995), Kyrgyzstan (1995), Belarus (1995), Slovenia (1995), Albania (1995), Azerbaijan (1995), Romania (1995), Armenia (1995), Moldova (1995), Georgia (1995), the Philippines (1995), Oman (1995), Egypt (1996), Bangladesh (1997), Lebanon (1997), Saudi Arabia (1997), Macedonia (1997)	36
2000–10	Qatar (2000), Bahrain (2000), Brunei (2000), Cambodia (2000), Syria (2001), Myanmar (2002), Yemen (2002), Iran (2005), Bosnia and Herzegovina (2005), India (2006), Latvia (2006), Czech Republic (2006), Slovakia (2007), Bulgaria (2007), Romania (2008), Israel (2009), Russia (2009)	17
2010–	Uzbekistan (2011)	1

Hence, they may be insufficient to protect China's outbound investment into BRI countries, where such political risks as the risk of expropriation are deserving of legal and policy responses.

A sensible approach to addressing those risks is to establish a BIT network, likely in the form of a mega-regional investment agreement, that covers China and all BRI countries and applies the doctrines of indirect expropriation and the Hull formula for compensating expropriated investments.

7

ASEAN Financial Integration and the Belt and Road Initiative

Legal Challenges and Opportunities for China in Southeast Asia

CHRISTOPHER CHEN

This chapter explores the legal challenges to Chinese financial institutions in Southeast Asia against the backdrop of China's grand 'Belt and Road Initiative' (BRI) and the establishment of the Association of Southeast Asian Nations (ASEAN) Economic Community. Banking and finance play important roles in promoting trade, investment and infrastructure projects. The development of ASEAN, an immense economic bloc located immediately south of China, will have an enormous effect on the BRI strategy. This chapter outlines the current development of financial integration within ASEAN with respect to the bloc's banking and insurance sectors. It also considers the legal obstacles and potential trade barriers facing Chinese banks and insurers offering credit facilities or insurance protection to projects implemented in ASEAN amidst further ASEAN financial integration and the ASEAN-China free trade agreement (FTA).

China announced its BRI plan in 2013 as an initiative to improve economic cooperation along the traditional Silk Road Economic Belt and 21st Century Maritime Silk Road (together, the New Silk Road). Given its geographic proximity, it is clear that Southeast Asia will play an important role in BRI projects. On the inland Silk Road, several Southeast Asian countries (e.g. Vietnam, Laos and Myanmar) are adjacent to the provinces of Guangxi and Yunnan, thus offering alternative land routes from China to the Indian Ocean. The maritime Silk Road, which passes through the South China Sea, will also traverse a number of Southeast Asian countries before entering the Indian Ocean and Arabian Sea. The BRI will clearly bring new opportunities to emerging Southeast

Asian economies. The member countries of ASEAN[1] have been slowly moving towards greater regional and economic integration, with intra-ASEAN trade almost quadrupling since 2000 to reach US$630 billion in 2013.[2] ASEAN also established the ASEAN Economic Community (AEC) in 2015. Such integration within ASEAN will inevitably affect the execution of the BRI.

In this chapter, the juncture of BRI and intra-ASEAN economic and financial integration is approached from the perspective of cross-border financial services. The chapter explores the existing commitments of ASEAN countries in terms of financial services and their ongoing financial integration. It also considers the position of the Chinese banks and insurers seeking to provide lending or insurance services to Chinese and/ or local firms working on infrastructure projects in Southeast Asia. According to the *Financial Times*, the New Silk Road is likely to require US$890 billion in investment.[3] The newly established Asian Infrastructure Investment Bank, as well as the Export-Import Bank of China and China Development Bank, may provide some of the funding required.[4] However, Chinese commercial banks are also expected to participate in some projects. It has been reported, for example, that the China Construction Bank (CCB) has agreed to partner with IE Singapore, a government body, to finance BRI projects 'with about US$22 billion in funding envisaged'.[5] Therefore, market access to Southeast Asia is likely to become a legal issue for Chinese banks looking to finance projects in ASEAN nations. Insurance companies will also play a role, offering essential services to Chinese and/or local firms engaging in BRI projects. Chinese investments and project output require protection from natural disasters such as tsunamis or earthquakes and from human hazards such as riots. It is also necessary to ensure the life and health of Chinese employees in Southeast Asia. Having proper protection may well encourage more investment by Chinese and local investors alike in the building of the New Silk Road.

[1] The ten ASEAN member states are Indonesia, Malaysia, the Philippines, Singapore, Thailand (the five original founding states), Brunei, Cambodia, Laos, Myanmar and Vietnam.
[2] Almekinders et al., 'ASEAN financial integration' (2015), IMF working paper WP/15/34, 5, accessed 8 June 2018, www.imf.org/external/pubs/ft/wp/2015/wp1534.pdf.
[3] James Kynge, 'How the Silk Road plans will be financed', *Financial Times*, 10 May 2016, accessed 8 June 2018 at www.ft.com/content/e83ced94-0bd8-11e6-9456-444ab5211a2f.
[4] Ibid.
[5] Ibid.

Although ASEAN integration is still underway and may take many years to progress further, this chapter explores some of the issues facing Chinese banks and insurers offering financial services in ASEAN to sponsor infrastructure projects or facilitate the trading and provision of other services. At the macro level, the successful implementation of BRI projects might give China a stronger voice in international governance issues, and the expansion of Chinese businesses abroad might in return help Chinese firms to improve their business practices both in and outside China. Whilst BRI's actual impact remains to be seen, this chapter argues that China's BRI-related ventures may in the long run help to raise rule-of-law standards in China itself.

The remainder of the chapter is organised as follows. Section 1 discusses the current stage of ASEAN integration with respect to financial services. Section 2 analyses the challenges that Chinese financial institutions face in entering the ASEAN market to offer lending and general insurance services, particularly in terms of cross-border supply and market access. The section also considers the BRI's potential long-term impact on China's standing with respect to international governance and the rule of law. Section 3 concludes the chapter.

1 ASEAN Financial Integration

1.1 Background: ASEAN and the AEC

ASEAN was established as an international organisation comprising Southeast Asian countries on 8 August 1967 with the signing of the ASEAN Declaration in Bangkok[6] ten years after the establishment of the European Economic Community (EEC). Since its establishment, ASEAN has become a platform for promoting 'cooperation in the economic, social, cultural, technical, educational and other fields, and in the promotion of regional peace and stability through abiding respect for justice and the rule of law and adherence to the principles of the United Nations Charter'.[7] However, unlike the European Union (EU) and its predecessor, the EEC, ASEAN has yet to create centralised institutions and a top-down regime to regulate the ASEAN market or harmonise

---

[6] ASEAN, 'About ASEAN', ASEAN website, accessed 8 June 2018 at www.asean.org/asean/about-asean/.

[7] ASEAN, 'History: the founding of ASEAN', ASEAN website, accessed 8 June 2018 at www.asean.org/asean/about-asean/history.

regulations across the region. Instead, we have the 'ASEAN Way', a commitment not to use 'collective defense to serve the interests of any among the big powers' and a promise to resort to 'the principle of consultation ... as the basis for settling differences among members'.[8] ASEAN's guiding principles are inclusiveness, transparency and reciprocity,[9] and the ASEAN Way is premised on the principle of consensus and non-interference in the internal affairs of member states, an approach that is applied to regional matters ranging from conflict management to economic development.[10]

The adoption of the ASEAN Way needs to be understood in light of the geopolitical and economic background of Southeast Asia, a region that varies widely in terms of economic development, cultures and political systems. For example, in per capita gross domestic product (GDP) terms, Singapore was the richest country in ASEAN in 2014, with GDP of US$56,284.30. Cambodia, in contrast, had per capita GDP of just US$1,094.60 that year, and the figure for Myanmar was US$1,203.80.[11] However, Singapore is also ASEAN's smallest country, and is surrounded by two large, predominantly Muslim countries (i.e. Malaysia and Indonesia). Hence, ASEAN faces challenges to regional integration that Europe has not seen in the past two decades.

Although Southeast Asia was in turmoil for several decades, partly owing to the Vietnam War and Cold War, the region has in general flourished in the past two decades. According to ASEAN figures, per capita GDP in ASEAN as a whole jumped from US$1.33 trillion in 2007 to US$2.57 trillion in 2014 (a 93 per cent increase), becoming the third largest economy in Asia (behind only China and India) and the seventh largest in the world.[12] With a population of 622 million,[13] its

[8] G. Goh, 'The "ASEAN way": non-intervention and ASEAN's role in conflict management' (2003) 3(1) *Stanford Journal of East Asian Affairs* 114.

[9] Alice Huang, 'The ABCs of ASEAN's economic and banking integration', Federal Reserve Bank of San Francisco: Pacific Exchange Blog, 16 November 2015, accessed 8 June 2018 at www.frbsf.org/banking/asia-program/pacific-exchange-blog/abcs-of-aseans-economic-and-banking-integration/.

[10] Elizabeth S. K. Ng, 'ASEAN IP harmonization: striking the delicate balance' (2013) 25 *Pace International Law Review* 129–58 at 134.

[11] Data extracted from the World Bank website, accessed 8 June 2018, http://data.world bank.org/indicator/NY.GDP.PCAP.CD.

[12] ASEAN, *A Blueprint for Growth – ASEAN Economic Community 2015: Progress and Key Achievements* (Jakarta: ASEAN Secretariat, 2015), p. 1, accessed 8 June 2018 at www.miti.gov.my/miti/resources/AEC_2015_Progress_and_Key_Achievement.pdf?mid=424.

[13] Ibid., pp. 1–2.

consumer base is bettered only by China and India.[14] ASEAN countries have agreed to open up cross-border trade and services based on the World Trade Organization (WTO) framework and, as noted, officially implemented the AEC in December 2015, marking a new era of economic integration. Initiatives to boost economic integration began to take shape after the first circulation of the Framework Agreement on Enhancing ASEAN Economic Cooperation in 1992.[15] Several key agreements have been signed and implemented in the years since, including the ASEAN FTA in 1992 (superseded by the ASEAN Trade in Goods Agreement in 2010), the ASEAN Framework Agreement on Services (AFAS) in 1995 and the Framework Agreement on ASEAN Investment Area in 2012.[16] The AEC's formation was first proposed in a 2003 summit before its official formation in 2015. The four pillars of the AEC and regional integration are '(a) a single market and production base, (b) a highly competitive economic region, (c) a region of equitable economic development, and (d) a region fully integrated into the global economy'.[17]

Economic development benefits not only the trading of physical goods but also cross-border services. Services accounted for between 35 per cent (in Myanmar) and more than 70 per cent (in Singapore) of overall ASEAN GDP in 2013.[18] The import and export of services within ASEAN have also increased since 2005.[19] However, the 'diverse development stages across the region have been a primary obstacle to the AEC's objective to promote a "free flow of services"'.[20] According to the International Monetary Fund (IMF), the total national GDP of ASEAN countries in 2013 ranged from as high as US$870 billion (Indonesia) to barely US$11 billion (Laos). As it did in 2014, Singapore also had the highest per capita GDP in 2013, US$55,182, whilst Indonesia recorded just US$3,510 and Laos US$1,594.[21] It has also been noted that '[m]ost ASEAN countries are still at a relative[ly] early stage of development and

---

[14] Ibid., p. 2.
[15] Ibid., p. 3.
[16] Ibid.
[17] Ibid., p. 5.
[18] ASEAN, *ASEAN Integration in Services* (Jakarta: ASEAN Secretariat, 2015), p. 7 (see Chart 1), accessed 8 June 2018 at www.asean.org/storage/2015/12/ASEAN-Integration-in-Services-(Dec 2015).pdf.
[19] Ibid., Chart 2.
[20] Pasha L. Hsieh, 'Liberalizing trade in legal services under Asia-Pacific FTAs: the ASEAN case' (2015) 18 *Journal of Economic Law* 153–85 at 155.
[21] Almekinders et al., 'ASEAN financial integration', 6.

have large infrastructure gap[s]'.[22] Different service sectors also face different challenges.[23] Nonetheless, economic development has in general paved the way for further financial integration within ASEAN.

1.2   ASEAN Financial Service Integration

Financial services constitute an important part of the AEC's plans, and the export of such services by ASEAN countries has increased significantly over time.[24] ASEAN recognises that an integrated regional financial system is 'a key catalyst for financial sector development, which, in turn, improves efficiencies and lowers the cost of capital'.[25] Further financial integration could achieve 'a well-functioning regional financial system with more liberalised financial services, capital account regimes and inter-linked capital markets, to facilitate greater trade and investment in the region'.[26] Accordingly, ensuring a stable and inclusive financial sector is a key goal for regional economic integration, and ASEAN has set three strategic objectives for achievement by 2025: financial integration, financial inclusion and financial stability.[27] Specific strategic measures include liberalising the financial service sector under the ASEAN Trade in Services Agreement to offer greater market access and operational flexibility for ASEAN banks, promote deeper insurance penetration, and deepen the interlinking of capital markets by progressing towards greater connectivity in clearing and settlement and custody services and the development of the bond market.[28] Key financial inclusion measures will enhance the financial ecosystem through collaboration, widen the scope of financial access and literacy and expand the distribution channels for financial products (e.g. micro-insurance).[29] All of these measures require strong financial stability within the region, which means that ASEAN must intensify the process of macroeconomic

---

[22] Ibid., 12.
[23] See, e.g. Hsieh, 'Liberalizing trade in legal services', for a general discussion of the legal service sector within ASEAN.
[24] ASEAN, *ASEAN Integration in Services*, p. 8 (Chart 4).
[25] ASEAN, *A Blueprint for Growth*, p. 14.
[26] Ibid.
[27] ASEAN, *ASEAN Economic Community Blueprint 2025* (Jakarta: ASEAN Secretariat, 2015), p. 16, accessed 8 June 2018 at www.asean.org/storage/2016/03/AECBP_2025r_FINAL.pdf.
[28] Ibid., p. 17.
[29] Ibid.

and financial surveillance and the implementation of cross-border cooperative arrangements for financial supervision.[30]

With respect to the banking industry, ASEAN members approved the ASEAN Banking Integration Framework (ABIF) in 2014. There has also been some collaboration amongst ASEAN states with the goal of forming ASEAN Exchanges to boost capital markets. The ASEAN Trading Link was launched in 2012 to provide investors with easier access to the stock markets of Singapore, Malaysia and Thailand to facilitate the trading of shares and to deepen the stock market pool.[31] In the insurance sector, ASEAN countries have agreed on the ASEAN Insurance Integration Framework (AIIF), which will – in principle – liberalise the cross-border supply of marine, aviation and goods in international transit (MAT) insurance[32] as part of the seventh package of financial sector commitments under AFAS, which was ratified in 23 June 2016.[33]

ABIF is structured under AFAS,[34] which, as noted, was signed on 15 December 1995.[35] According to the AFAS Annex on Financial Services,[36] each country is entitled to take prudential measures for the protection of investors, deposit holders and policy holders.[37] Member states are also allowed to implement exchange controls to ensure the stability of their exchange rates,[38] and may recognise the prudential measures of another state.[39] Thus, each member state is entitled to regulate its own financial institutions, whilst ABIF offers a foundation for mutual

---

[30] Ibid.
[31] ASEAN, *A Blueprint for Growth*, pp. 14–15.
[32] ASEAN, *Building the ASEAN Community – Insurance Sector Integration: Supporting Growth through Better Risk Management* (Jakarta: ASEAN Secretariat, 2015), accessed June 2018 at www.asean.org/storage/images/2015/October/outreach-document/Edited Insurance Sector Integration-1.pdf.
[33] 'ASEAN financial integration: where are we, where next?', Keynote address by Ravi Menon, Managing Director, Monetary Authority of Singapore, at ASEAN Banking Council Meeting on 12 June 2015, Monetary Authority of Singapore, accessed 8 June 2018 at www.mas.gov.sg/news-and-publications/speeches-and-monetary-policy-state ments/speeches/2015/asean-financial-integration-where-are-we-where-next.aspx.
[34] ASEAN, *Building the ASEAN Community – ASEAN Banking Integration: Strong Regional Banks, More Robust and Inclusive Growth* (Jakarta: ASEAN Secretariat, 2015), accessed 8 June 2018 at www.asean.org/storage/images/2015/October/outreach-document/Edited ASEAN Banking Integration Framework-1.pdf.
[35] See 'ASEAN financial integration: where are we, where next?'.
[36] See ASEAN website www.asean.org (accessed 8 June 2018)
[37] Paragraph 2(a) of AFAS Annex on Financial Services.
[38] Ibid.
[39] Ibid., para. 3(a).

recognition. ABIF was endorsed by ASEAN Central Bank Governors in December 2014[40] to provide a further step towards a more European-style 'single passport' concept for cross-border banking services within the ASEAN region.[41] The framework was officially enabled by the Protocol to Implement the Sixth Package of Commitment on Financial Services under AFAS, which was signed in March 2015 by ASEAN Finance Ministers.

There are two layers to ABIF. The first is a multilateral layer that creates ASEAN-wide guidelines for financial service integration. The second is a bilateral layer allowing two countries to conduct bilateral talks on greater access to qualified ASEAN banks (QABs) in each other's markets.[42] On this basis, ABIF grants banks that meet certain criteria (i.e. QABs) greater access and more flexibility to operate within the ASEAN market.[43] ABIF's purpose is to spur trade and investment within ASEAN and afford better access to finance for small to medium-sized enterprises (SMEs) and the unbanked.[44] Further financial integration may also boost growth, employment and financial inclusion and facilitate larger and deeper liquid financial markets, thereby lowering capital costs and improving resource allocation and risk diversification.[45]

Although the full details of the AIIF are not yet clear, it is evident that the framework will initially focus on transport- and shipping-related insurance (i.e. MAT insurance). The policy objective is obvious, as the MAT insurance sector is related to cross-border trade. Whether the AIIF will eventually cover other forms of general insurance or even life insurance remains to be seen.

Whilst the idea of financial service integration is sound, and the developments in that direction to date are encouraging, there are a number of challenges in opening up cross-border banking services within ASEAN. Such opening-up must be balanced against the risks of financial instability and financial contagion,[46] and more stringent supervision may be necessary. At the same time, the financial markets of ASEAN countries

---

[40] ASEAN, *Building the ASEAN Community – ASEAN Banking Integration*.

[41] Eli Remolona and Ilhyock Shim, 'The rise of regional banking in Asia and the Pacific' (2015) September *BIS Quarterly Review* 128.

[42] Yasmine Yahya, 'Banking on ASEAN banks to step up with AEC', *The Straits Times*, 9 December 2015, accessed 8 June 2018 at www.straitstimes.com/opinion/banking-on-asean-banks-to-step-up-with-aec.

[43] ASEAN, *Building the ASEAN Community – ASEAN Banking Integration*.

[44] Ibid.

[45] Almekinders et al., 'ASEAN financial integration', 13.

[46] ASEAN, *Building the ASEAN Community – ASEAN Banking Integration*.

are in different stages of development. For example, the cost-to-income ratio of Indonesian banks is much higher than that of other banks in the region.[47] The IMF has recommended that ASEAN countries at different stages of development implement different integration timelines.[48] It is hoped that the less developed countries in the region will ultimately catch up with their more advanced counterparts.

In contrast to the EU approach, ABIF was not imposed by a supranational body, and is not mandatory. ASEAN has adopted a two-track approach to phase out restrictions on wholesale banking while delaying the completion of retail banking liberalisation until a later stage.[49] ABIF is also built upon a three-dimensional framework under which equal access, equal treatment and an equal environment are the three long-term guiding principles.[50] Accordingly, ABIF offers only a framework by which two or more member states can negotiate the liberalisation of their banking sectors.[51] For example, the Bank of Indonesia, Financial Services Authority of Indonesia and Central Bank of Malaysia signed a bilateral agreement under the auspices of ABIF in 2014.[52] ASEAN countries must agree on a set of standards for QABs, and then these bilateral commitments are placed under each country's Consolidated Schedule of Specific Commitments on Financial Services (under the WTO structure).[53] Thus, the legal effect is not very strong. As the IMF notes, the ASEAN Way means that 'individual ASEAN member countries can take steps toward further financial sector liberalization and capital account liberalization if and when they believe [themselves] to be ready'.[54] Nonetheless, this is a first step towards a more integrated financial market.

2 Belt and Road Initiative in the Context of ASEAN Financial Integration

What might the establishment of the AEC and ASEAN financial integration mean for the BRI? Even with the establishment of the AEC and ABIF, considerable trade barriers remain, both amongst ASEAN states and between ASEAN states and third-party countries. The focus in this

---

[47] Huang, 'The ABCs of ASEAN's'.
[48] Almekinders et al., 'ASEAN financial integration', 15.
[49] Ibid., 15.
[50] Ibid.
[51] ASEAN, *ASEAN Economic Community Blueprint 2025*, p. 5.
[52] Remolona and Shim, 'The rise of regional banking in Asia', 128.
[53] ASEAN, *ASEAN Economic Community Blueprint 2025*, p. 5.
[54] Almekinders et al., 'ASEAN financial integration', 12.

section is on issues relating to the core financial services most closely connected with infrastructure projects in Southeast Asia. In particular, it focuses on the cross-border supply of credit facilities (e.g. syndicated loans led by Chinese banks) and on general insurance on properties or economic interests held by Chinese entities doing business in Southeast Asia, as well as the commercial presence of Chinese banks in the ASEAN region. These issues are examined from three perspectives. First, the section analyses the trade barriers faced by Chinese banks or insurers that enter Southeast Asia in the context of the FTA between China and ASEAN. Second, it analyses issues within ASEAN arising from the presence of Chinese financial firms in one or more ASEAN countries. Such analysis further allows examination of the potential opportunities presented by ASEAN financial integration to Chinese or other non-ASEAN financial institutions. Finally, the continued rise of the internet and combination of financial services and information technology have given rise to the 'fintech' phenomenon, which offers a further dimension of cross-border provision and financial service consumption that may challenge any existing regulatory frameworks and trade agreements.

2.1   Cross-Border Financial Services between China and ASEAN

At the international trade level, the extent to which Chinese financial institutions can offer financial services to Southeast Asia is defined by the FTA signed between China and ASEAN in November 2002 in the form of the Framework Agreement on Comprehensive Economic Co-operation between ASEAN and the People's Republic of China (China-ASEAN FTA hereafter).[55] The Agreement on Trade in Goods went into effect in July 2005, whilst the Agreement on Trade in Services was signed in January 2007 (effective July 2007).[56] This latter agreement lays out the framework for the cross-border supply and consumption of financial services between China and ASEAN. Pursuant to the China-ASEAN Agreement on Trade in Services, the GATS Annex on Financial Services is applicable,[57] meaning that China and ASEAN countries can for prudential reasons take measures to protect investors, deposit holders

---

[55] For the general background of the ASEAN-China FTA and free trade area, see Alyssa Greenwald, 'The ASEAN-China free trade area (ACFTA): a legal response to China's economic rise' (2006) 16 Duke Journal of Comparative and International Law 193–216.

[56] 'China FTA network', Ministry of Commerce of the People's Republic of China, accessed 8 June 2018 at http://fta.mofcom.gov.cn/topic/chinaasean.shtml.

[57] Article 28(1) of China-ASEAN Agreement on Trade in Services.

and policy holders to ensure the integrity and stability of the financial system.[58] A country may also recognise the 'prudential measures of any other country in determining how the Member's measures relating to financial services shall be applied' through harmonisation or an agreement.[59] Accordingly, each country is generally allowed to impose prudential regulations on financial institutions even if those regulations amount to trade barriers. The specific commitments made by each ASEAN country under the China-ASEAN FTA are reported in Table 7.1.

Table 7.1 covers the two main forms of financial service supply by way of the cross-border supply (i.e. Mode 1, see Table 7.3) of lending services by banks and the commercial presence (i.e. Mode 3, see Table 7.3) of foreign banks under the international trade framework. It is clear from the table that financial services between China and ASEAN are not fully open and that the degree of openness varies by country. In some ASEAN countries (e.g. Indonesia and the Philippines), financial services are not even on the agenda, whereas in others they are open to Chinese financial institutions as long as several conditions are fulfilled. As discussed further below, these conditions commonly include foreign ownership caps. Many countries choose to remain unbound for certain services to ensure that they remain free to apply local regulations to regulate foreign market participants. However, this environment has not deterred Chinese financial institutions from operating in Southeast Asia, as illustrated by Table 7.2, which shows the commercial presence of the five largest Chinese commercial banks in the region in 2015.

As Table 7.2 shows, the five largest banks in China all have branches in Singapore, reflecting the city-state's status as the financial centre of the region. Vietnam is another popular country, with four of the banks having a branch in either Ho Chi Minh City or Hanoi and the ABC having a representative office in Hanoi. However, the degree of the banks' commercial presence in other countries varies. Only the BOC has subsidiary banks in Malaysia and Thailand, as well as branches in four other ASEAN states. The ICBC has shown some interest in Cambodia and Laos, but its commercial presence in other ASEAN countries is more limited. With Myanmar opening up and ASEAN still enjoying good economic growth, there is certainly room for Chinese banks to expand their presence in Southeast Asia. However, Singapore is expected to be the most likely main entry point for Chinese financial institutions going forward.

---

[58] Article 2(a) of GATS Annex on Financial Services.
[59] Ibid., Article 3(a).

Table 7.1 *Limitations on Market Access under China-ASEAN FTA for Select Sectors*

Country/ Activity	Commercial Banking	Insurance
Brunei	Not listed in Specific Commitments.	Not listed in Specific Commitments.

Cambodia	1. Deposit-taking, lending and payment services:
	  a. No limitation except that deposits received from the public must be reinvested in Cambodia.
	  b. No limitation on commercial presence except through authorised financial institutions such as banks.
		1. For life business:
		  a. Cross-border supply is subject to local licensing requirements.
		  b. No limitation on commercial presence.
		2. For non-life business:
		  a. No limitation on cross-border supply for marine, aviation and transport insurance from 1 January 2009.
		  b. Otherwise, cross-border supply of non-life insurance service is subject to local licensing requirements.
		  c. No limitation on commercial presence.
		3. Reinsurance
		  a. No limitation on cross-border supply or commercial presence.

Indonesia	Not listed in Specific Commitments.	Not listed in Specific Commitments.
Laos	1. Not listed in Specific Commitments regarding deposit-taking or lending services.	1. Unbound regarding cross-border supply of insurance services (of any kind). 2. No limitation on commercial presence, although insurers must be in company form provided by Laos law.

Table 7.1 (*cont.*)

Country/ Activity	Commercial Banking	Insurance

Malaysia	1. Not listed in Specific Commitments regarding deposit-taking or lending services.	1. Director insurance:
		  a. Unbound for cross-border supply.
		  b. For commercial presence, foreign ownership cannot exceed 51%; new entry is limited to participation in a locally incorporated insurer; regulatory approval requires acquiring 5% or more of equity in a local insurer.

Myanmar	Not listed in Specific Commitments.	Not listed in Specific Commitments.
The Philippines	Not listed in Specific Commitments.	Not listed in Specific Commitments.

Singapore	1. Deposit-taking:
	  a. Unbound for cross-border supply.
	  b. Commercial presence: deposit-taking is subject to local licensing requirements.
	  c. No new full and wholesale commercial banks.
	2. Lending activities:
	  a. Unbound for cross-border supply.
	  b. Commercial presence: subject to limitations on national treatment.
	  c. Issuing credit cards is subject to local licensing requirements.
		1. Life business:
		  a. Unbound for cross-border supply.
		  b. No limitation on commercial presence except that a foreign party can only acquire up to 49% of a locally owned insurer.
		2. Non-life business:
		  a. Unbound for cross-border supply.
		  b. No limitation on commercial presence except that a foreign party can only acquire up to 49% of a locally owned insurer.
		3. Reinsurance:

Table 7.1 (*cont.*)

Country/ Activity	Commercial Banking	Insurance
	d. Foreign banks offering Singapore dollar credit facilities exceeding S$5 million must ensure the money is converted into a foreign currency.	a. Unbound for cross-border supply. b. Unbound except for admission of direct insurance and reinsurance brokers as locally incorporated subsidiaries.
Thailand	Not listed in Specific Commitments.	Not listed in Specific Commitments.
Vietnam	1. Regarding deposit-taking and lending: a. Unbound for cross-border supply. b. No limitation on commercial presence except that foreign banks can only establish branches, representative offices or joint-controlled banks (with equity no more than 50%).	1. No limitation on cross-border supply for (1) insurance services to foreigners working in Vietnam for foreign enterprises; (2) reinsurance services; and (3) insurance for international transport and goods in transit. 2. No limitation on commercial presence except no fully owned foreign insurer on mandatory insurance (such as motor insurance or workmen's compensation).

Source: website of the Ministry of Commerce of the People's Republic of China, accessed 5 June 2018, http://fta.mofcom.gov.cn/topic/chinaasean.shtml.

Table 7.2 *Commercial Presence of Selected Chinese Banks in Southeast Asia*

Country/ Activity	Subsidiary	Branch	Representative Office
Brunei			
Cambodia		ICBC (Phnom Penh)	
Indonesia		BOC (Jakarta)	
Laos		ICBC (Vientiane)	
Malaysia	BOC		
Myanmar			
The Philippines		BOC (Manila)	
Singapore		BOC, ICBC, CCB, ABC, BComm	
Thailand	BOC		
Vietnam		BOC, CCB and BComm (in Ho Chi Minh City); ICBC (Hanoi)	ABC (Hanoi)

List of Abbreviations:
ABC   Agricultural Bank of China.
BOC   Bank of China
BComm   Bank of Communication
CCB   China Construction Bank
ICBC   Industrial and Commercial Bank of China

In contrast to the banking sector, it is harder to paint an accurate picture of the Chinese presence in the Southeast Asian insurance market, as it is not always clear from the annual reports of insurers, although the situation varies for direct insurance and reinsurance. With respect to the former, some Chinese insurers have a presence in the retail markets of some ASEAN countries, selling direct insurance products to local customers. For example, China Insurance and China Taiping both have a wholly owned subsidiary in Singapore[60] selling life and general insurance

---

[60] China Life Insurance (Singapore) Pte Ltd and China Taiping Insurance (Singapore) Pte Ltd, respectively.

Table 7.3 *Specific Commitments Regarding Banking Services for Select ASEAN States*

Country/Activity	Mode 1[a]	Mode 3[b]
Brunei	Unbound	Subject to local licensing requirements.
Cambodia	None; deposits from the public must be reinvested in Cambodia.	None except through authorised financial institutions such as banks.
Indonesia	None	1. Bound only two sub-branches and two auxiliary offices for a foreign bank's branch office or a joint venture bank. 2. A foreign bank is allowed to establish or acquire a locally incorporated bank in cooperation with Indonesian nationals/entities. 3. Branch offices of a foreign bank may only open in some cities. 4. Foreign ownership capped at 51% if shares are listed for trading.
Laos	None	Subject to local regulations under the Commercial Banks Law.
Malaysia	Lending to residents in any currency in excess of RM 25 million must be undertaken jointly with a local bank.	1. Entry is subject to local incorporation of a joint venture with foreign ownership capped at 30%. 2. A representative office is allowed only for research and liaison services. 3. The provision of factoring services requires a separate entity with foreign ownership capped at 30%. 4. Investment banks cannot provide consumer credit or home mortgages.

Table 7.3 (*cont.*)

Country/Activity	Mode 1[a]	Mode 3[b]
		5. Only commercial banks are allowed to provide overdraft services.
		6. Offshore banks are permitted to lend in foreign currencies only.
Myanmar	Unbound for representative office services by a foreign bank.	Foreign banks are allowed to open representative offices in Myanmar.
The Philippines	Commercial presence required.	1. A widely held and listed foreign bank can take one form of commercial presence at a time but can still invest in up to 40% of voting stock of a local bank.
		2. Maximum six branches, with three by choice and three designated by the board.
		3. Acquisition of up to 60% of voting stock of an existing domestic bank or a newly incorporated local bank.
		4. Ownership by a non-bank financial service provider capped at 40%
Singapore	Unbound	1. Credit card can only be issued if approved by MAS [the central bank].
		2. Finance companies cannot extend S$ credit to non-resident financial entities.
Thailand	1. None for financial advisory and data processing.	1. None for representative office.
	2. Unbound for all other services.	2. Foreign bank branch:
		a. None for existing foreign bank branches under the present shareholding structure.

Table 7.3 (*cont.*)

Country/ Activity	Mode 1[a]	Mode 3[b]
		b. New establishment subject to licensing requirements.
		c. ATM operations permitted if joining ATM pool with other Thai banks or on own premises or sharing facilities with commercial banks in Thailand.
		d. None for participation in cheque-clearing system.
		3. Locally incorporated bank:
		a. Market access limited to acquisition of shares of existing banks.
		b. Shareholding by Thai nationals no less than 75% except by approval of the Bank of Thailand (but still up to only 49%).
		c. Thai government may take the necessary measures to support the financial system.
		d. At least three-quarters of directors must be Thai nationals.
Vietnam	Unbound except for the provision of financial information and advisory services.	None, except:
		1. Foreign bank's commercial presence:
		a. Foreign commercial bank: in the form of rep office or branch, joint venture bank with foreign capital not more than 50%, etc.

Table 7.3 (*cont.*)

Country/ Activity	Mode 1[a]	Mode 3[b]
		b. Foreign financial leasing company: rep office, branch, foreign joint venture leasing company or 100% foreign invested financial leasing company.
		2. Vietnam may limit equity participation by a foreign credit institution.
		3. A rep office is not allowed to open transaction points outside its branch office.

[a] Cross-border supply[61]
[b] Commercial presence
Source: Protocol to Implement the Sixth Package of Commitment on Financial Services under the ASEAN Framework Agreement on Services, accessed 5 June 2018, http://asean.org/storage/2016/12/Consolidated-AFAS-6-SOCs-with-ABIF-Commitments.pdf.

products to Singaporean customers. With respect to the latter, many reinsurers also have offices in Singapore, the largest reinsurance hub in Southeast Asia, to acquire insurance risk exposure. Chinese insurers may come to Singapore to seek reinsurance or to provide it to other direct insurers.

The next section explores whether Chinese banks can enter the ASEAN market through their commercial presence in ASEAN countries.

2.2   Financial Services within ASEAN

2.2.1   ABIF and Specific Commitments Regarding Core Banking Services within ASEAN

Even with the establishment of ABIF and the AEC, ASEAN countries still impose considerable trade barriers on the cross-border supply and

---

[61] See WTO, 'GATS training module: chapter 1 – basic purpose and concepts', accessed 8 June 2018 at www.wto.org/english/tratop_e/serv_e/cbt_course_e/c1s3p1_e.htm#boxa.

commercial presence of non-local financial institutions through the Protocol to Implement the Sixth Package of Commitment on Financial Services signed on 20 March 2015. This protocol is largely based on the commitments made by each ASEAN state within the WTO structure. Some of the key features of the cross-border supply (i.e. Mode 1) of lending services by banks and the commercial presence (i.e. Mode 3) of foreign banks in ASEAN states are summarised in Table 7.3.

It is worth noting that most of the ASEAN countries in Table 7.3 are committed to being unbound only with respect Mode 1, the only exceptions being Cambodia, Indonesia and Laos. Even Singapore, the de facto financial centre of the region, has declared itself unbound. The implication is that these countries want to 'remain free in the sector and the mode of supply to introduce or maintain measures that are inconsistent with market access or national treatment'.[62] In addition, some countries such as Indonesia have restricted the commercial presence (e.g. the number of branches or offices) of foreign banks. Under the present circumstances, if a Chinese bank plans to provide loans directly to borrowers (whether those borrowers be foreign firms, local firms or joint venture entities) in most ASEAN countries without going through branches or offices in those countries, it will be subject to local regulations. Commercial presence is even more heavily regulated. It is clear from Table 7.3 that there are a variety of markets access thresholds. More neutral requirements, such as in Brunei, are being subject to local licensing requirements in setting up a subsidiary, branch or representative office. In Europe, the single passport concept and harmonisation of licensing standards for banks may well help to eliminate between-country differences within the region.

In ASEAN, as noted earlier, the aim of ABIF is to advance regional banking integration. A QAB may be recognised without satisfying any additional local requirements. As the ABIF structure allows bilateral agreements between countries, we could in theory see as many as forty-five agreements of this kind signed within ASEAN in the future. Indonesia and Malaysia signed a 'Heads of Agreement' document in January 2015,[63] and more agreements have followed. Thailand signed letters of

---

[62] See the WTO's explanation in 'Guide to reading the GATS schedules of specific commitments and the list of article II exemptions', accessed 8 June 2018 at www.wto.org/english/tratop_e/serv_e/guide1_e.htm.

[63] See Charles Small, 'Indonesia-Malaysia financial agreement a model for bilateralism', ASEAN Briefing, 9 January 2015, accessed 8 June 2018 at www.aseanbriefing.com/news/2015/01/09/indonesia-malaysia-financial-agreement-model-bilateralism.html.

intent with Malaysia and Indonesia in March 2016 regarding the QAB framework,[64] and Bankko Sentral ng Pilipinas (BSP) in the Philippines and Bank Negara Malaysia signed entry agreements in early March of 2016.[65] In addition, Indonesia is reportedly in talks with Myanmar about a banking deal.[66] Malaysia and Indonesia seem to be the most active players at present. Interestingly, Singapore had not struck a deal with any other country as of June 2017.

However, as these agreements have not yet reached any public forum, the exact QAB criteria remain unclear. We can collect only gather indirect evidence from press releases. Pursuant to the media announcement made by BSP:

> A key provision ... [is] that it [the entry agreement] allows up to three QABs from each jurisdiction to operate in the other country. These QABs will enter the host jurisdiction only in the form of a subsidiary of the parent bank in the home jurisdiction in line with the principle of reciprocity. As these QABs from Malaysia enter the Philippines, they will then be regulated under applicable BSP regulations and within the legal framework defined under Republic Act No. 10641... QABs are strong and well-managed banks, headquartered in ASEAN and majority owned by ASEAN nationals. Banks that apply for QAB status must be endorsed by the home country regulator to and may be accepted by the host country regulator based on their bilateral agreement.[67]

There are several noteworthy points in this press release issued by the central bank of the Philippines. Pursuant to the Filipino-Malaysian agreement, only three banks from each country will be approved as QABs. It is suspected that there is likely a common standard for allowing three QABs from each country. Those QABs will still have to incorporate a local subsidiary to operate in the Philippines. Thus, the operation of a

---

[64] See 'The signing of the letter of intent on bilateral arrangement regarding qualified ASEAN banks between Thailand and Indonesia', Bank of Thailand press release issued on 31 March 2016, accessed 8 June 2018 at www.bot.or.th/Thai/PressandSpeeches/Press/News2559/n1659e.pdf#search=letter%2520of%2520intent.

[65] See 'Philippines and Malaysia sign agreement on entry of banks under ABIF', BSP media release issued on 14 March 2016, accessed 8 June 2018 at www.bsp.gov.ph/printpage.asp?ref=www.bsp.gov.ph/publications/media.asp%3Fid%3D4016; Mayvelin U. Caraballo, 'Malaysian bank seeks PH entry as QAB 2016', *The Manila Times*, 16 March 2016, accessed 8 June at www.manilatimes.net/malaysian-bank-seeks-ph-entry-as-qab/250795/.

[66] Grace D. Amianti, 'OJK expects to bag deal with Myanmar soon', *The Jakarta Post*, 15 October 2015, accessed 8 June 2018 at www.thejakartapost.com/news/2015/10/15/ojk-expects-bag-deal-with-myanmar-soon.html.

[67] See 'Philippines and Malaysia sign agreement on entry of banks under ABIF'.

QAB in a host state (e.g. the Philippines) is still well within the control of the host regulator (e.g. the BSP). In addition, the Filipino-Malaysian agreement also provides that a QAB must be headquartered in an ASEAN country and majority-owned by ASEAN nationals. It must also be sanctioned by the home country regulator to qualify as a QAB. Thus, there is still a considerable entry threshold even following ABIF's creation. In this sense, the idea of a single passport under ABIF is much more limited in scope than its counterpart in Europe. As ABIF remains in its infancy, we must wait for further developments.

2.2   Specific Commitments Regarding Insurance Services within ASEAN

Like the banking industry, the insurance sector is fraught with trade barriers, as shown in Table 7.4.

The opening of the insurance sector has lagged behind that of the banking sector, although the AIIF had not been fully agreed upon as of June 2017[68] Thus, until it is finalised it is difficult to predict exactly what the framework will look like or whether it will be akin to ABIF (in limiting each country to three QABs on a bilateral basis, for example). However, the Southeast Asian insurance market is far more fragmented and complex than the region's banking sector. Whilst there are several regional giants, including the Singapore-headquartered DBS Group and Oversea-Chinese Banking Corporation (OCBC) and Malaysia's CIMB Group, there is currently no large cross-ASEAN insurance group. Even in Singapore, the market is divided amongst a few large local insurers (e.g. Great Eastern and NTUC Income) and several foreign ones (e.g. Prudential and Manulife), with none dominating the market. The region thus holds promising opportunities for Chinese insurers.

Similar to the banking situation, most ASEAN countries have chosen to remain unbound with respect to the cross-border supply of insurance services to allow them to apply local regulations without making any commitments at the international trade level. However, a few, including Laos, do not restrict the cross-border supply of insurance products, and others have opened up their insurance markets on a more limited basis. Vietnam, for example, imposes no restrictions on the provision of insurance to foreign-invested enterprises and foreign workers, and the

---

[68] See Section 1.2 of this chapter.

Table 7.4 *Specific Commitments Regarding the Insurance Sector*

Country/ Activity	Mode 1[a]	Mode 3[b]
Brunei	Unbound	1. Subject to licensing requirements; locally incorporated company or branch required. 2. Approval from AMBD required to acquire control of a locally incorporated insurer.
Cambodia	1. None for marine, aviation and transport insurance, but before conditions are met, it has to be conducted with a licensed insurer in Cambodia. 2. Only by entering into a contract with licensed insurer in Cambodia.	None
Indonesia	Unbound	Subject to Indonesia's Horizontal Measures and General Conditions. Indonesia may impose foreign ownership restrictions.
Laos	None	None
Malaysia	1. Soliciting and advertising in Malaysia not allowed. 2. Approval of Central Bank required for direct placement of insurance abroad of properties in Malaysia and liability of residents of third party.	1. Permitted only through insurance companies and international Takaful operators. 2. Offshore insurers in Labuan not allowed to underwrite direct insurance of Malaysian risk.
Myanmar	Unclear	Unclear
The Philippines	Local risk shall be insured with companies authorised in the Philippines.	Subject to: 1. Acquisition of equity interest of a local insurer up to 100%.

Table 7.4 (*cont.*)

Country/ Activity	Mode 1[a]	Mode 3[b]
		2. Investment of a new locally incorporated insurer up to 100%.
		3. Participation of foreigners on the board of insurers is proportional to the percentage of foreign equity.
Singapore	Unbound	None except that foreign parties can only acquire equity stakes up to 49% in a local insurer (and cannot be the largest shareholder).
Thailand	Unbound except for international marine, aviation and transit and all classes of reinsurance.	1. Foreign ownership capped at 25%. 2. New establishment subject to licensing requirements.
Vietnam	None for: 1. Insurance provided to enterprises with foreign-invested capital and foreigners working in Vietnam. 2. Reinsurance. 3. Insurance for international transportation. 4. Insurance brokering. 5. Consultancy, actuarial, risk assessment and claim settlement services.	None except non-life branches of foreign insurance enterprises shall be permitted subject to prudential regulations.

[a] Cross-border supply
[b] Commercial presence
Source: Protocol to Implement the Sixth Package of Commitment on Financial Services under the ASEAN Framework Agreement on Services, accessed 8 June 2018 at http://asean.org/storage/2016/12/Consolidated-AFAS-6-SOCs-with-ABIF-Commitments.pdf.

situation in the Philippines is similar. Hence, Vietnam controls only insurance products sold to local Vietnamese, which should be understood in line with the country's commitment to attracting foreign direct investment. In addition, some ASEAN countries such as Cambodia and Thailand have opened their markets to marine, aviation and transport (MAT) insurance to promote the export and trade sectors.

Direct access to the insurance markets of ASEAN countries remains subject to the domestic licensing requirements for local subsidiaries or branches. It is not uncommon for there to be a cap on the foreign ownership of a domestic insurer, which affects foreign firms' ability to acquire an equity stake in them; for example, Thailand imposes a ceiling of 25 per cent. In contrast to the banking sector, the insurance sector boasts a number of insurance-related auxiliary services such as insurance brokerage, adjustment for marine losses, actuarial services and claim settlement services. These services are subject to local licensing requirements in the majority of ASEAN states that choose to remain unbound, although some, such as Vietnam, have committed to imposing no requirements on their cross-border supply.

2.3 Challenges to Chinese Financial Institutions

The China-ASEAN FTA and current state of ASEAN financial integration under ABIF and the pending AIIF create a number of challenges for Chinese banks seeking to advance further into Southeast Asia in support of BRI projects launched by Chinese or non-Chinese firms. For example, assuming that the definition of a QAB refers to a bank incorporated in ASEAN and owned by ASEAN nationals, Chinese banks will not be able to acquire QAB status in the short term unless ASEAN further opens up the banking sector, which means that they will have to establish a stronger commercial presence in the ASEAN countries that permit them to provide financial services to Chinese firms or the local citizenry. It is worth noting, however, that there are other – invisible – trade barriers that may deter foreign players. For example, a regulator may delay approval for particular activities in order to disadvantage particular market participants. Because many activities require regulatory approval (e.g. the appointment of directors, an increase in capital), regulators have many ways to affect foreign financial institutions operating in the domestic market. Although it may not be reflected in trade agreements or financial regulations, such regulatory leeway can create another set of trade barriers for foreign banks.

In addition, even if local licensing requirements do not present a major obstacle, there are potential foreign exchange controls in ASEAN, with every ASEAN country other than Singapore and Brunei having some form of such controls in place.[69] For example, the Philippines requires that all foreign borrowing should acquire prior approval from BSP,[70] and Malaysia still maintains foreign exchange controls under the Exchange Control Act of 1953.[71] These restrictions present challenges to cross-border cash flows, indirectly affecting foreign investment and the provision of cross-border financial services. Further, all clearing in Renminbi (RMB) in the region must go through Singapore (or Hong Kong). ICBC's Singapore branch has been the designated clearing bank for RMB in the city-state since 8 February 2013.[72] For this purpose, China's five largest banks all have a commercial presence in Singapore. BOC and ICBC have already acquired full banking licences in Singapore, meaning that they can carry out retail activities in both Singapore dollars and foreign currencies. CCB, ABC and BComm, in contrast, have wholesale licences, allowing them to provide financial services to financial institutions but not to retail customers. Nonetheless, as the three large banking groups in Singapore, namely, DBS, OCBC and United Overseas Bank (UOB), are the likeliest candidates for QAB status in Singapore, the chances of Chinese banks becoming QABs appear slim until future developments open up more opportunities for financial integration within ASEAN.

What are the implications for Chinese insurers who would like to sell insurance protection to firms working in Southeast Asia on a BRI project? Similar to the banking industry, the insurance sector also faces market access and licensing issues. However, insurance firms differ from institutions offering lending or deposit-taking services in several important ways.

First, a Chinese insurer may be able to circumvent trade barriers in Southeast Asia by structuring an insurance policy as a domestic policy in China. In that case, it is a Chinese insurer located in China insuring against a foreign risk (i.e. the insured's exposure in ASEAN) though a policy issued in Chinese territory. A similar situation would apply to a

---

[69] See 'Financial regulations', ASEAN website, accessed 8 June 201 at www.asean.org/?static_post=financial-regulations/.

[70] Ibid.

[71] Ibid.

[72] See 'Regional gateway for RMB', Monetary Authority of Singapore, accessed 8 June 2018 at www.mas.gov.sg/singapore-financial-centre/overview/regional-gateway-for-rmb.aspx.

policy issued by a Chinese insurer in China to insure the life and health of a Chinese person working overseas. Although such activities do not technically constitute the cross-border supply of insurance products, thus permitting Chinese insurers to circumvent the issues arising from international trade or the cross-border supply of insurance services, there may be legal issues in China. For example, it is unclear whether China Insurance Regulatory Commission (CIRC) regulations allow Chinese insurers to insure against overseas risks. In addition, the strategy might not work if an infrastructure project were being carried out by a locally incorporated joint venture or project company. In that case, the offering of insurance products by a Chinese insurer would amount to the cross-border supply of insurance products, and would thus face the entry requirements discussed above.

Second, Chinese insurers may acquire reinsurance coverage in ASEAN, notably in Singapore. In this situation, they would be seeking reinsurance protection as customers, which is not subject to local licensing requirements or market access thresholds. However, once again, whether such reinsurance would satisfy CIRC regulations remains an open question.

Third, the situation would differ if a Chinese insurer wanted to offer reinsurance to direct insurers covering losses stemming from projects in Southeast Asia. If a firm from an ASEAN country wanted to seek reinsurance coverage from Chinese reinsurers based in China, it would amount to overseas consumption by a local firm. Although such consumption is not a problem in most countries, there are restrictions in some. For example, overseas consumption in Indonesia is unbound, meaning that the Indonesian government is free to apply restrictions, except when no insurance company in Indonesia can handle the risk, no insurance company in Indonesia wants to provide coverage or the insured is not an Indonesian citizen. If, in contrast, a Chinese reinsurer wanted to offer reinsurance coverage from China to direct insurers from ASEAN states, doing so would trigger the restrictions on the cross-border supply of insurance products noted above.

Fourth, to have effective insurance coverage for potential losses, a firm must be able to reach a settlement for those losses in a timely fashion. In this respect, auxiliary services such as claim settlement and loss evaluation or adjustment can play an essential role in aiding Chinese firms working on infrastructure projects in Southeast Asia. The existence (or non-existence) of relevant services may complicate a firm's ability to seek payment for losses. Cross-border insurance products render the situation even more challenging for the insured firm and insurer alike. There is a significant legal risk for a Chinese firm that acquires an insurance product from a Chinese insurer in China. Unfortunately, as the ASEAN insurance market is far from integrated at present, it remains to be seen how the market will evolve post-AIIF.

For both banks and insurance firms, another way to bypass local licensing requirements is to acquire a local bank or insurer. However, some ASEAN countries have additional restrictions in this regard. For example, it is common for ASEAN financial regulators to control the transfer of substantial equity stakes in a bank or insurer, as we saw in Section 2.2, and prior regulatory approval is often required before a transfer of ownership is effected.[73] The rationale for such regulations lies in prudential regulation to ensure that banks and insurers are owned and managed by the proper persons to ensure the safety of financial institutions and the financial system. However, they also empower regulators to deter foreign ownership, and it is not uncommon for countries to impose direct restrictions on such ownership. As in the case of the insurance sector, for example, the Philippines limits foreign ownership of local banks to no more than 40 per cent of share capital, whilst Thailand requires at least 75 per cent of local bank shares to be held by Thai nationals, effectively limiting foreign ownership to a maximum of 25 per cent. The purpose of these restrictions is to ensure local ownership of the financial sector, and how far they can be justified by national security or other concerns is debatable.

Several countries also require foreign banks to form local partnerships before entering the market. For example, Indonesia allows a foreign bank to establish or acquire a locally incorporated bank in cooperation with Indonesian nationals/entities. In Malaysia, the commercial presence of a foreign bank is subject to the local incorporation of a joint venture with foreign ownership capped at 30 per cent. In Vietnam, a foreign bank may enter the Vietnamese market by opening a representative office, branch or joint venture bank with foreign ownership accounting for no more than 50 per cent. All of these restrictions constitute a form of protectionism, creating trade barriers for foreign banks wishing to enter the market. Accordingly, Chinese banks may be unable to obtain complete control over domestic banks in ASEAN countries, which may be undesirable for accounting or other reasons. Further, owing to the aforementioned protectionism rife in ASEAN, the chances of a Chinese bank acquiring

---

[73] For example, see Sections 15–18 of the Singapore Banking Act (Cap 19) and Section 28 of the Singapore Insurance Act (Cap 142).

a large local bank are likely very slim. Even the transfer of ownership from one owner to another within an ASEAN country may be blocked for political reasons. For instance, in 2012 after a five-year bid process, Temasek Holdings, Singapore's well-known sovereign wealth fund, announced its intention to sell its stake in Bank Danamon, the sixth largest bank in Indonesia, to DBS, a bank of which Temasek owns about 30 per cent of shares. However, the deal collapsed after Indonesia changed the law to cap single ownership in a domestic bank at 40 per cent (from 99 per cent).[74] This example is illustrative of the political risks and obstacles that Chinese banks are likely to face in attempting to enter Southeast Asia through mergers and acquisitions amidst China's expansion in the South China Sea and growing political and economic ambitions.

2.4   New Challenges from Financial Innovation

The twenty-first century is presenting new challenges to incumbent financial service providers, most notably the fintech phenomenon, which combines computing technology, Big Data and the internet with financial services. Whilst the fintech market is still developing, it is worth exploring some of the related issues taking place in parallel with ASEAN financial integration. Here, we briefly consider two broad developments that may change the financial landscape during execution of the BRI and construction of the New Silk Road.

First, new fintech firms can offer financial services to those who may have difficulty acquiring financing or insurance from traditional banks or insurers. For example, peer-to-peer (P2P) lenders may help to match SMEs with individuals who have extra cash to lend in exchange for higher interest income than that offered by banks. Europe has also seen the launch of P2P insurance (e.g. Friendsurance). These innovations may help to bridge the gap left by traditional domestic or foreign financial service providers. With computing power, Big Data and the availability of smartphones increasing even in emerging markets, it is only a matter of time before the fintech movement affects Southeast Asia in a big way. As Chinese firms are active and innovative players in that movement,

---

[74] Denny Thomas and Saeed Azhar, 'Temasek's Danamon suitors may now be Japanese, Chinese', *Reuters*, 1 August 2013, accessed 8 June 2018 at www.reuters.com/article/us-temasek-danamon-idUSBRE9700KT20130801.

they stand to benefit. For example, China is home to some of the world's largest P2P payment services (e.g. Alipay) and associated financial services (e.g. Alibaba's online investment account, *Yu E Bao*). Such services may help less developed countries such as Laos or Myanmar, and financial innovation may one day help foreign firms to bypass some of the red tape and trade barriers in place in ASEAN.

However, fintech firms face a number of legal risks, with some flourishing on the borderline of financial regulations. For example, P2P lenders can generally work around banking regulations if they offer a platform that matches lenders and borrowers but do not accept any deposits themselves. However, if a significant case of fraud or large-scale default were to occur, the regulators might be inclined to move towards greater regulation of such lending. In addition, managing the regulations of the ten ASEAN countries without a more uniform financial regulatory structure, such as that in the EU, is likely to be fraught with difficulty, as each member state may interpret the terms 'bank' and 'banking business' differently. This situation creates legal risks for Chinese fintech firms looking to benefit from the BRI by providing financial services to Southeast Asian states.

Second, the cross-border nature of financial technology and the internet will certainly challenge the current legal and regulatory framework for cross-border financial services in the future. For example, if a Chinese P2P platform attracts users from Southeast Asian countries who then take the initiative to acquire financing from Chinese lenders via the platform, does that constitute the cross-border supply of lending services? Although the answer is open to debate, the risks are likely to be high for a Chinese P2P operator actively seeking users in an ASEAN state even without answering the question of whether such operation amounts to lending. Unfortunately, these types of legal questions cannot be resolved by a single legal opinion, but they certainly demand the attention of both financial regulators and policymakers in the region in the near future.

2.5   Potential Impact on China's Role in International Governance and the Rule of Law

How are BRI projects and ASEAN financial integration likely to affect China's standing with respect to international governance and the rule of law in the long term? Whilst the answer depends on many factors,

ranging from the success of BRI implementation to political and economic conditions in China and surrounding countries, this chapter
argues for a potentially positive impact in the financial regulatory sphere
at both the micro and macro levels.

First, at the micro level, the presence of Chinese banks and financial
service providers supporting BRI projects in foreign territory will require
those banks/service providers to behave in a manner acceptable to the
host country. Such behaviour is often a condition of market access. For
banks, there are at least international standards to follow, such as the
Basel Accord on bank capital adequacy. However, financial service providers will have to accommodate relevant local regulations and licensing
standards if they want to expand their business beyond China's borders,
particularly when conducting business for which there are no established
global norms. Accordingly, Chinese financial service providers must find
commonly acceptable standards to conduct business, not only to satisfy
Chinese regulations (if any) but also those of host countries, much like
multinational banks and corporations are currently forced to do. Further
ASEAN financial integration down the road, if implemented successfully,
may also give ASEAN countries more clout in imposing regulations on
both domestic and foreign financial firms, whether they be well-established
financial institutions or new fintech firms. This has certainly been the case
in the EU. Such a scenario could well create a race-to-the-top momentum
that drives Chinese firms to raise their business practices and standards
in a uniform manner, which could in turn improve the rule of law in
China, premised of course on the ASEAN standards being more stringent
than their Chinese counterparts.

Second, at the macro level, Chinese-origin projects and China's mighty
political and economic power could create new international governance
norms. It is perhaps too early to claim that China will be able to call
the shots and lay down the international order as the United States did
after World War II. Also, with regard to trade issues, negotiations and
trade agreements between China and ASEAN will determine the mutual
flow of financial services and related products. However, with respect
to purely financial regulatory issues, and in the context of China's rise
as a superpower and its willingness to force the Chinese will through
the BRI, it is possible that the country may attempt to impose a new
international financial regulatory order based on its own needs. As Gao
and Chen argue, economic and market power are often driving forces
behind the migration of norms and rules in the financial regulatory

sphere.[75] Given China's immense economic and political power, it is not wholly impossible that the country will become the source of a new financial regulatory order in the future, superseding the role of the United States, United Kingdom and Europe.

International financial norms have traditionally been created by the Western powers and implemented via the so-called 'soft law' approach through a network of international organisations (i.e. such 'transnational regulatory networks'[76] as the Bank of International Settlement and Financial Stability Board) whose membership comprises the national regulators of major markets.[77] China and several ASEAN countries are also part of this international system.[78] From this perspective, there seems no need for China to impose its will and create a separate set of rules. Considering the current state of the ASEAN financial market, Southeast Asia is also far from being in any position to serve as a rule-maker. However, the question of whether uniform rules are an absolute good (or bad) remains subject to debate. Having uniform rules that apply everywhere provides a simple benchmark for market participants and regulators worldwide to make comparisons amongst banks and financial institutions, and may also help to connect different markets for various purposes (e.g. clearing and trading) and reduce the costs of market participants. However, such a one-size-fits-all approach set by the developed world may hinder competition, particularly for developing markets such as China and many ASEAN countries. With the rise of the fintech movement and growing power of Chinese e-commerce firms, there may be room for the development of separate regulatory standards or rules that deal with issues unaddressed by existing soft law standards. China's BRI may provide a platform for the development of bilateral or multilateral regulatory standards that facilitate the cross-border provision of financial

---

[75] See Simon Gao and Christopher Chen, 'Transnationalism and financial regulation change: a case of derivative markets' (2017) 18(1) *European Business Organization Law Review* 193–223.

[76] Stavros Gadinis, 'Three pathways to global standards: private, regulator, and ministry networks' (2015) 109(1) *American Journal of International Law* 1–57 at 1.

[77] See, generally, Chris Brummer, *Soft Law and the Global Financial System: Rule Making in the 21st Century* (Cambridge: Cambridge University Press, 2012).

[78] For example, China, Singapore and Indonesia are all members of the Financial Stability Board, although many other ASEAN countries, unlike the EU, do not have direct membership of this or other international organisations.

services by Chinese firms to other countries (or entry to China for non-Chinese firms). It could well be in ASEAN's interests to have regulatory standards in common with China or other neighbouring countries, not only to benefit from China's advanced e-commerce services but also to help local firms in Southeast Asia to take advantage of China's huge market and to ride the BRI development wave.

3 Conclusion

In conclusion, this chapter considers two geopolitical movements that are occurring simultaneously. China is seeking to build a New Silk Road under the auspices of the BRI, constructing both a land-based Silk Road through Central Asia and a maritime Silk Road traversing Southeast Asia and the Indian Ocean. At the same time, the countries of Southeast Asia have committed themselves to closer economic and financial integration in the coming decades. Although ASEAN does not function like the EU, it is expected to increase integration, albeit slowly, in the banking and insurance sectors following the announcement of ABIF and several bilateral agreements amongst ASEAN states, as well as the pending AIIF.

It is argued herein that Chinese banks and insurers may wish to offer essential financial services to advance the BRI concept. However, at present they will still face a great deal of red tape in seeking to provide lending or insurance services within the ASEAN region. As foreign firms, Chinese banks or insurers must generally comply with local licensing requirements to supply cross-border lending or insurance to or have a commercial presence in an ASEAN country. Several ASEAN member states also impose ceilings on the foreign ownership of domestic banks and insurers.

Even ABIF's passage has not necessarily made market entry easier for Chinese banks. Although there is a lack of transparency regarding the content of both that framework and bilateral agreements, QAB status is expected to apply primarily to banks incorporated in and owned by an ASEAN state. In other words, a certain degree of local protectionism is still permitted under the terms of ABIF. Therefore, the hands of Chinese banks and insurers remained tied in terms of cross-border lending and insurance service provision. However, the rise of the fintech movement and continued advancement of China's tech-savvy internet giants are likely to raise new issues for ASEAN politicians and regulators, particularly with respect to cross-border services. As ASEAN slowly moves towards further integration, the role of fintech firms is worth monitoring.

In the long run, the successful implementation of the BRI may afford China an opportunity to set international regulatory rules in cooperation with its partners in surrounding countries, including the ASEAN nations, and the globalisation of Chinese financial firms may help to raise the standard of business practices in China, thereby indirectly enhancing the rule of law.

8

A Prognostic View of the Applicable Law
for AIIB Loan Agreements

YUE PENG

The loans issued by multilateral development financial institutions (MDFIs) can be divided into two categories: loans to sovereign parties and loans to non-sovereign parties. MDFIs generally adopt international law as the applicable law in international arbitration concerning the former. However, the applicable law for loan agreements with non-sovereign parties may be either domestic law or international law. The primary focus of the newly established Asian Infrastructure Investment Bank (AIIB) is the provision of funding for infrastructure development in Asia. To facilitate coexistence and cooperation with other MDFIs, the AIIB needs to follow the traditional models established by the World Bank, International Finance Corporation (IFC) and Asian Development Bank (ADB), and adopt applicable laws in accordance with the nature of the loan agreement.

As an MDFI dominated by mainland China, the AIIB has been in the international spotlight since its inception at the end of 2015. Prior to its establishment, the International Bank for Reconstruction and Development (World Bank) and a number of regional development financial institutions, such as the Inter-American Development Bank (IDB), African Development Bank (ADB) and European Bank for Reconstruction and Development (EBRD), had been operating successfully for many years. Although MDFIs differ with respect to corporate purpose, business scope, managerial structure, codes of conduct and dispute settlement mechanisms, there are many similarities amongst them. By interacting closely with the International Monetary Fund (IMF) and other participants in the international capital market, MDFIs, as represented by the World Bank, constitute the fulcrum of the international financial system. Still in its start-up phase, the AIIB would do well to learn from the successful experience of its predecessors, and take appropriate actions in accordance with its institutional purpose: to strengthen infrastructural connectivity in Asia by providing large-scale capital for development purposes, particularly the construction of infrastructure and other productive sectors.[1] Accordingly, one of the AIIB's main business lines is issuing mid- to long-term loans to infrastructure projects in Asia. In the commercial world, the longer a project takes, the more numerous the risks involved. To avoid, or at least mitigate, potential legal risks, it is wise for lenders to choose a favourable applicable law in advance of future disputes. Hence, when signing international loan agreements with potential borrowers in Asia, the AIIB should carefully choose the proper laws applicable to those agreements. Otherwise, it may expose itself to legal risks arising from unexpected legal systems becoming involved in subsequent international disputes.

As noted, depending on the international legal status of the potential borrowers, loans issued by MDFIs can be divided into two categories: loans to sovereign parties and loans to non-sovereign parties. The former are loans provided to or guaranteed by a government, whilst the latter are loans provided to non-sovereign parties in the private sector or to public sector entities without government guarantees. When the loan agreement in question is with a sovereign party, MDFIs generally choose international law as the applicable law for international arbitration. However, where loan agreements with non-sovereign parties are concerned, either domestic law or international law may apply. The question is whether the AIIB, as the newcomer in town, should follow the traditional applicable law practices adopted by existing MDFIs to govern loan agreements, or whether it should develop a new legal model. The answer not only concerns the results of dispute settlement, but also affects the development of the international financial system.

The remainder of this chapter is organised as follows. Section 1 discusses the laws applicable to loan agreements between sovereign parties and traditional MDFIs. Section 2 focuses on how traditional MDFIs choose the proper law governing loans to non-sovereign parties. Section 3 then analyses the implications of traditional MDFI practices for the applicable law choices of the AIIB, and Section 4 concludes with a summary.

---

[1] See Art. 2(i) of the Articles of Agreement of the Asian Infrastructure Investment Bank (AIIB), which were opened for signature on 29 June 2015. Fifty-seven countries participated in negotiations over the Articles, with the final text adopted at the 5th Chief Negotiators' Meeting held in Singapore on 22 May 2015. Representatives from the fifty-seven prospective founding members gathered in Beijing on 29 June 2015 for an official signing ceremony, with fifty of those members ultimately signing the Articles.

1 Applicable Law for Loan Agreements with Sovereign Parties

1.1 Classification and Issues

Depending on the international legal status of the borrower, international loans can be classified as loans to sovereign parties with an international legal personality or loans to non-sovereign parties without an international legal personality. A sovereign party in this context refers to a sovereign state acting as a borrower (or guarantor). There are thus two types of loan agreements with sovereign parties: those signed between a non-subject of international law as lender and a borrower government and those signed between a subject of international law as lender and a borrower government. One view with respect to the former is that there is essentially no difference in content between this kind of agreement and agreements signed by two subjects of international law. Therefore, international law rather than domestic law should be applied to adjust the relationship in order to protect the interests of private creditors.[2] The tricky part of this view is that the generally accepted principle of *pacta sunt servanda* in international law can effectively prevent a sovereign borrower from unilaterally changing or terminating the terms of a loan agreement through domestic legislation, administrative measures or judicial decisions. However, seeking help from international law to protect private business interests is likely to encroach on a country's sovereignty. It may restrict the borrower's sovereign power to regulate the domestic economy or the right of the lender's home country to exercise diplomatic protection. In practice, unless otherwise agreed in the loan terms, international dispute settlement bodies and domestic courts will still classify such loans to sovereign countries as ordinary international commercial loans and presume that the loan agreements are thus subject to domestic laws.

In the context of international disputes, the dicta in the Serbian Loans Case and Brazilian Loans Case shed some light on the issue of applicable law in international loans between a non-subject of international law as lender and government as borrower. In these two cases, the governments of Serbia and Brazil issued bonds in France and other countries, respectively, and declared that the debts would be repaid in gold francs. However, they did not make clear which law would apply in the case of any related disputes. When the two governments subsequently failed to keep

---

[2] See M. Schmitthoff, 'The international government loan' (1937) 19 *Journal of Comparative Legislation and International Law* 179–96 at 183.

their promise to pay in gold francs, the French government exercised its diplomatic protection rights for French creditors. The negotiation between the government of France and those of Serbia and Brazil proved to be tedious and ultimately fruitless. The French government then resorted to the Permanent Court of International Justice (PCIJ). The two debtor governments claimed that French law should be applicable. However, according to French law, the *gold proviso clause* was unenforceable, and therefore the debtors could settle their debts with undervalued francs regardless of that clause. The PCIJ ruled that because there were no explicit terms concerning applicable law in the agreements, it should be presumed that the sovereign countries involved had intended to enter into a contract based on their own national laws. Because only one of the contracting parities in each case was a government, the court decided that Serbian law and Brazilian law were the applicable laws, and hence that both governments were bound by the gold proviso clause in repaying the bonds.[3]

According to the theory of dualism, international law and domestic law belong to different legal systems, each with its own legal sources, legal authorities and legal proceedings. The parallel operation of and interaction between the international legal system and a domestic legal system constitute a complex landscape of legal networks. Sometimes the rules of domestic law can be 'uploaded' to the international legal system, and sometimes the rules of international law can be 'downloaded' to a domestic legal system, and the interactions between the international and domestic systems help to establish the always-evolving legal ecology.[4] However, the rules or theories of international law cannot always be absorbed by a domestic legal system. For example, the aforementioned PCIJ decision has been rejected by some domestic courts in the context of domestic disputes. In a 1937 case, for example, the House of Lords in the UK found that the gold clause in dollar bonds issued in New York by the British government was unenforceable because legislation passed by the US Congress provided that such debt can be paid only in dollars according to its nominal amount.[5] Despite the conflict between this verdict by a British court and the PCIJ, there is some common ground:

---

[3] Serbian and Brazilian Loans Cases, PCIJ, Ser. A, Nos. 21 and 22 (1929).

[4] See Harold Honju Koh, 'Is there a "new" New Haven School of international law?' (2007) 32 *Yale Journal of International Law* 559–73 at 567.

[5] See *R. v. International Trustee for the Protection of Bondholders Aktiengesellschaft* [1937] AC 500.

if a loan is made to a sovereign party, and the lender is not a subject of international law and the contracting parties fail to specify the applicable law explicitly, then any dispute should be resolved by domestic rather than international law.

Loan agreements signed between two subjects of international law, in contrast, have long been recognised as contractual treaties in the international legal system. In such a case, one party cannot refuse to perform its international obligations under the veil of domestic mandatory rules, and, accordingly, it is unnecessary to state the applicable law explicitly in the loan agreement.[6] However, if the contracting party is not a government, but rather an independent public institution belonging to a government, the legal nature of that institution may affect the legal features of the agreement, and the applicable law will thus be determined on a case-by-case basis. Taking the framework agreement signed by the Ministry of Finance (MoF) of the People's Republic of China and the Export-Import Bank of the United States as an example,[7] Article 2 (Guarantee and Its Nature) stipulates that China's MoF will issue a guarantee for each export business covered by the agreement, and in the case of default under the credit articles therein, the Export-Import Bank can demand reimbursement from it. Article 4 (Statement and Assurance) states: 'The Export-Import Bank is an independent agency of the U.S. government and has the full power, authority and legal rights to sign and submit this framework agreement and to perform the obligations.' Although Article 7 of the framework agreement is entitled 'Applicable Law and Jurisdiction', it provides only that disputes should be resolved by means of an arbitration procedure:

> [Three] arbitrators appointed in accordance with the Arbitration Rules of the International Chamber of Commerce should bring in a final verdict according to the Arbitration Rules on any claim, divergent idea or dispute with the Framework Agreement or any relevant finance guarantee presented by the Export-Import Bank. The Arbitration shall be conducted in London. The working language of arbitration should be English and all the documents and testimony presented as evidence in the process of

---

[6] See Davidson Sommers, A. Broches and Georges R. Delaum, 'Conflict avoidance in international loans and monetary agreements' (1956) 21 *Law and Contemporary Problems* 463–82 at 481.

[7] No. 121 (2005) of the Ministry of Finance, 28 November 2005, accessed 21 June 2018 at www.fdi.gov.cn/1800000121_23_64419_0_7.html.

> arbitration should be translated into English. The chief arbitrator shall not
> be a citizen of the United States or China... [A d]ecision made by the
> arbitrators will be ... final and is binding upon both parties.

Due to the failure to specify the applicable law, legal disputes can be resolved in two ways: (i) if the Export-Import Bank is identified as an agency of the US government and does business for the benefit of the United States, the guarantee agreement between the bank and China's MoF should apply international law; (ii) otherwise, that is, if the bank is considered an independent agency doing business on its own account, the relevant guarantee agreement is likely to apply domestic law, creating uncertainty with respect to related legal disputes. From the perspective of the Chinese government, the latter is better than the former for the simple reason that the Chinese government can change domestic law to avoid its legal obligations if necessary.

1.2   Applicable Law Practice Concerning Traditional Loan
Agreements between Sovereign Parties and MDFIs

Different from the AIIB, traditional MDFIs are, in the main, dominated and managed by developed countries. In Asia, the World Bank and ADB are the predominant international financial institutions issuing loans to sovereign parties.

According to Article 3 of the Agreement of the International Bank for Reconstruction and Development (1944), with respect to loans to sovereign parties if the borrower is a member state, the World Bank should sign the loan agreement with the government of that state, whereas if the direct borrower is a state-owned enterprise, it should sign the guarantee agreement with the relevant government of the member state. In its early years of operation, the World Bank applied the then valid laws of New York State in interpreting the terms of loan agreements concluded with sovereign parties. However, the application of US law implied American hegemony owing to the dominant position of the United States globally, and such a practice was soon terminated. Thereafter, the World Bank enacted the General Conditions for Loans, which clearly exclude the application of domestic law, and proposed that relevant disputes be resolved through international arbitration. Under these arrangements, the World Bank incorporates loan agreements with sovereign parties into the international legal system, the legal system of the World Bank in particular, entirely excluding the influence of domestic law. As an important legal document of the World Bank, the General Conditions have changed several times in form and content, but the content concerning applicable law has remained essentially the same.

For instance, Article 8(01) of the 2017 General Conditions follows the content of the previous version,[8] that is, '[t]he rights and obligations of the Bank and the Loan Parties under the Legal Agreements shall be valid and enforceable in accordance with their terms notwithstanding the law of any state or political subdivision thereof to the contrary'. This article is certainly not a typical governing law provision, as it does not explicitly designate any particular legal system as the applicable law in potential disputes. However, Article 8(01) conveys one important message clearly: the parties involved shall not question the validity and enforceability of the loan agreement by reference to domestic law. It should be noted that this article excludes the application of domestic law without mentioning the role of international law. The mainstream view in academia is that the exclusion of domestic law means the application of international law in the terms of loans to sovereign parties.[9]

The World Bank's stipulation that loan agreements with sovereign parties be governed by international law has been wholly accepted by the ADB. For instance, both Article 11(01) of the ADB's current Ordinary Operations Loan Regulations and Article 10(01) of its Special Operations Loan Regulations[10] contain similar expressions to the provisions in the World Bank General Conditions. In addition, the former ADB document stipulates only that loan agreement disputes shall be settled through international arbitration without specifying any applicable law. The argument has been made that because the parties to the agreement are both subjects of international law, international law is the only choice, and it is thus unnecessary to specify the applicable law for loan agreements concluded between sovereign parties and the ADB.[11]

---

[8] The latest edition of the General Conditions of World Bank Loans was published on 14 July 2017, accessed 22 June 2018 at www.worldbank.org/en/topic/lawjusticeanddevel opment/publication/general-conditions.

[9] See Sommers et al., 'Conflict avoidance', 476.

[10] See ADB, *Ordinary Operations Loan Regulations*, accessed 15 June 2018 at www.adb.org/ sites/default/files/institutional-document/220606/ocr-loan-regulations-20170101.pdf; ADB, *Special Operations Loan Regulations*, accessed 15 June 2018 at www.adb.org/sites/default/ files/institutional-document/32555/files/special-operations.pdf.

[11] See Chun Pyo Jhong, 'The law applicable to the ADB and its transactions and techniques of settling disputes' (1966) 1 *Philippine Year Book of International Law* 183–96 at 185.

2 Applicable Law for Loan Agreements with Non-Sovereign Parties

2.1 Classification and Issues

In international legal relationships between lenders and borrowers, there are two types of loan agreements with non-sovereign parties, i.e. borrowers that are non-subjects of international law: those between two non-subjects of international law and those between a non-subject and a subject of international law. When legal disputes arise concerning either type, the two parties in question are, in theory, free to choose the applicable law from three options: (i) the domestic law of the country that is the host state or place of business of one party; (ii) the law that is generally applicable to similar loan contracts in accordance with customary business practices; or (iii) the law of a neutral third country. If both parties rely on the infrastructure or mechanisms of a particular capital market to conclude and perform in accordance with financial contracts, the local law of that market is generally applicable to the relevant loan agreement. For many years, financing in international capital markets was primarily bid in US dollars, a typical market being the Eurodollar market. Eurodollars initially referred to US dollar holdings in European commercial banks outside US territory. The existence and ongoing development of the Eurodollar market has been heavily dependent on world demand for US dollars. In the 1950s, many commercial banks had large dollar holdings. In the 1960s, Eurodollar markets were booming, and, in the 1970s, they diversified. In parallel with the fast growth of Eurodollar markets, various forms of borrowing in Eurodollars emerged, including standby arrangements, circulating credit and loans made through a bank consortium. Furthermore, numerous capital demanders with special identities (sovereign states and various government agencies) have swarmed into the Eurodollar markets. Early on, it was generally assumed that sovereign states and their public sectors would never breach their promises, an assumption that later proved very mistaken indeed. In any case, a large amount of international money flowed into public sectors worldwide. To increase the circulation of mid- and long-term Eurodollar loans and recycle capital as quickly as possible, the main international commercial banks gradually harmonised and unified the terms and standards in international loan agreements. In addition, secondary markets for the transaction of international loans have come into being in several international financial centres.

International commercial banks have employed two notable strategies during the concomitant processes of the localisation of international capital transactions and globalisation of the local laws of financial centres. First, most international commercial banks set a floating interest rate in accordance with the London Interbank Offered Rate (more commonly known as LIBOR), which ensures that various types of international loan agreements have a common measure of value and enhances transferability and negotiability. Second, after an international loan agreement is signed, regardless of whether the borrower draws money, the original lenders and participants in a bank consortium may transfer or distribute related loans to other financial institutions in the global capital market. As financial rights embedded in a concrete legal system, the financial rights in a central capital market are protected in a time of financial crisis at the cost of financial asset devaluation and chaos in peripheral capital markets,[12] and international loans focusing on liquidity and security are more inclined to apply the domestic law in which the international financial centre is located. As world capital is highly aggregated in a few capital markets and managed by a cluster of international commercial banks, the laws of those markets follow the circulation of capital and funds to ultimately become transnational law governing international financial transactions. In this way, the sovereign states that host international capital markets are able to 'export' their finance laws, whether private or public, to other countries, prompting those countries to sometimes complain that their sovereignty rights are being violated. However, this kind of jurisdiction is not the traditional jurisdiction of territory or community, which refers to a country's prerogative rights and power to control what happens in its territory or the conduct of its inhabitants, but rather the jurisdiction of governance. The governance dimension of jurisdiction tackles the regulative and ordering function of law.[13] Faced with the advent of a globalising economy, sovereign states and international organisations have had to adopt measures to regulate the negative impacts of economic globalisation. Every country has governance jurisdiction to deal with financial transactions, but only countries with international capital markets have the ability to influence the rest of the world by exporting their capital market regulatory laws.

Different from the financing patterns in capital markets, project financing is generally negotiated directly between borrowers and lenders.

---

[12] See Katharina Pistor, 'A legal theory of finance' (2013) 41 *Journal of Comparative Economics* 315–30 at 319.

[13] See Asha Kaushal, 'The politics of jurisdiction' (2105) 78 *Modern Law Review* 759–92 at 775.

Theoretically, the lenders that are party to project financing loan agreements can strengthen the liquidity of those agreements through the secondary market. However, because the agreements are associated with particular projects, it is difficult to standardise them without utilising the intricate process of securitisation. Therefore, when signing a project financing agreement, a lender will often take advantage of its superior position in the negotiation to impose the applicable law most favourable to itself. Of course, certain attached agreements, such as real estate guarantee agreements, may have to apply the domestic law of the property location. This exception is based primarily on implementation considerations.

As the amount of financing needed for projects of international scope is often too large to be satisfied by a single bank, a bank consortium may be formed to supply the necessary capital. In this situation, the law applicable to the project financing agreement will affect the rights and obligations of all participating banks. In addition, participating banks sometimes distribute their loans to non-participating banks. In that case, the newly involved banks cannot cherry-pick the applicable laws in the original agreements, as doing so would disturb the balance struck amongst the original bank signatories or affect the rights enjoyed by the original lenders and borrowers. Owing to business tradition and the US dollar's seemingly unshakeable internationally dominant position, the commercial banks that provide these types of loans are usually located in international financial centres in the United Kingdom or United States, namely, London and New York City. Accordingly, the available applicable laws for loan agreements are British law and New York State law. Even when sponsoring banks are not located in common law countries, in order to attract more banks to participate in project financing and to facilitate the marketing of the loans, those banks may prefer the law of the two financial centres as the applicable law.

Furthermore, it is widely accepted in the world of international finance that the adoption of the local laws of international financial centres helps to alleviate the endogenous uncertainty in loan agreements. Loan agreements are notorious for their minute details, but it is unrealistic to foresee and stipulate every possible situation that may arise within the four corners of a complex business contract. If disputes arise over the content or meaning of loan agreements, a particular methodological approach needs to be employed to clarify the uncertainties or fill the gaps therein. If the parties to a loan agreement fail to designate the local law of a particular financial centre, the arbitrators or judges will have to find other rules to resolve the dispute. Theoretically, when faced with incomplete contracts, adjudicators may employ a highly formalistic method called 'plain meaning' rules to solve the legal puzzles involved. Under such interpretive methodology, the adjudicators will read a contract term's meaning on its face. Adjudicators also sometimes adopt a method called the 'incorporation strategy', which incorporates context and commercial custom in filling gaps and defining terms.[14] Depending on the legal system, adjudicators may afford priority to one or the other of these interpretive methodologies. When the applicable law does not allow adjudicators to incorporate commercial customs into the contract and fill contract gaps, use of the adjudicators' discretion may wreak havoc with the dispute results. When the applicable law allows adjudicators to employ the incorporation strategy, the parties to the loan agreement will be unable to ascertain the kind of customs that will be incorporated into the contract because every capital market has its own commercial customs. However, if the contract parties select the local law of an international financial centre, use of the incorporation strategy may effectively reduce the legal uncertainties because the commercial customs in the international capital market are widely recognised worldwide and strongly endorsed by market participants. As most capital transactions currently take place in international financial centres, the local laws that prevail in those centres have evolved into the merchant law of the modern age.

2.2 Applicable Law Practice Concerning Traditional Loan Agreements between Non-Sovereign Parties and MDFIs

Worldwide, two models of applicable laws governing international loans to non-sovereign parties are adopted by traditional international financial institutions: the domestic law model represented by the ADB and IFC, a member of the World Bank Group, and the international law model represented by the EBRD. The World Bank and IFC are in charge of the World Bank Group's loan business to sovereign and non-sovereign parties, respectively. As noted above, World Bank loan agreements with sovereign parties are governed by international law because such agreements are signed by two subjects of international law. Logically then,

---

[14] See, e.g. Lisa Bernstein, 'Merchant law in a merchant court: rethinking the code's search for immanent business norms' (1996) 144 *University of Pennsylvania Law Review* 1765–821 at 1777.

a loan agreement signed between the IFC and a non-subject of international law such as a private enterprise should not be subject to international law, in which case a non-sovereign borrower might allege that certain requirements in the agreement, e.g. a duty to follow certain procedures for the procurement of goods or refrain from applying loan proceeds to the payment of taxes on goods imported into the country, are avoidable or unenforceable because of their inconsistency with local law. In practice, the IFC is usually able to utilise its advantageous negotiating position to choose New York State law as the applicable law. Similar to IFC loans, ADB loans to non-sovereign parties also face a dilemma in the choice and application of law. It is widely recognised that the application of Philippines law is not appropriate, even though the ADB is headquartered in Manila, and instead it is more reasonable to determine the arbitration law in each case according to the most significant relationship principle.[15]

The law applicable to the loan agreements signed by the World Bank, IFC and ABD traditionally features legal formalism: once the legal subject status of the agreement is determined, the applicable law is set down accordingly. In practice, however, the logic of such formalism sometimes proves ridiculous. For example, in the process of international arbitration, given that a party can now choose the law of a third country in accordance with the principle of party autonomy, there is no reason to deny parties the choice of international law as the governing law. Further, if international law is applicable, that does not mean that non-sovereign parties with no international legal personality are thereby converted into subjects of international law with an international legal personality, and nor can loan agreements with non-sovereign parties be converted into loan agreements with sovereign parties. However, if we consider the purpose of the World Bank, IFC and ADB, the rigidity of legal formalism has some merit, as it means these organisations can successfully commit themselves to not interfering with the internal affairs of member countries. When these MDFIs provide funding to promote economic development, they can remain free from external interference.

However, with the establishment of the EBRD, the longstanding tradition of MDFIs remaining estranged from politics was dramatically breached. Different from the aims of the World Bank, IFC and ADB,

---

[15] See Jhong, 'The law applicable to the AIIB', 93.

that of the ERBD is to promote the domestic political democratisation and economic marketisation and privatisation of Central and Eastern European countries:

> [T]hose Central and Eastern European countries with the commitment and application of multiparty democracy, pluralism and [a] market economy are encouraged to transit[ion] to an open market-oriented economy and [foster the] initiative spirits of individual[s] or enterprises[s] ... [and the EBRD] shall [therefore] assist and accept its member countries' implementation of structural and departmental economic reforms, including ... de-monopolization[,] de-centralization and privatization[,] in order to help these economic forms fully fit into the international economy.[16]

That aim necessitates the EBRD's interference in individual countries' political and economic development. The bank itself has taken on tremendous legal risks in issuing privatised loans to state-owned enterprises in countries that are in the process of political and economic transition, and it is therefore preferable for it to exclude the application of domestic law. From the perspective of the borrower and the borrower's country, compliance with an EBRD loan agreement can help to withstand the pressure of domestic opposition to reform and ensure the smooth course of privatisation. Accordingly, the EBRD does not strictly distinguish between loans to sovereign parties, i.e. member states, and loans to non-sovereign parties such as state-owned enterprises, applying international law in both cases. Different from the World Bank and ADB's practice of excluding the application of domestic law, however, the EBRD clearly lists the sources of international law. According to Clause 8(04) (b) (vi) of its Standards and Conditions for Loans, the sources of international law applicable for the purpose of arbitration by an arbitration tribunal include:

(A) the Agreement Establishing the bank and any relevant treaty obligations that are binding reciprocally on the parties;

(B) the provisions of any international conventions and treaties (whether or not they are binding directly as such on the parties) generally recognised as having codified or ripened into binding rules of customary law applicable to states and international financial institutions, as appropriate;

---

[16] Article 2.1 of the Agreement of Establishing the European Bank for Reconstruction and Development (EBRD), accessed 27 June at https://indevsync.azurewebsites.net/world/agreements/downloadFile.do?fullText=yes&treatyTransId=1357.

(C) other forms of international customs, including the practice of states
     and international financial institutions, of such generality, consist-
     ency and duration as to create legal obligation; and
(D) applicable general legal principles.[17]

The above enumeration of sources of international law for arbitration
purposes under an EBRD loan agreement roughly parallels the enumeration of sources in Article 38(1) of the Statute of the International Court
of Justice, which provides that the International Court of Justice shall
apply treaties, custom and general principles in deciding disputes submitted by sovereign states. There are thought to be two major reasons for
the EBRD to have adopted public international law as the proper law for
loan agreements: (i) when the EBRD were established, the international
community shared the widespread belief that, based on the principle of
party autonomy, even if one or more of the parties to an agreement was
not a subject of international law, the parties could still choose international law as the proper law; and (ii) the body of international law
defined by the EBRD Loan Standards and Conditions is now sufficiently
substantial and extensive, including not only treaties, international customs
and general legal principles, but also MDFI practices. It is also believed that
the EBRD's practices represent the latest developmental trend of MDFIs,
which is helpful for preventing future disputes.[18]

Dissenters to this view argue that it is improper to discuss the applicable law without considering the EBRD's different purpose from that
of other MDFIs, and further that the specific practices of the EBRD does
not mean the birth of supranational law.[19] A more authoritative view
is that agreement parties' choice of international law as the applicable
law means only that those parties have agreed to resolve disputes by
taking advantage of the substantive rules of international law. However, a
non-subject of international law cannot be transformed into a subject of
international law by that choice.[20] According to this view, even though

---

[17] See EBRD, 'Standard terms and conditions', 1 December 2012, accessed 15 June 2018 at
   lex.justice.md/UserFiles/File/2016/mo128-133md/b.e_43_eg.doc.
[18] See John W. Head, 'Evolution of the governing law for loan agreements of the World
   Bank and other multilateral development banks' (1996) 90 *American Journal of International Law* 214–34 at 228–9.
[19] See Aron Broches, Correspondence (1997) 91 *American Journal of International Law*
   489–90.
[20] 'A choice by the parties of public international law is assumed by some writers to place
   the contract on the international plane, but this cannot be correct since a state contract
   is not a treaty and cannot involve state responsibility as an international obligation.'

the legal responsibility of the loan agreement parties can be determined with reference to the rules of international law, that responsibility cannot be deemed the responsibility of a state. Therefore, the application of international law to loan agreements involving non-sovereign parties can only incorporate the relevant substantive rules of international law; it cannot replace the domestic law system with the international system.

3   Problems of the Application of Law for AIIB Loan Agreements

3.1   Option of Applicable Law Model

A legal system constitutes an essential framework for modern economic life. Human beings with rights *in rem* or *in personam* acquire a lasting sense of security from legal protection, whilst those who are promised something obtain a sense of security from the performance of an agreement. This sense of security arising from the law helps to maintain confidence in the market, and in turn reduce the cost of market transactions. With respect to loan agreements, MDFIs have traditionally adopted two models to achieve a sense of security. The first model is that adopted by the World Bank, IFC and ADB: loans are classified into loans to sovereign parties and loans to non-sovereign parties, with the former applying international law, and the latter domestic law. The second is that adopted by the EBRD, under which all loan agreements apply international law. When the AIIB supplies capital for infrastructure construction, it also needs to determine the applicable law from the perspectives of obtaining a sense of legal security and maintaining market confidence.

First of all, when it comes to loan agreements with sovereign parties, it is no surprise that the AIIB would choose international law as the governing law, as doing so effectively protects its rights from the encroachment of domestic law. However, the AIIB still has to decide which of the aforementioned models is more suitable with respect to the application of international law. In other words, the question is whether the AIIB have to explicitly list the sources of international law enumerated in Article 38(1) of the Statute of the International Court of Justice.[21] This chapter contends that the answer to that question largely depends on the

---

From Iran Brownlie, *Principles of Public International Law*, 7th edn. (Oxford: Oxford University Press, 2008), p. 549.

[21] See legal.un.org/avl/pdf/ha/sicj/icj_statute_e.pdf (accessed 15 June 2018).

AIIB's purpose and functions. If its infrastructure construction loans are complementary to rather than competitive with the World Bank's and ADB's related business lines in Asia, then the AIIB need not choose an applicable law model different from those adopted by the World Bank and ADB. Based on systematic complementation principles, the smaller the changes that need to be made, the higher the degree of coordination amongst the World Bank, ADB and AIIB that would be achieved. In this way, the implicated legal effect of AIIB loans to sovereign parties can be easily understood and estimated by other international financial institutions. Therefore, if the World Bank and ADB do not mention the applicable substantial law for international arbitration, then neither should the AIIB.

Second, with respect to loans to non-sovereign parties, the AIIB faces the temptation to adopt the EBRD's international law model to avoid the potential encroachment of domestic law. As noted above, there is no generally accepted doctrine on the application of law. However, the lack of legal restriction on the choice of law does not mean that the AIIB can completely separate itself from tradition. The anti-fundamentalists admit that although anything can in principle be questioned, everything cannot be challenged at the same time. Borrowing from Neurath's metaphor, the AIIB's reshaping of the international financial order is analogous to sailors' reconstruction of a ship at sea: sailors cannot disassemble and assemble the entire ship using the best materials as they would when in dry dock, but instead have to replace the boards one by one while also taking care that the ship remains afloat and equipped with stable navigation capability.[22] Therefore, to prevent fundamentalism from turning into nihilism, we should recognise conventionalism's positive role in the construction and maintenance of society, admitting that practice-based consensus is a solid cornerstone of social progress. If the AIIB has no good reason to question the generally applicable law practices pertaining to loans to non-sovereign parties adopted by the IFC and ADB, then it would do better to follow those practices than to pave a new path for the sake of adventure.

Hence, with respect to the applicable law for the AIIB's loan agreements with non-sovereign parties, this chapter argues that it is more suitable for it to follow the domestic law model adopted by the IFC and ADB rather than the international law model adopted by the EBRD

---

[22] See Eduardo Rabossi, 'Some notes on Neurath's ship and Quine's sailors' (2003) 7 *Principia* 171–84 at 174.

based on the three following considerations. First, the AIIB's main business focus is infrastructure construction in Asia, meaning there is considerable overlap with the business of the IFC and ADB. If the AIIB adopts a legal application model different from those of the IFC and ADB, it is likely to cause conflicts between laws, which goes against the generally admitted principle of coexistence and cooperation amongst MDFIs and would also be unfavourable to the AIIB's further cooperation with those institutions. Second, although the AIIB is an emerging MDFI whose main purpose is to provide funding to infrastructure construction projects in Asia, its loan agreements are closer in nature to ordinary commercial loans than to the loans issued by the IFC and ADB. If the loan agreements of those two institutions are able to apply domestic law as the substantive law of arbitration, there is no reason for the AIIB to refuse to adopt domestic law as the governing law. Finally, the EBRD's adoption of international law as the proper law for its loan agreements is closely bound up with its distinct mission to facilitate political democratisation and economic marketisation. The AIIB issues loans on the basis of commercial interests with no intention of interfering with the internal affairs of the recipient. Therefore, it should avoid transforming the loan agreements of an international organisation into international treaties and leave reasonable room for member countries to regulate their economies.

3.2   Applicable Law for AIIB Loan Agreements with Non-Sovereign Parties

If the AIIB should apply domestic law to loan agreements with non-sovereign parties, then a further question is which domestic law is applicable. The AIIB is headquartered in Beijing, the capital of China. Theoretically then, the AIIB could choose Chinese law. However, Chinese law is not suitable for adoption as the proper law for loan agreements for two reasons. First, compared with the universally applicable common law in the international capital market, the internationalisation of Chinese law is immature. In terms of form, the most widely used commercial language internationally is English, and, accordingly, global legal services are dominated by British and American law firms. Given the high barriers to entry, the comparative advantage of common law legal services would be difficult to undermine in the short run. In terms of content, although the Chinese economy occupies an important position in the global market, Chinese law holds peripheral status within the world legal system. Law is a systematic social project, and the understanding, interpretation and construction of any provision cannot be separated from its institutional context. China's financial law is highly domestically orientated, and is unfamiliar to most AIIB members. Those members and their companies would thus find it difficult to understand and apply Chinese law in international financial disputes. Both the language barrier and the marginalised status of Chinese law mean that China's legal internationalisation is likely to lag behind its economic internationalisation in the long run. It may be easy for China to export its products, but difficult for it to export its laws.

Second, the AIIB should not depend too much on the domestic law of its headquarters country for three reasons. First, the AIIB is an MDFI invested in and established by multiple states, and its main purpose is to provide capital for infrastructure projects in Asia. That purpose suggests that the bank should pay more attention to the selection, construction and delivery of particular projects than to the issuing, supervision and recovery of related loans. According to the closest connection principle, the law of a headquarters country is not necessarily the proper law for loan agreements. Second, in theory, AIIB headquarters could be located in any country, and it would thus be illogical to choose the law of China, the country that happens to be its headquarters, as the applicable law for loan agreements in the absence of other reasonable considerations. Third, to meet market demand, the AIIB may establish branches in the territories of its member states. If the headquarters country's domestic law is favourable to a loan agreement issued by the AIIB, then there is no reason to reject the proposal that loan agreements processed through its branches apply the laws of the countries in which those branches are situated.

At the same time, whilst the local law of the headquarters country is not suitable for AIIB loan agreements to non-sovereign parties, neither is the local law of the country in which a given infrastructure project takes place. Infrastructure construction in Asia carries considerable legal risks arising from changes in law in the countries in which they are situated, dealing a potentially devastating blow to the validity and enforceability of loan agreements. When a loan agreement is signed with a sovereign party, the AIIB can minimise the risks posed by domestic law changes with reference to international law. When the signatory is a non-sovereign party, however, if the domestic law of the country in which the infrastructure project is located is applicable, then it is difficult to prevent that country from manipulating its law to declare contract clauses invalid, suspend the fulfilment of contractual obligations, implement foreign exchange control or take other means to mitigate a loss or impose restrictions on a borrower's rights.

Therefore, until Chinese law becomes a leading member of international business law, which seems unlikely in the foreseeable future, the AIIB would be well advised to adopt the laws of countries in which international financial centres are located to settle disputes with non-sovereign parties. Currently, most of the countries that are home to these centres allow international loan agreements to apply local laws, regardless of whether the formation and performance of those agreements are locally relevant. In the UK, for example, the European Union's 2008 Law Applicable to Contractual Obligations (Rome I) (formerly known as the 1980 Convention on the Law Applicable to Contractual Obligations (Rome Convention)) adopts the principle of party autonomy.[23] In the USA, Article 1–105 of the Uniform Commercial Code requires that the law chosen by the parties concerned should be in reasonable conformity with the contract. In New York State, however, Article 5–14–1 of the 1984 General Liability Law expressly abolishes that requirement.[24] On 3 December 2015, the UK became the first country outside Asia and the first G7 member to ratify the AIIB's Articles of Agreement. Now that the UK is an official member of the AIIB, there are no political or legal obstacles to choosing English law as the applicable law for the bank's loan agreements with non-sovereign parties.

4   Conclusion

When the AIIB was first established, the countries that dominated the World Bank, IFC and ADB, such as the United States and Japan, regarded it as a threat to the existing international financial order. Since the entry of Western European countries led by the UK, however, the AIIB's international influence has grown rapidly. On its official website, the bank defines itself as 'a multilateral development bank with a mission to

---

[23] Regulation (EC) No 593/2008 of the European Parliament and of the Council of 17 June 2008 on the law applicable to contractual obligations (Rome I), accessed 15 June 2018 at https://eur-lex.europa.eu/legal-content/EN/TEXT/PDF/?uri=CELEX:32008R0593&from=EN.

[24] See Committee on Foreign & Comparative Law of New York City Bar, Governing Law in Sovereign Debt – Lessons from the Greek Crisis and Argentina Dispute of 2012 (February 2013), pp. 5–6, accessed 15 June 2018 at www.nycbar.org/pdf/report/uploads/20072390-GoverningLawinSovereignDebt.pdf.

improve social and economic outcomes in Asia and beyond', further noting that its foundation is built on 'the lessons of experience of successful private sector companies and existing multilateral development banks'.[25] Article 1(1) of the AIIB Articles of Agreement states: 'The purpose of the Bank shall be to: (i) foster sustainable economic development, create wealth and improve infrastructure connectivity in Asia by investing in infrastructure and other productive sectors; and (ii) promote regional cooperation and partnership in addressing development challenges by working in close collaboration with other multilateral and bilateral development institutions.' This wording suggests that the AIIB has no intention of challenging or replacing the world-leading position held by the World Bank or of changing the international financial system, including the long-established legal model under which it operates.

If the AIIB wants to cooperate with other MDFIs in Asia or supplement the business lines of those institutions, it needs to ensure that the laws applicable to relevant loan agreements are roughly consistent. If the AIIB follows the EBRD's example and insists on applying international law in its loan agreements with non-sovereign parties, it is likely to create conflicts with the laws applied by the IFC or ADB. As the AIIB has no political or economic mission, unlike the EBRD, it would be unwise to deviate from traditional applicable law practices governing loan agreements with non-sovereign parties. Similarly, where loan agreements with sovereign parties are concerned, the AIIB should follow the World Bank and ADB practices of incorporating a negative pledge clause to guarantee creditors' rights. Otherwise, conflicts with other MDFIs will likely arise.

It is necessary to point out that adopting the legal practices of the World Bank, IFC and ADB does not mean that those practices are perfect and unassailable. For example, the World Bank's negative pledge clause in loan agreements with sovereign parties has been widely criticised for the reason that the capital provided by traditional MDFIs is usually inadequate to meet a borrower's needs in full, and such a clause inevitably undermines the borrower's ability to obtain further funding from third parties. If the AIIB introduces a negative pledge clause to loan agreements with sovereign parties without any restrictions, it is bound to strengthen the position of MDFIs with the help of international law, thereby preventing additional market money from flowing into Asian infrastructure projects. Therefore, if the AIIB decides to incorporate such

[25] See the AIIB website, www.aiib.org/html/aboutus/introduction/aiib/?show=0.

a clause, it should do so in conjunction with exceptions necessary to facilitate the raising of money from other capital suppliers. When the AIIB cooperates with other MDFIs such as the World Bank or ADB, it should consult with its partners in making appropriate amendments to the negative pledge clause to allow the capital needs of Asian countries to be met.

In conclusion, there are many ongoing disputes concerning the AIIB's impact on the international financial architecture. According to the analysis in this chapter, this new MDFI player can be understood within the current framework of international finance law. As the newcomer in town, and to facilitate cooperation with other MDFIs, the AIIB has no choice but to adopt traditional modes of business and follow widely recognised legal practices. Doing so will also ensure that the AIIB is a constructor rather than a destroyer of the international financial order.

9

The Role of Environmental Impact Assessment in the Governance of the Nu-Salween River

A Comparative Study of the Chinese and Myanmar Approaches

YONGMIN BIAN[*]

1 Introduction

The countries covered by China's Belt and Road Initiative (BRI) are mainly developing states. It is a widespread assumption in China that the environmental standards of developing countries are much lower than those of developed states.[1] The prejudicial view that developing countries would like to make more of an environmental trade-off for economic development is misleading. This chapter takes Myanmar as a case study and compares it with Chinese environmental protection in the field of environmental impact assessment (EIA) rules and practice for hydropower projects. The failure to fully address environmental impacts caused by foreign investments explains in some part the failure of some of those investment projects in Myanmar. When implementing the BRI, China should have clearer guidelines on green development along the Belt and Road.

The Nu-Salween river[2] flows from China to Myanmar and Thailand. A total of 42 per cent of its river basin is in China, 53 per cent in

---

[*] This research has received support from the Professional Development of Water Govern-ance and Regional Development Practitioners in the Salween Basin led by the Center for Social Development Studies, Chulalongkorn University, Thailand.
[1] Juling Zhao, 'Zhong Guo Shi Xing Fa Zhan Zhong Guo Jia Zhi Liang Biao Zhun Yu Mei Guo You Cha Ju' [China Adopts the Environmental Standards for Developing States: Lower than American Ones], News.Eastday.com, 12 March 2011, accessed 8 June 2018 at http://news.eastday.com/c/2011lh/u1a5779317.html.
[2] The Myanmar name of this river is Thanlwin. Here we refer to the Chinese portion of the river as the Nu, and the Burmese/Thai portion as the Salween.

Myanmar and the other 5 per cent is in Thailand[3]. More than ten million people, representing at least thirteen different ethnic groups, depend on the Salween river basin for their livelihoods.[4] The mountains and valleys of the watershed are home to some of the most biologically and culturally diverse areas in the world.[5] As it flows down from the Tibet plateau, the river drops some 5,000 metres, much of that in steep gorges, making the Nu-Salween extremely attractive to hydropower developers.[6]

Both China and Myanmar have decided to develop hydropower projects on their shared Nu-Salween river. The early plan for the exploration of the Nu was to build thirteen cascades of dams.[7] After this plan was suspended by the former Chinese Premier Wen Jiabao,[8] the government made a second plan composed of five cascades of dams on the Nu in China's 12th Five-Year Plan.[9] But this second plan did not proceed.[10] The newly released 13th Five-Year Plan did not mention the development of the hydro-resources of the Nu river,[11] meaning the dam-building

---

[3] Jia Jianwei, Jiang Ming and Lu Sunyun, 'Zhong Mian Jing Nei Nu Jiang-Sa Er Wen Jiang Shui Wen Te Zheng Dui Bi Fen Xi' [Analysis of the Hydrological Features of Nu-Salween River in China and Myanmar] (2014) 45(S2) *Ren Min Chang Jiang* [*Yangtze River*] 9–11 at 9.

[4] Food and Agriculture Organization, 'Water Report 37: Salween Basin' (2011), accessed 8 June 2018 at www.fao.org/nr/water/aquastat/basins/salween/index.stm.

[5] Marrin Magee and Shawn Kelley, 'Damming the Salween River', in Francois Molle et al. (ed.) *Contested Waterscapes in the Mekong Region* (London: Earthscan, 2009), p. 115.

[6] Darrin Magee, 'Powershed politics: Yun Nan hydropower under great Western development' (2006) 185 *The China Quarterly* 23–41 at 23.

[7] Du Jing, 'Nu Jiang Zhong Xia You Shui Dian Kai Fa Bao Gao Zai Jing Tong Guo Shen Cha' [The Plan on Development of Hydropower in the Middle and Lower Reaches of Nu Was Adopted in Beijing], *Yun Nan Ri Bao* [*Yunnan Daily*], 15 August 2003, A01.

[8] Deng Jin, 'Huan Bao Xin Li Liang Deng Chang De Tai Qian Mu Hou' [The Context of Environmental NGOs Come to the Stage], *Nang Fang Zhou Mo* [*Nangfang Weekends*], 28 January 2005, accessed 8 June 2018 at www.people.com.cn/GB/huanbao/1072/3152 478.html. Also see Global Greengrants Fund, 'China: proposed dam project suspended – for now', 8 September 2005, accessed 27 June 2018 at www.greengrants.org/2005/09/08/china-proposed-dam-project-suspended-for-now/.

[9] State Council, 'Shi Er Wu Neng Yuan Fa Zhan Gui Hua' [The 12th Five-Year Development Plan of Energy], 1 January 2013, accessed 8 June 2018 at www.gov.cn/zwgk/2013-01/23/content_2318554.htm.

[10] The whole hydropower development plan in 12th Five-year Plan was fulfilled only about 50 per cent due to various difficulties, see Jia Kehua, 'Shui Dian Gui Hua Wan Cheng Qing Kuang Wei He Da Wu Zhe' [Why Only Half of the Hydropower Plan Was Finished], *Zhong Guo Neng Yuan Bao* [*China Energy News*], 2 May 2016, p. 1, http://paper.people.com.cn/zgnyb/html/2016-05/02/content_1676273.htm.

[11] The National Development and Reform Commission and National Energy Administration, *The 13th Five-Year Development Plan of the Electric Power*, 22 December 2016, accessed 8 June 2018 at http://mt.sohu.com/20161107/n472522229.shtml.

on the Nu river won't start until at least 2020. Downstream, Myanmar has planned six dams on the Salween.[12] These dams are in different stages of preparation: memoranda of agreement (MoUs) are being signed or environmental impact assessments (EIAs) are being conducted and so on. However, none of the projects are actually in construction. In October 2016 the Government of Myanmar commenced a strategic environmental assessment of its hydropower sector across the entire country, including proposed hydropower projects in the Nu-Salween basin.

This river is not only rich in hydropower, but also famous for biological and cultural diversity. The planned cascade of huge dams from upstream to downstream would cause significant changes to the current velocity, temperature, flow and other hydrological features of water, sediments and the habitat of aquatic organisms.[13] The lands that will be flooded to make reservoirs are home to many ethnic groups, endangered animals and precious plants. Fortunately both China and Myanmar have decided to use EIA in the decision-making process of hydropower projects to avoid substantial negative impacts to environment. This chapter compares the Chinese and Myanmar EIAs to analyse which country's approach might contribute more to sustainability. In light of the involvement of Chinese technology and capital invested in hydropower projects in Myanmar, this chapter further discusses the challenges for Chinese investors in Myanmar who have prior experience of conducting EIA in China.

From this research it will become clear how China and Myanmar can learn from each other in order to improve their EIA practice in utilizing their shared river. The comparison here is based on the provisions of EIA laws and practices in both countries. The Myanmar EIA laws scrutinised by this study are mainly the Environmental Conservation Law (2012),[14]

---

[12] Salween Watch, *Hydropower Projects on the Salween River, An Update*, 14 March 2014, accessed 27 June 2018 at www.internationalrivers.org/resources/hydropower-projects-on-the-salween-river-an-update-8258.

[13] Research has found that Chinese hydropower operations on the upstream Mekong have increased river flows in dry season and decreased flows in wet season. See Aalto University, 'Study shows China hydropower operations considerably increase dry season flows and decrease wet season flows', 6 January 2017, accessed 27 June 2018 at https://phys.org/news/2017-01-chinese-hydropower-considerably-season-decreased.html#jCp.

[14] Environmental Conservation Law of Myanmar, 2012, accessed 8 June at www.burmalibrary.org/docs15/2012-environmental_conservation_law-PH_law-09-2012-en.pdf.

Environmental Conservation Rules (2014)[15] and the Environmental Impact Assessment Procedure (2015). The EIA practice discussed, however, mainly concerns cases before the 2014 Environmental Conservation Rules and the 2015 EIA Procedure; EIA reports after the 2015 EIA Procedure, which was adopted in December 2015, were not available at the time of writing. The Chinese EIA laws are composed of the Law on Environmental Impact Assessment (2002)[16] revised in 2016 and a series of regulations and measures adopted to supplement this law. Since the EIA reports of projects on international rivers are not publicly available, the study of Chinese EIA of hydropower projects are based on released EIA reports of projects on Jinsha River, a tributary of the Yangtze river. The comparison follows three strands – the standards, the coverage and transparency – as these are critical for a successful EIA.

This chapter comprises six sections: Section 1, this introduction; Section 2, which argues that the role of EIA in governance of Nu-Salween river has not yet been effectively explored in China and Myanmar; Section 3, which finds that the provisions of Chinese EIA law is weaker in three respects than that of Myanmar EIA law, but in practice both Chinese and Myanmar EIAs downplayed the impacts of the hydropower projects; Section 4 observes the EIA practice by Chinese investors in Myanmar and their efforts to improve EIA; Section 5 discusses what China and Myanmar can learn from each other in using EIA as an instrument to better governance of Nu-Salween river; and Section 6 offers a brief conclusion.

2   Environmental Impact Assessment in Nu-Salween River: Potential Not Yet Fulfilled

Environmental Impact Assessment (EIA) is an instrument to help the decision-makers understand the environmental risks of proposed projects and plans in order to make decisions towards sustainability. China adopted its EIA law in 2002. Although this law requires both projects and

---

[15] The Ministry of Environmental Conservation and Forestry of the Republic of Union of Myanmar, Environmental Conservation Rules, Notification No. 50/2014, June 2014, accessed 8 June 2018 at www.burmalibrary.org/docs21/2014-06-Environmental_Conser vation_Rules-en.pdf.

[16] Law of Environmental Impact Assessment of China, 2002, English version, accessed 8 June 2018 at http://hk.lexiscn.com/law/law-of-the-peoples-republic-of-china-on-envir onment-impact-assessment.html.

plans to be subject to EIA,[17] the Regulation on Environmental Impact Assessment of Plans was not made until 2009.[18] For hydropower projects, EIA is required before project construction begins.[19] But according to the Provisions on State Secrets and Their Classification[20], information about international rivers is a state secret. Therefore the detailed EIA reports of hydropower projects on international rivers are not publicly accessible.

China has adopted a learning-by-doing approach to its EIA law and practice. Under such an approach, one cannot expect a highly effective implementation of EIA in the first few years. According to the Ministry of Environmental Protection of China, in the first two years after EIA law came into effect, problems were found in the process of large-scale construction, such as failure to implement environmental measures, varying levels of soil erosion and water shortages or drought downstream of the dam and the negative impact on the economy of the downstream community.[21] The Ministry of Environmental Protection renewed the Technical Guidelines to Environmental Impact Assessment in 2011, adding some new concepts such as social impact assessment, accumulative impact and public participation and so on.[22] Lack of sufficient protection of fisheries in hydro-projects gained the authority's attention in the tenth year of implementation of EIA law. The 'Notification to Enhance the Protection of Aquatic Organisms and Tighten the Administration of Environmental Impact Assessment' was issued by the Ministry of Environment and Ministry of Agriculture jointly in 2013, requiring, *inter alia*, to classify the aquatic organisms and their habits as sensitive

---

[17] Law of Environmental Impact Assessment of China, 2002, Article 3.

[18] State Council, *Regulation on Environmental Impact Assessment of Plans*, 2009, accessed 8 June 2018 at www.gov.cn/zwgk/2009-08/21/content_1398541.htm and also [in English] www.lawinfochina.com/display.aspx?lib=law&id=8158.

[19] Law of Environmental Impact Assessment of China, 2002, Article 25.

[20] Ministry of Water Resources and National Administration on the Protection of State Secrets, 'Shui Li Gong Zuo Zhong Guo Jia Mi Mi Ji Mi Ji Ju Ti Fan Wei De Gui Ding' [Provisions on State Secrets and Their Classification in Water Resources], 2013.

[21] Ministry of Environment and National Development and Reform Commission of China, 'Guan Yu Jia Qiang Shui Dian Jian She Huan Jing Bao Hu Gong Zuo De Tong Zhi' [Notification on Enhancing Environmental Protection in Hydropower Construction], *Huanfa* (2005) No. 13, 20 January 2005.

[22] Ministry of Environment of China, 'Huan Jing Ying Xiang Ping Jia Ji Shu Dao Ze' [The Technical Guidelines for Environmental Impact Assessment], *HJ* 2.1–2011, 1 September 2011, accessed 8 June 2018 at http://kjs.mep.gov.cn/hjbhbz/bzwb/other/pjjsdz/201109/t20110908_217113.htm.

and to take practical measures in accordance with the order to avoid or reduce the negative impact on them, or to restore aquatic resources.[23] This decree also requires the Ministry of Environment and Ministry of Agriculture to launch collaborative research on the methodology to assess this impact on aquatic organisms in order to provide 'credible' technical support and guidance on the protection of aquatic organisms in the EIA process.[24] The newest improvement of the EIA system happened in 2015 – a reform on the qualifications of EIA institutions[25]. Over time the EIA scheme has been improved, but during this process, many projects, including hydro-projects, had been approved despite their flaws, and there was also confusion over the terms of the schemes.

Myanmar started to require project workers to conduct EIA in 2012, a decade later than China. The Environmental Conservation Law of Myanmar authorised the then Ministry of Environmental Conservation and Forestry (MOECAF)[26] 'to lay down and carry out a system of environmental impact assessment and social impact assessment as to whether or not a project to be undertaken causing a significant impact on the environment'.[27] But this law did not provide detailed requirements about EIA. Chapter XI of the Environmental Conservation Rules (2014) establishes the framework of EIA. MOECAF is to determine which projects, categories of plans, businesses or activities, are required to conduct EIA,[28] which should be done by a third party with suitable

[23] Ministry of Environment and Ministry of Agriculture of China, 'Guan Yu Jin Yi Bu Jia Qiang Shui Sheng Sheng Wu Zi Yuan Bao Hu Yan Ge Huan Jing Ying Xiang Ping Jia Guan Li De Tong Zhi' [The Notification to Enhance the Protection of Aquatic Organism Tightens the Administration of Environmental Impact Assessment], *Huanfa* (2013) No. 86, 5 August 2013.

[24] Ibid., Article 5.

[25] Ministry of Environmental Protection, 'Jian She Xiang Mu Huan Jing Ying Xiang Zi Zhi Guan Li Ban Fa' [Measures on Administration of the Qualification of Environmental Impact Assessment of Projects], 28 September 2015, accessed 8 June 2018 at www.mep .gov.cn/gkml/hbb/bl/201510/t20151008_310733.htm.

[26] The MOECAF has been replaced by the Ministry of Natural Resources and Environment in 2016.

[27] The Republic of the Union of Myanmar, Ministry of Environmental Conservation and Forestry (MOECAF), *The Environmental Conservation Law 2012*, Article 7(m), accessed 8 June 2018 at www.myanmartradeportal.gov.mm/kcfinder/upload/files/The%20Environ mental%20Conservation%20Law(Eng).pdf.

[28] The Republic of the Union of Myanmar, Ministry of Environmental Conservation and Forestry (MOECAF), *Environmental Conservation Rules*, June 2014, Article 52, accessed 8 June 2018 at www.burmalibrary.org/docs21/2014-06-Environmental_Conservation_ Rules-en.pdf.

qualifications.[29] The EIA report will be reviewed by a Review Body composed of experts from government departments and organisations.[30] Private experts may also have chance to join the Review Body.[31] In the last month of 2015, the Ministry of Environmental Conservation and Forestry adopted the Environmental Impact Assessment Procedure (hereafter referred as 2015 EIA Procedure), which details the EIA system of Myanmar. This procedure sets out a two-tiered system of initial environmental examination (IEE) and EIA.[32] Whereas IEE applies to projects with limited scope or size, of a temporary nature, and with local and reversible environmental and social impacts, most hydro-projects have to go through EIA, not IEE. This also comes as a surprise for the investors and applies to any projects, field sites, factories or businesses that existed prior to the start of the procedure.[33] This means detailed work reviewing all the projects and businesses according to the Annex I 'Categorisation of Economic Activities for Assessment Purposes' to decide whether new conditions will be added to their permission or construction or operation. Hydro-projects such as the Mong Ton Dam[34] at Upper Salween are subject to this procedure.

Although the Myanmar EIA sets up comprehensive standards and detailed procedures to avoid or reduce adverse environmental or social impacts on Myanmar, it says nothing about transboundary impact assessment. The first dam on the Salween targeted for construction, the Hatgyi Dam near the Myanmar and Thailand border, may cause significant environmental impacts in both Myanmar and Thailand.[35] It is not clear

---

[29] Ibid., Article 56.

[30] Ibid., Article 58.

[31] Ibid., Article 59.

[32] MOECAF, *Environmental Impact Assessment Procedure*, Chapter IV IEE and Chapter V EIA, December 2015, accessed 8 June 2018 at www.aecen.org/sites/default/files/eia-procedures_en.pdf.

[33] MOECAF, *Environmental Conservation Rules*, June 2014, Article 55.

[34] The Mong Ton Dam is scheduled to be built in Shan State of Myanmar. The 241 metre high dam will produce 7000 megawatts of power, 90 per cent of which will be exported to Thailand. The developers involved in the project are China Three Gorges Corporation, EGAT International Co. Ltd of Thailand and International Group of Entrepreneurs Co. Ltd of Myanmar. See 'Naypyidaw must cancel its latest plans to build Upper Salween (Mong Ton) dam in Shan State', 9 June 2015, accessed 8 June 2018 at www.shanhuman rights.org/index.php/news-updates/216-naypyidaw-must-cancel-its-latest-plans-to-build-the-upper-salween-mong-ton-dam-in-shan-state.

[35] See the *Environmental Impact Assessment Report*, prepared by the Environment Research Institute of Chulalongkorn University, Thailand, 2008.

how Myanmar will address transboundary environmental impacts in its future governance of international rivers.

3 China's EIA Law Is Weak Compared with Myanmar's EIA Law

China's EIA can be described as a soft rein on a galloping horse: the economy. China's economy has experienced high-speed development over the past thirty years, especially from the second half of 1990s to the first decade of twenty-first century.[36] At the same time, this rapid economic growth resulted in high environmental and health costs.[37] The Proposal on the 10th Five-Year Plan by the Central Government of China stated that 'Development is the absolute principle, the key to solve all the problems of China'.[38] Under the absolute principle of development, environmental degradation is often seen as the trade-off that we have to accept. For some time, hydropower has been viewed as a clean and renewable energy, one important solution to China's energy shortage.[39] The huge investments in the local region and the potential economic income that would be generated almost always override the environmental concerns and risks detailed in the EIA reports. From the very beginning, there has been a huge imbalance between the environment and hydropower, with the environment suffering as a result. This may explain the weakness of China's EIA compared with Myanmar's.

---

[36] Based on the annual reports on statistics of economy released by the National Bureau of Statistics of China, accessed 8 June 2018 at http://data.stats.gov.cn/search.htm?s=GDP.

[37] World Bank and the State Environment Protection Administration of China, *Cost of Pollution in China: Economic Estimates of Physical Damages*, 2007, accessed 8 June 2018 at http://siteresources.worldbank.org/INTEAPREGTOPENVIRONMENT/Resources/China_Cost_of_Pollution.pdf.

[38] The Fifteenth Central Committee of the Communist Party of China, 'Zhong Gong Zhong Yang Guan Yu Zhi Ding Guo Min Jing Ji He She Hui Fa Zhan Di Shi Ge Wu Nian Gui Hua De Jian Yi' [The Proposal on the 10th Five-year Plan on National Economy and Social Development] 11 October 2000, accessed 8 June 2018 at www.people.com.cn/GB/paper39/1716/277521.html.

[39] See Junsong Gui and Yuewen Fu, 'Zhuan Fang Zhong Guo Shui Li Fa Dian Gong Cheng Xue Hui Chang Wu Mi Shu Zhang Wu Yi Hang' [Interview with Yihang Wu, the Vice Secretary-General of China's Hydropower Project Association], *Zhong Guo Neng Yuan Bao* [*China Energy Journal*, Issue 3], 15 June, 2015, p. 38, accessed 27 June 2018 at https://issuu.com/chinaenergyfundcommittee/docs/201507_ebook_cover_body2_e57c63784cb840.

3.1 Myanmar's EIA Clearly Refers to International Standards

Although Myanmar remains a developing country, its EIA procedure clearly refers to international standards in several respects. It defines 'good practice' as 'practice which is recognised by a consensus of relevant stakeholders (including without limitation government, industry, labour, financiers and academia) as having been adopted by leading, reputable companies of international standard ...'[40] For projects involving involuntary resettlement and indigenous peoples, the policies of the World Bank and Asia Development Bank are complied with before the Myanmar government issues any specific procedures.[41] The prevention and minimisation of pollution from a project should be based on the best available technology and good practice.[42] When MOECAF reviews and approves the conditions for issuing the environmental compliance certificate, the Ministry has the opportunity to refer to standards of good practice to determine how to reduce the adverse impacts of a project.[43]

The Chinese EIA law, regulations and technical guidelines do not refer to international standards. It cannot be argued that China's national standards are always lower than international standards however. It is beyond the scope of this research to compare China's national standards and international standards in detail but it is apparent that some international standards are missing from China's national standards. For example, the special protection to indigenous peoples – the concept of indigenous peoples is not in China's EIA legal system. Instead, the concept of minority or ethnic groups is adopted in Chinese law. But in the context of EIA, the rights of indigenous peoples are different from those of Chinese minorities defined by Chinese law. As stated in Article 19 of the UN Declaration on the Rights of Indigenous Peoples, 'The Declaration ... requires States to consult and cooperate in good faith with the indigenous peoples concerned through their own representative institutions in order to obtain their free, prior and informed consent before adopting and implementing legislative or administrative measures that may affect them'.[44] Article 28 continues: 'Furthermore, indigenous peoples who have unwillingly lost possession of their lands, when those

---

[40] MOECAF, EIA Procedure, 2015, Article 2(k), Chapter I.
[41] Ibid., Chapter II, Article 7.
[42] Ibid., Chapter II, Article 16(c)(ix).
[43] Ibid., Chapter VIII, Article 92(f).
[44] UN Declaration on the Rights of Indigenous Peoples, 2007, Article 19, accessed 8 June 2018 at www.un.org/esa/socdev/unpfii/documents/DRIPS_en.pdf.

lands have been "confiscated, taken, occupied or damaged without their free, prior and informed consent" are entitled to restitution or other appropriate redress'.[45] The Chinese minorities affected by hydropower projects were compensated according to the national and local standards for their loss of land and livelihood, but the compensation normally happens after the project has been approved by the authority. There is no procedure of free, prior and informed consent before the decision of occupying lands is made.[46]

In December 2015 Myanmar adopted National Environmental Quality (Emission) Guidelines made by the MOECAF. Article 3 of the Guidelines clearly states the relationship between this Myanmar standard and international standards: 'These Guidelines have been primarily excerpted from the International Finance Corporation (IFC) Environmental Health and Safety (EHS) Guidelines.'[47] Moreover, time and expertise are needed for codifying environmental standards, so this is a smart way to adopt international standards, unless any of them are proved inappropriate for Myanmar.

China has invested a great deal of resources to make and renew its own environmental standards, especially after 2006.[48] Now, China has established nearly 2,000 various environmental standards.[49] For international standards, China has adopted an approach that meets them step by step;[50] this is because the degradation of the environment by some industries is too severe to meet international standards any time soon. China has to start with some national standards that won't threaten the survival of most of its industries – a typical example is air quality. Consistency and integration are needed in the existing standards; for

---

[45] Ibid., Article 28.

[46] State Council of China, 'Da Zhong Xing Shui Li Shui Dian Gong Cheng Jian She Zheng Di Bu Chang He Yi Min An Zhi Tiao Li' [Regulation on Compensation for Expropriation of Land and Resettlement of Migrants], 2006, accessed 8 June 2018 at www.gov.cn/flfg/ 2006-08/13/content_367585.htm.

[47] Myanmar Center for Responsible Business, *National Environmental Quality (Emission) Guidelines*, 29 December 2015, accessed 27 June 2018 at www.myanmar-responsible business.org/pdf/2015-12-29-National-Environmental-Quality_Emission_Guidelines_ en.pdf.

[48] Ministry of Environment of China, 'Guo Jia Huan Jing Bao Hu Biao Zhun Shi Er Wu Gui Hua' [The 12th Five-Year Plan of National Environmental Standards], 17 February 2013, p. 7, accessed 8 June 2018 at www.mep.gov.cn/gkml/hbb/bwj/201302/t20130222_ 248380.htm (last visited 28 April 2016).

[49] Ibid., pp. 7 and 13.

[50] Ibid., p. 14.

example, there are now at least three standards for water: the quality of surface water, irrigation water and water for fisheries.[51] Compared with the willingness of Myanmar to respect international standards, the Chinese EIA cannot come into force when no national standards are available. The impact of hydropower projects on biological diversity, unfortunately, is one of the areas where there is a distinct lack of national standards.[52]

3.2   The Myanmar EIA Is More Transparent, Especially in Public Participation

According to Article 17 of Myanmar's 2015 EIA Procedure, either foreign or domestic organisations or third parties are qualified to undertake EIA if they are registered with the Department of Environment Conservation. The EIA of the Mong Ton Dam at Upper Salween was conducted by an Australian company, Snowy Mountains Engineering Corporation.[53] The EIA of Myitsone Dam at Ayeyawady River was conducted by the Changjiang Institute of Survey, Planning, Design and Research Limited Co. of China.[54] The EIA of Hutgyi Dam at the lower reaches of Salween was conducted by the Chulalongkorn University of Thailand.[55] In China, EIA has to be conducted by an organisation registered according to Chinese law and operating in China.[56] Before 2015, some organisations involved with EIA were actually affiliated to the

---

[51] Ibid., p. 10.
[52] Chen Kailin, Ge Huaifeng and Yan Xie, 'Shui Li Shui Dian Gong Cheng Zhong De Sheng Wu Duo Yang Xing Bao Hu – Jiang Sheng Wu Duo Yang Xing Ying Xiang Ping Jia Na Ru Shui Li Shui Dian Gong Cheng Huan Ping' [Biodiversity conservation in hydropower projects: introducing biodiversity impact assessment into environmental impact assessment of hydropower projects](2013) 44(5) *Shui Li Xue Bao* [*Hydropower Journal*] 608–14 at 612–13.
[53] Upper Thanlwin (Mong Ton) Hydropower Project, 22 January 2015, accessed 8 June 2018 at www.mongtonhydro.com/eportal/ui?pageId=133208.
[54] Changjing Survey, Planning, Design and Research Limited Co., 'Environmental Impact Report of Hydropower Development in Upper Reaches of Ayeyawady River', March 2010, accessed 27 June 2018 at www.uachc.com/ucan/uploads/1/file/public/201803/20180315102003_gmgds74ff4.pdf.
[55] Environmental Research Institute, Chulalongkorn University, 'Final Report of the Environmental Impact Assessment of the Hutgyi Hydropower Project', July 2008.
[56] Ministry of Environment of China, 'Jian She Xiang Mu Huan Jing Ying Xiang Ping Jia Zi Zhi Guan Li Ban Fa' [The Administration of the Qualification of Environmental Impact Assessment of Projects], November 2015, Articles 7 and 8, accessed 8 June 2018 at www.mep.gov.cn/gkml/hbb/bl/201510/t20151008_310733.htm.

environmental authorities at different levels. They often took advantage of the special relationship with the authority that approves the EIA reports to get 'unfair benefits'.[57] But these organisations have been forced to decouple from the environment authorities since late 2015 and they now operate under an open-market mechanism.

The transparency of the EIA process is apparent in the prior informed public participation. The current position of Myanmar in this regard is quite inspiring. First, the scope of the term 'public' is much wider than its counterpart in the Chinese EIA. Take the EIA process of Mong Ton Dam as an example: the participants of the first scoping meeting of EIA included four national parties, four government organisations, one international agency, the UNDP, eleven media organisations and twenty-four NGOs, as well as local residents and so on.[58] In China, environmental NGOs' participation in the EIA process is very rare. The 'public' is usually limited to local residents whose lives are directly affected by the project.[59] In fact, China's environmental NGOs have always advocated and proposed their rights and opportunities to participate in environmental decisions when the status of NGOs is not provided clearly by laws.[60] Chinese EIA organisations do use the media to post notifications and release project information, but traditional media seldom has an opportunity to participate in this type of consultation process.

The publication of EIA reports and the approval process for these reports by Myanmar are also (going to be) more transparent compared with Chinese law and practice. The 2015 EIA Procedure has very firm provisions concerning the publication of EIA reports. As Article 65 states, 'the Project Proponent shall disclose the EIA Report to civil society,

[57] Ministry of Environment of China, 'Jian She Xiang Mu Huan Jing Ying Xiang Ping Jia Zi Zhi Guan Li Ban Fa Xiu Gai Shuo Ming' [Amendment of the Administration of the Qualification of Environmental Impact Assessment of Projects], 6 March 2015, accessed 8 June 2018 at www.china-eia.com/xwzx/19163.htm.

[58] Snowy Mountains Engineering Corporation, Summary of Upper Thanlwin (Mong Ton) Hydropower Project Environmental Impact Assessment and Social Impact Assessment Scoping Meeting–Taunggyi District, 10 March 2015, accessed 8 June 2018 at www.mong tonhydro.com/eportal/ui?pageId=132815.

[59] Huadong Engineering Corporation, 'Jin Sha Jiang Bai He Tan Shui Dian Zhan Huan Jing Ying Xiang Ping Jia Bao Gao' [Environmental Impact Assessment Report of Bai He Tan Hydropower Project on Jin Sha River], 2014, pp. 1005–27.

[60] Hong Lin, 'Wo Guo Fei Zheng Fu Zu Zhi Zuo Wei Huan Jing Zhi Li Zhu Ti He Fa Xing De Gou Jian Lu Jing–Yi Huan Jing Bao Hu Fa Xiu Gai Guo Cheng Wei Li [The Road Map to Promote NGO's Position as Subjects in Environmental Governance: The Case of Revising the Law of Environmental Protection], in She Hui Fa Zhan Yan Jiu [Study of Social Development], April 2015, pp. 77–97.

PAPs [project-affected persons], local communities and other concerned stakeholders' no later than fifteen days after submission of the report to the Department of Environment Conservation (the Department) of Myanmar.[61] The Department 'shall invite comments and suggestions on the EIA Report from all relevant parties including involved government organizations, institutions, civil society organizations and PAPs' in reviewing and approving the process for EIA report.[62] It is not clear how Myanmar will deal with information of national security concern however; China has given the latter as the main reason why it won't publish EIA reports on hydropower projects on international rivers.[63]

In addition to there being insufficient information, we can also question to what degree does the public participation/consultation on EIA of a hydro-project really reflect public opinions in China.[64] In the winter of 2015, the Ministry of Environment of China launched a special investigation into public participation in EIA of projects, finding problems with fifteen projects; for instance, some interviewees denied that they had filled in the relevant questionnaire form, or they claimed that they had actually opposed the project, or they could not be reached and so on. The Ministry's conclusion drawn from this investigation was that in some cases the methods used for public participation 'failed to protect public interest'.[65] The Xia Men PX Chemical Project[66] reported vividly the sharp difference between real and unclear public participation. The EIA of this project was approved in July 2005.[67] Although the local

[61] MOECAF, EIA Procedure, 2015, Article 65.
[62] Ibid., Article 67.
[63] Ministry of Water Resources, 'Shui Li Guo Jia Mi Mi Gui Ding' [Provisions on State Secrets in Water Resources], 2013.
[64] Interview with an anonymous leader of an NGO that is very active in river protection in China.
[65] Ministry of Environment of China, 'Guan Yu Jian She Xiang Mu Huan Jing Ying Xiang Ping Jia Gong Zhong Can Yu Zhuang Xiang Zheng Zhi Gong Zuo De Tong Bao [Report on Special Campaign of Rectification of Problems in Public Participation in the Environmental Impact Assessment of Construction Projects], 20 November 2015, accessed 8 June 2018 at www.zhb.gov.cn/gkml/hbb/bgth/201511/t20151126_317789.htm.
[66] Xinhua, 'Xia men suspends controversial chemical project', China Daily, 30 May 2007, accessed 8 June 2018 at www.chinadaily.com.cn/bizchina/2007-05/30/content_883440.htm.
[67] Qian Zhu, 'Kang Zheng Zhong De Huan Jing Xin Xi Ying Gai Ji Shi Gong Kai – Ping Xia Men PX Xiang Mu Yu Cheng Shi Zong Ti Gui Hua Huan Ping' [Environmental Information Should Be Published on Time: Comments on the EIA of Xia Men PX Project and City Development Plan], Fa Xue [Law Science] January 2008, p. 9.

environment agency claimed the public had been consulted,[68] the people of Xia Men City only found out about this project when the construction of the project had started in November 2006.[69] After many months of public protest led by local elites, a real consultation was organised for this project. More than 90 per cent of the public representatives voted against the project,[70] and it was finally abandoned by Xia Men City. Another similar example is the huge blast at a chemical warehouse in Tianjin in the summer of 2015 when 173 people were killed.[71] Although the EIA of the warehouse project stated that more than half of the public consulted supported the project, the residents living just a few hundred metres from the warehouse claimed they had never received the questionnaire about the project, or had been consulted.[72]

3.3   The Coverage of Myanmar EIA Is Broader than That of Chinese EIA

Myanmar EIA covers environmental, occupational, social, cultural, socio-economical, public and community health as well as safety issues.[73] As stated in Article 2(i) of the EIA Procedure, '[the] cumulative impact ... or impacts which in itself or themselves may not be significant but may become significant when added to the existing and potential impacts eventuating from similar or diverse Projects or undertakings in the same

---

[68] Xia Men Municipal Government, 'Hai Cang PX Xiang Mu Yi An Guo Jia Fa Ding Cheng Xu Pi Zhun Zai Jian' [Haicang PX Chemical Project Was in Construction in Due Course Approved by the State], May 29 2007, accessed 27 June 2018 at www.xm.gov.cn/xmyw/200705/t20070529_164540.htm. Haicang was the site planned for this chemical project in Xia Men.

[69] Zhu, 'Huan Jing Xin Xi Ying Gai Ji Shi Gong Kai' [Environmental Information Should Be Published on Time], p. 11.

[70] Xianghui Liu and Lina Zhou, 'Li Shi De Jian Zheng – Xia Men PX Shi Jian Shi Mo' [A Historical Mirror: The Course of Xia Men PX Event], *Zhong Guo Xin Wen Zhou Kan* [*China News Weekly*], 31 December 2007 p. 56.

[71] Susan Lloyd McGarry and Satchit Balsari, et al., Preventing the Preventable: The 2015 Tianjin Explosion, FXB/DPRI Case Study Series, Case 4, FXB Center for Health & Human Rights, Harvard University, February 2017, accessed 4 August 2018 at http://www.hkjcdpri.org.hk/download/casestudies/Tianjin_CASE.pdf.

[72] Jiaofeng Qin, Kun Li et al., 'Tian Jin Bao Zha She Shi Gong Si Cheng Huan Ping Wu Fan Dui Yi Jian Ju Min Bu Zhi Qing' [The Company in Tian Jin Blasting Claimed No Objections to EIA But Residents Claimed They Were Never Informed], 18 August 2015, accessed 8 June 2018 at http://news.qq.com/a/20150818/001844.htm.

[73] MOECAF, EIA Procedure, Article 2(h).

geographic area or region' shall be taken into consideration.[74] Even before the 2015 EIA Procedure was released, some EIA practices in Myanmar covered broader subjects than EIA practices in China. The criticised EIA report of Myitsone Hydropower project contained several paragraphs on the project's impacts on religion and ethnic culture.[75] The EIA report of Hutgyi Dam assessed the project's impacts on, *inter alia*, culture, aesthetics and recreation.[76] For Mong Ton Dam, both environmental and social impacts were conducted.[77]

The Chinese EIA Law (2002) did not define the coverage of environmental impact assessment; but the General Program of the Technical Guidelines of Environmental Impact Assessment (2011) contains the proviso that the social impacts of a project should also be assessed.[78] Social impacts include the impacts to places of cultural heritage and also the health of the population.[79] But the author of this chapter did not find any anthropology or social science experts in the EIA team of the Bai He Tan hydropower project.[80] The EIA reports show very weak assessments of the impacts to ethnic groups and their culture and religion. For example, the EIA report of Wu De Dong hydropower project on Jinsha River stated that, in total, twenty-six ethnic minorities lived in ten counties affected by the Wu De Dong hydropower project area, before the dam was built.[81] The section on 'social impacts analysis' of the EIA

---

[74] Ibid., Article 2(i).

[75] Changjiang Survey, Planning, Design and Research Limited Co., *Environmental Impact Report of Hydropower Development in Upper Reaches of Ayeyawady River*, pp. 209–11, accessed 27 June 2018 at www.uachc.com/ucan/uploads/1/file/public/201803/20180315102003_gmgds74ff4.pdf.

[76] Environment Research Institute, Chulalongkorn University, *Final Report of Environment Impact Assessment of Hutgyi Hydropower Project*, July 2008.

[77] China Three Gorges (Group) Corporation, *EIA and SIA of Upper Thanlwin (Mong Ton) Hydropower Project*, accessed 8 June 2018 at www.mongtonhydro.com/eportal/ui?pageId=132069.

[78] Ministry of Environment, *Technical Guidelines for Environmental Impact Assessment: General Programme*, 2011, Article 7, accessed 27 June 2018 at http://english.sepa.gov.cn/Resources/standards/others1/Technical_Guideline_EIA/201201/W020110908499252096304.pdf.

[79] Ibid.

[80] Huadong Engineering Corporation, 'Jin Sha Jiang Bai He Tan Shui Dian Zhan Huang Jing Ying Xiang Ping Jia Bao Gao Shu' [Environmental Impact Assessment for the Bai He Tan Hydropower on Jin Sha River], Table of team members with their duties and technical titles, July 2014.

[81] Changjiang Water Resource Protection Institute, 'Jin Sha Jiang Wu De Dong Shui Dian Zhan Huan Jing Ying Xiang Ping Jia Bao Gao Shu' [Environmental Impact Assessment for the Wu De Dong Hydropower on Jin Sha River], 2014, pp. 276–7, www.ctgpc.com.cn/news/files/036005/89590.pdf.

report covered social economy, health, transportation, cultural relics and so on,[82] but it did not mention any impacts on ethnic minorities, their special way of living or their religion. In the case of Bai He Tan hydropower project, seven counties, including a Miao and Yi autonomous county, were affected by the dam construction.[83] Again the 'social impacts analysis' did not mention any special impacts on minorities, whilst assessment of the impacts on transportation, economy, access to water, land use, tourist attractions, cultural relics and so on was stated.[84]

3.4   EIA Practices of Both China and Myanmar Sometimes Downplay the Environmental Impacts

Myanmar is eager to grow its economy. The Chinese economy has been booming for more than thirty years and the current government expects it to keep growing at 6–7 per cent every year.[85] Both countries are facing the challenge of balancing economic and environmental interests in their pursuit of sustainable development. When economic development was set as a fundamental principle for solving all the problems of China,[86] it was too much to expect that EIA would change a decision on hydropower investment, which might involve several dozen billion US dollars.

The EIA reports of hydropower projects sometimes downplay the negative impacts of the dams. For example, the EIA report of Bai He Tan hydropower project states that several endangered species live in the dam area.[87] But for endangered animals it holds that either there won't be any negative impacts, or the animals will find a way to flee from the danger. For endangered plants, the EIA report argues that the same plants will remain living nearby although some of them will be destroyed by construction. To cite one example, the dam area covers part of the habitat of the *Neofelis nebulosa* (a member of the cat family), a national

[82] Ibid., pp. 659–67.
[83] Huadong Engineering Corporation, 'Bai He Tan Huan Ping Bao Gao' [Environmental Impact Assessment Report of Bai He Tan Hydropower Project], 2014, p. 263.
[84] Ibid., pp. 579–84.
[85] Keqiang Li, '2016 Zheng Fu Gong Zuo Bao Gao' [Report on Government's Work of 2016], 5 March 2016, accessed 8 June 2018 at http://news.xinhuanet.com/fortune/2016-03/05/c_128775704.htm.
[86] The Fifteenth Central Committee of the Communist Party of China, 'Zhong Yang Guan Yu Shi Wu Gui Hua Jian Yi' [The Proposal on the 10th Five-Year Plan].
[87] Huadong Engineering Corporation, 'Bai He Tan Huan Ping Bao Gao' [Environmental Impact Assessment Report of Bai He Tan Hydropower Project], pp. 486–526.

Class I protected animal. But the report concludes that the construction and operation of dam won't affect *Neofelis nebulosa* because it has a wide range of activities.[88] Three groups of *Macaca mulatta* (a member of the primate species), a national Class II protected animal, were seen living in dam area by the staff members of the corporation which conducted the investigation for EIA before the dam project. Later the three groups of *Macaca mulatta* had to migrate to other places due to road construction for the dam. The EIA report, however, argues that there is no impact to *Macaca mulatta* because they were no longer living in dam area by the time the report was finished.[89]

Although in the past three years, the Chinese government has paid more attention to environmental issues, the slowing economy seems unable to withstand intensive environmental measures. Hopefully, under pressure from the target of creating an eco-civilisation, as advocated by the current government,[90] EIA can play a more influential role than it has in the past.

It is not clear how strictly the new government of Myanmar, led by National League of Democracy, implements its EIA law. The old EIA practices that were in use before the current government were unsatisfactory for many stakeholders. The EIA of the Myitsone Dam and Burma-China Pipeline, as discussed in Section 4.1, are examples. The EIA of the Thilawa Special Economic Zone, the largest cooperation project between Japan and Myanmar, was conducted in accordance with Japan's International Cooperation Agency's Guidelines for Environmental and Social Considerations.[91] It was criticised for its failure to consider, among other things, potential air pollution and emissions sources, an unsatisfactory water management system, including for hazardous waste, and a limited investigation of the water supply and its impacts on local communities and so on.[92]

---

[88] Ibid., p. 497.

[89] Ibid.

[90] President Xi Jinping has talked about eco-civilisation several times. See 'Xi Jinping Tan Sheng Tai Wen Ming' [Xi Jingpin Talking about Eco-Civilisation], edited by the Communist Party of China, 29 August 2014, accessed 27 June 2018 at http://cpc.people.com .cn/n/2014/0829/c164113-25567379.html.

[91] Earthrights International, *Analysis of the EIA for Phase I Thilawa SEZ*, November 2014, accessed 8 June 2018 at www.earthrights.org/es/publication/analysis-eia-phase-i-thilawa-sez.

[92] Ibid., p. 1.

4 Chinese Investors in Myanmar: Learning to Meet High Standards

One significant difference between China and the US and European states is that of environmental regulation. It is taken for granted by many Chinese that as China is still a developing state, its environmental policy is not as effective as that of the US and European states. China has had to live with a certain amount of environmental pollution, accepting this as a trade-off during the process of economic development.[93] It is not clear to what degree Chinese investors think the developing host states for Chinese investment share this value; i.e. that poor developing countries should choose a low standard for their environment. This hypothesis is proved to be true in many cases, but not all of them. The environment of many developing states is even more fragile than that of developed states. To start the process of industrialisation without keeping a tight rein on environmental impacts can result in painful pollution costs[94] and jeopardise states' capacity to sustain their economies.

Myanmar is a state in transition from a weak protector of its environment to having a serious commitment to environment protection in line with international standards. Chinese investment once ranked highest among all foreign investment in Myanmar.[95] Because this investment was mainly in infrastructure – oil pipelines, mining and hydropower etc. – its potential impacts on the environment needed to be dealt with carefully to secure interest in the long run.

4.1 Half Way to Meet High Standards

Chinese investors in Myanmar had paid attention to environmental concerns of their investment even though the old Myanmar law did not require a compulsory EIA. The Myitsone Dam and the oil pipeline were good examples.

---

[93] Junjie Zhang, 'Is China doing enough for the Environment?', *Chinafile*, 11 March 2016, accessed 8 June 2018 at www.chinafile.com/conversation/china-doing-enough-environment.

[94] World Bank and the State Environmental Protection Administration of China, *Cost of Pollution in China*, 2007.

[95] Yu Dingcheng, 'Yi Dai Yi Lu Zhan Lue Shi Ye Zhong De Zhong Guo Dui Mian Dian Tou Zi' [Chinese Investment to Myanmar under the Belt and Road Initiative], *Zhong Guo Ling Dao Ke Xue* [China Leadership Science], February 2016, p. 38.

Although environmental concern was only one of the reasons that the controversial Myitsone Dam was suspended,[96] it could hardly be denied that the EIA report that covers the Myitsone Dam, done in 2010, was very weak especially in its assessment over the impacts on cultural and biological heritage. The EIA report spent 100 pages describing the vegetation and animals living in the area potentially affected by the dam. The author of the EIA also reported that many of the flora and fauna were on IUCN's Red List or CITES Appendices.[97] But when the report came to assess the impacts on the plants and animals, it was not persuasive in some of its conclusions. For example, according to the EIA report, there were only less than 100 *Orcaelia brevirostris* (a kind of dolphin) in Asia, even based on optimistic estimation, and most of them live in the Ayeyawady River (whose source is where the intended dam was to be built) and the Mekong River. The Myitsone Dam was going to cause a change in outflow of water in both the high and low flow period of the Ayeyawady river. Against these descriptions of the *Orcaelia brevirostris*, without justification, the author drew a conclusion that 'the hydropower development has less influence on hydrological conditions in the protection area of *Orcaella brevirostris*, so it will not affect *Orcaella brevirostris*'.[98]

The Burma-China Pipeline project also attracted a lot of attention from the perspective of human rights and environmental protection. The project was led by China National Petroleum Oil Corporation (CNPC), one company from South Korea and one from India in partnership with the Myanmar Oil and Gas Enterprise.[99] As the Earthrights International report states, 'CNPC commissioned and carried out a quantitative Social Impact Assessment (SIA) in portions of the pipeline

---

[96] Xianghui Zhu, Tira Foran and David Fullbrook, 'Hydropower Decision Making in Myanmar: Insights from Myitsone Dam', in David Blake and Lisa Robins (eds.), Water Governance Dynamics in the Mekong Region, (Malaysia: Strategic Information and Research Development Center, 2016), p. 149.

[97] See Changjiang Survey, Planning, Design and Research Limited Co., *Environmental Impact Report of Hydropower Development in Upper Reaches of Ayeyawady River*, March 2010, pp. 63–70, accessed 27 June 2018 at www.uachc.com/ucan/uploads/1/file/public/201803/20180315102003_gmgds74ff4.pdf. (IUCN is the International Union for Conservation of Nature and Natural Resources. CITES is the Convention on International Trade in Endangered Species.)

[98] Ibid., p. 173.

[99] Earthrights International, *The Burma-China Pipelines: Human Rights Violations, Applicable Law and Revenue Secrecy*, Situation Briefer No. 1, March 2011, accessed 8 June 2018 at https://earthrights.org/wp-content/uploads/the-burma-china-pipelines.pdf.

route. There were reportedly 3,600 households surveyed in 12 townships along the pipeline route'.[100] Earthrights International commented this 'is a positive and welcome development'.[101] But the details of the EIA and SIA are not publicly available. The SIA conducted by CNPC actually began after the construction of the project started.[102] Since the impact assessments lacked transparency and were shrouded from public scrutiny, the core function of the assessment was diminished substantially.[103]

4.2   Marching to Be More Responsible

The suspension of Myitsone Dam, which cost the Chinese developer US $1.2 billion, obviously sent a loud warning to late investors, especially in projects that may cause significant environmental impacts, even though the decision of suspension was not only due to environmental impacts.[104] Three years later, the EIA of Mong Ton Dam, led by a Chinese consortium, was conducted by an Australian company seeking a more transparent and effective assessment. This process was much more transparent than that of the EIA of hydropower projects in China. The public were provided with chances to participate in the consultation, raise questions and demonstrate their opposition if they so wished.[105] The EIA report of the Mong Ton Dam is not yet available, but should be released before it is submitted for official review.

In the case of the Letpadaung copper mine in Myanmar, Chinese Wanbao Mining Ltd suffered severe protests from the local communities against human rights abuse and negative environmental impacts.[106] According to the findings of the independent Letpadaung Taung Investigation Commission, the copper mine started to develop without prior

---

[100] Ibid., p. 17.
[101] Ibid.
[102] Ibid.
[103] Ibid., p. 18.
[104] Zhu et al., 'Hydropower Decision Making in Myanmar'.
[105] Shan Human Rights Foundation, 'Mong Ton Villagers Protest Against Salween Dam at Consultation Meeting', 7 April, 2015, accessed 8 June 2018 at www.shanhuman rights.org/index.php/news-updates/209-mong-ton-villagers-protest-against-salween-dam-at-consultation-meeting.
[106] Cecilia Jamasmie, 'One dead, 20 hurt in protest copper mine in Myanmar', Mining.com, 22 December 2014, accessed 8 June 2018 at www.mining.com/one-dead-20-hurt-in-protests-against-copper-mine-in-myanmar-76686/.

EIA, or SIA or health impact assessment (HIA) and without an environmental management plan.[107] Wanbao Mining Ltd has taken great efforts
to gain 'social license' from the local community, including making and
releasing its policy on social responsibility.[108] Wanbao is expecting a
'new dawn' for continuing its business in Myanmar;[109] however, it is not
clear when the new dawn will arrive.

5   Use EIA As an Instrument towards Better Governance of Nu-Salween

5.1   China's Potential Leadership and Contribution to Better Governance

China probably won't easily give up its plan to build hydropower projects
on the main watercourse of Nu river. And Myanmar intends to explore
the Salween river also. If there is no way to stop the dam-building on the
Nu-Salween river, EIA will be the most effective instrument to help
reduce the negative impacts to the biggest degree. Given that the value
of EIA has been appreciated by both China and Myanmar, it is possible
for these two neighbours to share their experience and lessons in order to
benefit from the EIA scheme.

China is much more powerful compared with Myanmar in many
respects; and China has more resources and potential pathways available
to lead a better governance of the Nu-Salween river. China is not only
one of the main riparian states of Nu-Salween river and embraces just
under half of the river in its territory, but it is also the most important
financial source and developer of the hydropower projects on Salween
river in Myanmar territory.

To take the leader in better governance of the Nu-Salween river, China
should think about its obligations to conduct transboundary EIAs of the

---

[107] Charltons, *Letpadaung Investigation Commission Issues Final Report*, April 2013, accessed 8 June 2018 at www.charltonslaw.com/letpadaung-investigation-commission-issues-final-report/.

[108] 'Wanbao Mining Company reaches out with CSR program, innovative video', *Mizzima*, 27 April 2016, accessed 8 June 2018 at http://mizzima.com/news-domestic/wanbao-mining-company-reaches-out-csr-programme-innovative-video.

[109] Mining.com editor, 'Myanmar Wanbao: A New Dawn For Chinese Copper Miner', *Mining.com*, 20 April 2016, www.mining.com/myanmar-wanbao-a-new-dawn-for-the-chinese-copper-miner/.

projects planned on the Nu river.[110] Now that Myanmar has planned several dams on the Salween and EIAs have been done for some of them, Myanmar's expectations are that the future upstream dams in China won't deprive downstream dams in Myanmar of the capacity to generate power, or in any way deplete such capacity. There are precedents for this: for instance, in the Lake Lanoux arbitration case, the tribunal stated that in carrying out works for utilisation of the waters of Lake Lanoux, France, the upstream state should take the right and interests of Spain, the downstream state, into consideration.[111] Also, the arbitral tribunal of the Kinshanganga case held that in constructing Kinsheanganga project on the shared river with Pakistan, India bore the obligation of mitigating significant harm to Pakistan.[112] Without an EIA including consideration of transboundary impacts, it could be hard for China to argue that it has fulfilled its duty of due diligence.

In fact China could have a lot of experience and lessons to share with its neighbour with regard to improving the role of EIA in decision-making towards sustainable development. After implementing the EIA law for more than a decade, the Chinese Ministry of Environment has adopted a series of rules and guidelines as well as standards relating to EIA on projects and plans. It also learns how to work shoulder by shoulder with other governmental organs, such as the Bureau of Fisheries, Ministry of Agriculture and Rural Affairs and the Ministry of Water Resources and so on. China has an especially rich experience of mitigating the negative environmental impacts on the health of rivers and the conservation of plants and animals, including fish. Some of these lessons were learned at great cost due to the partial failure of previous projects.[113] These lessons can help the Myanmar government to administrate and supervise the implementation of EIA law in Myanmar.

---

[110] Nadia Sanchez and Yongmin Bian, 'China's obligation to conduct Transboundary Environmental Impact Assessment (TEIA) in utilizing its shared water resources' (2014) 55 *Natural Resource Journal* 105–25.

[111] Lake Lanoux Arbitration (*France v. Spain*), 24 International Law Reports, 1957, p. 101.

[112] Final Award in the Matter of Indus Waters Kinshanganga Arbitration, December 2013, p. 112, accessed 27 June 2018 at https://pcacases.com/web/sendAttach/48.

[113] For example, the diversion type of hydropower projects has caused problems such as water interception, loss of habitat of aquatic organisms, degradation of the eco-system along river banks and derogation of eco-service of the river especially in the south-east area of China. See Min Zhao, Chengjuan Xu, 'Yin Shui Shi Dian Zhan Dui Xi Nan Shan Qu He Liu Jian Kang Ying Xiang De Ping Jia Zhi Biao Ti Xi Yan Jiu' [Research of the Index System for Evaluating the Health of Rivers Affected by Diversion Type of Hydropower Projects] (2015) 43(7) *Journal of Anhui Agriculture Science* 357–8 at 357.

5.2   Promise and Challenge of Myanmar EIA to Contribute to Better Governance

As discussed in the previous sections, the current Myanmar EIA law is very strong on protecting the environment. Myanmar is lucky to have such an instrument as they start to pursue economic development under a democratic government. If Myanmar can implement its EIA law effectively, it will be able to demonstrate how a more transparent and robust EIA may contribute to better governance of Nu-Salween river. Since the 2015 EIA Procedure was adopted only recently, it is still too early to have a clear picture about its implementation.

Good EIA law keeps the EIA process on track, but there are several difficulties for Myanmar to overcome before reaching its destination. First, to integrate environmental and social justice into its economic plan is always a challenge for a poor developing country like Myanmar. The biggest attraction of the hydropower projects planned on Salween river is money, as the electricity generated will mainly be sold either to Thailand or to China.[114] Therefore it is up to Myanmar to balance the environmental and social costs against the economic benefits. The social structure of Myanmar is quite different from that of China. In case of the proposed Salween hydropower projects, the reservoirs will flood important areas of land in the local communities, but it is unlikely that the revenue from the projects will be used for the benefit of local people. Second, even if Myanmar intends to take the EIA very seriously, it is not easy to supervise and evaluate the EIA without good expertise and detailed data of the Myanmar eco-system as well as the capacity to process, analyse and understand data. Dr Mar Mar Aye from the Botany Department of Lashio University claims that in an area near the site of Mong Ton hydropower project she has found seven species of plants whose medicinal uses have never been documented officially.[115] Her

---

[114] It is said that 90 per cent of the electricity of Mong Ton Dam will be sold to Thailand. Watcharapong Thongrung, 'MoU for Salween Hydropower project to be signed between Thailand, Myanmar, China', *The Nation*, 15 July 2015, accessed 8 June 2018 at www .nationmultimedia.com/business/MoU-for-Salween-hydropower-project-to-be-signed-be-30264423.html. The electricity of Hutgyi dam was also to be sold to Thailand. See 'Myanmar, Thailand to implement one more hydropower project', *Xinhua News Agency*, 4 April 2006, accessed 8 June 2018 at http://en.people.cn/200604/04/eng20060404_255814.html.

[115] The author has discovered that Dr Mar Mar Aye was working on the 'Ethnobotanical study on some plants growing along the Thanlwin river of Lashio District, Northern Shan State, Myanmar', 12 November 2016, Lashio University, Botany Department,

research reveals that there is a risk, due to the hydropower project, that some precious organisms could be destroyed even before we have the opportunity to study them. Because some areas of Myanmar have suffered from military conflicts for several decades, and it is hard for outside experts to access to the areas of conflict to investigate the environment and consult the local people, the conclusions of EIA based on 'best knowledge of the current information', may be equivalent to decisions based on little or insufficient research. Third, the retroactive application of the 2015 EIA rules can be a serious concern for foreign investors in Myanmar. It remains unclear whether the purpose of the retroactive application will only enable the current government to understand and foresee the environmental costs of the projects approved by the previous government, or whether it will also regulate those old projects in line with the new rules, and cancel, suspend or change any projects. In the latter case, the Myanmar government may violate the agreements signed with the previous government representing Myanmar and foreign investors.

6   Conclusion

This comparative study of the Myanmar and Chinese Laws on EIA finds that the Myanmar EIA law requires a more transparent EIA covering not only environmental issues, but also social and cultural health concerns. Over the past ten years, the Chinese environmental authority has kept improving its EIA scheme, by adding supplements to the regulations regarding the EIA of plans, information disclosure, public participation, the protection of fisheries and the qualifications of entities doing EIA. But detailed EIA reports of projects on international rivers such as Nu river are not publicly accessible. Therefore the domestic and transboundary impacts of those planned hydropower projects are unclear for the public and downstream riparian states.

When Chinese investors come to Myanmar to invest in hydropower projects, they must be prepared to follow higher standards of EIA than they once did in China. The case of Myanmar is not exceptional in Southeast Asia. Thailand, Vietnam, Laos and Cambodia have all adopted

accessed 8 June 2018 at https://static1.squarespace.com/static/575fb39762cd94c2d69dc556/t/5932f5e915d5dba280099357/1496511983277/No.32_P766_796_Mar+Mar+Aye.pdf.

EIA law, although the implementation of these laws varies.[116] Chinese investors are in the main good at engineering projects to generate power, but might not be the best exemplars of how to conserve rivers; and the Chinese experience of EIA in hydropower projects might not be sufficient for the sustainable use of rivers shared by China and her neighbours. The marked degradation of water quality and river ecosystems in the Chinese domestic rivers will hopefully not be repeated in rest of Southeast Asia.

[116] Yongmin Bian and Bin Peng, 'The influence of the environmental impact assessment laws of the countries in Mekong River Basin on foreign investment' (2016) 48(6) *Journal of Yun Nan Normal University* 73–81.

10

The Role of Regional Space Cooperation in Procuring Space Security in the Asia-Pacific Region

Prospects for the Future

YUN ZHAO*

Space security has become a hot topic in recent years, with space cooperation, regional space cooperation in particular, believed to be the major mechanism for realising and maintaining such security. This chapter examines the role of regional cooperation in the Asia-Pacific region and discusses how such cooperation can contribute to the maintenance of space security. Drawing on the successful experience of Europe, the chapter explores possible ways of furthering space cooperation in the Asia-Pacific region. It also outlines the principles and guidelines that should be followed in pursuing future regional space cooperation in the Asia-Pacific. The chapter concludes by arguing that regional space cooperation is crucial to furthering space security, and thus that the Asia-Pacific region needs to step up its efforts in this arena.

The development of space technologies has important implications for both state security and perceived military imperatives,[1] particularly given the increasing number of space activities taking place worldwide. The issue of space security has become a focus of interest in the space arena partly because of the inclusiveness of the term 'space security' itself and partly because of the challenges posed to international society with regard to the peaceful uses of space. Since the start of the space era in 1957, international society has emphasised the importance of international cooperation in space activities. Such cooperation results in mutual

---

* The author is grateful to the research assistance provided by Long Jie, a PhD candidate at the University of Hong Kong.
[1] Columba Peoples, 'New space for security?: geopolitics and sustainability in a changing world', in C. Al-Ekabi et al. (eds.), *Yearbook on Space Policy 2012/2013* (Vienna: Springer-Verlag, 2015), p. 210.

respect for and understanding of the space activities of various countries, consequently contributing to the peaceful uses of space. International cooperation can take place in various forms and at various levels.

Regional cooperation, a subcategory of international cooperation, is particularly helpful in addressing concerns over space security. We have already witnessed successful regional cooperation in the case of Europe. However, cooperation within the Asia-Pacific region does not appear to have led to fruitful results as yet. The launch of China's Belt and Road initiative (BRI) provides an excellent opportunity to re-examine the current situation and future development of space cooperation in the Asia-Pacific region. Under the auspices of the BRI, countries in the region can be encouraged to work more closely with one another to realise space security.

Following this introduction, Section 1 of this chapter addresses the relationship between space security and space cooperation. A proper understanding of the term 'space security' is vital to any further consideration of space cooperation. Thus, this section of the chapter presents the various contemporary understandings of the term to set the stage for the discussion in the subsequent sections. Section 2 then examines the current status of regional space cooperation in Asia-Pacific, showing it to be far from satisfactory at present. In making suggestions for improved space cooperation within the region, Section 3 takes regional space cooperation in Europe as an example, demonstrating how successful such cooperation has been in helping Europe to realise space security. With the successful European experience in mind, Section 4 then discusses possible ways of furthering space cooperation in the Asia-Pacific region and proposes principles and guidelines to follow in future. The chapter concludes by arguing in Section 5 that regional space cooperation is so vital to ensuring space security that the Asia-Pacific region would be well advised to step up its game in this arena.

1   Space Security and Space Cooperation

The international community was quick to respond to the development of space technologies and space activities. During the Cold War era, five major multilateral space treaties[2] were enacted under the aegis of the

---

[2] The five treaties are the 1967 Outer Space Treaty (Treaty on Principles Governing the Activities of States in the Exploration and Use of Outer Space, including the Moon and Other Celestial Bodies, opened for signature 27 January 1967, 610 United Nations Treaty

United Nations, setting out basic principles for space activities. These treaties filled the gaps in the space regulations of that period, and ensured the smooth development of space activities over the next three decades or so. However, it must be noted that all five treaties were enacted at a time when states were the sole actors in space exploration, a very different situation from today's active involvement of private entities in the ongoing process of space commercialisation and privatisation. Although they provide a skeletal legal framework for space activities, the five treaties fail to deal with new issues arising from the commercial and/or private space-related initiatives that constitute one of the world's fastest growing industries. Space investment currently accounts for the major share of developments in communications infrastructure, including telecommunications and broadcasting services for weather and geological monitoring and disaster management. Against this backdrop, one of the black holes deterring further space development and investment is the absence of an international governance structure to ensure space security. Consequently, the pursuit of space cooperation to procure such security has become a topic of interest to the international community and academia alike.

Different scholars and officials have different understandings of the meaning and scope of space security, and reaching a consensus about the definition of the term has proved a difficult task. Space security can have 'different meanings in different context[s], reflecting the dual-nature of space capabilities'.[3] Former European Commission (EC) President José Manuel Barroso has argued for the importance of considering security in and from space in a more expansive and comprehensive manner,[4]

Series (UNTS) 205, 18 United States Treaties and Other International Agreements (UST) 2410); the 1968 Rescue Agreement (Agreement on the Rescue of Astronauts, the Return of Astronauts and the Return of Objects Launched into Outer Space, opened for signature 22 April 1968, 672 UNTS 119); the 1972 Liability Convention (Convention on International Liability for Damage Caused by Space Objects, opened for signature 29 March 1972, 961 UNTS 187); the 1975 Registration Agreement (Convention on Registration of Objects Launched into Outer Space, 14 January 1975, 28 UST 695, Treaties and Other International Acts Series (TIAS) 8480); and the 1979 Moon Agreement (Agreement Governing the Activities of States on the Moon and Other Celestial, opened for signature 18 December 1979, 1363 UNTS 21).

[3] Scott Pace, 'Security in space' (2015) 33 *Space Policy* 52.

[4] Columba Peoples, 'The growing "securitization" of outer space' (2010) 26 *Space Policy* 207.

encompassing not only the issue of attacks on space assets but also such issues as space debris, the space environment and natural and manmade hazards.[5]

Joseph Pelton and Ram Jakhu took up the challenging task of defining 'space safety', instead of 'space security', as 'the protection of human life and/or spacecraft during all phases of a space mission, regardless of whether this is a "manned" or "unmanned" activity'. They defined the scope of space safety as including '(a) all aspects from pre-launch, launch, orbital or sub-orbital operations, through re-entry and landing; (b) the protection of ground and flight facilities and surrounding population and buildings in proximity to launch sites; and (c) the protection of space-based services, infrastructure and unmanned satellites'.[6] Whilst 'space security' cannot be equated to 'space safety', the difficulty in defining the term is clear. Accordingly, a pragmatic approach would be to list all possible issues that may affect space security in its broadest sense. To date, several issues have been highlighted in international discussions of space security. For example, Pelton and Jakhu posit that 'a prerequisite for [the] safe and sustainable use of space' implies at least the following: (i) the control of space debris mitigation and improved space situational awareness; (ii) international space traffic rules, international management and controls to ensure spacecraft safety; (iii) internationally agreed standards and rules to achieve compatibility amongst different space systems and facilities, as well as improved safety and reliability; (iv) the systematic elimination of weapons and other threats from space; and (v) the protection of people and facilities on Earth from direct hazards and indirect environmental effects.[7]

---

[5] José Manuel Durão Barroso, 'The ambitions of Europe in space', speech delivered at Conference on European Space Policy, Brussels, 15 October 2009, accessed 15 June 2018 at http://europa.eu/rapid/press-release_SPEECH-09-476_en.htm. In discussing the need for security in space and from space, Barroso declared: '[O]ur space assets and infrastructure are indispensable for our economy and security and we need to protect them. The EU should develop an independent capacity to monitor satellites and debris orbiting the Earth and the space environment, and tackle possible hazards. We should also exploit the potential of space infrastructure (already available, for example, through GMES) to protect our citizens and our ground infrastructure against natural and man-made hazards and to be at the service of European Security and Defence Policy goals. These capacities should be developed in partnership with Member States.'

[6] Joseph N. Pelton and Ram Jakhu (eds.), *Space Safety Regulations and Standards* (Oxford: Elsevier, 2010), p. xli.

[7] Ibid.

The Space Security Index defines space security as 'the secure and sustainable access to, and use of, space and freedom from space-based threats'.[8] It also states that any definition of space security should be in line with 'the express intent of the 1967 Outer Space Treaty that space should be preserved as a global commons to be used by all for peaceful purposes'.[9] According to Abeyratne, nine indicators have been identified to elaborate the term 'space security': 'the space environment; space situational awareness; space security laws, policies and doctrines; civil space programs and global utilities; commercial space; space support for terrestrial military operations; space systems protection; space systems negation; and space-based strike weapons.'[10] In *Space Security 2010*, an important distinction is made between the militarisation and weaponisation of space.[11]

Whilst no consensus has been reached regarding the essence and scope of space security, the international community has a common understanding of the important role of international cooperation in achieving such security. It has been noted that the Cold War period, whilst being preoccupied with fierce competition between the world's two superpowers, the United States and Soviet Union, was at the same time characterised by 'an enormous amount of international cooperation' in the space arena.[12] The Secure World Foundation, a key non-governmental organisation that is actively involved in the promotion of space sustainability, has observed that 'ensuring that all humanity can continue to use

---

[8] Robert Lawson, 'The space security index' (2004) 2(2) *Astropolitics: International Journal of Space Politics Policy* 177.

[9] Space Security Index, *Space Security 2009*, Sixth Annual Report, Spacesecurityindex.org, accessed 15 June 2018 at http://spacesecurityindex.org/wp-content/uploads/2014/10/SSI 2009.pdf.

[10] Ruwantissa Abeyratne, *Space Security Law* (Berlin; Heidelberg: Springer-Verlag, 2011), p. 15.

[11] Casar Jaramillo (ed.), *Space Security 2010* (Waterloo, ON: spacesecurity.org, 2010), p. 8, accessed 15 June 2018 at http://swfound.org/media/29039/space%20security%20index %202010%20full%20report.pdf. As explained in this document, the militarisation of space is a reality, but space weaponisation lacks documented evidence at the moment: 'Although the use of space assets for military applications such as reconnaissance, intelligence, and troop support has been ubiquitous for several years, space apparently has remained weapons-free. To maintain this state, the prevention of an arms race in outer space remains a priority for policymakers at various international forums, since it is assumed that once a state places weapons in space, others will follow suit.'

[12] Michael Sheehan, *The International Politics of Outer Space* (Oxford: Routledge, 2007), p. 55.

outer space for peaceful purposes and socioeconomic benefit in the long term ... will require international cooperation, discussion and agreements designed to ensure that space is safe, secure and peaceful'.[13]

International space cooperation has been an important principle from the very beginning of the Space Age. As early as 1961, the United Nations General Assembly (UNGA) adopted Resolution 1721(XVI), which specifies international cooperation in its subtitle and emphasises the importance of strengthening space cooperation to ensure the peaceful use of outer space. The 1967 Outer Space Treaty then formally adopted that principle as a fundamental principle for space activities.[14] The treaty recognises outer space as the province of all mankind, and calls for its peaceful use as an area of international cooperation.[15] The principle received further impetus in 1996 when the UNGA adopted a resolution providing further details of its application.[16] The 1996 resolution encourages space cooperation at various levels and in various formats.

By engaging in international cooperation, the international community was able to conclude five international space treaties during the 1967–79 period, the first just a decade after the launch of the first manmade satellite in 1957. However, with more nations with divergent national interests joining the space club, international space legislation is facing a variety of challenges. Under these circumstances, given the geographical proximity and similar historical and cultural backgrounds of the states in a particular region, regional space cooperation appears to be a more realistic prospect. In arguing for ASEAN[17] space cooperation, for example, Noichim lists several substantial benefits of such cooperation in a given geographical region: 'reducing natural resources consumption; increasing employment capacities; increasing economic development; building knowledge of space together[;] and decreasing

---

[13] Secure World Foundation, *Space Sustainability: A Practical Guide* (Broomfield, CO: 2014), p. 4, accessed 15 June 2018 at http://swfound.org/media/121399/swf_space_sus tainability-a_practical_guide_2014__1_.pdf.

[14] Article IX of the Outer Space Treaty provides that 'States Parties to the Treaty shall be guided by the principle of cooperation and mutual assistance and shall conduct all their activities in outer space...'.

[15] Outer Space Treaty, preamble and Article I.

[16] Declaration on International Cooperation, UNGA Resolution 51/122 (13 December 1996).

[17] The Association of Southeast Asian Nations. The ten ASEAN member states are Indonesia, Malaysia, the Philippines, Singapore, Thailand, Brunei, Cambodia, Laos, Myanmar and Vietnam.

competition among the cooperating countries.'[18] Regional cooperation is also the best way to ensure space security in a region.

2   Regional Space Cooperation in the Asia-Pacific Region

Space cooperation is already in place in the Asia-Pacific region, which currently boasts three space cooperation platforms. Japan and India host two regional forums, the Asia-Pacific Regional Space Agency Forum (APRSAF) (1993)[19] and the Centre for Space Science and Technology Education in Asia and the Pacific (CSSTEAP) (1995), respectively. APRSAF is a loose platform for the voluntary exchange of information on an annual basis. It does not pursue legally binding agreements, but 'rather provides a flexible framework to promote regional cooperation in space development and utilization through voluntary cooperative efforts of participating countries and organizations'.[20] CSSTEAP is affiliated with the United Nations and provides developing countries with research and education opportunities.[21] It was established as an education and research institution 'capable of high attainments in the development and transmission of knowledge in all relevant fields of space science and technology'.[22] The third regional platform, the eight-member Asia-Pacific Space Cooperation Organization (APSCO),[23] is the only inter-governmental space organisation in the region. It operates on a non-profit basis with full international legal status. According to the APSCO Convention, the field of cooperation for APSCO members includes

> 1. Space technology and programs of its applications; 2. Earth observation, disaster management, environmental protection, satellite communications and satellite navigation and positioning; 3. Space science research; 4. Education, training and exchange of scientists/technologists; 5. Establishment of a central data bank for development of programs of the Organization and dissemination of technical and other information relating to the programs and activities of the Organization.[24]

[18] Chukeat Noichim, 'Promoting ASEAN space cooperation' (2008) 24 *Space Policy* 11.
[19] See APRSAF website, accessed 15 June 2018 at www.aprsaf.org.
[20] APRSAF Secretariat, *APRSAF: Asia-Pacific Regional Space Agency Forum* (Tokyo: APRSAF, 2016), accessed 15 June 2018 at www.aprsaf.org/about/leaflet/APRSAF_leaflet_en.pdf.
[21] See CSSTEAP website, accessed 15 June 2018 at www.cssteap.org.
[22] Ibid., 'Background', accessed 15 June 2018 at www.cssteap.org/background.
[23] The eight APSCO member countries are Bangladesh, China, Iran, Mongolia, Pakistan, Peru, Thailand and Turkey.
[24] Article 6 of the APSCO Convention.

The convention further outlines the basic activities of member states, which include

> a) establishing ... the Organization's plans for space activities and devel-
> opment; b) carrying out fundamental research concerning space technol-
> ogy and its applications; c) extending the applications of matured space
> technology; d) conducting education and training activities concerning
> space science and technology and their applications; e) managing and
> maintaining the branch offices and the relevant facilities as well as the
> network system of the Organization; f) undertaking other necessary
> activities to achieve the objectives of the Organization.[25]

It is clear that the APSCO Convention was drafted in a very broad manner to incorporate many possible ways for members to cooperate. This open approach to encourage regional cooperation is meaningful, but the organisation's limited number of members must be borne in mind. Such limited participation inevitably weakens the desired effects within the region.

3   Space Cooperation in Europe: A Case Study

Europe boasts the world's most successful example of regional space cooperation. Space cooperation emerged on the continent as early as the 1960s with the establishment of the European Space Research Organ-isation (ESRO)[26] and European Launcher Development Organisation (ELDO),[27] which led to the formation of the European Space Agency (ESA) in 1975.[28] The European Space Policy (ESP), released in 2007, covers a wide range of space-related issues in Europe,[29] and is seen as an integrated aspect of the overall efforts of all countries and institutions in the European Union (EU).[30] Whilst it has been argued that the EU is

---

[25] Article 7(1) of the APSCO Convention.
[26] ESRO was established in accordance with the Convention for the Establishment of a European Space Research Organisation, Paris, 14 June 1962, 58 UNTS 35 (1965).
[27] ELDO was established in accordance with the Convention for the Establishment of a European Organisation for the Development and Construction of Space Vehicle Launchers, with Annexes, Financial Protocol and Protocol Concerning Certain Responsi-bilities in Connection with the Initial Programme, London, 29 March 1962, 507 UNTS 177 (1964).
[28] ESA, Basic Texts of the European Space Agency, Vol. 1, A-6, Paris, 1 September 1977.
[29] Council of the European Union, Resolution on the European Space Policy, Brussels, April 2007.
[30] M. Cervino, S. Corradini and S. Davolio, 'Is the "peaceful use" of outer space being ruled out?' (2003) 19 Space Policy 232.

still searching for a coherent space security strategy,[31] its highly integrated institutional and legal framework helps to realise such security in the region, and thus provides an excellent example in seeking ways to improve space cooperation in the Asia-Pacific region. As it is not possible to examine all aspects of space cooperation in Europe, the present discussion focuses on cooperation in the standard-setting arena in view of the ongoing space commercialisation process taking place worldwide.

In Europe, national space agencies and national standards bodies were the main players in drafting and implementing national security standards before 1993, leading to cross-border incompatibilities and prompting calls for greater cooperation in view of the dual advent of regionalisation and commercialisation on the continent.[32] However, European cooperation in the space arena needed to 'overcome national sovereignty issues by pooling funding and capacities' to realise the ultimate goal of strategic autonomy in space.[33] As the regional space organisation responsible for intra-European cooperation, the ESA actively participates in international forums to influence the formulation of international space rules at two levels. At the internal level, the ESA hosts consultations between member states to encourage a unified stance concerning particular legal issues. At the external level, it represents ESA members at international meetings to voice their concerns and common position.[34] ESA has also taken the initiative to work closely with national space agencies in Europe to develop a set of unified rules and minimum standards to ensure space security within the region. Its geographic return policy, which allows technology transfers amongst ESA members, also provides important policy support for space commercialisation.

The EU, by including the space industry in its common market plan, works together with ESA to harmonise security standards and improve interoperability for the space industry. The emergence of commercial space companies with strong interests necessitated the production of an up-to-date, objective set of standards for space products and services. In view of global competition and economic viability, the standardisation of

---

[31] Max M. Mutschler and Christophe Venet, 'The European Union as an emerging actor in space security?' (2012) 28 *Space Policy* 118.

[32] Pelton and Jakhu, *Space Safety Regulations*, p. 31.

[33] Marcel Dickow, 'The pursuit of collective autonomy? Europe's autonomy in "space and security" lacks a joint vision', in C. Al-Ekabi et al. (eds.), *Yearbook on Space Policy 2012/2013* (Vienna: Springer-Verlag, 2015), p. 114.

[34] Roy Gibson, 'Law and security in outer space international regional role – focus on the European Space Agency' (1983) 11 *Journal of Space Law* 17.

a European space security framework is vital to enhancing the competitive edge of European space companies in the international marketplace. Accordingly, serious measures have been taken at the European level to facilitate space commercialisation on the one hand and ensure space security on the other. It is clear from the European example that space commercialisation and regional cooperation go hand in hand, particularly the harmonisation of security and other relevant standards, with the ultimate goal of realising regional space security and safety.

Years of regional cooperation have proved fruitful in harmonising regional security and safety standards. Upon the endorsement of the ESA standardisation boards and ESA Standardization Steering Board, ESA periodically issues a List of ESA Approved Standards in the areas of management, product assurance and engineering that are to be used in the implementation of all ESA space projects and activities. Within the ESA, a dedicated Quality, Dependability and Safety Division, which covers the three crucial criteria for the success of space missions, is charged with overseeing the quality of all ESA space-related products and services, whilst the ESA Product Assurance and Safety Office bears responsibility for setting the safety standards governing human space flight.[35] Further, European Cooperation for Space Standardization (ECSS) is an organisation tasked with facilitating the development of standards for the European space industry.[36] The organisation provides an essential platform for the formulation of space security standards in the region. Whilst ESA and ECSS play important roles in standardising space-related products and services in Europe, a number of other institutions, including the EC, European Committee for Standardization, European Committee for Electrotechnical Standardization and European Telecommunications Standards Institute, are also heavily involved in the process, either individually or jointly.

It is clear that Europe's space security standards constitute the first truly international set of space safety standards.[37] The space safety standard-setting process is a typical example of European cooperation in realising space security. With the active participation of both member states and interest groups in the standard-setting process, the standards drafted under the auspices of the aforementioned regional organisations

---

[35] Gerardine Meishan Goh, 'Space safety standards in Europe', in Joseph N. Pelton and Ram Jakhu (eds.), *Space Safety Regulations and Standards* (Oxford: Elsevier, 2010), p. 35.

[36] See ECSS website, accessed 15 June 2018 at www.ecss.nl.

[37] Pelton and Jakhu, *Space Safety Regulations*, p. 44.

help the European space industry to remain competitive in a rapidly evolving technical and economic environment. It should be noted that the heavy involvement of interest groups helps to ensure that the drafting process results in standards that truly reflect the real needs of the space industry and contributes to their effective implementation. Also worthy of note is that European regional cooperation exists at various levels and is implemented by various entities rather than being monopolised by space agencies, a situation that helps to create a healthy environment for regional cooperation in the space arena.

Another distinct feature of regional cooperation in Europe is that 'safety standards are no longer targeted solely for the benefit of the space system or the astronaut. Rather, a broad and robust approach has been undertaken to consider the safety of ground personnel and private individuals, avoidance of property damage and environmental protection'.[38] Consequently, regional cooperation in the standard-setting process helps to ensure space security in a broader sense, extending the benefits from procuring the safety of a particular space project to broader areas such as environmental protection in outer space.

Moving beyond the standard-setting arena, the formalisation of the first ESP in 2007 is further evidence of European cooperation. It was followed by the definition of 'space and security' as a new priority area in the Space Council Resolution in September 2009.[39] A more recent document, entitled 'Towards a Space Strategy of the European Union that Benefits its Citizens', acknowledges the importance of space infrastructure to the security and defence of the EU.[40] European countries cooperate with one another to present a common position on space security internationally. Led by the European External Action Service, the EU produced an International Code of Conduct for Outer Space Activities in 2007 to cope with the issue of space security.[41] Its aim was to codify a set

---

[38] Ibid., pp. 44–5.

[39] Frank Asbeck and Jana Robinson, 'Europe's space security contingencies and preparedness', in C. Al-Ekabi et al. (eds.), *Yearbook on Space Policy 2012/2013* (Vienna: Springer-Verlag, 2015), p. 105.

[40] Council of the European Union, 'Towards a space strategy of the European Union that benefits its citizens: council conclusions', 3094th Competitiveness (Internal Market, Industry, Research and Space) Council Meeting, Brussels, 31 May 2011, accessed 15 June 2018 at www.consilium.europa.eu/uedocs/cms_data/docs/pressdata/en/intm/122342.pdf.

[41] European Union External Action, 'EU proposal for an international space code of conduct, draft', 31 March 2014, accessed 15 June 2018 at https://eeas.europa.eu/topics/disarmament-non-proliferation-and-arms-export-control/14715_en.

of transparency and confidence-building measures for space activities.[42]
Such concerted Europe-wide efforts in the space security arena have
helped Europe to 'establish itself as a norm entrepreneur in the context
of space security and promote norms that are in line with its interests
and values'.[43]

4   Further Development of Space Cooperation in the Asia-Pacific Region

Compared with Europe, the Asia-Pacific region lags far behind when it
comes to space cooperation, a situation that is not conducive to the
maintenance of space security. In view of the divergent cultural and
historical background of the region's numerous nations, we need to
formulate a viable approach to promoting regional cooperation on space
activities. It is vitally important that a climate of trust and cooperation
is created and that common ground amongst states is sought. At the
international level, the concept of transparency and confidence-building
measures (TCBMs) has been put forward to build confidence amongst
members of the international community. TCBMs can play an important
role in 'clarifying the intentions of space actors and reducing the risk of
misperception and erroneous assessment of the activities of States in
outer space, thus helping to foster regional and global stability'.[44] These
or similar measures appear essential to building trust in the Asia-Pacific
region. Possible other measures include the drafting of operational rules
and/or guidelines for space activities in the region, information-sharing
activities and regular regional consultative meetings.

Space cooperation must be carried out in an open and flexible manner,
and states within the region must cooperate in good faith. Amongst the
numerous issues in the space arena, space security is the most deserving
of urgent attention. To a large extent, regional space cooperation and
regional space security are both mutually compatible and interdependent. Although the issues involved in space security are wide-ranging,
Asia-Pacific countries could begin cooperating by initiating program-
mes and taking measures in neutral and/or less controversial areas. For

---

[42] Cesar Jaramillo, 'The multifaceted nature of space security challenges' (2015) 32 *Space Policy* 64.

[43] Mutschler and Venet, 'The European Union as an emerging actor', 123.

[44] Peter Martinez et al., 'Criteria for developing and testing transparency and confidence-building measures (TCBMs) for outer space activities' (2014) 30 *Space Policy* 92.

example, as the region is highly vulnerable to natural disasters, Asia-Pacific countries recognise the urgency of cooperating on environmental monitoring and disaster relief at the regional level.[45] Possible cooperation on the use of space technologies and facilities to tackle these issues would be an ideal way for these countries to reach a consensus.

It has been argued that 'cooperation between nations and coordination of programs undertaken by organization[s] of the international scientific community are envisaged as elements of the pattern for space research and operations'.[46] In view of the ongoing space commercialisation process, the legal status of private entities involved in space activities should be clarified, and their interests emphasised in regional space cooperation; this would maximise their vast potential ability to strengthen space security. It thus seems feasible to set up a working group to investigate the possibility of establishing compulsory and/or optional commercial standards for the space industry in the areas of management, product assurance and engineering.

A sustainable institutional arrangement is important for regional space cooperation. An agency such as ESA has obvious advantages for furthering space cooperation in Europe. APSCO, currently the only intergovernmental organisation in the Asia-Pacific region, could take up a similar role to ESA, providing an ideal platform for the harmonisation of space security standards within the region. At present, however, APSCO has only eight member states, with China the only spacefaring nation amongst them, which may raise doubts over the organisation's ability to truly represent the region's countries, particularly given the enduring political and cultural differences and mistrust amongst them.

We should not exclude the possibility of other standards of organisations or non-governmental organisations in the region playing a role in formulating space security standards. Whilst not legally binding per se, such standards could be made applicable to contracts and projects through their inclusion in cooperation agreements. In the era of increasing space commercialisation and privatisation, such standards would be meaningful when drawing up contracts involving private entities that want to carry out their space activities more securely. However, with different organisations playing a part in establishing space security standards, it is

---

[45] James Clay Moltz, 'China, the United States, and prospects for Asian space cooperation' (2011) 20 *Journal of Contemporary China* 82.

[46] Eilene Galloway, 'World security and the peaceful uses of outer space', XIth International Astronautical Congress Stockholm, (1960) 3 *Proceedings on Law of Outer Space* 95.

necessary for the various institutions and national space agencies involved to engage in dialogue and exchange to avoid the duplication of standards.

5   Conclusion

The development of space technologies is seen as an important component of the military and economic power of a state. With a growing number of space activities taking place on a daily basis, it has become necessary to think about strategies to ensure that those activities are carried out in an orderly manner and that space objects are well protected. Accordingly, space security has become a hot topic worldwide. As some scholars have observed, space technologies have important consequences for space security.[47] As discussed throughout the chapter, existing space treaties are ill-equipped to deal with the new issues arising in the era of space privatisation and commercialisation, and thus efforts should be made to lay the foundations for international cooperation in the interests of all.[48] It is widely accepted that space cooperation is the major mechanism for realising space security. As Basiuk has correctly observed: '[A]dvanced technologies, because of their huge costs, large scale, and, in the case of nuclear weapons, immense destructive power, provide an important impetus for international cooperation'.[49]

Space cooperation at the regional level has moved to a higher level on the international agenda after almost six decades of space technology and space activity development. Although some progress has been achieved in regional cooperation within the Asia-Pacific region, including the establishment of the region's first intergovernmental organisation, APSCO, we must be cognisant of the reality that substantial space cooperation at the regional level will require considerably more time and effort than many had anticipated.[50] In this regard, the Belt and Road initiative, most of

---

[47] David Wright, Laura Grego and Lisbeth Gronlund, *The Physics of Space Security: A Reference Manual* (Cambridge, MA: American Academy of Arts and Science, 2005), pp. 1–11.

[48] Colleen M. Driscoll, 'Redefining national security and the role of international law to secure peaceful uses of outer space', 4th Eilene Galloway Symposium on Critical Space Law Issues: International Cooperation for Peaceful Purposes, (2010) 52 *Proceedings of the International Institute of Space Law* 529.

[49] Victor Basiuk, *Technology, World Politics, and American Policy* (New York: Columbia University Press, 1977), p. 7.

[50] Yasuhito Fukushima, 'An Asian perspective on the new US space policy: the emphasis on international cooperation and its relevance to Asia' (2011) 27 *Space Policy* 6.

whose member states are in the Asia-Pacific region, provides an ideal platform for regional cooperation in the space arena. Such cooperation would help to create a secure environment for the sustainable development of the space industry and safeguard the interests of space companies by providing legal certainty and clarity. The realisation of space security in the Asia-Pacific region through regional space cooperation would undoubtedly help to establish a mutually beneficial development mode for cooperating parties, and ultimately promote space security for the wider international community.

PART III

Development of International Dispute Resolution under the Belt and Road Initiative

11

Regional Dispute Resolution

An International Civil Dispute Resolution
Model for East Asia

YUHONG CHAI

There is growing concern over how conspicuous a role regional dispute resolution will play in international dispute resolution concerning China's Belt and Road Initiative (BRI), particularly at a time when international civil dispute resolution tends to be similar to international commercial arbitration (ICA). Deep deliberation is needed to balance the relationship between regional and international dispute resolution from the angles of competition and cooperation. This chapter analyses ICA and related factors in three countries: mainland China, Japan and South Korea (Korea hereafter), to develop a model of international civil dispute resolution for East Asia.

1 International Commercial Arbitration Law in China, Japan and South Korea

In today's globalised world, ICA is the most widely used form of international civil dispute resolution. Since the 1920s, a global legal system of ICA has gradually been built through international cooperation. However, the ever-increasing globalisation of ICA highlights its importance for regional dispute resolution, particularly in the case of the BRI. Hence, this chapter begins with a brief analysis of the ICA systems in three East Asian countries, namely, China, Japan and Korea, their legal systems, arbitration institutions and dispute settlement mechanisms in particular. The following paragraphs address each country in turn.

From an international perspective, China's response to the ICA law regime is relatively backward. The Arbitration Law of the People's Republic of China was adopted during the Ninth Meeting of the Standing Committee of the Eighth National People's Congress on 31 August 1994 and came into force on 1 September 1995 (1995 Arbitration Law hereafter).

The 1995 Arbitration Law is ranked lower than the Chinese Constitution, but higher than any regulations formulated by the State Council or local legislatures. It constituted China's first dedicated regulation of the country's arbitration system, and has thus been praised as a milestone in its arbitration history. The 1995 Arbitration Law sets out the basic principles and systems of arbitration law, institutions and procedures, as well as judicial supervision. Although it lags behind international standards, the law equipped China with a modern arbitration system, albeit not one that follows the Model Law[1] on International Commercial Arbitration promulgated by the United Nations Commission on International Trade Law (UNCITRAL)[2] on 21 June 1985. The UNCITRAL Model Law provides states with a template for an effective, comprehensive and modern arbitration system. To date, seventy-two states in 102 jurisdictions have adopted legislation based on the Model Law.[3] Following the promulgation of the 1995 Arbitration Law, attempts were made through Supreme People's Court (SPC) interpretations, for example, the SPC's Interpretation on Several Issues Concerning Application of the Arbitration Law of the People's Republic of China (Judicial Interpretation (2006) No. 7),[4] to close the gap with international standards, but fundamental problems remain. In Hong Kong, a common law jurisdiction that has been a Special Administrative Region of China (HKSAR) for the past twenty years, a new Arbitration Ordinance whose content is based on the UNCITRAL Model Law, and thus differs from the 1995 Arbitration Law, took effect on 1 June 2011.

There are also obvious gaps between the 1995 Arbitration Law and Japanese and Korean arbitration law. Japan's current Arbitration Law is the 2003 version (2003 Arbitration Law hereafter), with the law having passed through three stages, the third of which is ongoing. The first stage was the period before 1890. Although limited information is available prior to 1890, it is clear that Japan had a long-standing arbitration system, such as the 'five group system' of the Tokugawa era. The second

---

[1] The UNCITRAL Arbitration Model Law (Model Law hereafter) has played an important role in creating international standards for international commercial arbitration (ICA). The 1985 Model Law was subsequently amended during the thirty-ninth UNCITRAL meeting on 7 July 2006, in accordance with ICA practice.

[2] UNCITRAL was established during the twenty-second UN General Assembly in December 1966 to promote the harmonisation and unification of international trade law.

[3] See the UNCITRAL website, accessed 15 June 2018 at www.uncitral.org/uncitral/en/uncitral_texts/arbitration/1985Model_arbitration_status.html.

[4] This interpretation was promulgated by the SPC on 23 August 2006 and took effect on 8 August 2006.

stage was from 1890 to 2003. At the beginning of that period, arbitration matters were settled with reference to Section 8 of Japan's old Code of Civil Procedure Law (1890), which marks the start of the country's modern (imported) arbitration system.[5] The provisions concerning arbitration proceedings in Section 8 of the old code are almost an exact replica of those in Section 10 of the 1877 German Code of Civil Procedure Law. Although Japan's Code of Civil Procedure Law was completely revised in 1926, the section concerning arbitration law has been maintained until the present day, although it was renamed the Public Notice Procedure and Arbitration Procedure Law in 1996.[6] The third, ongoing, stage comprises the years since passage of the 2003 Arbitration Law, which was passed on 1 August 2003 and came into effect on 1 March 2004. In the first two stages, there was no substantial alteration to the Japanese system of arbitration, which is modelled on the German system, since its introduction in 1890, although some modifications were made in 1926 to suit the needs of the era. In the years up to 2003, many countries adopted the UNCITRAL Model Law in establishing their own arbitration laws, and, accordingly, Japan also modelled its 2003 Arbitration Law on the Model Law to bring the Japanese arbitration system into compliance with international standards. Hence, great expectations were placed on the 2003 Arbitration Law with respect to promoting the utilisation of Japanese ICA. Although it complies with the UNCITRAL Model Law in essence, however, some of the 2003 Arbitration Law's legislative provisions have been adapted to Japanese dispute resolution practice, and there are moves afoot to further improve the arbitration system, for example, by harmonising it with the overall legal system.

Korea's arbitration law has gone through two phases, the first prior to application of the UNCITRAL Model Law. In the first half of the twentieth century, Korea was a Japanese colony, and, according to Article 1 of the Korean Civil Decree No. 13, legal regulations relating to arbitration should comply with Japan's Code of Civil Procedure Law. The Korean arbitration system also underwent modernisation in 1912. Although Korea gained independence from Japan after World War II and became a new nation in 1948, Section 8 of the old Japanese Code of Civil Procedure Law continued to apply to arbitration. In 1960, however, with the formulation of a new Korean Civil Procedure Law, only the old

---

[5] Matsuura Kaoru and Aoyama Yoshimitsu, *Modern Arbitration Law Issues* (Tokyo: Yuhikaku, 1998), p. 4.

[6] Takeshi Kojima and Akira Takakuwa, *Explanations and Comments on Arbitration Law* (Tokyo: Seirinsyoin Press, 2007), p. 4.

arbitration law in the Labour Dispute Adjustment Act was kept, with other parts of the act eliminated. Korea's first five-year economic development plan was implemented in 1961, triggering a rise in international trade with Korea, as well as a significant increase in the number of international trade disputes. Because Korea is an output-oriented market economy, the Korean government and business community recognised the necessity of promoting the use of a dispute-resolution system rather than litigation to ensure the smooth development and flow of international trade. Based on that recognition, the Korean National Assembly passed an Arbitration Act establishing the Arbitration Law of Korea on 31 December 1965. The law then took effect on 6 March 1966. The arbitration proceeding provisions in the Arbitration Law of Korea are patterned on the provisions of Section 10 of the 1877 German Code of Civil Procedure Law, but also refer to other civil law jurisdictions, such as France and Japan. To further expand the utilisation of arbitration, Korea's Arbitration Law was amended in 1973, 1993 and 1997.

The second phase was during application of the UNCITRAL Model Law. The development of arbitration practices in Korea, as well as the influence of the world's major arbitration institutions, sparked calls to adopt the Model Law in the early 1990s, and a series of arbitration seminars held by the Korean Commercial Arbitration Board (KCAB) and related organisations furthered interest in such a move. The international trend towards adoption of the Model Law and Korea's implementation of a policy of globalisation in 1994 led to an independent committee being established within the Ministry of Justice in December 1998. In the first six months of the following year, the committee drafted an Arbitration Amendment Act in accordance with the UNCITRAL Model Law, together with a number of amendments. The act was then approved by the Korean National Assembly on 2 December 1999, and entered into force on 31 December of the same year. Because Korea's Arbitration Law applies the UNCITRAL Model Law, it is consistent with international standards. The law was subsequently amended in 2001, 2002 and 2010, although its fundamental content and structure have remained the same. The 2010 Arbitration Law is currently in force.

1.1   Commercial Arbitration Institutions in East Asia

The number of arbitration institutions in China has risen from seven to 244 since implementation of the 1995 Arbitration Law. The country's fast-paced economic development and regional differences in economic development are partially responsible for the rise. The major arbitration institutions in China include the China International Economic and Trade Arbitration Commission (CIETAC), the Beijing Arbitration Commission (BAC) and a number of other well-known institutions. However, the nature and position of arbitration bodies have long been uncertain in China, leading to confusion during the course of their development. Although those bodies make efforts to meet international standards, those efforts are not sufficient to improve the image of mainland Chinese arbitration internationally.

The situation is very different for the Hong Kong International Arbitration Centre (HKIAC), which was established in 1985 as a non-profit organisation. According to an interpretation of the provisions of Article 2 of the Hong Kong Arbitration Ordinance (Cap 609), the HKIAC is incorporated in Hong Kong under the Companies Ordinance (Cap 32) as a company limited by guarantee. A company limited by guarantee is an alternative type of corporation used primarily by non-profit organisations. It has members who act as guarantors covering a certain, usually nominal, amount of the company's debt that is explicitly stated in the company's memorandum. In the event of bankruptcy owing to insufficient assets, members of the company assume the amount of debt previously guaranteed to fulfil their corresponding obligations. Although the HKIAC received support from the Hong Kong Government and Hong Kong business community when it was established, it is now completely independent, both financially and administratively. It is operated by the HKIAC Council, and is neither influenced nor controlled by any other organ or person. Since its establishment in 1985, the number of cases heard by the HKIAC has risen steadily, and the centre has become increasingly prominent worldwide as a trusted international arbitration institution. In addition, the International Chamber of Commerce (ICC) opened an Asian office in Hong Kong in 2008.[7] Hong Kong is also home to CIETAC's first arbitration centre outside mainland China, namely, the China International Economic and Trade Arbitration Commission Hong Kong Arbitration Centre (CIETACHKAC), which began operating in 2012.

---

[7] Michael J. Moser and John Choong (eds.), *Asia Arbitration Handbook* (Oxford: Oxford University Press, 2011), p. 200.

In Japan, the Japan Commercial Arbitration Association (JCAA) is currently the only arbitration institution that handles ICA, although the Japan Shipping Exchange and Japan Intellectual Property Arbitration Center handle related areas. The JCAA deals with both domestic and international commercial arbitration cases. It was established in 1950 by the Japan Chamber of Commerce and Industry (JCCI) with the support of six other business organisations, including the Japan Federation of Economic Organizations, Japan Foreign Trade Council and Federation of Banking Associations of Japan, to settle commercial disputes and promote international trade. With further growth in international trade, the JCAA's arbitration committee became independent of the JCAA in 1953. Since 2009, it has operated as general association corporation. The JCAA is headquartered in Tokyo, and has offices in Osaka, Kobe, Nagoya and Yokohama. The Tokyo and Osaka offices have dedicated staff who handle arbitration cases directly. Nagoya serves as the boundary for determining which jurisdiction, i.e. Tokyo or Osaka, will hear an arbitration case: if the parties agree that Nagoya, Yokohama or Tokyo is the place (or seat) of arbitration, the case will be settled in the Tokyo office, whereas the Osaka office will deal with disputes in all other places. The Kobe, Yokohama and Nagoya offices receive people and material resources from the JCCI. The trends in the number of arbitration cases handled by the JCAA from 2000 to 2010 can be seen in Figure 11.1.[8]

Moving to Korea, the Korean Commercial Arbitration Board (KCAB) was established as an independent arbitration institution in 1970. It is the only authorised institution of its kind in Korea, and is a non-profit association corporation operated by the KCAB Council, which comprises a chairperson, president and fifteen directors. The KCAB Secretariat deals with daily business. Korea is also home to a Commercial Arbitration Law Commission and General Affairs Department of Management and Arbitration. KCAB deals with disputes arising from domestic and international trade in Korea, and has dealt with approximately

---

[8] Nakamura Tatsuya, *The Current Situation and Problems of International Commercial Arbitration in Tokyo*, AIB Transaction No. 14 (East Lansing, MI: Academy for International Business, 2012), p. 231.

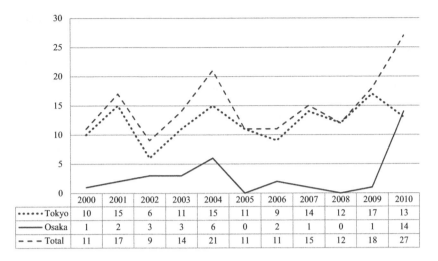

	2000	2001	2002	2003	2004	2005	2006	2007	2008	2009	2010
⋯⋯ Tokyo	10	15	6	11	15	11	9	14	12	17	13
— Osaka	1	2	3	3	6	0	2	1	0	1	14
– – Total	11	17	9	14	21	11	11	15	12	18	27

Figure 11.1   Arbitration Cases Heard by the Japan Commercial Arbitration Association between 2000 and 2010[9]

4,000 arbitration domestic and international cases since its establishment.[10] Statistics show that the board handles approximately fifty ICA cases per year on average. For example, of the eighty-five international cases KCAB processed in 2012, sixty-three were related to ICA. Five were maritime cases, two intellectual property cases, one a labour case, four financial cases and the remainder concerned a variety of other issues. Of the seventy-seven and fifty-two cases dealt with in 2010 and 2011, ICA cases accounted for thirty-nine and fifty-three, respectively.[11] The chart depicted in Table 11.1 shows the number of cases processed by KCAB in relation to those handled by the world's major ICA institutions.[12]

---

[9] Ibid.
[10] Korean Commercial Arbitration Board (KCAB), *2012 Annual Report* (Seoul: KCAB, 2012), p. 5.
[11] Ibid.
[12] The Singapore data come from the homepage of the Singapore International Arbitration Centre (SIAC).

Table 11.1 *International Cases Handled by Arbitral Institutions Globally*

Arbitral institution	2000	2001	2002	2003	2004	2005	2006	2007	2008	2009	2010
AAA-ICDR	510	649	672	646	614	580	586	621	703	836	888
ICC	541	566	593	580	561	521	593	599	663	817	793
CIETAC	543	562	468	422	461	427	442	429	548	560	418
LCIA	87	71	88	104	87	118	133	137	213	272	237
HKIAC	NA	NA	NA	NA	NA	NA	NA	139	173	212	175
SIAC	37	39	34	23	39	29	47	55	71	114	140
SCC	66	68	50	77	45	53	64	81	74	96	91
KCAB	40	65	47	38	46	53	47	59	47	78	52
BAC	11	20	19	33	30	53	53	37	59	72	32
JCAA	8	16	8	14	15	9	11	15	12	17	26

1.2   East Asian Dispute Settlement System

Mainland Chinese arbitration institutions have used a combination of arbitration and mediation in dispute resolution since CIETAC first adopted the approach in the 1950s. CIETAC was the country's first arbitration institution to adopt the combined dispute resolution method. In the 1950s, CIETAC was not a well-known ICA institution. Between January 1956 and October 1966, it received only twenty-seven cases, of which a few were resolved through arbitration alone and the remainder through a combination of arbitration and mediation. The Arbitration Regulation issued by CIETAC in 1988 clearly defines the combined approach in Article 37. It is also mandated by the 1995 Arbitration Law in Article 51.[13]

The combination of arbitration and mediation has its own rationale and effectiveness in the dispute resolution systems of East Asia. For example, the 2 December 2011 decision in the Gao Haiyan arbitration case in mainland China was later supported by the HKSAR Court of Appeal, thereby affording Hong Kong Court approval to the combined

---

[13] Article 51 of the 1995 Arbitration Law stipulates that an arbitration tribunal may first attempt to conciliate before giving an award. If the parties apply for conciliation voluntarily, the arbitration tribunal shall conciliate. If conciliation is unsuccessful, an award shall be made promptly. When a settlement agreement is reached by conciliation, the arbitration tribunal shall prepare the conciliation statement or award based on the results of the settlement agreement, and the conciliation statement shall have the same legal force as that of an award.

approach. This development trend can also be seen in the mediation systems of Hong Kong and Japan. For example, Article 28 of the 2013 HKIAC Rules and Articles 52 and 53 of the revised JCAA Arbitration Rules stipulate the combination of arbitration and mediation in dispute resolution. Although there is no such provision in KCAB's International Arbitration Rules at the pre-proceedings stage, the combined dispute settlement procedure has been called a last-chance procedure.[14] According to Article 34[15] of those rules, the final outcome of mediation to resolve disputes is binding on the parties concerned.

The foregoing analysis of the ICA situation in China, Japan and Korea shows that, with the exception of China, arbitration law and ICA institutions have reached generally recognised international standards. However, the actual practice of ICA in Japan and Korea has long been somewhat stagnated. Whilst both countries have taken some measures to revitalise that practice, with Korea arguably making more progress than Japan, the effectiveness of the combination of arbitration and mediation in their dispute settlement systems has not yet been fully realised. The remainder of this chapter explores the East Asian model of international civil dispute resolution from the perspective of the international progress achieved in ICA to elucidate the efficiency and economics of such resolution.

2 Key Factors in International Commercial Arbitration in East Asia

2.1 Dispute Resolution Culture in East Asia

China, Japan and Korea are all members of East Asia, and in addition to their geographic proximity they also have similar legal systems, cultures, languages and habits, and their histories are intertwined. With the exception of the HKSAR, all three countries also practise civil law. Before the Meiji Restoration (*Meiji Ishin*) in Japan in 1868, the nations of East Asia

---

[14] Shahla F. Ali, *Resolving Disputes in the Asia-Pacific Region: International Arbitration and Mediation in East Asia and the West* (London: Routledge, 2012), p. 39.

[15] Article 34 covers awards by consent. It states that if the parties concerned reach a settlement after a request has been filed and advance costs have been paid, the arbitral tribunal may render a consent award recording the settlement if any party so requests. If the parties do not require a consent award, then upon written confirmation by the parties to the secretariat that a settlement has been made, the arbitral tribunal shall be discharged and the reference to arbitration concluded, subject to payment by the parties of any outstanding costs of the arbitration.

were centred on Chinese culture, with a wide range of cultural exchanges taking place amongst them. Chinese culture was thus the foundation of the traditional common culture in East Asia.[16] That culture is heavily influenced by Confucianism, which is deeply rooted in China, Japan and Korea. Under the influence of Confucian culture, the primary means of dispute resolution in East Asia has traditionally been reconciliation. Although each East Asian nation has its own language, there are similarities amongst them, and China, Japan and Korea all use some Chinese characters. The three countries also share legal terminology.

2.2 Place of Arbitration

The place (or seat) of arbitration is a very important concept in ICA, and is usually stipulated in the arbitration clause or agreement. Although there are divergent views on the place of arbitration concept and how to determine that place,[17] it is generally considered to be the place where the arbitration award is to be made or where the bulk of the arbitration proceedings are to be held.[18] In other words, the place of arbitration has two important legal consequences. First, it determines which jurisdiction's arbitration laws apply to the proceedings and which courts may exercise supportive and supervisory powers over the arbitration. Second, it determines the place of the arbitration award for international enforcement purposes.

Although the place of arbitration is not clearly provided in the 1995 Arbitration Law, Article 20 of the Hong Kong Arbitration Ordinance, Article 28 of Japan's Arbitration Law and Article 21 of Korea's Arbitration Law convey the following common understanding. First, the parties to the dispute have the right to choose the place of arbitration by agreement. Second, if the parties cannot reach agreement on the place of arbitration, then the arbitration tribunal shall determine it in accordance with the interests and convenience of the parties and the relevant circumstances. However, the place of arbitration is just a formal concept in law, and hence the arbitration tribunal can carry out the arbitration proceeding in locales other than the place of arbitration. In other words, the place

---

[16] Masaji Chiba, *The Pluralistic Structure of Asian Law* (Tokyo: Seibundo, 1998), pp. 89–99, 99–102.

[17] Kojima and Takakuwa, *Explanations and Comments*, p. 14.

[18] Akira Takakura, *A Collection of Essays about International Civil Procedure Law: Private International Law* (Tokyo: Toshindo, 2011), p. 360.

of the arbitration hearing and the place of arbitration do not have to be the same.[19] Also, the place of arbitration may not be stated explicitly in the arbitration award. Finally, paragraphs 1(a) and (d) of Article 5 of the New York Convention (NYC)[20] and paragraph 2 of Article 1 of the UNCITRAL Model Law highlight the importance of the place of arbitration in ICA. It is necessary to choose that place to render a certain degree of assistance and intervention possible. Because the place of arbitration plays such an important role in the ICA system, arbitration will face a crisis if no such place is specified. First, the assistance obligation of the court in the place of arbitration will be excluded, although not judicial relief. Second, at the arbitral award enforcement stage, if the place of arbitration is unclear, the NYC applies in the case of any problems.

Because the place of arbitration can be selected through agreement, it would be in the interests of the parties to international civil disputes to select a place that is as neutral as possible to meet their diverse needs. A neutral place of arbitration is also one in which the legal system is capable of carrying out ICA smoothly. Accordingly, the importance of the place of arbitration has exerted a considerable impact on the overall ICA trend in East Asia. The choice of a jurisdiction as the place of arbitration is not simple, and should be based on comprehensive consideration of a variety of factors. For example, when the parties concerned are making their selection, they will consider whether the place is geographically convenient, whether it is neutral with respect to politically sensitive cases, whether entry visas can be easily obtained and whether the judicial system is trustworthy, as well as the nature of the surrounding social environment, the convenience of the transport system and the legal system the jurisdiction applies. With respect to the legal system alone, there are numerous factors to consider, which can produce a variety of effects. Most parties to international disputes will look, for example, for arbitration institutions that operate in accordance with international standards, arbitration law that is enacted in accordance with the UNCITRAL Model Law and enforced by a court that understands and supports ICA, and law firms staffed with lawyers who have ICA experience.

From a comparative perspective in the current East Asian context, it is obvious that Hong Kong constitutes a neutral place of arbitration.

---

[19] Masato Dougauti, 'The meaning and function of the place of arbitration in international commercial arbitration' (2004) 51(12) *JCA Journal* 62.

[20] The 1958 Convention on the Recognition and Enforcement of Foreign Arbitral Awards.

Hong Kong has many advantages, including a world-class airport, a reliable legal system based on common law, a compatible legal culture, lawyers with rich ICA experience, the possibility of resolving a dispute in multiple languages and the stability of arbitration awards enforced in mainland China. In addition, Hong Kong is home to a number of well-respected arbitration institutions, including the HKIAC, ICC and CIETACHKAC.

No arbitration institutions in China, Japan or Korea are comparable to those in Hong Kong. Although China has several arbitration institutions with the same standards as international arbitration institutions, such as CIETAC and the BAC, problems remain with the 1995 Arbitration Law and the uncertainty surrounding the nature of the country's arbitration institutions. Similarly, although the JCAA, KCAB and Seoul International Dispute Resolution Center (Seoul IDRC) also meet international standards, in comparison with Hong Kong's arbitration institutions they lack practical ICA experience. If East Asia is to form an economic circle comparable in strength to Europe's, it is essential that it establishes world-class arbitration institutions capable of resolving international civil disputes objectively.

2.3   Functional Expansion of International Commercial Arbitration Institutions

Another eye-catching development in dispute resolution through arbitration is the cooperation between arbitration institutions for the purpose of promoting one another. The signing of agreements between arbitration institutions and establishment of arbitration organisations amongst institutions are the usual methods of cooperation. For example, the JCAA signed an agreement with KCAB in 1973 and with CIETAC and the HKIAC in 2009.[21] Furthermore, the Asia Pacific Regional Arbitration Group (APRAG), which had thirty member organisations as of 2016, was established in 2004. Despite such cooperation, the continued rise of ICA cases has sparked fierce competition amongst arbitration institutions. However, precisely because each institution tries its best to become the centre of ICA in its region, the ICA environment continues to improve, which serves to encourage cooperation. A case in point is Maxwell Chambers, which was established in Singapore in 2010, with major

---

[21] See the JCAA website, accessed 15 June 2018 at www.jcaa.or.jp/e/.

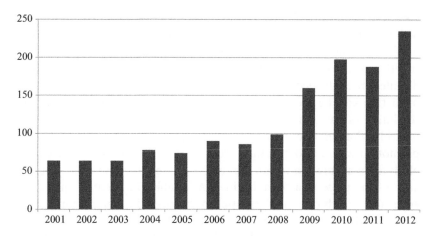

Figure 11.2   Singapore International Arbitration Centre Cases from 2001 to 2012

international arbitration and other dispute resolution institutions, including the Singapore International Arbitration Centre (SIAC), the ICC and the American Arbitration Association's International Centre for Dispute Resolution subsequently joining it. These entities provide support and services to those who desire to resolve their disputes via ICA. Figure 11.2 shows the increase in cases following the establishment of Maxwell Chambers.[22]

According to a 2012 SIAC report, prior to the establishment of Maxwell Chambers, the highest number of cases accepted in a single year was 160 in 2009. Subsequent to it, in the three years from 2010 to 2012, SIAC accepted 198, 188 and 235 cases, respectively. It can thus be inferred that the establishment of Maxwell Chambers had a profound effect on the development of commercial arbitration in Singapore. Korea set up the Seoul IDRC on 27 May 2013. Similar to Maxwell Chambers, it is not an arbitration institution, but provides a site and equipment to support international arbitration and other forms of dispute resolution.

3   Conclusion

The analysis of ICA in East Asia in this chapter makes clear the challenges and opportunities of such arbitration and the direction it needs to

---

[22] SIAC, *2012 Annual Report*, accessed 27 June 2018 at www.siac.org.sg/images/stories/articles/annual_report/siac_annual_report_2012_new.pdf.

take to develop further in the region. First, the combination of arbitration with mediation is based on the form of dispute resolution that prevails in East Asian cultures. East Asians, in general, perceive mediation to be a superior form of such resolution, and thus consciously try to resolve disputes through mediation. Thus, the combination of arbitration with mediation can be seen as a typical feature of and model for dispute resolution in East Asia, and may serve to promote the region as a place of arbitration in international civil dispute resolution. Of course, its promotion would also give the parties to such disputes a greater choice of places of arbitration within the region. Second, because of the importance of the place of arbitration in ICA, establishing neutral and efficient places of arbitration is essential to the overall development of ICA in East Asia. On the one hand, such establishment would reduce the current differences amongst the arbitration institutions of China, Japan and Korea. On the other, it would enhance the competitiveness of ICA in East Asia. At present, it is reasonable to take full advantage of Hong Kong as a place of arbitration. Third, the region should look south to Singapore for an example of a composite pattern that gives full play to the functions of arbitration institutions. At present, the only organisation in East Asia established on that pattern is the Seoul IDRC in Korea. However, the composite pattern could prove a very effective way for China and Japan to promote the development of ICA in a similar way to Korea. In the case of mainland China, however, because ad hoc arbitration is not recognised, the necessity for outside arbitration institutions to set up shop on the mainland is not obvious. Thus, establishing the Singapore-type composite pattern in Hong Kong would likely be more appropriate for ICA institutions. That pattern can also be used to promote the development of ICA in Japan. Attracting the world's major international commercial arbitration institutions to join such an entity would promote the development of arbitration, accumulate practical ICA experience and deepen understanding of ICA in Japan.

For all of these reasons, and in the spirit of cooperation and competition, in this final section of the chapter I discuss the prospects of international civil dispute resolution in East Asia from the perspective of ICA institutions. First, agreements should be concluded to set up an office in another arbitration institution. The function of that office would not necessarily be to deal with cases directly, but rather to collect information, including business contacts, and for promotional purposes. Cooperation between arbitration institutions can reduce the cost of maintaining separate offices and improve efficiency. At present, it would be feasible

Table 11.2[23] *Mainland China-Related Cases Accepted by the HKIAC from 2007 to 2012*

Year	International arbitration (excluding domestic arbitration)	Number of cases involving mainland parties	Mainland parties versus others (mainland parties as claimants)	Others versus mainland parties (mainland parties as respondents)	Mainland versus mainland
2007	139	82	N/A	N/A	N/A
2008	173	85	N/A	N/A	N/A
2009	212	119	N/A	N/A	N/A
2010	175	91	25	65	1
2011	178	87	20	51	16
2012	293	144	N/A	N/A	N/A

for one arbitration institution to establish an office in another in East Asia. Such a measure would ease some of the problems that international civil dispute resolution currently faces in the region. It would also serve as a transitional step towards a composite pattern of international civil dispute resolution. Second, an East Asian international civil dispute resolution centre should be established in Hong Kong. Although the Seoul IDRC already exists, the establishment of such a centre in Hong Kong would have several advantages, not least Hong Kong's position as a meeting place of Eastern and Western cultures and special status as a neutral place of arbitration in international civil dispute resolution. Table 11.2 reports statistics on mainland China-related cases accepted by the HKIAC from 2007 to 2012.

It can be seen from the Table 11.2 that the HKIAC dealt with 293 international cases in 2012, of which 144 concerned mainland parties.[24] The data therein clearly show that Hong Kong is an important choice of location in international arbitration cases relating to mainland China. Third, the ideal model for resolving international civil disputes in East

---

[23] These data were provided by Guan Zhong of the Hong Kong International Arbitration Centre (HKIAC).

[24] Guan Zhong provided this information during my visit to the HKIAC in March 2013. He also informed me that more than 40 per cent of the international cases handled by the HKIAC relate to mainland Chinese parties.

Table 11.3 *International Commercial Arbitration Cases in East Asia Settled by the International Chamber of Commerce from 1998 to 2009*

Country	98	99	00	01	02	03	04	05	06	07	08	09	Total
Korea	21	12	22	27	34	23	27	13	37	40	30	31	317
Japan	20	18	7	31	23	19	23	27	15	20	13	26	242
Mainland China	11	9	14	7	10	15	24	26	22	22	20	33	213
Hong Kong	11	13	12	15	8	7	8	8	15	5	18	15	135

Asia would be to set up several international civil dispute resolution centres in China, Japan and Korea. The parties to such disputes would then have a choice of places of arbitration depending on the circumstances of the case. It would also allow ICA cases in East Asia to be resolved internally. Improving the overall competitiveness of international civil dispute resolution services in East Asia would also make it possible for institutions within the region to handle ICA cases from other regions. The necessity of this ideal model is illustrated by the ICC data presented in Table 11.3.[25]

The statistical data in Table 11.3 refer to the number of East Asian cases settled by the ICC alone. In addition, many other cases were settled by institutions outside the region, including SIAC and the London Court of International Arbitration. In conclusion, maximising the utilisation of dispute resolution resources in East Asia through this ideal model would greatly help to improve the prospects of the BRI in East Asia and beyond.

---

[25] Data are taken from Kevin Kim Kap-You and John P. Bang, *Arbitration Law of Korea: Practice and Procedure* (New York: Juris, 2012), p. 4.

12

Enforcement of Arbitral Awards in Asia under the Belt and Road Initiative

Implications for International Governance and the Chinese Rule of Law

WEIXIA GU*

The accomplishments of a broadly homogenised global arbitration system have been made possible by international embracement of three UN-initiated arbitration devices: the Convention on the Recognition and Enforcement of Foreign Arbitral Awards (the New York Convention hereafter),[1] UNCITRAL Model Law on International Commercial Arbitration (Model Law hereafter)[2] and UNCITRAL Arbitration Rules (UNCITRAL Rules hereafter).[3] However, a truly harmonised system of international commercial arbitration has thus far been foiled by the 'public policy' exception in the enforcement of arbitral awards under the New York Convention, Article V2(b) which stipulates that '[r]ecognition and enforcement of an arbitral award may also be refused if the competent authority in the country where recognition and enforcement is sought finds that . . . (b) [t]he recognition or enforcement of the award would be contrary to the public policy of that country.'[4] Indeed, it was Burrough J of the English Court of the Exchequer who famously proclaimed in 1824 that public policy 'is a very unruly horse, and once you get astride it you never

* The writing of this chapter benefited from the support of the Hong Kong Government Research Grants Council's General Research Fund (Project Code: HKU 17617416H). I thank Emily Chan for her helpful research assistance. All errors remain my own.
[1] The Convention on the Recognition and Enforcement of Foreign Arbitral Awards was agreed in New York on 10 June 1958: 21 UST 2517, TIAS No. 6997, 330 UNTS 38.
[2] UNCITRAL is the United Nations Commission on International Trade Law. The 1985 UNCITRAL Model Law on International Commercial Arbitration was adopted in Vienna on 21 June 1985, with amendments adopted in 2006: 24 ILM 1302.
[3] UNCITRAL Arbitration Rules (revised in 2010 and 2013), 15 December 1967, UN Doc. A/RES/31/98; 15 ILM 701.
[4] Article V2(b) of the New York Convention

know where it will carry you'.[5] The 'unruly horse' metaphor aptly captures the indeterminacy of the public policy exception within international commercial arbitration, a substantial and recurring obstacle to both the finality and enforceability of arbitral agreements and awards. The existence of differing conceptions of public policy amongst legal systems, traditions and jurisdictions generates substantial uncertainty as to the conditions of international arbitral award enforcement in both theory and practice. True harmonisation of the nebulous public policy exception is thus necessary to fashion a cogent, coherent arbitral enforcement system that is applicable across the globe.

Within Asia, the aim of China's proposed Belt and Road Initiative (BRI) is to bolster regional connectivity, promote cross-border investment and strengthen economic coordination across the Eurasian nations located along the historic Silk Road.[6] In light of the large volume of cross-border contractual disputes expected to arise as a result of the BRI, the importance of arbitration as the preferred means of commercial dispute resolution is expected to grow, particularly given its ability to mitigate conflicts between different legal systems.[7] This chapter contends that the BRI provides an ideal context for contemplating the possibility of the regional or 'geo-legal' harmonisation of the public policy concept in the cross-border enforcement of arbitral awards within Asia. Whilst the abundance of different legal cultures in Asia presents formidable challenges to harmonisation, bringing consistency to the public policy exception is likely to yield substantive benefits in the arena of commercial certainty and, as a natural corollary, stimuli for boosting investment amongst the Belt and Road nations. Such developments will pave the way towards the ultimate goal of 'true harmonisation' of the international commercial arbitration system.

---

[5] *Richardson* v. *Mellish* (1824) 2 Bing at 229, [1824–34] All ER 258 at 266 per Burrough J.

[6] National Development and Reform Commission (NDRC), Ministry of Foreign Affairs and Ministry of Commerce (MOFCOM), 'Vision and actions on jointly building Silk Road Economic Belt and 21st-Century Maritime Silk Road', NDRC, 28 March 2015, accessed 15 June 2018 at http://en.ndrc.gov.cn/newsrelease/201503/t20150330_669367.html.

[7] Indeed, Hong Kong Secretary for Justice Rimsky Yuen envisioned that opportunities for outward expansion of the local legal and arbitration sectors lay in providing services to alleviate the 'legal uncertainties' along the Belt and Road route. See Department of Justice (Hong Kong), 'Secretary for Justice promotes Hong Kong's legal and dispute resolution services in Beijing (with photos)', Department of Justice, 18 August 2015, accessed 15 June 2018 at www.doj.gov.hk/mobile/eng/public/pr/20150818_pr.html.

1 Barriers to the Enforcement of Foreign Arbitral Awards: Taming the Untamed Horse

1.1 The Public Policy Exception under Article V2(b) of the New York Convention

Under Article V2(b) of the New York Convention, the recognition or enforcement of an arbitral award within a given jurisdiction may be declined by a contracting state if such recognition or enforcement is considered by the courts of that state to contravene public policy.[8] As the peripheries of public policy are neither restricted nor defined by the convention, contracting states are essentially free to determine the substantive content and limits of their nation-specific public policy.

The controversy in international legal jurisprudence surrounding this 'free-for-all' public policy exception is rooted in its bestowal upon national judicial systems of ultimate control over the recognition and enforcement of (perhaps) otherwise valid arbitral awards, along with the unpredictability and irregularity of its application. It has been noted that the power of refusal to recognise or enforce arbitral awards goes 'to the heart' of the New York Convention.[9] The primary objective of the convention is to advance collective legislative standards for the enhanced recognition and enforcement of cross-border arbitral awards. A broad interpretation of the public policy exception thus frustrates the effective functioning of the convention and, by extension, the efficient operation of the international arbitration system.[10]

Even within national boundaries, the vagueness of the article V2(b) exception is encapsulated in the general dearth of statutory definitions of 'public policy'.[11] A general survey of the public policy definitions advanced by various jurisdictions, however, reveals a common thread in that violation of public policy implies contravention of 'fundamental' or 'basic'

---

[8] Article V2(b) of the New York Convention

[9] Richard A. Cole, 'The public policy exception to the New York Convention on the Recognition and Enforcement of Arbitral Awards' (1985) 1 *Ohio State Journal on Dispute Resolution* 365–83 at 372.

[10] Ibid., 366.

[11] A recent report issued by the International Bar Association (IBA) Subcommittee on Recognition and Enforcement of Arbitration found that of the more than forty jurisdictions surveyed, only two (Australia and the United Arab Emirates) had developed explicit statutory definitions for the concept of public policy. See IBA Subcommittee on Recognition and Enforcement of Arbitral Awards, *Report on the Public Policy Exception in the New York Convention* (London: IBA, October 2015), p. 2. General reports and country reports are available from the IBA website, accessed 15 June 2018 at www.ibanet.org.

principles.[12] Hence, the minimum content of a state party's public policy lies in the fundamental principles or values underscoring its legal order and social fabric, whatever those normative standards and values are determined to be.

However, the indeterminacy of public policy's definition can be mitigated to some extent by dividing it into two dimensions: the procedural and the substantive. Procedural public policy is concerned with upholding formal justice between two arbitrating parties, for instance, in matters relating to the right of due process or the refusal to enforce awards obtained by fraud or falsification.[13] Substantive public policy, in contrast, involves value-laden norms that inform the interests of public policy, for instance, the general common law prohibition against punitive damages unrelated to formal equality.[14] As discussed later in the chapter, procedural public policy based on securing fair procedure is often viewed as less contentious than substantive public policy, which may mandate the acceptance of certain norms based on state-specific priorities or other normative judgments.

Nonetheless, fears over the indeterminacy of the public policy exception in Article V2(b) may be more academic than factually based. Owing to the narrow construction afforded that exception by most state parties, coupled with the pro-enforcement bias of foreign arbitral awards in many jurisdictions, even when the exception is raised, it is far more often rejected than accepted.[15] In China, of the seventeen cases reported to the Supreme People's Court (SPC) in which a foreign arbitral award was refused recognition or enforcement under Article V of the New York Convention, only one succeeded on the public policy ground offered by Article V2(b).[16] This lack of success highlights the pro-enforcement policy adopted by the Chinese judiciary. Only with the SPC's permission can the lower courts refuse to recognise or enforce foreign arbitral

---

[12] IBA Subcommittee, *Report on the Public Policy Exception*, p. 6. The report further notes that 'fundamental' and 'basic' principles are expressed differently by common law and civil law jurisdictions: the former refer to 'basic principles or values' forming the basis of society, whilst the latter refer to more precise – albeit still vague – 'communal values'.

[13] Ibid., p. 15.

[14] Ibid., p. 17.

[15] Ibid., p. 12.

[16] Xiaohong Xia, 'Implementation of the New York Convention in China' (2011) 1 *Arbitration Brief* 20–4 at 23.

awards.[17] The result is a lack of clear legislative guidance concerning the Chinese conception of public policy, which, whilst indeterminate, does not in practice seem to raise any issues vis-à-vis enforcement. The same applies with respect to other member states of the New York Convention.

1.2   Competing Paradigms: Seat Theory Versus Delocalisation Theory

An appeal for harmonisation of the public policy exception invites scrutiny of the two main contending theories underpinning the normative foundations upon which international commercial arbitration ought to develop. Known respectively as seat theory and delocalisation theory, each paradigm addresses the issue of whether the fact that parties have opted for a particular jurisdictional 'seat' for their arbitral proceedings means that the applicable national procedural laws, or *lex arbitri*, of that jurisdiction ought to govern the arbitral process.[18] On a more abstract level, each theory may be considered to pertain to the source of the legal validity of arbitral awards.[19] Whilst orthodox state practice has thus far tended towards the adoption of seat theory,[20] it is argued herein that the delocalisation of arbitral norms is preferred in the interests of homogenisation. It should be noted, however, that the seat and delocalisation theories represent only the two most prominent theories concerning the foundations of international commercial arbitration.[21]

1.2.1   Seat Theory

Seat theory advances the primacy of the territorial seat of international commercial arbitration proceedings, whereby the relevant national procedural laws of that seat are considered to hold an automatic and

---

[17] Supreme People's Court of the People's Republic of China, Circular of the Supreme People's Court on Issues in the People's Courts Handling of Foreign-Related Arbitration and Foreign Arbitration Matters, a Fa [1995] No. 18, 28 August 1995. A translation of this document may be found at CIETAC's website, accessed 15 June 2018 at www.cietac.org/index.php?m=Article&a=show&id=2414&l=en.

[18] Masood Ahmed, 'The influence of the delocalization and seat theories upon judicial attitudes towards international commercial arbitration' (2011) 77 *Arbitration* 406–22 at 407.

[19] Matthew Barry, 'The role of the seat in international arbitration: theory, practice, and implications for Australian courts' (2015) 32 *Journal of International Arbitration* 289–323 at 295.

[20] Ahmed, 'The influence of the delocalization and seat theories', 412–17.

[21] Barry, 'The role of the seat', 294–300.

legitimate mandate to supervise the proceedings.[22] The arbitral process is, by extension, thus shaped by legal standards specific to the arbitration location, which forms the normative backdrop against which the parties concerned determine the arbitral proceeding procedure. Enforcement courts, if located outside the seat jurisdiction, must generally defer to the decisions of the seat, unless doing so would violate the public policy of the enforcement jurisdiction under Article V2(b) of the New York Convention

Given the traditional Westphalian focus on national sovereignty and state positivism, a substantial number of states and their judicial systems, have both explicitly and implicitly adopted seat theory, conferring upon their courts a mandate to supervise arbitral proceedings via state-specific *lex arbitri*.[23] Under this paradigm, a party seeking to enforce a cross-border arbitral award is subjected to two sets of controls: arbitration proceedings are first governed by the *lex arbitri* of the seat – in addition to the rules and procedures chosen by both parties – before then being enforced by an alternate jurisdiction with its own distinct considerations concerning recognition and enforcement. It is thus contended in this chapter that this dual system is both inefficient and uncertain in that it creates a superfluous hurdle for parties who have obtained an arbitral award in one jurisdiction, but seek to enforce it in another. Delocalisation theory provides a potential solution for this particular predicament.

1.2.2   Delocalisation Theory

Delocalisation theory envisions an international commercial arbitration system liberated from the influence of the *lex arbitri* of the arbitral seat.[24] In other words, arbitration parties are free to determine the form and procedure of their arbitral proceedings without regard to the need to adhere to the law of arbitration within the seat jurisdiction. Redfern couches such freedom in the language of a 'universal' *lex arbitri* such that all laws regulating the arbitral process are the same.[25] The implication is the homogenisation of arbitral procedural laws between jurisdictions in that there are no longer any state-specific procedural requirements applicable above the usual. In the delocalisation paradigm, the only national legal

---

[22] Ahmed, 'The influence of the delocalization and seat theories', 412–13.
[23] Ibid.
[24] Ibid., 478.
[25] Alan Redfern and Martin Hunter, *Law and Practice of International Commercial Arbitration* (London: Sweet & Maxwell, 2004), p. 89.

consideration that plays a legitimate role in the arbitration process is the public policy of the enforcement court. In contrast to the dual control imposed first by *lex arbitri* and then the enforcement court, the sole point of control – along with its public policy considerations – is now the enforcement jurisdiction.[26]

To use the terminology of delocalisation proponent Jan Paulsson, unlike the case under seat theory, the arbitral process is not 'anchored' within the national norms of that arbitral seat, but rather both 'floats' and 'drifts' in its capacity to be recognised by the arbitral systems in other jurisdictions.[27] Delocalisation theories thus naturally promote party autonomy, allowing greater leeway for parties to determine the resolution of their disputes free from the constraints of national public policy.[28] Paulsson also favours the delocalisation approach for another reason: whilst the foregoing discussion revolves around governance of the arbitration process rather than enforcement of the arbitral award, it is contended that the same rationale of homogenisation may be applied to the enforcement position, thereby lending legal certainty to commercial considerations under a global rule of law. Similar to Redfern's proposal of a universal *lex arbitri*, a universal set of enforcement standards, including grounds for exclusion under the public policy exception, would create a 'level playing field'[29] for recognition and enforcement regardless of where the parties concerned sought to enforce the award.

Having set forth the delocalisation and harmonisation of public policy norms and the international arbitral system as the desired end, a question arises as to the means by which such arbitral norms – whether they relate to regulation or enforcement – may be so homogenised.

2   Harmonisation of Public Policy Exception in Asia under the BRI

2.1   The BRI: China's Infrastructural Development Strategy

Promoted by Chinese President Xi Jinping during his visit to Indonesia in 2013, the ambitious Silk Road Economic Belt and 21st-Century

---

[26]   Ibid., p. 90.
[27]   Ahmed, 'The influence of the delocalization and seat theories', 408. See, generally, Jan Paulsson, 'Arbitration unbound: award detached from the law of its country of origin' (1981) 30 *International & Comparative Law Quarterly* 358–87.
[28]   Ahmed, 'The influence of the delocalization and seat theories', 409.
[29]   This phrase is used by Redfern in Redfern and Hunter, *Law and Practice*, p. 89.

Maritime Silk Road project – pithily referred to as the Belt and Road Initiative (BRI) – is China's keystone national development strategy. Its aim is to expand economic cooperation and foster closer connections amongst Eurasian countries along the historic Silk Road and beyond.[30] With its focus on infrastructural growth and development, a particular aim of the BRI is to open up markets and expand the volume of trade within Asia by connecting the resource-rich regions of Western and Central Asia with emerging economies in South and Southeast Asia.[31] Further, China's transition to the 'new normal' of slower, more stable economic growth provides an incentive for the creation of new economic opportunities by reaping the benefits of exporting the overcapacity of domestic industries via the BRI. Some commentators have interpreted the BRI as an attempt by China not only to engage in external trade, but also to strengthen the position of the Chinese currency within the international financial arena.[32]

The development of infrastructure projects has thus far been augmented by a US$40 million Silk Road Fund, which was established in December 2014 as a limited liability company to invest in infrastructure and resources, as well as to facilitate financial cooperation with the Belt and Road nations.[33] In addition, Asian Infrastructure Investment Bank (AIIB), comprised of fifty-seven members, was established in 2015 as a novel multilateral development bank with a view to addressing the infrastructural development needs of Asia, particularly in the areas of transport, telecommunications, rural infrastructure, urban development and logistics within the continent's less-developed nations.[34] The building of transport corridors, high-speed rail lines and maritime connection points will strengthen logistical routes and countries' capacity to handle large amounts of freight, thereby bolstering the transfer of both commercial goods and raw materials[35] that will benefit not only less economically developed nations – i.e. by the construction of essential infrastructure

---

[30] NDRC, 'Vision and actions'.

[31] Geethanjali Nataraj and Richa Sekhani, 'China's One Belt One Road – an Indian perspective' (2015) 1 *Economic & Political Weekly* 67–71 at 67.

[32] Ibid., 68.

[33] Hong Kong Trade Development Council (HKTDC), 'The Belt and Road initiative', HKTDC Research, 21 January 2016, accessed 15 June 2018 at http://china-trade-research .hktdc.com/business-news/article/One-Belt-One-Road/The-Belt-and-Road-Initiative/obor/ en/1/1X000000/1X0A36B7.htm.

[34] Ibid.

[35] Nataraj and Sekhani, 'China's One Belt One Road', 68.

that strengthens their economies – but also China. However, the BRI is viewed by some Western scholars as being motivated by and reflective of China's desire to shift the current global power dynamics, and consolidate soft power within the BRI region, by wielding both economic hard power and bolstering cultural soft power through the operation of the BRI and related policies.[36] Moreover, the BRI promises to stimulate an array of commercial and trade opportunities, with the following consequences.

2.2   Arbitration as a Primary Vehicle of International Commercial Dispute Resolution under the BRI

Given the projected increase in trade and commercial opportunities within the Belt and Road nations, commercial disputes are inevitable. It is posited here that for China the advantages of international arbitration over litigation will render it the preferred mode of dispute resolution between foreign parties in the BRI context.

Owing to the complexities of the commercial realm, the cardinal need to preserve business relationships and interests is better served through arbitration than the often adversarial system of litigation. Arbitration is frequently preferred to complex disputes by the parties concerned because of the freedom to elect their own arbitrator.[37] In the particular context of disputes over infrastructure projects, an arbitrator with construction expertise is likely to have a better understanding of the dispute in question and the interests of the parties concerned – e.g. a contractor and the subcontractor to whom work has been delegated – than a Chinese judge, who, whilst well-versed in the law, may be unfamiliar with the intricacies of infrastructure-related disputes. As Cole notes, the ability to choose one's arbitrator 'eliminates the possibility of the legal system of a country unfairly favouring its own citizen'.[38] Such freedom of choice is particularly significant in the Asian judicial context, where

---

[36] Francis Fukuyama, 'Exporting the Chinese model', *Project Syndicate*, 12 January 2016, accessed 15 June 2018 at www.project-syndicate.org/commentary/china-one-belt-one-road-strategy-by-francis-fukuyama-2016-01. See also Michael Clarke, 'Beijing's march West: "One Belt, One Road" and China's continental frontiers into the 21st century', The Political Studies Association, accessed 15 June 2018 at www.psa.ac.uk/sites/default/files/conference/papers/2016/Clarke-PSA-2016-paper.pdf.

[37] Cole, 'Public policy exception', 367.

[38] Ibid.

concerns over internal corruption and protectionism are rife.[39] In addition, whilst the Chinese courts are relatively efficient in their handling of disputes, the speed and simplicity of arbitration – which is within the control of the parties concerned – help to reduce costs. Arbitration further preserves confidentiality, an essential ingredient in the protection and preservation of business relationships. In the context of economic cooperation, it makes sense that parties would prefer to resolve their differences amicably whenever possible for the benefit of future cooperation. Cole further notes that 'the use of arbitration increases the security of international transactions and thus eases the barriers to international trade',[40] which is precisely the goal of the BRI.

Within the Chinese context, international commercial arbitration institutions such as the China International Economic and Trade Arbitration Commission (CIETAC) inspire greater confidence in arbitration processes than in local litigation.[41] CIETAC, as well as the Beijing Arbitration Commission (BAC) and Shenzhen Court of International Arbitration (SCIA), has expanded internationally in recent years and compiled an impressive array of international experience. Hence, recourse to these bodies is arguably more suitable for international parties than utilising the Chinese judicial system.[42] Other jurisdictions on the Belt and Road route – particularly such strongholds of arbitration as Hong Kong and Singapore – can also provide dispute resolution services that cater directly to the needs of parties involved in international commerce. It is thus envisioned by scholars and policymakers alike that arbitration will constitute the primary vehicle for international commercial dispute resolution under the BRI, with many welcoming the opportunities the initiative will

---

[39] See Y. Wang, 'Court funding and judicial corruption in China' (2013) 69 *The China Journal* 43–63.

[40] Cole, 'Public policy exception', 367.

[41] China International Economic and Trade Arbitration Commission (CIETAC), 'CIETAC has great potential in foreign-related commercial arbitration', CIETAC, 25 February 2014, accessed 15 June 2018 at www.cietac.org/index.php?m=Article&a=show&id=2491&l=en. In 2013, CIETAC accepted 1,256 economic or trade dispute cases, of which almost 25 per cent were foreign-related.

[42] Jie Zheng, 'Competition between arbitral institutions in China – fighting for a better system?', Kluwer Arbitration Blog, 16 October 2015, accessed 15 June 2018 at http://kluwerarbitrationblog.com/2015/10/16/competition-between-arbitral-institutions-in-china-fighting-for-a-better-system/.

provide for the development of an arbitral commission and arbitral institutions.[43] One outstanding issue, however, is the issue of recognition and enforcement, an issue encapsulated in the public policy exception.

2.3 Prospects of Regional Harmonisation through BRI Public Policy Exception

The BRI provides cause to envision the regional harmonisation of the public policy exception across Asia. To secure the initiative's success, China and the other Belt and Road jurisdictions have an interest in ensuring the enforcement of arbitral awards in the commercial disputes that are bound to arise as a result of increased economic cooperation.[44] The China-led BRI calls for greater economic integration between the Belt and Road countries, forming a sphere of economic influence within the region similar to that of the EU in Europe. Although the creation of the AIIB and Silk Road Fund is promoting closer economic integration in the region, increased economic cooperation and commercial opportunities have also given rise to the need for a better regulatory system that will make doing business within the region feel more secure. The BRI's aim is not only to increase China's cooperation with other countries in the region, but also to strengthen the trade links amongst those countries.[45] Given the resulting increase in commercial activity, a strong dispute resolution system is imperative. In the particular context of infrastructure projects – a clear focus of the BRI – the public policy exception cannot be used as a barrier, given the size and scale of such projects. After all, there is no point in obtaining an arbitral award if it is not enforceable.[46] To boost the confidence of investors or other parties and ensure commercial certainty, the public policy exception – as the greatest barrier to arbitral enforcement – must be clarified or at least harmonised. Given the cultural proximity of many of the Asian nations involved in the BRI, such harmonisation seems a real possibility.

---

[43] Department of Justice (Hong Kong), 'Secretary for justice promotes Hong Kong's legal and dispute resolution services in Beijing', Department of Justice, 18 August 2015, accessed 27 June 2018 at www.info.gov.hk/gia/general/201508/18/P201508180765.htm.

[44] Cole, 'Public policy exception', 367.

[45] Nataraj and Sekhani, 'China's One Belt One Road', 68.

[46] Cole, 'Public policy exception', 367.

2.4   Content of Harmonised Public Policy Exception

Whilst it is beyond the scope of this chapter to discuss the substantive content of a Pan-Asian public policy, several comments can be made. The present hindrance to navigating the international commercial arbitration system is the need to fulfil the different procedural requirements of seat jurisdictions, with reference to seat theory, to secure a valid arbitral order.[47] The harmonisation of such requirements within the Belt and Road nations would greatly simplify the international arbitral process, creating the business-friendly environment necessary to encourage commercial participation and manpower investment in the BRI. By applying a delocalisation approach in promoting a Pan-Asian *lex arbitri*,[48] the users of the international system within the Belt and Road nations could rely on the arbitral procedure with relative ease.

The main issue, however, is that of the denial of arbitral award enforcement and recognition under the public policy exception of Article V2(b) of the New York Convention. With regard to the enforcement jurisdiction, it is tentatively contended that the usual culprits of public policy contravention – namely, procedural deficits – would be relatively uncontroversial in being part of a collective public policy.[49] Such considerations, whilst rooted in the desire to secure procedural fairness, are likely to be agreed by most nations. Indeed, the existing discrepancies are unlikely to be great, particularly amongst countries with similar legal systems. Thus, the arbitral rule harmonisation of geo-legally similar jurisdictions – e.g. Hong Kong and Singapore, two common law jurisdictions in Asia – is easily foreseeable, and would pave the way towards harmonisation between different legal systems. The substantive considerations for public policy – often informed by the values or morals of individual nations – are obviously more contentious given the role that culture plays in determining their content.[50] However, it is possible that from a geo-cultural perspective some consensus may be reached.

---

[47] Redfern and Hunter, *Law and Practice*, p. 89.

[48] Ibid., pp. 89–90.

[49] IBA Subcommittee, *Report on the Public Policy Exception*, pp. 14–15. Although the report differentiates the main manifestations of violations of procedural public policy – for instance, violation of the right of due process or the right to present one's case – from procedural issues 'not affecting public policy in most of the other covered jurisdictions', such as the 'lack of reasons supporting an award', it also notes that most successful instances of the invocation of Article V2(b) of the New York Convention are on procedural grounds.

[50] Ibid., pp. 17–18.

The goal would not necessarily be to draw up an exhaustive, all-compassing definition of 'public policy'. Rather, the harmonisation of certain grounds mutually considered to violate Asian public policy may be agreed upon by specific countries within the region encompassed by the BRI. However, this possibility perhaps remains in the domain of theory if we consider the International Bar Association reports that suggest the greatest barrier to public policy enforcement is procedural defects rather than 'vaguely defined' substantive policy.[51]

2.5   Challenges to Pan-Asian Harmonisation of Cross-Border Arbitral Enforcement

2.5.1   Social and Cultural Discrepancies amongst Belt and Road Nations

The challenges of harmonising cross-border arbitral enforcement systems, or for that matter any cross-border system, lie in the fragmentation of various jurisdictions along social, cultural, ethnic and religious lines.[52] Social, cultural, ethnic and religious values are manifested in the unique social characteristics underlying the integral values and interests of a nation, an issue that goes to the root of the undefined nature of the public policy exception.[53] As stated previously, it is contended in this chapter that whilst nations are likely to be able to agree on such vague substantive concepts as justice or fairness, differences in cultural characteristics do not necessarily prevent countries from agreeing on minimum standards of procedural fairness, e.g. the absence of fraud and the impartiality of the mediator. Hence, although public policy may be incompletely defined, a positive first step would be to draw up a non-exhaustive list of procedural defects that would contravene the public policy of the Belt and Road nations, and thus be unenforceable. Whilst the 'true' harmonisation of the public policy exception is likely to prove difficult, harmonising the less contentious aspects of that exception would be instrumental in increasing both commercial certainty and investor confidence.

---

[51] Ibid., p. 8.

[52] This is a concern highlighted in Mohamed Al-Nasair, 'The effect of public policy on the enforcement of foreign arbitral awards in Bahrain and UAE' (2013) 16(3) *International Arbitration Law Review* 88–96.

[53] See the discussion in IBA Subcommittee, *Report on the Public Policy Exception*, p. 6, wherein the judicial definition of public policy as a ground for the refusal to enforce or recognise foreign awards hinges upon the 'fundamental values' of a legal system or culture.

2.5.2   Different Legal Systems in Belt and Road Jurisdictions

Another difficulty lies in reconciling the different legal systems that prevail amongst the Belt and Road nations. As the metaphorical Silk Road extends across Asia, the Middle East, Europe and parts of Africa, the BRI encompasses the common law, civil law and even Islamic law traditions.[54] It is inevitable that each legal tradition has a different idea of what can be considered public policy. As in the case discussed above, substantive differences may be ignored in favour of imposing procedural defects as defined content that contravenes public policy. However, the logistics of top-down harmonisation efforts directed at specific legal systems remain unclear. For instance, common law systems operate by *stare decisis* and the doctrine of binding precedent. One may consider the example of the UK and its conflicting approach to the European Convention on Human Rights for an example of the tension between a national legal system and the legal position of externally decided norms.[55] 'Harmonised' norms will likely have to be incorporated into and embedded in national legislation to have an enforceable effect, which is expected to introduce a host of political difficulties, further leading to the difficulty of straddling the distinction between Macdonald's 'transplantation' and 'harmonisation'.[56] Whilst harmonisation is the goal, the act of harmonising will likely involve some form of transplantation of a set of agreed standards. Unless the various legal systems find a viable means of coordination to embed common standards with regard to public policy enforcement, harmonisation efforts could easily be frustrated by the misapplication of transplanted standards.

2.5.3   Creation of 'Transnational' Public Policy

Another concern is that harmonisation of the public policy exception may inch towards or imply the creation of a 'transnational' public policy. Such a policy is advocated by Adeline Chong, who argues that aside from domestic and international public policy, there is a third type of public policy that seeks to protect interests across borders.[57] However, such a

---

[54] HKTDC, 'The Belt and Road Initiative'.

[55] See Jessica Elgot, 'British judges not bound by European Court of Human Rights', *The Guardian*, 24 May 2015, accessed 15 June 2018 at www.theguardian.com/law/2015/may/24/british-courts-echr-leveson.

[56] Roderick A. Macdonald, 'Three metaphors of norm migration in international context' (2009) 34 *Brooklyn Journal of International Law* 603–53 at 612.

[57] Adeline Chong, 'Transnational public policy in civil and commercial matters' (2012) 128 *Law Quarterly Review* 88–113 at 89.

transnational policy is difficult to reconcile with the public policy exception in the New York Convention, which expressly refers to the public policy considerations of specific countries.[58] This brings us to what may be the most fundamental technical challenge to the harmonisation of that exception – whether in Asia under the BRI or elsewhere: it does not accord with the drafters of the New York Convention. Nonetheless, it is submitted here that this is no reason to baulk at harmonisation: harmonisation does not *necessarily* limit a country's ability to define its own public policy; it simply brings different systems into harmony with one another. Whether the chosen berth is wide or narrow is irrelevant. Of course, the question that now arises is the extent to which it is possible to bring such disparate systems into harmony.

3 Shifting Power Dynamics: Implications of the BRI for International Commercial Arbitration and Beyond

3.1 The Sleeping Dragon Awakes: BRI Contextualised in Regional Dynamics

We have all heard the famous aphorism frequently attributed to Napoleon: 'China is a sleeping dragon. Let her sleep; for once she wakes, she will shake the world.'[59] Many have resorted to the sleeping dragon metaphor when discussing the country's economic rise at the opening of the twenty-first century. Today, China – sitting at the cusp of further economic development – boasts the world's second largest economy and is exerting a growing influence on international affairs.[60] Indeed, according to Zicheng Ye, 'there is a close connection between the rejuvenation of the Chinese nation and China's becoming a world power ... only when it becomes a world power can we say that the total rejuvenation of the Chinese nation has been achieved'.[61] Whether or not world power status is the aspiration of the Chinese government, Francis Fukuyama has interpreted the BRI as representing a departure in policy whereby Beijing

---

[58] IBA Subcommittee, *Report on the Public Policy Exception*, p. 8.
[59] 'China's fitful sleep', *The Economist*, 17 July 1997, accessed 15 June 2018 at www.econo mist.com/node/151617.
[60] The World Bank, 'Overview: China', The World Bank, accessed 15 June 2018, www.world bank.org/en/country/china/overview.
[61] Zicheng Ye, *Inside China's Grand Strategy: The Perspective from the People's Republic*, (Kentucky, University Press of Kentucky: 2011) p. 74.

is seeking to 'export its development model to other countries'.[62] The potential of the BRI lies in its ability to turn China into an economic regional superpower and a central commercial hub for investors and businesses in the region. By opening up new markets, the BRI will not only boost China's commercial opportunities, but also exert both hard and soft power influences on surrounding jurisdictions. This dynamic was clearly seen in the establishment of the AIIB, which many observers saw as an attempt by China to shift the power dynamics of international banking. However, the BRI also presents another, as yet overlooked, opportunity for China: the opportunity to rewrite international legal norms. By pioneering a harmonised Asian public policy under the auspices of the BRI, China can not only exert influence monetarily, but also write the rules of a new international system. This is a significant opportunity, particularly in terms of the international arbitration system, which, owing to the public policy exception, remains fragmented and disorganised with respect to enforcement.

3.2 The Future of the BRI

Fukuyama has called into doubt the likelihood of the BRI's success, noting that although infrastructure-led growth has been dominant in China owing to the government's ability to control the political environment, extraneous factors such as instability and corruption are likely to render infrastructure projects outside China less effective in securing returns.[63] For Fukuyama, the success of the BRI – or lack thereof – may well determine the future of global politics.[64] However, for naysayers and proponents alike, the BRI's success remains to be seen. Whilst the returns – both economic and power-based – of China's infrastructure investments in Belt and Road countries have yet to be realised, the economic growth and increased trade driven by the initiative are undeniable. Regardless of whether it succeeds, the vast opportunities for the development and construction of infrastructure indicate a vast market for international arbitration within the region and, in turn, an opportunity to square the circle and harmonise the regulatory domain, including the public policy exception.

---

[62] Fukuyama, 'Exporting the Chinese model'.
[63] Ibid.
[64] Ibid.

3.3   Relevance of International Governance and Chinese Rule of Law

In October 2014, the Fourth Plenum of the 18th Central Committee of the Communist Party of China took advancement of the rule of law as its dominant theme.[65] Affirming the Chinese Constitution as forming the crux of the country's legal system and promoting wide-ranging judicial reforms to tackle institutionalised corruption, the Party lauded a 'new era' in committing to a 'Chinese rule of law' suited to existing 'national conditions'. Advancement of the rule of law has long been viewed as crucial to the development of China's market economy, as well as to the bolstering of investor confidence and encouragement of continued economic growth.[66] Another integral aspect of the development of a Chinese rule of law is bringing China into line with the First World nations that have traditionally dominated the international governance arena.

As discussed above, the opportunities presented by the BRI place China in a prime position to pioneer and promote harmonisation of the public policy exception through the active formulation of widely agreed public policy norms. In addition to permitting China to take on a more proactive role in writing norms within the traditional global order, such a formulation has positive implications for China's demonstrated commitment to promoting and adhering to the rule of law – not only within its own borders, but also across the Asian region. As China assumes the helm of economic leadership within Asia, it may well demonstrate further capacity to lead in the formulation of legal norms, inspiring greater confidence in the international diplomatic community in its ability to not simply take part in all aspects of international governance but to lead.

4   Conclusion

Given the successes of the New York Convention, Model Law and UNCITRAL Rules in promoting the harmonisation of the international arbitration system thus far, it would be ironic if the goal of internal consistency was defeated by the whims of a national public policy

---

[65] 'Promoting rule of law crucial to development of market economy', *English.news.cn*, 27 October 2014, accessed 15 June 2018 at http://news.xinhuanet.com/english/indepth/2014–10/27/c_133745913.htm.

[66] Ibid.

concerning enforcement. While granting that the public policy exception was drafted with the interests of individual countries in mind,[67] where that exception holds potential for unnecessary uncertainty it ought to be subjected to scrutiny. Harmonisation of the public policy exception would yield considerable benefits, not only for the internal consistency of the international arbitration system at large, but also for individual nations themselves, by increasing certainty. Whilst seat theory has traditionally formed the basis for the development of the international arbitral system, true harmonisation under Macdonald's three metaphors for norm propagation may mandate greater scrutiny of delocalising efforts.

China's BRI provides a not-to-be-missed opportunity to consider the possibility of harmonising the public policy exception within Asia on the basis of geo-legal similarity. The harmonisation of cross-border arbitral enforcement along the Silk Road would provide the legal certainty required to bolster investor and commercial confidence in the success of China's ambitious initiative. The BRI's future hinges on investor confidence in the massive-scale infrastructure projects being proposed by China. To secure such confidence, a strong dispute resolution system for effectively and decisively resolving commercial disputes must be in place. Such a system may in fact be the make-or-break factor in the success or otherwise of China's Belt and Road development policy. Further, finding a way to tame the 'unruly horse' in the Asian context and reconciling national policy with the need to forge a coherent system of international arbitration would set a valuable precedent, and place renewed emphasis on China and Asia as pioneers of international economic and legal power. Finally, as the true harmonisation of the international arbitral system is one of the most important goals of an increasingly interdependent and globalised world, the opportunities that the BRI affords for realising that goal within Asia are exciting indeed.

---

[67] IBA Subcommittee, *Report on the Public Policy Exception*, p. 8.

13

Establishment of an International Trade Dispute Settlement Mechanism under the Belt and Road Initiative

SHENGLI JIANG

The fast-paced development of China's 'Belt and Road Initiative' (BRI) requires an effective and reasonable means of resolving the international trade disputes likely to arise between China and the other countries involved. Because the initiative differs from traditional regional economic cooperation models, and because of the considerable differences in economic level and trade policy amongst the numerous countries involved, it is not feasible to resolve those disputes by copying or straightforwardly applying existing global or regional trade dispute settlement mechanisms. Therefore, a new mechanism is needed to resolve international trade disputes under the BRI. That mechanism should be based on full consideration of the initiative's factual circumstances, with reference to the merits of existing mechanisms. A flexible mechanism that takes arbitration and diplomatic measures as its primary and secondary dispute settlement measures, respectively, is needed. In addition to detailed standards, it is argued that a specialised dispute settlement institution with optional compulsory jurisdiction over disputes amongst Belt and Road member countries is necessary and that compulsory measures should be avoided in implementing dispute settlement resolutions whenever possible.

In the years since Chinese President Xi Jinping first proposed the joint construction of the Silk Road Economic Belt and 21st-Century Maritime Silk Road on visits to Central Asia and Southeast Asia in September and October 2013, respectively, the BRI has gradually begun to take shape and attract worldwide attention. The Vision and Actions on Jointly Building [a] Silk Road Economic Belt and 21st-Century Maritime Silk Road (Vision and Actions hereafter),[1] issued by the National

---

[1] National Development and Reform Commission (NDRC), Ministry of Foreign Affairs, Ministry of Commerce of the People's Republic of China, *Vision and Actions on Jointly*

Development and Reform Commission, Ministry of Foreign Affairs and Ministry of Commerce, under the authority of the State Council of the People's Republic of China, on 28 March 2015, offered the Chinese government's first official interpretation of the initiative and defined the aim and route of its material and normative progress. Although the continued development of the BRI will improve bilateral, multilateral and regional economic cooperation between China and the other countries along the Belt and Road, trade disputes and conflicts are inevitable. Accordingly, an international trade dispute settlement mechanism under the auspices of the BRI[2] that is acceptable to all of the countries involved is a priority if the initiative's aim of promoting regional trade cooperation is to be realised.

1   Unsuitability of Existing Mechanisms

Since the proposal of the BRI in 2013, China has concluded agreements or reached consensus on trade cooperation with quite a few countries along the Belt and Road. However, most of these are bilateral arrangements, meaning that we are still far away from a routine system of regional trade cooperation amongst China and the other Belt and Road participant countries. As a consequence, there is also no dispute settlement mechanism under the auspices of the initiative that is applicable to resolving the trade disputes likely to be brought by the countries involved. Although it might seem at first glance that copying or straightforwardly using existing international trade dispute settlement mechanisms would be an economical way of resolving trade disputes quickly and conveniently, the considerable differences in economic level and trade policy amongst the numerous countries along the Belt and Road renders those mechanisms unsuitable for a number of reasons.

1.1   Issues with Copying or Straightforwardly Applying Global Mechanisms

As the world's most important and representative international trade cooperation organisation, the World Trade Organization (WTO) enjoys

---

Building Silk Road Economic Belt and the 21st-Century Maritime Silk Road, 28 March 2015, accessed 15 June 2018 at http://en.ndrc.gov.cn/newsrelease/201503/t20150330_669367.html.

[2] Junbing Guan, 'The choice of the regional trade dispute settlement mode for China under the context of "One Belt One Road"' (2015) 8 *Modern SOE Research* 21.

a reputation as 'the Economic United Nations', and its dispute settlement mechanism, praised as 'the jewel in the crown of the WTO regime', is currently the most successful mechanism for resolving international trade disputes.[3] Since the WTO's establishment on 1 January 1995, its Dispute Settlement Body (DSB) has heard 553 international trade disputes (as of 18 June 2018),[4] and the credibility of the WTO dispute settlement mechanism is accepted by all WTO members.[5] Nevertheless, with respect to international trade disputes under the BRI, copying or straightforwardly applying that mechanism is likely to lead to serious, if not insurmountable, problems. For example, there are 164 WTO member states.[6] Of the sixty-five countries along the Belt and Road,[7] however, fifteen are not WTO members,[8] accounting for almost one-quarter of all Belt and Road participants. Because the WTO dispute settlement mechanism, namely, the rules and procedures outlined in the Understanding on Rules and Procedures Governing the Settlement of Disputes, or Dispute Settlement Understanding (DSU), is applicable only to the resolution of trade disputes brought by WTO members, it cannot be automatically applied to disputes brought by the fifteen non-WTO members of the Belt and Road.

In addition, it must be admitted that the main reason for a country to refuse to join the WTO is that the WTO's legal system, including its

---

[3] Donald McRae, 'The WTO in international law: tradition continued or new frontier?' (2003) 3 *Journal of International Economic Law* 38.

[4] World Trade Organization (WTO), 'Chronological list of disputes cases', accessed 15 June 2018 at www.wto.org/english/tratop_e/dispu_e/dispu_status_e.htm.

[5] Jianming Cao and Xiaoyong He, *World Trade Organization*, 3rd edn (Beijing: Law Press, 2011), pp. 85–6.

[6] WTO, 'Members and observers', accessed 15 June 2018 at www.wto.org/english/thewto_e/whatis_e/tif_e/org6_e.htm.

[7] To date, neither Vision and Actions nor any other official document released by the Chinese government has published the full list of countries along the Belt and Road. However, analysis of a variety of relevant data support the preliminary conclusion that there are sixty-five such countries/territories, namely: China, Russia, Mongolia, Indonesia, Thailand, Malaysia, Vietnam, Singapore, the Philippines, Myanmar (Burma), Cambodia, Laos, Brunei, East Timor, India, Pakistan, Bangladesh, Sri Lanka, Afghanistan, Nepal, the Maldives, Bhutan, Saudi Arabia, the United Arab Emirates, Oman, Iran, Turkey, Israel, Egypt, Kuwait, Iraq, Qatar, Jordan, Lebanon, Bahrain, Yemen, Syria, the Palestinian Territories, Poland, Romania, the Czech Republic, Slovakia, Bulgaria, Hungary, Latvia, Lithuania, Slovenia, Estonia, Croatia, Albania, Serbia, Macedonia, Bosnia and Herzegovina, Montenegro, Kazakhstan, Uzbekistan, Tajikistan, Turkmenistan, Kyrgyzstan, Ukraine, Belarus, Georgia, Azerbaijan, Armenia and Moldova.

[8] Of the countries along the Belt and Road, the non-members of the WTO are East Timor, Afghanistan, Bhutan, Iran, Iraq, Lebanon, Syria, the Palestinian Territories, Serbia, Bosnia and Herzegovina, Uzbekistan, Turkmenistan, Kyrgyzstan, Belarus and Azerbaijan.

dispute settlement mechanism, is simply unacceptable to that country because of its factual circumstances or other factors. As a consequence, a non-WTO member country is likely to object to any attempt to apply the WTO mechanism to any international trade dispute in which it is involved as a compulsory measure. It is therefore obvious that the WTO dispute settlement mechanism is unworkable for a considerable number of countries along the Belt and Road. Furthermore, even when dealing with trade disputes brought by Belt and Road participants that are WTO members, it remains unfeasible to copy or straightforwardly apply the WTO dispute settlement mechanism in the Belt and Road context for several reasons.

First, as stated in Article 1, paragraph 1 of the DSU, application of the WTO dispute settlement mechanism is limited to the settlement of disputes under the agreements listed in Appendix 1 to the DSU (Covered Agreements hereafter) and the Agreement Establishing the World Trade Organization (WTO Agreement hereafter). In the Belt and Road context, trade disputes that arise between countries along the Belt and Road are brought pursuant to the bilateral or multilateral trade agreements those countries concluded under the initiative, which are beyond the scope of either the Covered Agreements or WTO Agreement. The interpretation and application of these 'non-WTO laws' will be allowed only if explicitly provided for in the text of the Covered Agreements or WTO Agreement.[9] In most cases, however, there is no such provision, and hence the WTO dispute settlement mechanism is not applicable even if both parties to the dispute are WTO members.

Second, of the fifty-one WTO member countries along the Belt and Road, only eleven countries are developed economies. The remaining forty countries, that is, nearly four-fifths of the whole, are developing economies.[10] It is not cheap to bring disputes and seek settlement under the WTO dispute settlement mechanism, and cost considerations have thus inhibited many developing countries from taking full advantage of

---

[9] Nguyen Tan Son, 'The applicability of RTA jurisdiction clauses in WTO dispute settlement' (2013) 15 *International Trade and Business Law Review* 262.

[10] According to the latest clarification of the level of economic development amongst countries worldwide. See United Nations Development Programme (UNDP), *2015 Human Development Report* (New York: UNDP, 2015). Of the WTO members along the Belt and Road, Singapore, Brunei, Bahrain, Israel, the Czech Republic, Slovakia, Slovenia, Estonia, the United Arab Emirates, Qatar and Poland are considered developed economies.

that mechanism.[11] Therefore, the high cost of raising a dispute under the WTO dispute settlement mechanism has forced most of the WTO member countries along the Belt and Road to give up their due rights and equal opportunities to resolve international trade disputes under this progressive mechanism, at least as plaintiffs.

Third, because WTO dispute settlement operates under a multilateral trade system, it cannot be denied that the WTO, when faced with international disputes, has to consider the interests of all WTO members or those of various interest groups within the organisation, balance the interests and demands of both developed and developing countries, and coordinate conflicts of interest between the South and North.[12] According to Article 11 of the DSU, the function of a panel appointed by the DSB is to make 'an objective assessment of the matter before it'. Because this provision does not specify the precise nature or intensity of the review of factual and legal issues that the panel must perform, however, it is the panel or appellate body itself that decides how intensively a particular matter should be reviewed and how much deference should be granted to national authorities.[13] As a consequence, the standards of review, which express the deliberate allocation of power between the national authority taking a measure and the judicial organ reviewing it, gain unprecedented political and systemic significance in panel or appellate body proceedings.[14] Therefore, an international trade dispute decision made by the WTO DSB, regardless of the panel or appellate body involved, is to some extent the outcome of balancing and coordinating the interests, demands and conflicts of opposing parties, or the interested third parties behind them, which implies that the WTO dispute settlement mechanism places greater emphasis on the formal resolution of trade disputes brought by WTO members than on the substantive fairness of their settlement.

The BRI, in contrast, at least according to the Vision and Actions, is 'a road for win-win cooperation of promoting common development and realizing common prosperity, and a road of peace and friendship through

---

[11] Keisuke Iida, 'Is WTO dispute settlement effective?' (2004) 10 *Global Governance* 217.

[12] Yaping Mu and Li Xiao, 'To create a dispute settlement body for CEPA' (2004) 4 *Journal of Sun Yatsen University (Social Science Edition)* 45–6.

[13] Claus-Dieter Ehlermann and Nicolas Lockhart, 'Standard of review in WTO law' (2004) 7 *Journal of International Economic Law* 491.

[14] Matthias Oesch, 'Standards of review in WTO dispute resolution' (2003) 6 *Journal of International Economic Law* 635.

enhancing mutual understanding and trust, and strengthening all-round exchanges'.[15] Owing to the initiative's principle of seeking harmony, comprehensiveness and mutual benefit, although conflicts of interest may occur amongst the countries involved, their interests are likely to be convergent on the whole. In other words, the relationships amongst the countries along the Belt and Road are likely to be cooperative rather than contradictory. Therefore, the settlement of disputes under the BRI is likely to focus more on substantive fairness than the WTO dispute settlement mechanism, which has an inclination towards formal fairness.

1.2   Issues with Copying or Straightforwardly Applying Regional Mechanisms

As one element of the framework of the BRI is the promotion of regional trade cooperation, and as the initiative is also aimed at establishing a broader, more comprehensive trade cooperation system in the Belt and Road region, superficially it appears that regional dispute settlement mechanisms may be more suitable than global mechanisms, such as the WTO mechanism, for meeting the actual demand for international trade dispute resolution under the BRI. Along these lines, at the High-level Forum of China Development organised by the Development Research Center of the State Council on 22 March 2015, McKinsey & Company Chairman and Global CEO Dominic Barton recommended that the NAFTA dispute settlement mechanism be followed in resolving international trade disputes under the BRI.[16] That point of view is supported by a number of Chinese scholars who argue that copying existing regional trade dispute settlement mechanisms of sufficient maturity, or straightforwardly applying the mechanism specified by the regional trade agreement (RTA) to which the opposing parties to the dispute are members, such as that outlined in the China-ASEAN Free Trade Agreement (CAFTA), would be the best option for resolving international trade disputes under the BRI. However, the feasibility of such replication/straightforward application is limited by the particularity of the initiative itself and the complexity of the countries involved.

[15] NDRC, *Vision and Actions.*

[16] 'McKinsey chairman Baod Min: "along the way" to learn the North American Free Trade Area dispute settlement mechanism', Caijing.com.cn, 22 March 2015, accessed 15 June 2018 at http://economy.caijing.com.cn/20150322/3845409.shtml.

At present, all existing regional trade dispute settlement mechanisms were established under regional economic zones built in accordance with relevant RTAs. The most significant characteristic of such regional agreements or zones is that they require a close cooperative relationship amongst their members. Although the aim of the BRI is to establish a regional trade cooperation system amongst all of the countries involved, it seeks to build a more open and comprehensive regional 'zonal economic sphere' rather than a regional economic zone. As a consequence, the initiative does not restrict the number of countries involved, and the trade cooperation arrangement it envisions does not require close economic integration of those countries.[17] Therefore, owing to the particularity of the BRI in breaking through the traditional regional economic cooperation model offered by the most common RTAs, existing regional dispute settlement mechanisms that are specifically applicable to regional economic zones are unsuitable for resolving international trade disputes under the initiative.

Furthermore, as several scholars have pointed out, fewer than half the countries along the Belt and Road are members of any existing RTA. Further, the marketisation of most of the countries involved remains weak and unstable, and few recognise the general rules of international trade.[18] Therefore, if neither party to an international trade dispute under the BRI is a member of any RTA, there is no existing regional mechanism applicable to resolving that dispute. At the same time, it would be an enormous challenge to change the negative attitude towards generally accepted international trade rules held by most countries along the Belt and Road into acceptance of the application of advanced regional dispute settlement mechanisms.

2 Framework for Mechanism Establishment under the BRI

As the foregoing section makes clear, the particularity of the BRI and factual circumstances of the participating countries make it unfeasible in practice to copy or straightforwardly apply existing global or regional

---

[17] Wang et al., 'The background, potential challenges and future tendency of the "Silk Road Economic Belt" initiative' (2014) 4 *Russian, Central Asian and East European Market* 5–7.

[18] Yan Liu and Xiang Huang, 'National risk prevention and control in the construction of "One Belt One Road": under the view of international law' (2015) 8 *Journal of International Economic Cooperation* 27.

mechanisms to resolve international trade disputes. However, that does not mean that there is nothing to be learnt from those mechanisms in establishing an international trade dispute settlement mechanism under and suited to that initiative. As there are huge gaps in the knowledge needed for the establishment of such a mechanism, it is essential that the merits of existing mechanisms be taken into account in devising it, with adaptations made to meet the actual demands of international trade dispute resolution under the BRI.[19] It is argued here that the establishment of a BRI-specific international trade dispute settlement mechanism should follow the framework laid out in the following paragraphs.

2.1   The Need for a Flexible, Diverse Format

Owing to its basic characteristics of openness and comprehensiveness, the BRI does not require participant countries to build a regional economic zone or traditional RTA. Instead, its aim is to construct a flexible regional trade cooperation system under the principle of, according to Wang et al., 'either the bilateral cooperation mode or the multilateral cooperation mode ... depending on which one is more suitable to the [initiative's] aim [and] the bilateral cooperation mode should promote the multilateral one, while the multilateral cooperation mode should drive the bilateral one as well'.[20] Furthermore, in terms of content the initiative is not limited to a particular programme or field, but rather looks towards a multi-programme, multi-field regional trade cooperation system.

Because of these factors, the international trade dispute settlement mechanism established under the BRI requires both flexibility and diversity to allow adaptation to suit the initiative's factual circumstances and basic characteristics. Accordingly, the mechanism should not require all countries along the Belt and Road to comply with a single body of dispute settlement rules and procedures. Instead, it should allow each country to determine the material rules and procedures in conjunction with the other countries involved in both the bilateral and multilateral spheres in accordance with the factual circumstances of the regional trade cooperation system and actual demands of the trade disputes that arise therein.[21]

---

[19] Guan, 'The choice of the regional trade dispute settlement mode', 22.

[20] Wang et al., 'The background, potential challenges and future tendency', 5–7

[21] Yuncheng Bao, 'Legal thinking on the construction of "One Belt One Road"' (2015) 1 *Forward Position* 67.

In determining those material rules and procedures, China, as the initiator of the BRI, may provide a model that offers alternative means of dispute resolution and corresponding basic rules and procedures for the reference of the other countries involved in the initiative. Then, by negotiating with and revising the China model, those countries can determine the material rules and procedures best suited to resolving specific international trade disputes. Establishing an international dispute settlement mechanism under the BRI in such a flexible, diverse manner will not only guarantee acceptance of the mechanism's rules and procedures amongst the countries along the Belt and Road, but will also help to enforce the dispute settlement resolutions made under that mechanism.

2.2 The Need for Arbitration as a Primary Dispute Settlement Measure

Whilst there are a variety of differences amongst existing international trade dispute settlement measures, scholars have discovered that almost all RTAs provide for at least one of three measures in their dispute settlement mechanisms: diplomatic measures (including negotiation, intervention and mediation); judicial measures (through the setting up of a permanent court or other permanent judicial institution); and/or arbitration. Although most RTAs tend to take negotiation as the first step in settling an international trade dispute, arbitration is the most popular dispute settlement measure in almost all regional mechanisms.[22]

In fact, the advantages of arbitration as the main means of international trade dispute settlement are quite obvious. First, a well-established institution that is independent of all parties involved takes responsibility for the arrangements of the entire arbitration proceedings. Second, in addition to the relevant *jus cogens*, arbitration must also comply with its own substantive and procedural rules, namely, the detailed and transparent arbitration rules established by the aforementioned institution or decided by the parties to the dispute. Finally, a resolution reached by arbitration is legally binding on the opposing parties, and its enforcement is guaranteed by adequate coercive measures.

For these reasons, compared with other measures, dispute settlement resolutions reached by arbitration are more predictable and stable,

---

[22] Amelia Porges, 'Dispute settlement', in Jean-Pierre Chauffour and Jean-Christophe Maur (eds.), *Preferential Trade Agreement Policies for Development: A Handbook* (Washington, DC: The World Bank, 2011), pp. 467–71.

serving not only to supply a reliable guarantee of the legitimate rights of the parties to an RTA, but also to promote the smooth operation of the overall regional trade cooperation system. Therefore, as noted, most of the world's RTAs specify arbitration as the main measure for the resolution of international trade disputes, and have established dispute settlement mechanisms accordingly. Although the BRI is not aimed at building a rigid regional economic zone such as those created by existing RTAs, taking arbitration as the main international trade dispute settlement measure and setting up a corresponding dispute settlement mechanism would facilitate the initiative's aim of building a flexible, smoothly operating regional trade cooperation system.

2.3 Diplomatic Measures as a Secondary Dispute Settlement Mechanism

Specifying arbitration as the main means of international trade dispute settlement does not mean that diplomatic measures should be excluded from the dispute settlement mechanism of the BRI.

Diplomatic measures play an important role in resolving international trade disputes, and are widely used in existing global and regional dispute settlement mechanisms. For example, under the WTO dispute settlement mechanism, the entire consultation procedure provided for in Article 4 of the DSU is a measure allowing WTO members to resolve disputes in a diplomatic manner. Further, according to Article 6 of the DSU, consultation, as a diplomatic measure, is so important that it is the prepositive procedure for establishing a panel: the opposing parties cannot demand the establishment of a panel unless they have already completed the consultation procedure. Article 5 of the DSU provides for other diplomatic measures, including good offices, conciliation and mediation, as voluntary procedures for facilitating dispute resolution between WTO members. Similarly, many RTAs also specify such common diplomatic measures as negotiation, intervention and mediation as subsidiary means of resolving international trade disputes in their dispute settlement mechanisms, and such diplomatic measures are always given priority over arbitration or other legal measures.[23] Therefore, diplomatic measures are of crucial importance to the settlement of international trade disputes.

---

[23] Lihu Chen and Yanmin Zhao, 'The dispute settlement mechanisms in RTAs that China is involved in' (2007) 3 *Contemporary Law Review* 86.

Furthermore, because most of the countries along the Belt and Road are developing countries, or even amongst the world's least developed countries (e.g. Afghanistan, Bhutan), in addition to lagging behind in marketisation and economic development, many also face turbulent political circumstances and a poor security situation. The Syrian civil war and rise of the terrorist group known as ISIS in recent years have further exacerbated the difficult regional situation. Hence, preventing or at least minimising the political risks in promoting trade cooperation with Belt and Road member states is a core component of the initiative's legalisation.

In this regard, particularly when dealing with international trade disputes driven by political risks, in addition to arbitration and/or other legal measures, it is essential that a consultative dialogue mechanism between countries in dispute be established. For example, a consultation conference attended by the state leaders or trade representatives of the opposing parties could be held, and such common diplomatic measures as negotiation, intervention and mediation will also prove indispensable.[24] However, it is very important that in establishing diplomatic measures to resolve international trade disputes under the BRI, care is taken to avoid the countries involved in the dispute using the settlement mechanism as a show of national strength. The overarching aim should be maintaining equity between and the mutual benefit of all countries along the Belt and Road.

3 Detailed Standards for Mechanism Establishment under the BRI

Now that we have laid out a framework and ideas for establishing an international trade dispute settlement mechanism under the BRI, it is important to perfect the detailed content of and standards for establishing that mechanism for the reference of China and the other countries involved when determining material dispute settlement rules and procedures for resolving specific international trade disputes.

---

[24] Jingdong Liu, 'Thinking on the legalization of the "One Belt One Road" initiative', CSSN, 30 April 2015, accessed 15 June 2018 at www.cssn.cn/fx/fx_gjfx/201504/t20150430_1716617.shtml.

3.1   The Need for a Specialised Dispute Settlement Institution

Establishing a specialised dispute settlement institution will not only provide basic institutional assurance for the international trade dispute settlement mechanism set up under the BRI, such an establishment will also be an indispensable foundation of that mechanism's effective operation. The serious problems caused by the absence of such an institution in existing international trade dispute settlement mechanisms, particularly in regional mechanisms, should be avoided at all costs.

For example, one of the significant characteristics of the CAFTA dispute settlement mechanism is that it does not require the establishment of a specialised dispute settlement institution, but rather tasks its members with setting up their own agencies responsible for the communication of all matters relevant to the dispute settlement in question. As a consequence, although arbitration is the main dispute settlement measure under CAFTA, the lack of a specialised institution to provide an arbitrator list means that even before the official start of arbitration proceedings, CAFTA members in dispute encounter difficulties choosing arbitrators. Further, according to Article 7 of the CAFTA Dispute Settlement Mechanism Agreement, if two opposing parties cannot agree on the tribunal president, they must ask the WTO rather than CAFTA itself for help, allowing the director general of the WTO to appoint the president of a tribunal whose objective is to solve a dispute that has arisen under CAFTA.[25]

CAFTA is just one notable example. In the case of global or regional mechanisms, the absence of a specialised dispute settlement institution can delay the entire dispute settlement proceedings. Also, when arbitration is adopted as the dispute settlement measure, the lack of such an institution will introduce an element of randomness into the choice of arbitrators, in turn exerting a negative influence on the independence of the tribunal and fairness of the arbitration award.[26] Therefore, it is essential that a specialised institution be set up within the international trade dispute settlement mechanism established under the BRI in either the bilateral or multilateral sphere.

---

[25] Dukgeun Ahn, 'Dispute settlement systems in Asian FTAs: issues and problems' (2013) 8 *Asian Journal of WTO and International Health Law and Policy* 429.

[26] Xixiang Song and Peng Wu, 'The dispute settlement mechanism of China-ASEAN free trade area' (2006) 5 *Present Day Law Science* 95.

The functions of that institution should include but not be limited to the following: (i) before an arbitration proceeding, the institution should first assist the countries involved in trying to resolve the dispute through diplomatic measures; (ii) it should coordinate communication between the opposing parties, and urge both to implement negotiation, intervention or mediation; (iii) then, before the official start of the arbitration proceeding, the institution should help the parties to choose the arbitrators; (iv) in addition to preparing an arbitrator list comprising qualified governmental or non-governmental arbitrators, the institution should take responsibility for directly appointing a tribunal president if the opposing parties cannot reach an accord; (v) after the arbitration proceeding has concluded, the institution should supervise implementation of the arbitration award decreed by the tribunal, and prevent either party from taking arbitrary retaliatory measures; and finally (vi), the institution should also be responsible for the delivery of legal instruments, management of all documents and files relevant to the dispute, regular publishing of information and all other routine work.

3.2   The Need for Optional Compulsory Jurisdiction over Disputes

As previously noted, amongst the countries along the Belt and Road, fifteen are non-members of the WTO, and more than half do not belong to any existing RTA. Nevertheless, fifty-one WTO members are included amongst the Belt and Road countries, some of which are also signatories to RTAs.[27] Accordingly, regardless of whether the substantive rights and obligations of the countries along the Belt and Road (which may or may not be WTO members or parties to RTAs) are inconsistent or even contradictory under various international trade rules, because of overlaps between the BRI and WTO or RTA rules, any international trade dispute that arises between China and the other participating countries will be doomed, leading to jurisdictional conflict.[28]

---

[27] For example, all of the ASEAN countries are also countries along the Belt and Road, and both they and China are also members of the China-ASEAN Free Trade Area.

[28] A conflict of jurisdiction arises if a dispute can be brought in full or part before two or more different courts or tribunals. See International Law Commission, *Report of the Study Group of the International Law Commission on Fragmentation of International Law: Difficulties Arising from the Diversification and Expansion of International Law*, UN Document A/CN.4/L.682 (13 April 2006), pp. 23–5.

In this respect, although Article 23 of the DSU provides for exclusive jurisdiction of all disputes arising under the Covered Agreements and WTO Agreement, not only is it possible for the parties in dispute to seek arbitration as an alternative recourse, but the 'specific rules and procedures on dispute settlement contained in the covered agreements', such as Article 11, paragraph 3 of the Agreement on the Application of Sanitary and Phytosanitary Measures, can also override that exclusive jurisdiction; this means that adjudicators may still be confronted with jurisdictional conflict between the WTO dispute settlement mechanism and other dispute settlement forums and find that such conflict cannot be resolved by the provision in DSU Article 23 alone.[29] Furthermore, some scholars argue that because Article XXIV of the General Agreement on Tariffs and Trade (GATT) clearly acknowledges the existence of RTAs within the GATT/WTO system, WTO members are allowed to use RTA dispute settlement mechanisms to settle disputes under WTO-compatible RTAs.[30] Therefore, jurisdictional conflict may not be eliminated by existing rules.

It is thus proposed in this chapter that optional compulsory jurisdiction may be a suitable way of resolving the problem of jurisdictional conflict. That approach, which is quite different from the concept in Article 36, clause 2 of the Statute of the International Court of Justice, refers to opposing parties being free to jointly choose the dispute settlement mechanism established under the BRI, the WTO mechanism or a mechanism specified in a specific RTA before or after an international trade dispute occurs. Further, as long as the parties agree on which dispute settlement mechanism to use in resolving their dispute, and once the corresponding dispute settlement proceeding has begun, that mechanism then has exclusive jurisdiction over the dispute, and neither party has recourse to any other mechanism.

There are several reasons for recommending optional compulsory jurisdiction in the Belt and Road context. First, the approach is widely accepted by RTAs worldwide, and has already become the main way of resolving the jurisdictional conflict that arises from overlaps between the

---

[29] Tim Graewert, 'Conflicting laws and jurisdictions in the dispute settlement process of regional trade agreements and the WTO' (2008) 1 *Contemporary Asia Arbitration Journal* 293–4.

[30] Jennifer Hillman, 'Conflicts between dispute settlement mechanisms in regional trade agreements and the WTO: what should the WTO do?' (2009) 43 *Cornell International Law Journal* 197.

dispute settlement mechanisms of RTAs and the WTO.[31] Second, if exclusive jurisdiction were imposed, namely, forcing the countries along the Belt and Road to resolve international trade disputes solely with reference to the settlement mechanism established under the initiative, not only would that mechanism be rendered too rigid, but the Belt and Road countries would have cause to doubt the fairness of any settlement so reached, as the mechanism would be directed by China. Opting for optional compulsory jurisdiction instead is likely to avoid these issues.

That said, however, although the approach affords countries in dispute the freedom to choose amongst dispute settlement mechanisms, it would be better if the mechanism under the BRI could still be given priority. Only then can both WTO members and non-WTO members and both members and non-members of existing RTAs look to the same dispute settlement mechanism for resolution, thereby guaranteeing formal fairness and promoting the substantive fairness of international trade dispute settlement under the BRI.

3.3   Avoidance of Compulsory Measures in Implementing Dispute Settlement Resolutions

Most of the existing global or regional dispute settlement mechanisms in the international trade arena allow for compulsory measures to be taken as a last resort to guarantee the practical implementation of dispute resolutions. The WTO dispute settlement mechanism, for example, according to Article 22, paragraph 1 of the DSU, stipulates that compensation and the suspension of concessions or other obligations are available as compulsory measures in the event that the recommendations and rulings of the DSB are not implemented within a reasonable period of time. Further, according to paragraph 2 of the article, whilst compensation is voluntary and should be negotiated and agreed upon by both opposing parties with a view to mutual acceptance, the suspension of concessions or other obligations is to be authorised directly by the DSB if satisfactory compensation cannot be agreed through negotiations within a reasonable time-frame.

It is true that the availability of compulsory measures can provide a reliable guarantee of dispute settlement implementation to a certain

---

[31] Nguyen Tan Son, 'Towards a compatible interaction between dispute settlement under the WTO and regional trade agreements' (2008) 5 *Macquarie Journal of Business Law* 125–7.

extent, and even enhances the effectiveness and credibility of a dispute settlement mechanism. In addition, the principles of harmony, comprehensiveness and the pursuit of mutual benefit of the BRI do not require a country that is party to an international trade dispute to sustain trade cooperation with the opposing party, even at the cost of sacrificing economic benefits, if that party fails to meet its obligations and rejects a dispute settlement. However, the imposition of compulsory measures would likely dampen enthusiasm for joining the initiative, particularly amongst the developing and least developed countries along the Belt and Road, thereby hindering the realisation of the initiative's aim of establishing a broader, more comprehensive trade cooperation system.

For these reasons, as well as to allow greater mechanism adaptability, softer implementation measures are preferred to compulsory measures, and the specialised dispute settlement institution established under the BRI should take responsibility for supervising the implementation of all international trade dispute settlement resolutions. Once such a resolution has been reached, the institution should assist both parties in negotiating its implementation and urge them to determine a reasonable period of time for implementation. However, if the two parties cannot agree on a reasonable period of time, then the tribunal that made the resolution should be in charge of determining it. After such determination, the institution should then submit the implementation conditions of the losing party to a supervision procedure, regularly supervising and assessing those conditions until the resolution is fully implemented. If the losing party has reasonable grounds for failing to implement the resolution in full, the institution should urge the two parties to reach a compensation agreement as a substitute for implementation before expiry of the established time-frame. Finally, only if the losing party fails to implement the resolution and the two parties cannot reach a compensation agreement within that time-frame can the winning party request the tribunal to authorise the suspension of concessions or other obligations to the losing party. In this case, the level of the complaining party's suspension of concessions/obligations needs to meet the requirement of proportionality, namely, the level of suspension must be proportionate to the level of damage suffered by the complaining party as a result of the losing party's failure to implement the resolution.[32]

---

[32] Ahn, 'Dispute settlement systems in Asian FTAs', 425.

4 Conclusion

The establishment of an international trade dispute settlement mechanism under the BRI should strictly follow the principle of adaptability to the actual demand for international trade dispute resolution under the initiative. Because the simple copying or straightforward use of existing global or regional dispute settlement mechanisms cannot meet that principle, a dispute settlement mechanism should be established in full consideration of the initiative's factual circumstances, including the particularity of the initiative itself and the complexity of the countries along the Belt and Road. However, it should also be established with reference to the merits of existing mechanisms, albeit with a flexible and diverse framework. For example, it should permit any country involved to determine the material rules and procedures of dispute settlement with others in both the bilateral and multilateral sphere. Further, the mechanism should also adopt arbitration as its primary means of dispute settlement and diplomatic measures as a subsidiary measure. The mechanism's detailed measures have yet to be perfected. However, in essence, the establishment of a specialised dispute settlement institution responsible for all routine work related to the entire arbitration proceedings is necessary. In addition, although the mechanism should permit optional compulsory jurisdiction over disputes arising amongst the countries along the Belt and Road, the mechanism established under the BRI should be afforded priority, and compulsory measures should be avoided in the implementation of dispute settlement resolutions to the greatest extent possible.

INDEX

ABIF. *See* ASEAN Banking Integration
Framework
abuse of market dominance, AML and,
101
ACFTA. *See* ASEAN-China Free Trade
Area
ACP. *See* African, Caribbean and
Pacific Group of States
ADB. *See* Asian Development Bank
administrative enforcement, of merger
control, 91
AEC. *See* ASEAN Economic
Community
AFAS. *See* ASEAN Framework
Agreement on Services
Africa, Chinese FDI in, 136–7
African, Caribbean and Pacific Group
of States (ACP), 69
African Development Bank, 197
Agreement on Subsidies and
Countervailing Measures (SCM
Agreement), 74–8
assistance provisions in, 75
general infrastructure of, 75–8
defined, 75–6
Vienna Convention on the Law of
Treaties and, 75–6
subsidy definitions, 77
Agreement on Trade in Goods, 118,
172–3
AIIB. *See* Asian Infrastructure
Investment Bank
AIIF. *See* ASEAN Insurance Integration
Framework
Alvarez, Alejandro, 38
AML. *See* Anti-Monopoly Law

anti-competitive behavior
under AML, 92
cross-border, 113, 121, 126, 129
Anti-Monopoly Law (AML) (China).
See also mergers
abuse of market dominance and,
101
anti-competitive behavior under,
92
antitrust enforcement cooperation
under, 121–2
BRI under, 99–101
enforcement of
control definitions and, 89
private, 96–8
SPC provisions, 96–8
juridical interpretations of, 82–91
SOEs under, 99–101
market dominance of, 100
state monopolies under, 99–101
Anti-Monopoly Law Enforcement
Agency. *See* Ministry of
Commerce
antitrust, 98, 104, 110, 113, 123–9,
131
antitrust enforcement cooperation
under AML, 121–2
comity arrangements, 127–8
for export cartels, 121–3
against margin squeeze, 122–3
MOUs for, 126–7
against predatory pricing, 122
rule of law and, 125
transnational, 123, 125
vertical restraints in, 123
anti-unfair competition, 114, 228–9